Pati reveals that the people at these embattled sites engage with the state's acquisition processes in unanticipated ways: they were neither always confrontational, nor merely resigned to their fates. Instead, the author uses life stories, court judgments, architectural forms, local political institutions and urban rental markets to provide a rich description, arguing that people often participated actively and purposefully in the process by which agricultural land became private urban property. This work should animate, for a long time to come, discussions about styles of urbanisation, economic growth and political forms of villages incorporated into the city.

—**Janaki Nair**, author of *Mysore Modern: Reconceptualising the Region under Princely Rule*

Pati's dexterous research and elegant prose takes us on an engaging journey through Delhi's 'urban villages' that shows us the importance of attending to the vernacularisation of capital through deeply situated dynamics of rent. We will be learning from this book for quite a while yet.

—**Sharad Chari**, author of *Fraternal Capital: Peasant-Workers, Self-Made Men, and Globalization in Provincial India*

Properties of Rent catalyses new thinking about the entanglements of land, labour and capital in urbanising India, the vital roles urban villages perform in Delhi's urban mosaic, and the neglected social life of rent in shaping cityscapes and caste futures. Desire, loss, alienation, violence and hope all collide in Pati's evocative book. Ethnographically rich and conceptually bold, *Properties of Rent* makes a range of provocative interventions, in debates spanning geographical political economy, anthropologies of capitalism and urban theory.

—**Vinay Gidwani**, author of *Capital, Interrupted: Agrarian Development and the Politics of Work in India*

Properties of Rent

We live in cities whose borders have always been subject to expansion. What does such transformation of rural spaces mean for cities and vice versa? This book looks at the spatial transformation of villages brought into Delhi's urban fray in the 1950s. As these villages transform physically, their residents, an agrarian-pastoralist community—the Jats—also transform into dabblers in real estate. A study of two villages, Munirka and Shahpur Jat, both in the heart of the bustling urban economies of Delhi, reveal that it is 'rent' that could define this suburbanisation. *Bhaichara*, once a form of land ownership in colonial times, transforms into an affective claim of belonging and managing urban property in the face of urbanisation. *Properties of Rent* is a study of how the vernacular form of capitalism and its various affects shape up in opposition to state, finance capital and the city in contemporary urban Delhi.

Sushmita Pati teaches political science at National Law School of India University, Bengaluru. Her research interests are urban politics, political economy, state and democracy.

METAMORPHOSES OF THE POLITICAL: MULTIDISCIPLINARY APPROACHES

The Series is a publishing collaboration of Cambridge University Press with The M. S. Merian–R. Tagore International Centre of Advanced Studies 'Metamorphoses of the Political' (ICAS:MP). It seeks to publish new books that both expand and de-centre current perspectives on politics and the 'political' in the contemporary world. It examines, from a wide array of disciplinary and methodological approaches, how the 'political' has been conceptualized, articulated and transformed in specific arenas of contestation during the 'long twentieth century'. Though primarily located in India and the Global South, the Series seeks to interrogate and contribute to wider debates about global processes and politics. It is in this sense that the Series is imagined as one that is regionally focused but globally engaged, providing a context for interrogations of universalized theories of self, society and politics.

Series Editors:
- Niraja Gopal Jayal, formerly at Jawaharlal Nehru University, New Delhi
- Shail Mayaram, formerly at Centre for the Study of Developing Societies, Delhi
- Samita Sen, University of Cambridge, Cambridge
- Awadhendra Sharan, Centre for the Study of Developing Societies, Delhi
- Sanjay Srivastava, University College London, UK
- Ravi Vasudevan, Centre for the Study of Developing Societies, Delhi
- Sebastian Vollmer, University of Göttingen, Germany

ICAS:MP is an Indo-German research collaboration of six Indian and German institutions. It combines the benefits of an open, interdisciplinary forum for intellectual exchange with the advantages of a cutting-edge research centre. Located in New Delhi, ICAS:MP critically intervenes in global debates in the social sciences and humanities.

Other Titles in the Series
- *The Secret Life of AnOther Indian Nationalism: Transitions from the Pax Britannica to the Pax Americana* • Shail Mayaram
- *Debt, Trust, and Reputation: Extra-legal Finance in Northern India* • Sebastian Schwecke
- *Saffron Republic: Hindu Nationalism and State Power in India* • Edited by Thomas Blom Hansen and Srirupa Roy
- *Women, Gender and Religious Nationalism* • Edited by Amrita Basu and Tanika Sarkar

Properties of Rent

Community, Capital and Politics in Globalising Delhi

Sushmita Pati

Metamorphoses of the Political
Merian Tagore International Centre of Advanced Studies

CAMBRIDGE
UNIVERSITY PRESS

Shaftesbury Road, Cambridge CB2 8EA, United Kingdom

One Liberty Plaza, 20th Floor, New York, NY 10006, USA

477 Williamstown Road, Port Melbourne, vic 3207, Australia

314 to 321, 3rd Floor, Plot No.3, Splendor Forum, Jasola District Centre, New Delhi 110025, India

103 Penang Road, #05–06/07, Visioncrest Commercial, Singapore 238467

Cambridge University Press is part of the University of Cambridge.

It furthers the University's mission by disseminating knowledge in the pursuit of education, learning and research at the highest international levels of excellence.

www.cambridge.org
Information on this title: www.cambridge.org/9781316517277

© Sushmita Pati 2022

This publication is in copyright. Subject to statutory exception and to the provisions of relevant collective licensing agreements, no reproduction of any part may take place without the written permission of Cambridge University Press.

First published 2022
Reprint 2023, 2025

Printed in India by Repro India Ltd.

A catalogue record for this publication is available from the British Library

ISBN 978-1-316-51727-7 Hardback

Cambridge University Press has no responsibility for the persistence or accuracy of URLs for external or third-party internet websites referred to in this publication, and does not guarantee that any content on such websites is, or will remain, accurate or appropriate.

Contents

List of Maps and Figures	ix
Acknowledgements	xi
List of Permissions	xv
List of Abbreviations	xvii
Units of Measurement	xix
Maps	xxi
Introduction	1
1. Creating Values of Land: Law, Records and *Kabza*	33
2. From Buying Land, Owning Taxis to Becoming Landlords: The Changing Economic Landscape of Villages	59
3. Villages of the City: Ordering Spaces and Aspirations in Neoliberal Times	86
4. In the Shadows of the State: Community as a Mode of Political and Economic Organisation	116
5. Culture, Gender and Belongingness? City and the Violence of Rent	144
6. The Fringes of the Cartel: How the Marginalised Become Landlords	174
7. The Allure of Politics: The Candidates, the Cadre and the Euphoria of Elections	199
Epilogue	229
Glossary	245
Bibliography	248
Index	283

Maps and Figures

Maps

1.	Delhi's Urban Villages	xxi
2.	Munirka, 1960s (*top*); Munirka, 1980s–1990s (*bottom*)	xxii
3.	Post-2000s Munirka	xxiii
4.	Shahpur Jat, 1960s–1970s (*top*); Shahpur Jat, 1970s–1990s (*bottom*)	xxiv
5.	Shahpur Jat after 2000	xxv

Figures

I.1	A lane in Shahpur Jat during the monsoon season	8
1.1	Market area close to the Ring Road	42
3.1	Hundreds of buildings like these house the numerous 'one-room sets' in Munirka	93
3.2	A regular working day in a garment workshop in Shahpur Jat	96
5.1	A shop selling 'Northeast items' and 'Himalayan Chinese' food in Munirka	146
5.2	The pamphlet issued by Adhikar Darshan Manch	156
E.1	A building that collapsed in February 2020 in Munirka village	230

Acknowledgements

The idea of this book took shape as a PhD proposal in the year 2011, completely oblivious of how things were going to change around us radically. While the storm brew over the horizon, we were obsessing over research questions and methodology, over student politics, at different canteens and *dhaba*s across Jawaharlal Nehru University (JNU). By the time we were finishing, in the summer of 2016, much had changed. JNU had become the centre of newsroom debates. From being a premier national institute in 2011, it had ended up at the receiving end of a national ire.

I had entered JNU in the year 2009 as a wide-eyed master's student. Each day was a lesson in political theory in the classroom and politics on campus. JNU gave me the independence to be, something I had not experienced ever before. It opened me up to debates on historiography, modern Indian social thought, art history and so much more beyond the confines of my discipline. I am eternally grateful to the teachers who taught me how to think. Anupama Roy, Amir Ali, Gopal Guru and Valerian Rodrigues, among several others, have shaped different parts of how I think. As a teacher now, I am becoming increasingly aware of their influence on my thinking. I owe my biggest intellectual debt, however, to Rajarshi Dasgupta—my supervisor for both my MPhil and PhD. He opened up new intellectual terrains and pushed me to be unafraid of disciplinary boundaries. He taught me what it is to be passionate about research. He showed faith in me, especially in moments when I had none. It hurts to see the same place and the same people under constant attack—in every sense of the term.

My first and foremost gratitude would go to my respondents, without whom this book would not be possible. I cannot take names, but some respondents have been critical to my entry into the lifeworld of these villages. This book was written across various institutions and I am indebted to each one of them for the time, resources and mentorship that they provided. I am grateful to the engagement and feedback that this work has received at the Centre for Studies in Developing Societies (CSDS), Centre for Policy Research (CPR), Centre for Studies in Law and Governance (CSLG) at JNU, School of Oriental and African Studies (SOAS) and Mahanirban Calcutta Research Group (MCRG), among several others. As a visiting PhD fellow at the Centre for Modern Indian Studies at University of Göttingen, Germany, I had four valuable months to think through and write up my chapters. I am especially grateful to

Nate Roberts, Ravi Ahuja and Srirupa Roy for their comments on some very early, garbled drafts, many of which stayed with me for really long. In 2018, I spent a glorious summer in the University of Victoria, Canada, as a QES-AS early career scholar where I could work single-mindedly and managed to finish the first draft to my publisher for review. At UVic, Helen Lansdowne and Victor Ramaraj went out of their way to make us comfortable. They took a lot of care so that our stay was productive and I am deeply grateful for that. In 2019, I went back to Delhi as an ICAS-MP postdoctoral fellow for five months, where I was able to finish massive amounts of rewriting. Laila-Abu-El Rub, Martin Fuchs and Shail Mayaram made sure that the environment was a deeply stimulating one. Conversations with co-fellows at ICAS, Arnaud Kaba, Nandini Sundar and Shankar Jayaram made me ask questions of the material that I had not specifically asked myself. But to each of these institutes, I am thankful for providing me with that one thing that my home institutions had not—a room of one's own. Having an office to oneself brought in almost child-like enthusiasm to make the most of it, and I am happy I did.

I am deeply thankful to Anant Maringanti and Solomon Benjamin my PhD examiners, who gave me extensive feedback on my thesis, much of which formed the backbone of the work I did after my PhD. AbdouMaliq Simone, Amita Baviskar and Awadhendra Sharan have helped shape up several parts of my writing. At the School of Policy and Governance at Azim Premji University, my colleagues have been extremely indulgent. I have probably misused the Thursday seminars to inflict my terrible drafts on my colleagues over and over. Both Moyukh and Vishnu gave extensive comments on two very crucial chapters. While Ajit brought an economist's lens, Krishna, Ram and Siddharth brought in their unique sensibilities of studying politics to many of those discussions. Conversations with Champaka about urban planning brought a different kind of clarity to my understanding. Arun has always been a comforting presence with generosity—both intellectually and otherwise—that comes so naturally to him. I am glad he is my go-to person. Sudhir has been exceptionally encouraging as a director. He enabled research, thought and writing, which is sadly not the easiest to find among directors. Anshuman, Asha, Kanika, Neeraj and Prateeti always made Thursday talks more exciting with drinking plans that followed after. Sunayana did the noble job of keeping me company in Victoria. At the School of Development, I spent much less time, but ended up making good friends with Shreelata, Vandana and later, Indrani. I am thankful to Azim Premji University's internal grant, which funded my two months of research in 2018. I am also thankful to the librarians at APU, especially Aditya and Praveena, who went out of their way to help me.

I moved to National Law School India University in the middle of the pandemic. The pandemic has made it difficult to get to know new colleagues and students, but I am grateful to the students who keep up the collective spirits despite the challenges of online teaching and learning. I am also thankful to Sarasu and Sudhir who made my transition into a new institution so smooth. I am looking forward to my time in NLSIU and to see how a law college changes the way I understand politics. And I am looking forward to using the office space that I now finally have.

My fascination with Delhi as a city has a lot to do with my own journey. I came to Delhi as an 18-year-old from a small-town, sheltered life and exploring the city became my way of exploring my own freedoms. From film festivals to aimless traipsing around, I fell in love with the city. I am deeply indebted to my female friendships for being constant companions through much of this tomfoolery. Their eccentricities and passions rubbed off on me and exposed me to so much that I would not have known, if not for them. I am indebted to them for their sense of humour, for their intellectual honesty and generosity, for the love and emotional support that they have given me. Sharmin, Shivani, Shruti and I have shared the travails of writing exams, papers and dissertation chapters, tempered with cheap wine and anxiety over more than 15 years of trying to find our place in this academic world. Shruti and I have often been confused for the other, and that's for good reason. They collectively hold the unenviable record of reading almost every word that I have written—at least twice over. This work has their imprint all over. Kasturi, Khatija, Reva and Sana have been my source of bad jokes and outlandish plans. Our debates and disagreements have been the basis of my moral compass. Individually, we may do stupid things, but collectively, I think we have always been wise beyond our years.

I met Pooja much later in life, but her friendship has been inspiring and deeply affirming. Aditi and Deepasri have goaded me to think differently. But more importantly, they have pushed me to be unafraid in my writing. Sana and her mother took care of me for days when I had fallen sick. Bhoomika suggested that the only way to end pandemic-induced isolation was to start an online writing group and soon, those discussions with Bhoomika, Sharmin, Shivani and Tanvi became that one thing to look forward to through the drudgery of a lockdown. Reva and Ritambhara opened up their home for me when I needed a place to live in Delhi. Those happy, music-filled mornings and evenings will be something I will always want to keep coming back to. I am very proud to say that I am a product of women's solidarities and friendships. They have been the biggest source of joy, intellectual camaraderie and support in my life, and I do not think I can ever thank them enough.

A long-drawn conversation with Debarati and Ritajyoti over two days put numerous things in perspective. That one weekend in peak winter in Mohali clarified several things conceptually. Ritajyoti's comments on my work have helped me tie many loose ends. His conceptual clarity is something I have deeply admired. Himadri accompanied me to my field once, and he saw so many things that I had not. Amitanshu accompanied me to a *panchayat* all the way to Jind, apart from sharing his rooted understanding of Indian electoral politics. Anubhav, Pooja, Swastee and Tarangini's very incisive comments on early chapter drafts made me look into my material again. Akash, being my only friend from JNU in Bangalore, who I still regularly have *chai* with, has been such a relieving presence. Swathi's comments on an earlier PhD draft went a long way in reframing the project for my manuscript. Countless numbers of friends and 'friends of friends' helped with contacts and anecdotes, which I am so very grateful for. Devadeep, Dilip and Ritambhara were valiant warriors who got me the images I needed, just in the nick of time. This book would have been so much poorer without them. But all aside, everybody needs a crazy, totally out-there *mallu* friend in their lives. And I must say, Saharu has not disappointed in this respect.

Arpita Das's editorial insights into my writing have made this book read infinitely better. I am deeply grateful to her for noticing things that I had missed and pushing me to write more clearly. Nithya Subramanian's immense patience has seen through the making of these maps. I am delighted that Pia Alizé Hazarika agreed to do the cover. It is magical to witness your work transform into a work of art. I am deeply thankful to Anwesha Rana, Debjani Mazumder, Priya Das and Qudsiya Ahmed for smoothening the process of publishing with Cambridge University Press. I would also like to express my gratitude to the two blind peer reviewers whose extensive and crucial comments on my work led me to rethink several parts of my writing far more deeply than I otherwise would have.

Anand and Shilpa have quickly become the younger siblings that I never had. Amma and Appa have been the most easygoing and generous in-laws ever. Amma's sambhar has saved us on many a day. Praveen came in with his good humour and immense patience just at the right time in my life. His insistence and passion for good storytelling has rubbed off on me, though I wish I could do it as well as him. For every doomsday scenario I have painted in my anxious moments, he has always asked me, 'What is the worst-case scenario?' And while conjuring up these worst-case scenarios in my head, what I actually figured was that he is my best-case scenario.

And finally, my parents. But above all, Ma, my most ardent cheerleader. Who made everything possible. Who unflinchingly stood up for me at the most crucial time in my life. She would be the proudest holding this book in her hands. I dedicate this book to her.

February 2021 **Sushmita Pati**

Bengaluru

Permissions

A part of Chapter 1 was published as 'The Productive Fuzziness of Land Documents: The State and Processes of Accumulation in Urban Villages of Delhi' in *Contributions to Indian Sociology* 53, no. 2 (2019): 249–71.

A part of Chapter 5 was published as 'Accumulation by Possession: The Social Process of Rent Seeking in Urban Delhi', in *Accumulation in Postcolonial Capitalism*, ed. Iman Mitra, Ranabir Samaddar and Samita Sen (Singapore: Springer, 2016), 93–108.

A part of Chapter 7 was published as 'Anxieties of "Dabanggai": Tales from Delhi's Urban Villages', in special issue edited by Madhura Lohokare on Masculinities of Urban India: Of Contradictions, Dilemmas and Uncertainties for *Café Dissensus* 35 (2017).

The image of the 'Collapsed Building in Munirka' is used with permission from Hindustan Times Digital Services.

Abbreviations

AAP	Aam Aadmi Party
ACC	Associated Cement Company Limited
ADM	Adhikar Darshan Manch
BKD	Bharatiya Kisan Dal
BKU	Bharatiya Kisan Union
BJP	Bharatiya Janata Party
BSI	Buddhist Society of India
BPO	business process outsourcing
BSP	Bahujan Samajwadi Party
CCTV	closed-circuit television
CPWD	Central Public Works Department
CNG	compressed natural gas
DDA	Delhi Development Authority
DDMA	Delhi Disaster Management Authority
DLF	Delhi Land and Finance
DTC	Delhi Transport Corporation
EMI	equated monthly instalment
FCSD	Food and Civil Supplies Department
GPA	General Power of Attorney
IAS	Indian Administrative Service
INC	Indian National Congress
INLD	Indian National Lok Dal
JCB	Joseph Cyril Bamford
JNU	Jawaharlal Nehru University
LCD TV	liquid crystal display television
LGBTQ	lesbian, gay, bisexual, transgender, queer
MCD	Municipal Corporation of Delhi
MLA	member of legislative assembly
NCT	National Capital Territory
NRC	National Register of Citizens
NRI	non-resident Indian

OBC	other backward classes
OPEC	Organisation of Petroleum Exporting Countries
PDS	Public Distribution System
PG	paying guest
PIL	public interest litigation
RWA	resident welfare association
SAF Games	South Asian Federation Games
SC/ST	scheduled caste/scheduled tribe
SDMC	South Delhi Municipal Corporation
SEZ	special economic zone
SHO	station house officer
STC	State Trading Corporation
STUD	Student Tenants' Union of Delhi
UPA	United Progressive Alliance
UPSC	Union Public Service Commission
YBM	Youth Brigade Munirka

Units of Measurement

1 *biswa* = 50 square yards

1 *bigha* = 1,000 square yards

1 *anna* = 1/16th of a rupee

1 lakh = 100,000

1 crore = 10,000,000

Maps

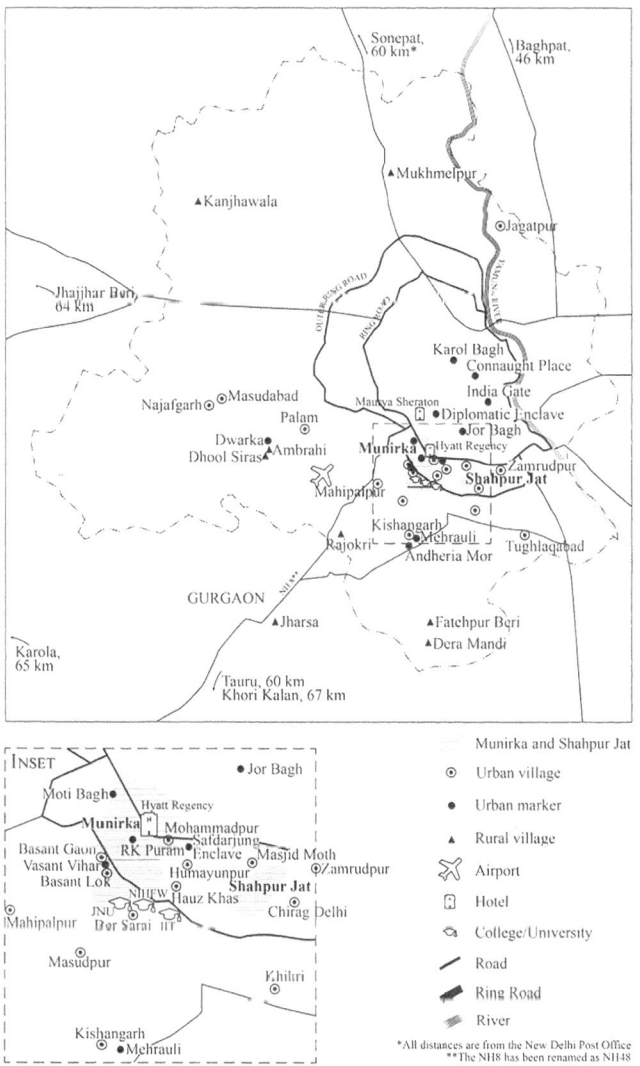

Map 1 Delhi's Urban Villages

Source: Author.

Map 2 Munirka, 1960s (*top*); Munirka, 1980s–1990s (*bottom*)

Source: Author.

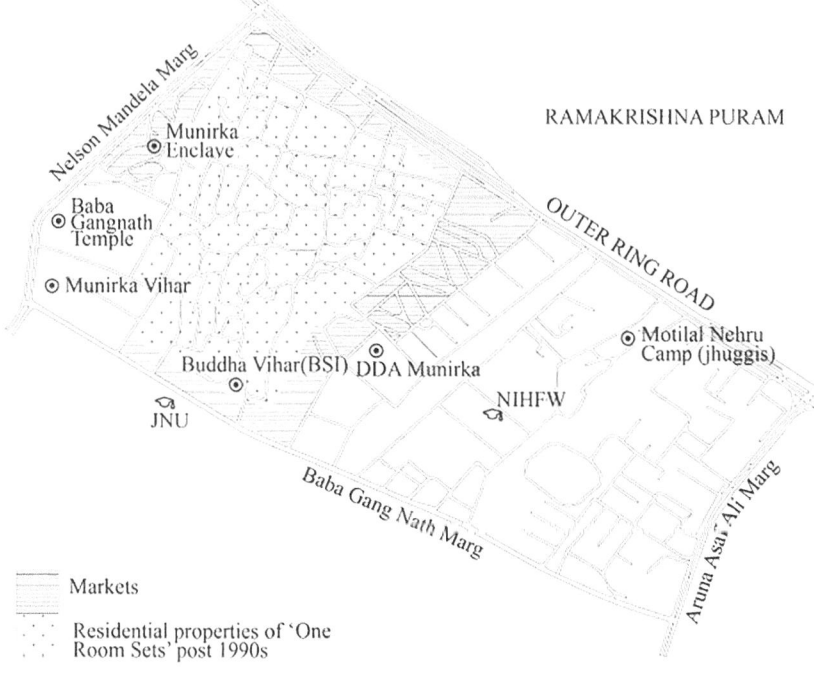

Map 3 Post-2000s Munirka

Source: Author.

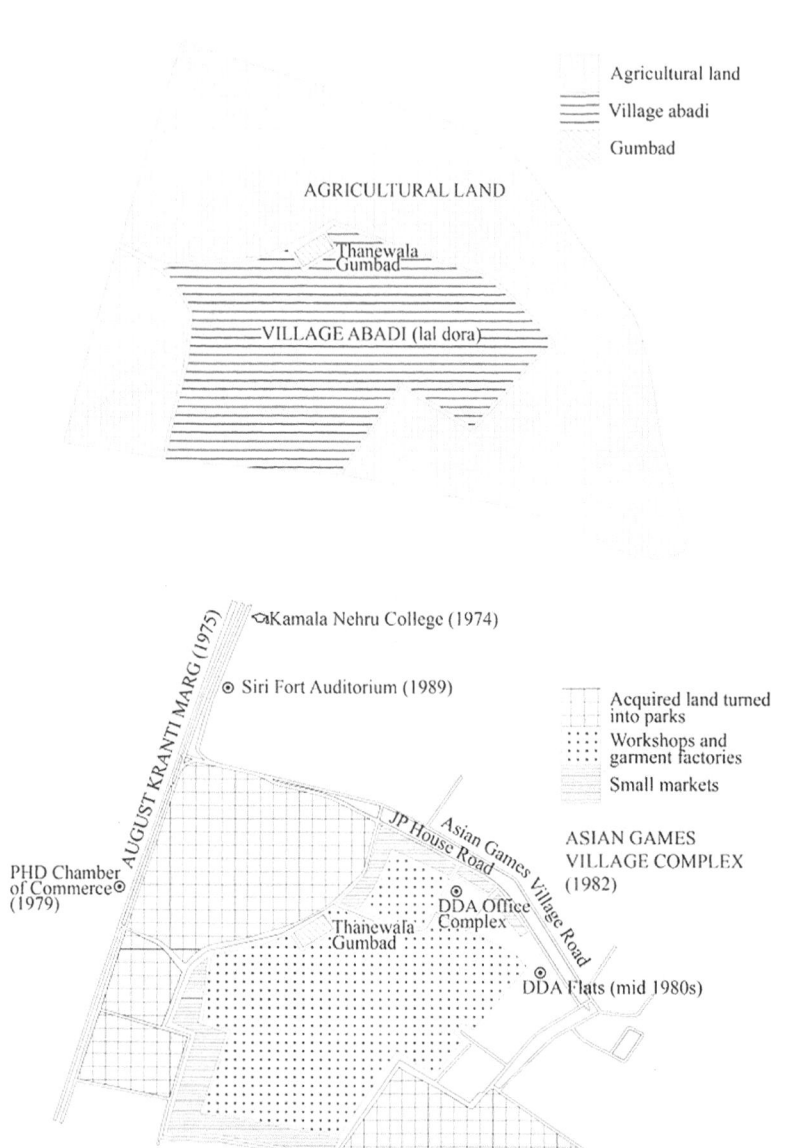

Map 4 Shahpur Jat, 1960s–1970s (*top*); Shahpur Jat, 1970s–1990s (*bottom*)
Source: Author.

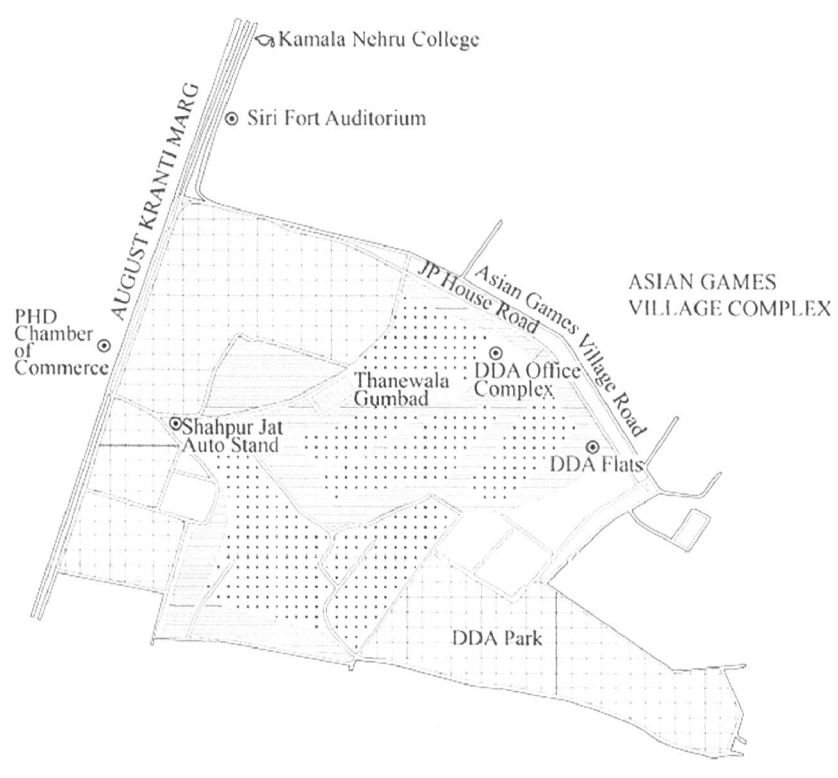

Map 5 Shahpur Jat after 2000

Source: Author.

Introduction

… the bewitched, distorted and upside-down world haunted by Monsieur le Capital and Madame la Terre, who are at the same time social characters and mere things.
—Karl Marx, *Capital*, vol. 3

Balbir Singh, a resident of Shahpur Jat, then a village in the outskirts of Delhi, remembers the time when land acquisition began taking place in the year 1958. The news had first come to them wafting in as a rumour, but it grew limbs and fangs to become reality soon enough. He remembers having accompanied a group of villagers headed by Dalip Singh Panwar, a local Congress leader, to appeal to Jawaharlal Nehru, the then prime minister, to not acquire the land. Nehru had merely thrown up his hands in despair, expressing his helplessness in the matter and said, 'Badhte hue bachhe aur badhte hue shahar ko main nahi rok sakta.'*

There probably could be no better analogy than the one Nehru had used. In the life of a newly independent nation, in the heyday of Nehruvian socialism, cities were indeed like children. They needed to be nurtured, nourished and sacrificed for. It is entirely another matter that cities as we know them today are less like growing children and more like insatiable monsters, which demand blood sacrifices on a regular basis. Their appetite for resources has only grown exponentially. So much so that these monstrous cities devour almost everything that falls in their way. And while cities devour and keep growing bigger, they end up changing the entire morphology of the spaces that they consume. Quite like how Nehru saw the fate of these villages in Delhi's hinterlands, the question of rural dispossession has been treated akin to 'collateral damage'. For the monstrous city, the periphery is the space waiting, like a sacrificial goat, for its turn to be consumed. But zooming closer, the city appears more like a bored and slow sloth, which creates a trail

---

* 'I cannot stop a growing child and a growing city.'

of half-eaten, half-chewed out debris. In the process, urbanisation does not look like a sharp, linear transition, but rather a curious mosaic made of such semi-devoured landscapes. For the purposes of the present work, I would like to focus the reader's attention on one such half-eaten form: the urban villages of Delhi.

Sixty years after the time when Balbir Singh's story was set, Shahpur Jat now exists as an 'urban village' in the administrative lexicon. In a way, it is only justified that these spaces are called urban villages: they neither look like cities nor are they entirely village-like. Clumps of electric wires hang overhead and broken patches of concrete that can hardly be called roads give away the shoddy state of public utilities in the area. In the cacophony of busy markets, and the sounds of bicycles, scooters, cars and their honking, the one noise that remains omnipresent is the sound of construction drilling. Oscillating between a constant drone in the backdrop and almost a deafening, overpowering din, the sound of drilling follows you around. The sound of constant drilling is a reminder of how construction and renovation have come to become the backbone of this economy. This book attempts to tell the story of this transformation.

These urban villages are products of Delhi's southward-bound growth in the post-independence phase. In political economy discourse, this onslaught of capitalist forces on rural lands has been termed 'primitive accumulation'. Farmlands transform into private enclosures, and the serfs, now dispossessed, begin to move to cities as a reserve army of labour.[1] In the Indian context, David Harvey's formulation, *accumulation by dispossession*,[2] has been extremely influential in studying how capital has changed our cities. We have encountered several ways in which urbanisation has happened through rural dispossession. Agricultural lands have increasingly turned into special economic zones (SEZs).[3] Slums and squatter settlements in cities have been finding it increasingly difficult to withstand the pressures of gentrification.[4] In other cases, corporate interests, bourgeois environmentalists, urban planners and courts have worked together in cohorts and declared inhabitations of the poor illegal.[5] The story of *accumulation by dispossession* becomes one of exploited, dispossessed farmers on the one hand and an extractive state and capital forces on the other.

The urban villages that I speak of are somewhat similar. But they do not quite fit into this mould. Theirs is not a standard story of dispossession. These urban villages, despite occupying prime urban land, despite their tenuous status in modern property regimes, are here to stay. They have come to manifest a permanent condition of impermanence within the supposed formal, legal cityscape. In fact, I argue that these tenuous property titles and the strong community ties in these villages have proved to be particularly productive in the global economy. These villages and their inhabitants, I argue, have come to find their place in and as the underbellies of the city: an inchoate, messy form which absorbs the contradictions of capital.

On 13 November 1959, in a bid to create a modern postcolonial city and, along with it, modern citizens, the Delhi Development Authority (DDA), a statutory body created in 1957, passed an order to acquire 34,070 acres of land under Section 4 of the Land Acquisition Act, 1894. Most of these villages happened to be Jat- and Gujjar-dominated villages lying on the southern side of the city precincts. The land settlement report of 1908–09 had marked the village *abadi* (settlement area) as separate from the agricultural land of the village through a line drawn in red ink on the village map. The line that was once used to demarcate taxable agricultural land from the non-taxable residential settlement area of the village had now emerged as the frontier of this legal demarcation of the rural as opposed to the urban.[6] The agricultural land was acquired, and the village settlement land within the red line, or the *lal dora*, was left as it is. Currently, there are some 135 such urban villages, or *lal dora* villages, dotting the urban landscape of Delhi. The reasons for not acquiring the village settlement in such a curious fashion are not very clear. A fair guess suggests that this strategy speeded up and cheapened the process of acquisition. In their grandiose scheme of wanting to create an urban revolution through a regional plan, the planning authorities could not be too bothered about the question of these newly created 'urban villages'. It would be decades before the urban authorities were haunted by these unruly spaces, by then no longer tameable by law. It might be said, therefore, that urban villages are ironically a by-product of the Delhi Master Plan, 1962, the modern, regional plan that was supposed to end all the woes of the city.

I look at two such villages in this book: Munirka and Shahpur Jat. Both villages now thrive in the middle of South Delhi, home to probably some of the most expensive real estate in India. Munirka's urbanisation started with the South Delhi Municipal Committee vide Chief Commissioner's Notification dated 4 March 1954.[7] It was one of the first villages that lay right outside the then precincts of Delhi to be acquired. The proposed Ring Road, an arterial road that was to be the marker of a planned new city, and new government housing were to come up on what used to be Munirka's agricultural land.

Shahpur Jat's farmlands, on the other hand, were acquired in 1958. However, the land was not immediately taken over. The villagers were allowed to cultivate it as tenants until 1978, when the farmlands had to give way for the construction of the Asiad Games Village to house the players and delegates attending the Asian Games in 1982.[8] The residential part of Shahpur Jat, tucked away from any major roads, did not see much transformation in the early years. In time, garment workers and garment workshops came to be the mainstay of Shahpur Jat's economy. From the late 1990s onwards, a niche, customised fashion hub began to emerge here, with several fashion designers opening up their boutiques. Easy availability of workers and cheaper rents have made Shahpur Jat a favourable location both for these specialised enterprises and their workers.

In this work, we look at two kinds of built forms that dominate the rental market in the two villages: the 'one-room set', a roughly 8 x 8 feet living space complete with a kitchen and a bathroom for renting out to the migrants; and the *adda*, independent units with 6–8 workers for garment manufacture.[9] The fast transformation of the economy and the city, which opened up opportunities for young people, only heightened the migration of lowly paid workers into the service sector. The business process outsourcing (BPO) sector boomed, and restaurants, shops and malls mushroomed all over the city, increasing the demand for younger migrant workers, especially from northeast India, who are considered smarter and more articulate but are invariably poorly paid.[10] On the other hand, the garment industry of Shahpur Jat houses garment artisans in thousands; cooped up in countless small *adda*s and factories are the foot soldiers of the fashion industry.

Villages of the Master Plan

The Delhi Master Plan, in its megalomania of developing a region, was never sure about what to do with the urban villages. The Draft Plan was released in the year 1960 along with two volumes of the Work Studies Report, which contained the details of the committee's research. The Work Studies Report, which preceded the Master Plan, imagined a concentric circle form of structure for the villages in which they would be connected to each other through their small-scale trades and markets. The Work Studies Report stated:

> The development of rural trades and crafts in small villages and light to medium industries located in Delhi and in the other ring towns is strongly recommended. In such an organisation it is hoped that the small centres will experience a co-operative interest in the bigger ones and these will develop a genuinely supporting, instead of an exploitative relationship towards the industries located in the smaller towns and the countryside.[11]

Though it was vaguely imagined that villages in Delhi would be home to small and medium enterprises, not much was said about their feasibility in an urban space. There is almost a reticence on these 'urban villages to-be', which were too close to the city to sustain a rural economy like before. The Work Studies Report further stated:

> Villagers situated very close to Delhi are dying out due to their increasing inability to sustain the population. Consequently, the rural environment is deteriorating. To close our eyes to the rural sector of Delhi, which is getting impoverished due to efflux of people, will be to let the malady grow worse. It is, therefore, necessary to check the mass movement of people from the countryside and to put the rural sector in the right gear through proper planning.[12]

The final Master Plan document released in 1962, however, said precious little with respect to these urban villages, leaving much to the imagination of people and the administration. Awadhendra Sharan points out that the zoning strategy that the Master Plan of 1962 used to keep out 'noxious and hazardous' industries from the city had no clarity on what trades and crafts it categorised as rural and for what reason.[13] The document at best gave out only confusing signals about the future of these villages. But as Sharan puts it aptly, 'The rural stood as a marker of that which the city must expel.'[14] In continuation of this ambiguity, in the year 1963, a notification by the DDA declared that *lal dora* villages do not need to subscribe to the modern plan. The 1963 notification was, therefore, one of the first moves by the state to officially 'forget' these villages. But, at the same time, they were supposed to become spaces that encouraged 'rural crafts': a vague set of professions and trades that the city needed but could not bear to hold. These villages then kept growing in the shadows of the city and its needs and, conversely, the opportunities that it threw up.

But there was a time when these villages were carefully constructed through surveys and maps for revenue collection by the colonial government.[15] After 1947, villages had slowly become places which promised little value. The value regimes had changed radically. Within the scheme of Nehruvian modernity, as agriculture slowly began to give way to industrialisation, value now clearly lay in the ability of localities in becoming 'urban' land. In such a situation, once the vast majority of agricultural land was acquired, the villages per se had little to offer in terms of value. Far from the Gandhian utopia of creating village republics, these villages had turned into zones where the 'unsightly' within the cities would be dumped: cows, small-scale factories and informal labour. The exceptions created for urban villages, therefore, became the mode through which institutional forgetting took place in this case.[16] Along with the villages, the cattle, the grimy small-scale factories and its poor inhabitants could all be forgotten.

This kind of forgetting is not peculiar to Delhi. Urban planners frequently forget 'unruly' spaces while making their lofty plans look like a success. Desakota[17] regions in the Philippines and Chengzongcun in China are some examples of similar forms that have emerged at the interface of such a rural–urban continuum. These villages may be peculiar to the city of Delhi, but almost all cities are familiar with spaces such as these—ghettos of New York, banlieues of Paris, favelas of Rio de Janeiro—that are products of urban planning's failures to build inclusive, equitable cities.[18] Urban planning derived from Eurocentric notions of organising space spawned immense speculation over land value and, consequently, a housing shortage for the working classes across the world, leading ultimately to homelessness.[19] The new 'public' spaces thus now need to be consistently cordoned off from the homeless and squatters by adding spikes and barbed wire to these spaces.[20] The Delhi Master Plan, 1962, was no different. In its obsession to create neat, ordered cities, and responding to fears of 'congestion',[21] the Plan appeared clueless about how to deal with the question of working-class housing.

In Indian cities, which witnessed a growth spurt following liberalisation in the 1990s, there was an intensification of the housing problem. As the demand for cheap labour and small enterprises grew manifold, the zones laid out in the Master Plan proved to be even more impractical and inefficient. As a result, these villages, which the plans decided to overlook, became alive with enterprise. Some came to be known for godowns, such as Ghitorni, or *momo* factories, such as Chiragh Dilli.[22] Some others came to be known for garment workshops, such as Lado Sarai, or budget hotels, such as Yusuf Sarai and Mahipalpur.[23] By the 1990s, as the need for a class of precariat blue-collar workers increased with the rise of service-led growth, these villages began to evolve to provide cheap housing. As factories also changed into their post-Fordist[24] form, urban villages became hosts to them as well. Despite all that has changed in the rural ways of living, the villagers continue to retain a dogged affinity towards their deeply traditional forms of social life. These villages soon came to occupy an important space in the city's entrepreneurial economy. But rural, kinship-based networks continued to persist in Delhi's otherwise swiftly transforming urban villages.

These villages rest over a conflict over 'value'. Value is as much about economic value as it is about emotions and sensibilities that completely defy the language of economic value. Keeping this in mind, in the subsequent chapters, I open up the question of value to a range of different kinds of logics and scrutiny. David Graeber writes, 'Value will necessarily be a key issue if we see social worlds not just as a collection of persons and things but rather as a project of mutual creation, as something collectively made and remade.'[25] Value then becomes more than its monetary representation. As values of land and their enterprises have grown, their sense of having lost out on social registers of value has also intensified. In this book, I look at this tension between the rapidly changing economic realities and the parallel attempt to hold on to kinship associations, as well as traditional notions of respect and honour. I argue that, in fact, this tension has distinctly shaped the very forms of accumulation that have evolved in spaces like these urban villages. I look specifically at the Jat community—the dominant caste in several of these villages, a community known for its hardworking farmers and chivalrous warriors in the northwest region of India—to understand what forms their interface with global capital takes at various points.

Though these villages were transforming quite fast because of their proximity to the city, a mad rush to construct by the 1990s went on to change the village landscape unrecognisably. Furthermore, due to the 'exemptions' in building bye-laws for these *lal dora* spaces, and extensive land grabbing, the villages ended up growing in unpredictable ways. Over a period of time, urban villages began to resemble unauthorised colonies, the term used for informal, unplanned residential clusters that routinely come up to house the urban poor. In fact, out of 135 villages spread over Delhi, 81 are already part of such unauthorised colonies. Mostly made with cheap building material, stacked on top of each other, these buildings resemble a poorly played game of Tetris. Oddly built, these villages seem like the ultimate nightmare for a planner. Today, these urban villages are at least five–six times more densely populated than the non-urban village areas. Moreover, a complex, mixed land-use pattern allows them to carry on residential, commercial and often industrial functions in the same space. While sewer and clean water pipelines were provided, these were never equipped to cater to such a large number of inhabitants. Rainwater and sludge flood the lanes in the monsoon (Figure I.1). Many of these villages have inferior sewage systems and the inadequate Delhi Jal Board water supply is compensated for by an informal network of water providers.

Figure I.1 A lane in Shahpur Jat during the monsoon season

Source: Photo by author.

Rent and the Making of Delhi

Scholars have now begun to question the neat divide between 'urban' and 'rural', leading to two different fields of study: urban studies and rural studies. Satendra Kumar's work on rural socialities in north India speaks of how they are being configured anew through migration, social media and smartphones.[26] He shows how villages have neither remained like villages nor have they become like 'cities', but instead have emerged as something else altogether.[27] Similarly, works in urban studies are also increasingly speaking of new kinds of spaces that again defy both labels of rural and urban. Shubhra Gururani and Sai Balakrishnan make a rather convincing case that if these new spaces are to be understood then agrarian studies and urban studies would need to speak to each other.[28]

These villages I speak of are neither entirely dispossessed nor are they waiting to be gobbled up by real estate pressures. The spatial structure of the residential village, its caste order and the community life it was familiar with continued as the city mushroomed in its full abundance all around it. The community and caste order adapted themselves to their new urbanised lives and the global economy and, of course, the modern state.[29] Keeping this in mind, the book traverses a complex landscape of caste, enterprise, racial violence and electoral politics in a space that is both rural and urban at the same time. My narrative is as much about the changing landscape of the village as it is about its inhabitants. I demonstrate the ways in which colonial land relations and traditional kinship associations like the *panchayat* have found their way into extractive processes in the global city. The dominant lens of 'capital' views spaces like urban villages as transient 'phases'. But I argue that in order to really understand these processes of suburbanisation, we need more lenses than the ones proffered by capital.

I, therefore, foreground the phenomenon of rent in this discussion. Rent, unlike capital, is not produced by labour. Simply put, rent is an expression of possession. Karl Marx wrote, 'Landed property presupposes that certain persons enjoy the monopoly of disposing of particular portions of the globe as exclusive spheres of their private will to the exclusion of all others.'[30] There has been a general consensus among classical political economists— Adam Smith, David Ricardo and Marx—that value is generated by labour and, therefore, rent is not productive. As a result, rent has often not been given the attention it deserves. Fernando Coronil critiques this understanding and argues that an excessive focus on labour has led these scholars to ignore the role of natural resources in creating unequal social relations.[31] Clearly, an analysis purely based on capital only takes us so far.

Kalyan Sanyal shows us how postcolonial capitalism integrates capital and non-capital in a way that it ceases to be a narrative of transition.[32] I enter this conversation through rent's place in urban political economy. Urban political economy, too, has for long been dominated by the analytical framework of capital. But anybody who has ever written on rent would agree that rent is slippery as a concept. Rent is best understood as a 'product of an economy where capital is privately owned'.[33] But with financialisation, it has become extremely hard to distinguish between value extraction and value production.[34] Modern banking, Mariana Mazzucato argues, even though it is not engaged in what would be understood as usurious in the 19th century, is now considered to be producing value.[35] Both rent and capital are extractive; they both work in conjunction with each other and create cities that thrive on their violence. But they are also deeply divergent in many ways. Capital and rent together, through their flows and frictions,[36] constitute spaces and sociabilities that together go on to make these city spaces.

Of late, Marx's assertion of the role of monopoly landed property as being both a historic precondition and a permanent foundation for the capitalist mode of production has found currency.[37] Thomas Piketty invokes rent in order to distinguish between income and wealth and how differential wealth has gone on to exacerbate inequality across the globe.[38] But this is also where the problem begins. Rent has been seen as either an annoyance or as a faithful ally in the process of accumulation of capital. Which is why the question of value has continued to plague rent. While scholars such as Lapavitsas and Andreucci et al. believe that rent does not generate any value and merely grabs it,[39] some others like Anne Haila argue that maybe a modern theory of rent can be seen as productive.[40] But time and again, we see that the relationship between value, rent and finance is not necessarily very seamless; all the same, it continues to be at the heart of capitalist production.[41]

This relationship between capital and rent has been, as a result, quite tenuous. How is rent different from profit? Can rent carry value? How does rent transform from Marx's agrarian context to an urban one? Clearly these intense debates are a result of rent's centrality in financial capital. In this book, I turn this logic on its head. I instead try to look at global capital from the vantage point of vernacular rent.[42] If rent in this context is defined by possession, how then do these urban villages, owned by landlords, find their space in the political economy of a global city? As an expression of 'possession', rent, in this case, goes against the very ethos of speculation that is at the heart of financialisation today. Nowhere is this opposition more apparent than with respect to urbanisation. On the one hand, financialisation has gone on to convert land to real estate, but land still continues to hold emotive value. In the age of quick selling and buying, here is a community—the Jats in this case—which steadfastly holds on to its possession: the village homestead land. The homestead land, marked off by a red line (*lal dora*) from the revenue-generating agricultural land, becomes the source of its income and livelihood by renting property, while ownership of the land also remains the basis of their community pride and belongingness. When these villages are left out of the acquisition plan and are not uprooted from their village lands, their older notions of hierarchies and possessions enter the urban frame, marching into the age of neoliberalism. As a result, we see the emergence of a rent market in the post-liberalisation era, albeit one that is governed by community control.

And in doing that, as much as rent gets embedded in the world of global capital, it also claims its independence from it. As these smaller, vernacular economies begin to get intrinsically linked with global capital, it has been easy for much of scholarship to paint everything with the same broad brush stoke of capital. I argue, however, that invoking a concept like rent allows us to see much more. If global capital is built along notions of risks and speculation, rent is strongly organised around the spine of a community. Global capital makes space for these exceptions, which, in turn, go on to make space for these messy, grey zones like the villages that can absorb the contradictions of the city produced by capital. But these zones themselves are not entirely governed by global capital. To understand these spaces better, categories such as rent provide us with a new lens. Rent then needs to be understood in relation to global capital, in the ways in which they converge and diverge. Rent and capital chafe against each other, but they make accumulation possible. Locating urban villages within the flows of capital and spatial transformation, we also see how seemingly premodern associational bonds of kinship, *kunba*, *bhaichara* and *panchayat*s transform in response to village land transforming into real estate. In doing so, they begin to play a crucial role in both accumulation and modern electoral politics. After all, accumulation through rent requires a steady discourse around community pride and confidence.

In interacting with the world of capital, the notion of this ethnically, kinship-bound 'community' constantly feels anxious about its own existence. Trapped in a state of siege in the city, the community's own rural and familial values tend to get heightened with the perceived onslaught of the urban on its world. Consequently, even as rent ensures accumulation, it also functions as a node around which existing notions of prestige are reinforced, if not reconstituted. However, the fact that this rent continually operates within the context of global urban capital produces generalised conditions of fear and anxiety. In this sphere of an otherwise productive and extremely profitable interaction between rent and capital, the social interaction between the two is not necessarily pleasant. This anxiety then gets reproduced in the disdain the posh, urbane residents of South Delhi have for the Jat landlords. The Jat landlords reciprocate quite generously with equal amount of disdain, flaunting both their wealth and culture, which is considered 'crass'.

Being Brothers in the City: Caste, Kinship and the Notion of *Bhaichara*

My contention throughout this work is that rent is the essential puzzle that needs to be cracked open if urbanisms of the Global South have to be understood. The Jats, the dominant caste and also the biggest landowners in the area, have used the land and social capital they already possessed to work around the new urban realities by way of rent. In this negotiation, neither community nor capital remained pristine or untouched.

The village land in Munirka had traditionally belonged to the Jats from the Tokas clan.[43] Reflective of the process of splintering of villages, which goes on to create a *got*-[44] based territorial unit, Mohammadpur, a village close to the upmarket South Delhi locality of Safdarjung Enclave was set up as an offshoot of the Tokas clan from Munirka. To date, they consider each other as kin villages and there is no intermarriage between families of the two villages. They are also considered a part of the same unit in the hierarchy of *panchayat*s. Their collective memory speaks of having migrated from Behraur district in Rajasthan, arguably around the early 16th century. Later, the Jats from another clan 'Rathi' came to settle in Munirka as well and were given land on the periphery of the village. Over time, members of other castes, Brahmins, Kumhars, Jatavs and Balmikis, also settled in the village and organised themselves around the Jats, who continued to remain the dominant caste.[45] Once their land was acquired in the late 1950s, many of the villagers took up government jobs through the sports quota.[46]

Unlike Munirka, Shahpur Jat had far less expanse of land but owned many more fertile tracts. Shahpur Jat, it is believed, was part of the historical city of Siri, established by Alauddin Khilji, a ruler of the Delhi Sultanate in the 13th century. The village is still dotted with the ruins of ramparts and tombs dating back to that time. Shahpur Jat is dominated by the Panwar *got* of the Jat community. It is said that the village originally belonged to another Jat clan, the Dagars. The Panwars settled here much later. Over a few generations, the Dagars have dwindled in number due to fewer marriages and progeny. Ber Sarai, adjacent to the IIT campus in South Delhi, is a splinter village of Shahpur Jat. These villages have historically followed the land tenure system of *bhaichara*. They are a part of a territorial consolidation that was achieved by the Jats most successfully during colonial times.

Neeladri Bhattacharya shows how eclectic forms of land tenure systems in northwest India were consolidated under standardised forms, one of them being *bhaichara* (roughly translated as brotherhood). The *bhaichara* system was based on joint proprietorship of land, which in principle undercut the possibility of emergence of an individual power figure: the *zamindar*, popular in other forms of land tenure systems.[47] B. H. Baden-Powell, an English civil servant, notes that the term *bhaichara*, in the context of land tenure, began to encompass a much broader set of practices. Often, a group of adventurers would move to a new place, and colonise and settle on a different patch of land,

and yet continue to retain their ties with the mother village, thus extending the expanse of *bhaichara*.[48]

Munirka and Shahpur Jat are part of a longer territorial consolidation by the Jats across the northwestern part of India, mainly Delhi, western Uttar Pradesh and Haryana. According to a colonial Settlement Report from 1885, out of the 519,000 acres under cultivation in the Delhi district, nearly half of it was cultivated by the Jats.[49] Along with the Ahirs, the Jats were considered by British administrators to be one of the best cultivator communities in India.[50] Unsurprisingly, therefore, and as we shall see in the course of this book, as a community with a deep historical affinity to land, there are continuities between this affinity and the Jats' contemporary ownership of property.

Eric Stokes points out that while the Jats were numerically dominant, they were not a caste in themselves; instead, they were a broad category of warrior–cultivators who had absorbed many outsiders within their ranks.[51] Because of their origin outside the Hindu fold, the Jats are spread across three religious communities today: Sikhs, Hindus and Muslims. Moreover, male Jats married into a whole range of lower agricultural and entrepreneurial castes.[52] Stokes writes that their social mores were grounded more in a form of tribal nationalism instead of caste identity.[53] All this begins to change around the turn of the 20th century when the Jats start to transform from being a syncretic and fluid community to a more organised one as a result of the Arya Samaj Movement.[54] Colonial administrators saw the Jats as hardworking and brave,[55] thereby declaring them a martial race. This had a significant impact on the community's self-perception. The Jats' dominance over land, strengthened by the colonial administration, helped establish their social dominance, which was recognised both by themselves and other castes.[56] Their strong sense of community, their hold over land and their self-perception regarding their valour and, by extension, their masculinity has allowed for the creation of a strong community identity based on pride.[57] It might indeed be stated that the one factor that is historically specific to the Jats is their community solidarity, articulated through the institution of *khap panchayat*s. Through the system of *khap*s, the Jats were able to forge a regional identity that was the result of a more territorial and not simply a communitarian consolidation.[58]

Christopher Bayly writes that the Jats were able to establish their dominance over southeast Delhi by 1710 by moving into the Gangetic plains in two phases in the 17th and 18th centuries.[59] But only after the 1857 revolt, which marked the downfall of the Mughals in particular and the Islamic culture of Delhi in general, did the Jats start working towards steadily increasing their landholdings in the region, sometimes through deceit and at other times through bribery.⁶⁰ The strong community network was further consolidated as the Punjab Land Alienation Act, 1900, which forbade the sale of land to communities that were not recognised by the British government as agrarian.⁶¹ Jat kinship networks, as a consequence, expanded throughout the region. As mentioned earlier, even after settling down in a new territory, the splinter groups would invariably maintain close relations with the parent village through kinship ties mediated by *gotra* or *got*. This form of association between villages became the basis for an elaborate *panchayat* system, of which these urban villages constitute the lowest tier. Till date, villages that are considered to be connected through *got* are not allowed to marry into each other.⁶² *Bhaichara* travels well beyond merely being a form of land ownership. *Bhaichara*, which means brotherhood, is also an affect, a way of being within a community.

> Bound together by the ties of blood, connection, and above all common interest, like the bundle of sticks, they are difficult to break. Drought may wither their crops, famine and disease may depopulate their houses their fields may be deserted for a time, but when the storm blows over, and if any survive, they are certain to return. If an accident happens to any individual, he is assisted and befriended by his *bhybunds*....⁶³

The key to the ascension of the Jats, however, lies in the fact that they have been a community of landowners. In the Delhi district alone, the Jats owned 48 per cent of land in 1912.⁶⁴ And as this land acquired higher value, as speculation over land began to rage, the Jats automatically entered the centre stage of all the hyperactivity around urban real estate. Notions of *bhaichara* and institutions such as the *kunba* and *panchayat* began to respond to the changing realities of the political economy around land. Their historical ownership of land has led the community to organise a property market around rent. But the fact that these 'village economies' have shaped up to provide ancillary services to global capital ensures that the two work closely together.

Through a historical narrative of the Jat regional solidarities, I show in the course of this narrative how their moral economies are crucial for them to hold on to.⁶⁵ It would be a mistake to believe that contemporary neoliberal order works to produce only a particular kind of rational utilitarian subjects. In fact, neoliberalism produces diverse moralities and moral subjects.⁶⁶ The villagers continue to feel derided and looked down upon by the city dwellers and cheated by the state. Though they have benefited from neoliberal finance capital, they also feel mistrusted by the same, and for good reason. The friction between the world of capital and the world of rent goes on to produce subjectivities around loss, pride, anger and hurt. These frictions, like Anna Tsing suggested, do not necessarily mean resistance but keep these global connections in motion.⁶⁷ Keeping these factors in mind, instead of looking at how state, capital and everyday practices transform urbanism, I wish to explore how community, rent and everyday practices transform the nature of urbanisation. It is vital to point out, however, that this 'community' is far from stable.

What's in It for Urban Theory?

In the scholarship around urbanism from South Asia, there is a burgeoning body of literature which ties together the global, planetary nature of capital and the deeply localised nature of spatial practices. They have shown how neoliberal capital, in cahoots with the state, has transformed urban realities. For instance, there has been a sustained interest in looking at gentrified aesthetics driving 'world-class' urbanism,⁶⁸ real estate magnates and SEZs changing the landscape of the city,⁶⁹ and speculation-driven urban development.⁷⁰ A second set of scholarship on cities speaks of popular resistance in the face of an onslaught from both the state and the market.⁷¹ From literature on dispossession to increased violence towards the working classes, there has been a sustained interest in neoliberalism's impact on city spaces. Perspectives on forms of *accumulation by dispossession* are therefore central to both these sets of literature. The moral lines are pretty clearly drawn between the large, monstrous forces of capital that dispossess people and marginalised communities who work around these onslaughts to make a living and live a life of dignity. In doing this, neoliberalism has been understood as a totalising force that engulfs everything. While that may be partly true, neoliberalism, if it has to hold any meaning, needs to be defined precisely.⁷² I would lean on Aihwa Ong's formulation of neoliberalism with a small 'n', which speaks of a 'relationship between the governing and the governed, power and knowledge and sovereignty and territoriality'.⁷³ Neoliberalism then does not seem like a monolithic force, but rather a series of disconnected forms that shape up through a complex interaction between vernacular institutions and practices, and global capital.

There is another set of literature that acknowledges a far more conducive relationship between global forces of capital and communities. Work on the Marwaris, Gounders and Chettiars shows that industrious caste-based communities with adequate social and economic capital have been able to make inroads into avenues created by capital to further their economic interests. Many of these works are historical studies, grounded in studying capitalism as a lived form. Ritu Birla marks law as an important register, across which Marwaris transformed themselves into modern subjects, by slowly moving from the 'illegal' vernacular world of mercantile capital into the world of 'legal' industrial capital through market governance.[74] The problem with this articulation of 'vernacular forms of capitalism' is that they seem to be playing by the same rules of global capitalism in their smaller microcosms. The Marwaris trade and bet in the world of commodity trading, the Chinese businessmen use social networks[75] and the Italian businessmen toe the family line to make profits.[76] How do we then study these precise cultural forms without making them look like minor case studies, or cases of Chinese capitalism, Italian capitalism and Indian capitalism?

The latter corpus of literature, however, is also not concerned with the problem of urban transformation. The gap is filled with the work of Sharad Chari, Carol Upadhya, Sai Balakrishnan and Sanam Roohi.[77] Together, they show how caste and community networks embed themselves into neoliberal modes of urban speculation over land that is fast transforming from rural farmlands to urban capital. Debjani Bhattacharyya shows how even Marwari capital was essentially tied up in urban speculation and drawing rents.[78] With land values spiralling upwards, land speculation takes place along community lines. In showing how this happens, scholars such as Upadhya, Roohi and Balakrishnan complicate the nature of neoliberal capital and see it in continuation with pre-existing structures of power. Balakrishnan's work, for instance, looks at how a caste of sugarcane cultivators and beneficiaries of the Green Revolution in Pune, Maharashtra, are able to mobilise their existing networks to become successful stakeholders in the upcoming real estate market. Shubhra Gururani lists compensation (*muawaza*), capture (*kabza*) and rents (*kiraya*) as the three contested nodes around which these mediations take place. Gururani also looks at erstwhile farmers from Gurgaon who have entered the realm of real estate speculation. In another article co-authored with Rajarshi Dasgupta, they discuss what 'frontier urbanism' could mean conceptually and argue that the rural–urban continuum has failed to understand how the agrarian and the urban are materially and symbolically co-produced.[79] Gururani enters the question of decimating the boundaries between agrarian and urban studies from the vantage point of suburbanisation. For her, these interventions are important to debunk Eurocentric categories and generate new analytical frameworks. As important as these interventions are, Balakrishnan does not step outside the dominant category of global capital; and Gururani does not make explicit how her understanding of agrarian urbanism may change our understanding of capital.

Tom Cowan, however, enters the discussion on the rural–urban continuum through the category of rent. He looks at two examples of rentier capitalism in Gurgaon: the village rentier, who rents out cheap housing to migrant workers; and the elite rentier, a wealthy agriculturist who made enough money through private land acquisition and derives his income from expensive property.[80] Cowan locates the village rentier and elite rentier within the larger conceptual framework of rent located within speculative real estate.[81] While 'property' has been a useful analytic so far, by shifting the focus onto rent, I believe we can break into newer conceptual and political terrains. I posit that looking at political economy from these granular perspectives allows us to open up the black box of neoliberalism. It shows us that the state is not the only source of regulation and control. Rent is erected on very closely bound networks of landlords, circulation of funds in illicit chains of hard cash, and emotionally, on a discourse of anger and hurt towards the city and the state. And if this edifice needs to be understood, then neoliberalism or capital alone are not adequate lenses to work with.

Doing 'Small' Political Economy in the World of 'Big' Theory

Political economy has for the most part been spoken of in the language of 'big' concepts. Capital that gets fixed in spaces[82] appears infinite as an amorphous, freely floating force that fills all spaces like air. It presents itself as a decentred, de-territorialised apparatus that is no longer bounded by borders.[83] The scale of studying political economy has always been grand. In the 19th century, political economists were busy studying the national and imperial political economy of Britain. Political economists of today are studying global capital, where the scale has become even grander. London, New York and Tokyo are spoken of in one breath, as are Rio de Janeiro, New Delhi and Accra. Cities come and go in planetary urbanism literature to show the assemblages that capital can create and disrupt, as examples of the grand scale of global capital. Anna Tsing critiques this approach to understanding political economy through 'bigness' as a masculine way of trying to understand capitalism.[84] Tsing picks a battle with the works of Hardt and Negri, which speak of global capital as an empire. She argues that the nature of capitalism cannot be understood if it is not situated in localised, contingent forms that use the local vulnerabilities of their labour. Capitalism is not one monolithic force; it breaks itself into multiple shards. For feminist ethnographers, she argues, intersectionalities of race, caste and gender are at the heart of these various capitalisms. But while the 'big' political economists would always speak of the importance of these local, 'small' scholarships, they are often understood as lesser works. They are seen as too local, maybe a case study, at best an anthropological insight into the 'big' theory of capital. Tsing, therefore, provokes us to think how such feminist methods of doing political economy should be imagined, written and produced in ways that seem 'big enough' to non-feminist readers.[85]

Taking up Tsing's gauntlet, then, I look at the concept of rent. In the grand political economy scheme, rent has rarely found a place. In the context of urbanisation, David Harvey was one of the first theorists who brought rent back into the conversation on urbanisation. Harvey set up the question of rent as class-monopoly rent rather succinctly way back in 1974.[86] As urbanisation creates a 'relatively permanent, man-made resource', he argued, it becomes harder to distinguish between rent and profit. However, soon, he also moved away from looking at rent on its own terms and located it as an appendage to global finance capital.[87] His analysis around rent slowly began to congeal around a more planetary, global perspective. The other perspective, of understanding rent as a social relationship located in production of space through everyday practices,[88] hardly received any traction. In the context of India, David Harvey's influence on urban studies has been long lasting. In fact, *accumulation by dispossession* and Gentrification theory,[89] the most popular frameworks to study urbanism in India, both draw their genesis from Harvey's later writings.

This book attempts to piece together Harvey's earlier provocations from 1974 on class-monopoly rent (before he moved towards a more planetary scale) with Tsing's provocation to do 'small' political economy. I attempt to sketch a social history of rent and juxtapose it with 'big' political economy. Through a close look at the two urban villages of Delhi, I analyse how rent shapes up in the shadows of global capital. Rent here is not just a political economic category but also a lived one. These two conceptions of rent, the abstract and the lived, may not always map onto each other, but they reveal a conversation, a productive tension. I choose to look at rent as it operates in the lives of these villages and its inhabitants, and their changing social relations. If rent is primarily about control over resources, then it is vital to follow how this 'control' is sociologically and historically produced. The 'control' appears in two forms. One, where 'control' is expressed through an emotive expression of the value of belongingness, community, honour and *bhaichara*, and the other, where 'control' takes a particular socio-economic form whereby channels of extraction 'grab' economic value. This double function of value is essentially the conflict between 'use value' and 'exchange value' that goes on to constitute any commodity. As Marx wrote, use value remains unquantifiable and in many senses also inalienable. For any community, especially an agrarian one like the Jats, land's use value is not just instrumental. Exchange value, on the other hand, can be completely divorced from use value. Every commodity carries within it this duality, this opposition. Commodities come into the world as use values, but in the world of market, they need to be bearers of exchange value.[90] Value has to make its appearance in its 'phantom-like objectivity', quantifiable and comprised of congealed labour. Use value and exchange value constitute each other, but their oppositional relationship gets reproduced in the social relationship around village homestead land.[91]

Whether a commodity like land, produced by nature, embodies value or not is contested. But I show that the two kinds of values that constitute these lands, use value and exchange value, are in a state of a perpetual conflict. Land's use value continues to cast its long shadow over its exchange value, sometimes even to bolster exchange value. But in many others, these two notions of value clash to create very particular kinds of social relations. I argue that use value finds expression in the language of possession of rent, while its exchange value continues to be articulated in the real estate valuation terms of global finance capital. Use value and exchange value, or, in other words, the world of rent and capital, mutually sustain each other, but at the same time continue to remain uncomfortable bedfellows.

Rent circulates within the logic of 'money' that works within community chains as opposed to that of 'finance'. 'Finance' moves ahead by multiplying and dispersing control and ownership, but 'money' ensures that control and ownership, which are essential to rent, do not become anonymised. And if land has to be controlled, then channels of investments also need to be controlled through personalised networks that I am calling 'money'. They are embedded in the world of global capital both by accommodation and friction. The two forms of values are inscribed on different registers, but they do not inhabit mutually exclusive worlds. In fact, as the chapters will go on to show, these values reproduce each other. Rent mimics and taps into the world of capital but remains perpetually suspicious of it. Rent and capital have overlapping careers, but they don't become one. Rent is at home in the world of global capital, but then again, not quite. The uneven process of primitive accumulation, the monster that leaves behind half-chewed out spaces, is then precisely the way in which capital operates. 'Like the Proverbial Sisyphus, capital is engaged in a task that is never accomplished.'[92]

I look at this micro process of one such form of engagement with capital and non-capital from a granular perspective. I believe I am able to make these 'big' claims, beyond *accumulation by dispossession*, beyond the totalising force of capital, only because I attempted to see political economy in its 'smallness'.

Mapping the Book

Chapter 1 looks at the period of land acquisition in Delhi in the late 1950s and 1960s and the accompanying process of transformation of rural property to urban property. Through a series of land acquisition awards and court cases, it maps the changing mode of valuation of land. The rural land, hitherto divided into individual property, village land and village commons, follows different trajectories into eventually becoming urban private property; first, through land acquisition, and then, through *kabza*, or 'capture'. In this chapter, we see how a whole spectrum of property relations gets created through both legal and extra-legal processes.

In Chapter 2, I focus on how land acquisition forced dispossessed people to venture into various pursuits that in turn went into making the city from the 1960s to the 1990s, by investing their money in three endeavours: buying more rural land, construction and transport. We also see Jat landlords increasingly plugging into the lower ends of rent-seeking networks of the licence-permit state to enter these very same businesses. Through their individual stories, we follow their highs and lows, their windfalls and their moments of irrecoverable losses. In this chapter, we also begin to locate how their fates began to become intrinsically tied to the city.

Chapter 3 takes the reader to post-liberalisation Delhi, when these villages ultimately acquire 'real estate' value. While Munirka becomes home to lower-middle-class migrants employed in the service economy looking for cheap but apart-style accommodation, Shahpur Jat emerges first as a place for small garment factories and *kaarigars*, and eventually turns into a curated chic place full of boutiques and lifestyle stores. The chapter marks this vital turn. As the landscape begins to change drastically because of increased real estate pressures since the 1990s, it also marks a shift in the way the state begins to approach these spaces in contrast to how it had hitherto done.

Chapter 4 turns its attention towards community forms and how they modify themselves in the light of the changing urban political economy. Cartel-like *panchayat*s, vernacular forms of joint-stock companies based on the *kunba* structure, and new community-based forms of moneylending come to dominate the economic life within these villages. We see how older *bhaichara* forms of sociabilities acquire a new life in times of global capital. In this chapter, I foreground vernacular capitalism as driven by rent.

In Chapter 5, I take up incidents of racial and sexual violence within these villages, and their hyperbolic representation on platforms like YouTube, to speak of the frictions between rent and capital. The fact that this accumulation needs 'outsiders' cultivates a deep-seated anxiety among the landlords, focused on a loss of culture, masculine self-worth and control over women. The racialised tension speaks to this catch-22 situation where the landlords are both dependent on the tenants and at the same time repulsed by them.

Chapter 6 shows how this changing urban economy allows Dalits to follow in the footsteps of the Jats to become landlords as well. Their entry into the market disrupts older understandings of community. We see how the exhortations to community have had to change because the Jats are no longer synonymous with being the only landlords. If cartels have to be successful, they have to reach out to the Dalits as well. This chapter, thus, highlights the fissures and cracks that exist not just between the Jats and Dalits but also within different Dalit groups.

Chapter 7 engages the reader's attention with electoral politics and how accumulation through rent has effectively heightened people's aspirations to join it. Individuals located at different levels of the rent-market structure participate in this 'sport'. At the same time, the chapter notes the breakdown of the older territorial association of the Jats as neoliberalism creeps in to create irreparable schisms between the rural Jats of Haryana and Uttar Pradesh and the urban Jats of Delhi, and reveals how rent has transformed their kinship and political relations as well.

Methodology

I had come to Delhi in 2004 from a small town in Jharkhand, as an 18-year-old to pursue an undergraduate degree. Like countless other students who come to Delhi University anxious about which college they would end up studying in, it soon translates into another concern: which paying guest accommodation would you stay in? I had found a place in a three-seater all-girls 'paying guest' (PG) in a village called Zamrudpur, that happened to be bang opposite my college. By paying guest, most readers would assume a living arrangement with a middle-class family in a middle-class locality. This PG establishment was nowhere close to that. The building was barren, with bare brick walls and rats scurrying along the kitchen. The only thing that qualified it to be a PG was the fact that it was only meant for women, and the Gujjar family that owned the building lived on the first floor and maintained strict surveillance of the inmates. The landlord also ran a small *dhaba* (eatery) from the same building, catering to several other migrants living in the village, including us. As a young adult, my efforts to make sense of the world around me initially constituted a struggle to negotiate my space in my college and the PG. Across the road from each other, these two buildings constituted my sense of alienation in the big city in radically different ways. As a more privileged migrant to the city, I soon moved into the university hostel accommodation within Jawaharlal Nehru University, but our student lives continued to be entwined with the economy of another village across the road: Munirka. Munirka happens to be a treasure trove for students low on cash. From cheap food to cheap accommodation to cheap almost everything, there is nothing you could not find in that village. In the nine years of university life, several friends found accommodation there. Munirka, like for most students, was an extension of our university lives. And yet, the violence of that life, both covert and overt, was not lost on anyone. This book does not directly look at tenants. But it is this collective experience that frames this work. Rent, therefore, could not just be a political-economic abstract term to me. It also had to be 'lived'. And so methodologically, it only made sense to speak of these two sensibilities of rent together.

Though I formally studied only two villages, my fieldwork took me to several more. Tracking down entrepreneurs, landlords, tenants who had already made their exit, members of the Palam *panchayat*, and noted political figures from the community often required me to go beyond the village. Several threads of inquiry led me to other villages like Palam, Mohammadpur, Masoodpur and Masjid Moth, which made apparent to me the deep socio-economic ties that existed between these villages. These networks also took me as far as Jind in Haryana. A significant section of the fieldwork was conducted at the revenue offices of the villages amidst land record documents. Though I do not speak much about other villages here and the kinds of networks that exist between them, following those threads allowed me to frame the territorial question in particular ways.

Gender has been an absent presence in my fieldwork.[93] As a woman researcher amidst predominantly male respondents, gender was always something that needed to be negotiated. Young women, even though assertive, have little mobility within the village. If rent's use value in this case rests upon notions of community and its honour, one can argue that gender relations are at the heart of this social life of rent. But my access to women, especially young ones, was quite limited. In so many years of my work there, I was rarely invited by Jat men into their homes.[94] My presence in their inner places—including their 'offices'—a modern reincarnation of *baithaks*[95] could very rarely be purposeless. Offices made sure that I, like other outsiders (including men from their own community), had no access to their private spaces. Even though my outsider-researcher status gave me access to spaces that traditionally were not accessible to women, I could only hope for so much. There was a general reluctance to talk about property to an outsider, since property, land and investments are considered appropriate subjects of discussion only with other similarly aged and ranked men. Talking about property to a 'chit of a girl' seemed odd to them. Suspicion and sometimes even hostility loomed large, which precluded possibilities of developing a personal rapport with many. But I was also as suspicious of them as they were of me. However, the interactions were not necessarily hostile. They behaved extremely warmly with me; I was almost immediately addressed as a *beti*.[†] Younger men were, however, a different deal. They neither had access to offices nor did they suffer any discomfort. They were as curious about me as I was about them. With them, my constant struggle was to keep the interaction as de-sexualised as possible, sometimes by not objecting to being called 'Madam'[96] or by addressing them with the respectable suffix 'ji' to their names.

Ultimately, a city is built as much by administrative planning as much as it is by human acts. In this case, urban villages are a result of planning processes as well as the human spirit to make lives better, even if it is at someone else's cost. Strewn across this book are such stories about all kinds of wheeling and dealing, about some striking gold overnight and many more hoping to do so by dabbling in different endeavours, ranging from the transport business to property dealership. While some stories are about human resilience, friendships and collaborations, quite a few of them are also about greed and deceit or just sheer opportunism. The book is essentially about a rural community making its space within the urban through a process that finds little redemption. In the end, I only hope that I am able to tell the story of the city's making, both by bricks and mortar as well as human aspirations in black, white and several shades of grey in between.

[†] 'Daughter'.

Notes

1. Karl Marx, *Capital: A Critique of Political Economy*, vol. 1, trans. Ben Fowkes (London: Penguin Classics, 1994).
2. David Harvey, *The New Imperialism* (New York: Oxford University Press, 2003). By 'accumulation by dispossession', Harvey meant that the primitive accumulation that Marx conceptualised was not a one-time historical affair but rather an ongoing one. He argues that neoliberal capital has, in fact, accelerated the process of dispossession across the world through an economy of debt, structural adjustment programmes and financialisation.
3. Michael Levien, 'Special Economic Zones and Accumulation by Dispossession in India', *Journal of Agrarian Change* 11, no. 4 (2011); Swapna Bannerjee-Guha, 'Space Relations of Capital and Significance of New Economic Enclaves: SEZs in India', *Economic and Political Weekly* 43, no. 47 (2008).
4. Sapana Doshi, 'The Politics of the Evicted: Redevelopment, Subjectivity, and Difference in Mumbai's Slum Frontier', *Antipode* 45, no. 4 (2013); Andre C. Ortega, 'Manila's Metropolitan Landscape of Gentrification: Global Urban Development, Accumulation by Dispossession and Neoliberal Warfare against Informality', *Geoforum* 70 (2016).
5. Amita Baviskar, 'Between Violence and Desire: Space, Power, and Identity in the Making of Metropolitan Delhi', *International Social Science Journal* 55, no. 175 (2003): 89–98; Véronique Dupont and Usha Ramanathan, 'The Courts and the Squatter Settlements in Delhi: Or the Intervention of the Judiciary in Urban Governance', in *New Forms of Urban Governance in India: Shifts, Models, Networks, and Contestations*, ed. I. S. A. Baud and Joop de Wit (New Delhi: Sage, 2008).
6. Ministry of Urban Development, *Report of the Expert Committee on Lal Dora and Extended Lal Dora in Delhi* (New Delhi, 2007), 15.
7. Ajay K. Mehra, 'Urban Villages of Delhi', in *Urbanization and Governance in India*, ed. Evelyn Hust and Michael Mann (New Delhi: Manohar, 2005), 298.
8. The Asian Games was more than a sporting event. It was meant to skyrocket Delhi and India on to the international platform.
9. The Delhi Master Plan, 1962, designated manufacturing zones in the city but did not designate living spaces for the same working class that was supposed to work in those manufacturing units. Therefore, slums continued to proliferate and the colonial obsession over 'congestion' and consequently slum clearance remained steadfast. Also, industrial zoning as a strategy failed because industries never stopped proliferating in non-designated areas of Delhi, partly out of lack of requisite infrastructure or partly out

of infeasibility. See Awadhendra Sharan, *In the City, Out of Place: Nuisance, Pollution and Dwelling in Delhi, c. 1850–2000* (New Delhi: Oxford University Press, 2014), 211.
10. The migrants from Northeast India have been exceptionally high in demand in these sectors also because of their racially different features which makes them 'more presentable' in the global economy. Here I am using the term 'Northeast Migrants' as a shorthand for the people from Manipur and other states in Northeast India as well as Sikkim, Darjeeling in North Bengal and across the border in Nepal who have Tai, Tibeto-Burman and Mon Khmer lineages, which makes them racially distinct from the rest of the people of India. See Duncan McDuie-Ra, *Northeast Migrants in Delhi: Race, Refuge and Retail* (Amsterdam: Amsterdam University Press, 2012), 27–32, for a discussion on how the phrases 'Northeastern migrants' might be extremely problematic to refer to them as a collective. These terms take for granted the territorial fixity of the nation state and do not take into account the aspirations of several groups that constitute that geographical territory. However, due to our own conceptual confines, 'Northeastern migrants' might just be the most feasible term when discussing them as a collective for this particular work.
11. Delhi Development Authority, *Work Studies Relating to the Preparation of the Master Plan Report*, vol. 3 (New Delhi, 1957), 795.
12. Ibid., 812.
13. Sharan, *In the City, Out of Place*, 192.
14. Ibid., 193.
15. Neeladri Bhattacharya, *The Great Agrarian Conquest: The Colonial Reshaping of a Rural World* (Ranikhet: Permanent Black, 2018).
16. Gavin Shatkin, 'Planning to Forget: Informal Settlements as "Forgotten Places" in Globalising Metro Manila', *Urban Studies* 41, no. 2 (2004): 2472. Gavin Shatkin calls these spaces 'Forgotten Places' in the context of global city-regions emerging in Asia.
17. Desakota refers to the densely populated agricultural hinterlands in Asia which lie outside the limits of the mega urban regions. Desakota is a term that has been coined by clubbing two words in Indonesian: *desa*, which means 'village', and *kota*, which means 'town'. Terry McGee, 'The Spatiality of Urbanization: The Policy Challenges of Mega-Urban and Desakota Regions of Southeast Asia' (working paper no. 161, Institute of Advanced Studies, United Nations University, 2009), 8.
18. The failure of the Delhi Master Plan, 1962, to provide affordable housing to the poor has been extensively written about. See Gautam Bhan, 'Planned Illegalities: Housing and the Failure of Planning, 1947–2010',

Economic and Political Weekly 48, no. 24 (2013). For a detailed discussion of how the DDA becomes an institution that speculates on land through the extensive implementation of the Delhi Master Plan, see Ravi Sundaram, *Pirate Modernity: Delhi's Media Urbanism* (Oxford; New York: Routledge, 2010), 28–66.

19. Increasingly, world over cities have refused to pump taxes into constructing housing for the poor and other public facilities, leading to demands for housing justice across the world.
20. Winnie Hu, '"Hostile Architecture": How Public Spaces Keep the Public Out', *New York Times*, 8 November 2019, https://www.nytimes.com/2019/11/08/nyregion/hostile-architecture-nyc.html (accessed 20 March 2020).
21. There is a longer history to the short-sightedness of these massive plans. The Regional Plan was technically a successor of the Garden City Plan, another comprehensive plan, that had failed miserably. Anthony D. King, *Urbanism, Colonialism and the World-Economy: Cultural and Spatial Foundations of the World Urban System* (London; New York: Routledge, 1990).
22. Nipesh Narayan Palat and René Véron, 'Informal Production of the City: Momos, Migrants, and an Urban Village in Delhi', *Environment and Planning D: Society and Space* 36, no. 6 (2018).
23. Surajit Chakravarty, 'Between Informalities: Mahipalpur Village as an Entrepreneurial Space', in *Space, Planning and Everyday Contestations in Delhi*, ed. Surajit Chakravarty and Rohit Negi (New Delhi: Springer, 2016).
24. Fordism refers to a process of mass production carried out through big assembly line production. Made iconic by Henry Ford's General Motors, it revolutionised mass production in the early 20th century. Post-Fordism would refer to the industrial age which began to see such massive factories as a more unwieldy form of production and started outsourcing its production to adapt to more flexible forms of manufacturing, with far more precarious work conditions. The transition from Fordism to Post-Fordism, however, is not necessarily very pronounced in countries like India because large factory-based production never really was the most dominant form of production here. Small-scale, family-based, informal manufacturing has been the most pervasive form of production since the beginning of industrialisation in India.
25. David Graeber, 'It Is Value That Brings Universes into Being', *HAU: Journal of Ethnographic Theory* 3, no. 2 (2013): 222.
26. Satendra Kumar, *Badalta Gaon, Badalta Dehat: Nai Samajikta Ka Uday* (New Delhi: Oxford University Press, 2018).

27. Ibid., 122.
28. Shubhra Gururani, 'Cities in the World of Villages: Agrarian Urbanism and the Making of India's Urbanizing Frontiers', *Urban Geography* 41, no. 7 (2020); Sai Balakrishnan, *Shareholder Cities: Land Transformations along Urban Corridors in India* (Philadelphia: University of Pennsylvania Press, 2019).
29. There is a clear overlap between the kinship and ethnically bounded notion of 'community' and Partha Chatterjee's notion of political community: a modern, governmentally and electorally bound collective. See Partha Chatterjee, *The Politics of the Governed: Reflections on Popular Politics in Most of the World* (New York: Columbia University Press, 2004).
30. Karl Marx, *Capital: A Critique of Political Economy*, vol. 3, trans. David Fernbach (London: Penguin Classics, 1991), 752.
31. Fernando Coronil, *The Magical State. Nature, Money, Modernity in Venezuela* (Chicago; London: University of Chicago Press), 41.
32. Kalyan Sanyal, *Rethinking Capitalist Development: Primitive Accumulation, Governmentality and Post-Colonial Capitalism* (New Delhi: Routledge, 2007).
33. Thomas Piketty, *Capital in the Twenty-First Century*, trans. Arthur Goldhammer (Cambridge, MA; London: The Bellknap Press, 2017), 537.
34. Mariana Mazzucato, *The Value of Everything: Making and Taking in the Global Economy* (London: Allen Lane, 2018), 6. Mazzucato's fantastic study also shows how neoclassical economics systematically pushed for an argument that even income from rent should be understood as value production. Ibid., 71–74. Carlo Vercellone, 'The Becoming Rent of Profit? The New Articulation of Wage Rent and Profit', *Knowledge Cultures* 1, no. 2 (2013); Christian Marazzi, *The Violence of Financial Capitalism*, trans. Kristina Lebedeva (Los Angeles: Semiotext(e), 2010).
35. Mazzucato, *The Value of Everything*, 106.
36. I would like to invoke Anna Tsing's formulation of the term 'friction' to understand global connectedness. Writing against the grain of understanding global connectedness through the metaphor of 'flows', Tsing speaks of looking at 'frictions', the uneven and awkward links that go on to constitute global commodity chains. Anna Lowenhaupt Tsing, *Friction: An Ethnography of Global Connection* (New Jersey: Princeton University Press, 2005).
37. Marx, *Capital*, vol. 3, 754.
38. Piketty, *Capital in the Twenty-First Century*.
39. Costas Lapavitsas, 'The Financialization of Capitalism: Profiting without Producing', *City* 17, no. 6 (2013); Melissa Garcia-Lamarca Andreucci, Jonah

Wedekind and Erik Swyngedouw, 'Value Grabbing: A Political Ecology of Rent', *Capitalism, Nature, Socialism* 28, no. 3 (2017).

40. Anne Haila, *Urban Land Rent: Singapore as a Property State* (Chicester: Wiley-Blackwell, 2015).
41. Thomas Purcell, Alex Loftus and Hug March, 'Value–Rent–Finance', *Progress in Human Geography* 44, no. 3 (2020). Marx notes the complexity of the relationship between capital–profit, land–ground rent and labour–wages. For Marx, this 'Trinity Formula' encompasses the mysterious relationship of social production. Marx, *Capital*, vol. 3, 953.
42. By vernacular rent, I am essentially trying to distinguish it from rent that is deeply enmeshed with financial capital.
43. A category of people called '*bhaat*s' who maintain handwritten familial and clan records claim that the Tokas clan moved into Munirka around 1503. Ruddh Singh Tokas, to whom the village traces its origin, began to sell milk here. By some turn of events that are not clear, the local noble Munir Khan came to owe 600 rupees to Ruddh Singh and consequently had to part with 7,000 *bigha*s of land as repayment. This story is recounted in a local history book written by Chaudhary Mahendra Singh Tokas titled *Munirka: Dilli Dehat Ke Reeti-Riwaaz*.
44. *Got* or *gotra* (Sanskritised version of the term) is an exogamous familial unit comprising descendants following from one common male ancestor.
45. According to their oral history, Brahmins are said to have come from Bahadurgarh in Haryana and the Lohars from Alwar in Rajasthan. The Nais came from Amer in Rajasthan, then moved to Khera in Delhi and eventually to Munirka. The Jatavs are said to have come from Babarpur in Delhi. While the exact time period of Jatavs' migration into Munirka is not clear, it seems that it mostly happened around the late 19th to the early 20th century.
46. The Government of India, in order to promote sports in the country, allocates reserved seats in colleges and government jobs for candidates who excel in sports.
47. Baden-Powell writes,

> ... as our revenue system, borrowed from the North-West Provinces, at once assumed these village bodies to be joint and entitled to all the land inside their local village area, and as the feelings of the people evidently fell in with this position, it is impossible to suggest any antecedent condition and any subsequent growth of a landlord class, or gradual development of landlord claims.

See B. H. Baden-Powell, *The Land Systems of British India*, vol. 1 (Oxford: Oxford University Press, 1974), 139.

48. Ibid., 163.
49. Oswald Wood and R. Maconachie, *Final Report on the Settlement of Land Revenue in the Delhi District* (Lahore: Victoria Press, 1882), 3.
50. Ibid., 3.
51. Eric Stokes, *Peasant and the Raj: Studies in Agrarian Society and Peasant Rebellion in Colonial India* (Cambridge: Cambridge University Press, 1980).
52. Ibid., 58.
53. Ibid.; Nonica Datta, too, writes, 'They were not a rigid caste, but a socially inclusive group with a capacity to incorporate different peasant castes, military adventurers and groups living on the fringes of settled agriculture.' See Nonica Datta, *Forming an Identity: A Social History of Jats* (New Delhi: Oxford University Press, 1999), 11.
54. Ibid.
55. Colonial administrators and writers often sang paeans to the Jats who were capable of immense hard work. William Crooke, who wrote the book titled *The North Western Provinces* (London 1897), wrote that, 'in all of India, there is no finer raw material than the Jats'. Quoted in Stokes, *The Peasant and the Raj*, 233.
56. Suhas Palshikar, 'Caste Politics through the Prism of Region', in *Region, Culture and Politics in India*, ed. Vora Rajendra and Anne Feldhaus (New Delhi: Manohar, 2006), 271–98.
57. The idea of Jat pride is a complex one with no clear answers. Much of it is owed to the fact that Jats were enumerated as a martial race during colonial times, which made it possible for them to enter the armed forces directly, which further lent to them a discourse of masculinity. Baden-Powell noted in the year 1892 that Jats and Gujjars, owing to their strong sense of 'tribe', had been able to exert communal control over village land and therefore had a feeling of superiority over other castes, members of which helped them cultivate these lands. See Baden-Powell, *The Land Systems in British India*, vol. 1, 107. Another originary matter of pride finds its source in mythical stories of the *khap panchayat*s having revolted against Muslim 'invaders' like Qutubuddin Aibak, Taimur Lan, Babur and Ahmed Shah Abdali; this has become a part of their oral history and is frequently cited in contemporary times in the context of the Jats being the first 'freedom fighters'. See Suraj Bhan Bharadwaj, 'Myth and Reality of the Khap Panchayats: A Historical Analysis of the Panchayat and Khap Panchayat', *Studies in History* 28, no. 43 (2012).
58. Suhas Palshikar, 'Caste Politics through the Prism of Region'.
59. See Christopher Bayly, *Rulers, Townsmen and Bazaars: North Indian Society in the Age of British Expansion 1770–1870* (New Delhi: Oxford University Press, 2012), 26–27.

60. Kai Friese, 'Peasant Communities and Agrarian Capitalism,' *Economic and Political Weekly* 25, no. 39 (1990): A-137.
61. M. Mufakharul Islam, 'The Punjab Land Alienation Act and the Professional Moneylenders', *Modern Asian Studies* 29, no. 2 (1995).
62. Shahpur Jat is related to Ber Sarai and Munirka to Mohammadpur through these exogamous networks of kinship.
63. Wood and Maconachie, *Final Report on the Settlement*, 4.
64. Ibid., 38.
65. The reference to 'moral economy' has been made by historian E. P. Thompson, who wrote about the English crowds dating back to the 18th century, which would 'riot' each time the bread prices would rise to a level that they would collectively perceive as unjust. But this moral economy is far from Thompson's. These erstwhile farmers are not necessarily plainly victims of market. They are enthusiastic participants in it. E. P. Thompson, 'The Moral Economy of the English Crowd in the Eighteenth Century', *Past and Present* 50, no. 1 (1971): 76–136.
66. Andrea Muelbach, *The Moral Neoliberal: Welfare and Citizenship in Italy* (Chicago: University of Chicago Press, 2012).
67. Tsing, *Friction*, 6.
68. D. Asher Ghertner, *Rule by Aesthetics: World-Class City Making in Delhi* (New York: Oxford University Press, 2015).
69. Llerena Guiu Searle, *Landscapes of Accumulation: Real Estate and the Neoliberal Imagination in Contemporary India* (Chicago: University of Chicago Press, 2016); Preeti Sampat, 'Special Economic Zones in India: Reconfiguring Displacement in a Neoliberal Order?' *City and Society* 22, no. 2 (2010).
70. Michael Goldman, 'Speculative Urbanism and the Making of the Next World City', *International Journal of Urban and Regional Research* 35, no. 3 (2011).
71. Solomon Benjamin, 'Occupancy Urbanism: Radicalizing Politics and Economy beyond Policy and Programs', *International Journal of Urban and Regional Research* 32, no. 3 (2008); Lisa Weinstein and Xuefei Ren, 'The Changing Right to the City: Urban Renewal and Housing Rights in Globalizing Shanghai and Mumbai', *City and Community* 8, no. 4 (2009).
72. Rajesh Venugopal, 'Neoliberalism as Concept', *Economy and Society* 44, no. 2 (2015).
73. Aihwa Ong, 'Introduction: Neoliberalism as Exception, Exception to Neoliberalism', in *Neoliberalism as Exception: Mutations in Citizenship and Sovereignty*, ed. Aihwa Ong (Durham; London: Duke University Press, 2006), 3.

74. Ritu Birla, *Stages of Capital: Law, Culture and Market Governance in Late Colonial India* (Durham; London, Duke University Press, 2009).
75. I am referring to the extensive work done on *guanxi*, or the use of social capital by Chinese businessmen. A. B. Kipnis, *Producing Guanxi: Sentiment, Self, and Subculture in a North China Village* (Durham: Duke University Press, 1997); John Osburg, *Anxious Wealth: Money and Morality among China's New Rich* (Stanford: Stanford University Press, 2013); Alan Smart, 'Gifts, Bribes, and Guanxi: A Reconsideration of Bourdieu's Social Capital', *Cultural Anthropology* 8, no. 3 (1993).
76. Sylvia Junko Yanagisako, *Producing Culture and Capital: Family Firms in Italy* (Princeton; Oxford: Princeton University Press, 2002).
77. Sharad Chari, *Fraternal Capital: Peasant Workers, Self-Made Men and Globalisation in Provincial India* (Stanford; New Delhi: Permanent Black, 2004); Carol Upadhya, 'The Farmer-Capitalists of Coastal Andhra Pradesh', *Economic and Political Weekly* 23, no. 28 (1988); Balakrishnan, *Shareholder Cities*; Sanam Roohi, 'Anticipating Future Capital: Regional Caste Contestations, Speculation and Silent Dispossession in Andhra Pradesh', *Journal of Contemporary Asia* 50, no. 5 (2020).
78. Debjani Bhattacharyya, *Empire and Ecology in the Bengal Delta: The Making of Calcutta* (New Delhi: Cambridge University Press, 2019), 169–200.
79. Shubhra Gururani and Rajarshi Dasgupta, 'Frontier Urbanism: Urbanisation beyond Cities in South Asia', *Economic and Political Weekly* 53, no. 12 (2018).
80. Tom Cowan, 'The Urban Village, Agrarian Transformation, and Rentier Capitalism in Gurgaon, India', *Antipode* 50, no. 5 (2018).
81. Ibid., 5.
82. David Harvey, *Conditions of Postmodernity: An Enquiry into the Origins of Cultural Change* (Cambridge; Oxford: Blackwell, 1989).
83. Michael Hardt and Antonio Negri, *Empire* (Cambridge; London: Harvard University Press, 2001), xii.
84. Anna Lowenhaupt Tsing, 'Supply Chains and the Human Condition', *Rethinking Marxism: A Journal of Economics, Culture and Society* 21, no. 2 (2009).
85. Ibid., 152.
86. David Harvey, 'Class-Monopoly Rent, Finance Capital and the Urban Revolution', *Regional Studies* 8, no. 3 (1974).
87. In *Limits to Capital*, David Harvey's primary concern is how to think about rent in the context of financialisation. David Harvey, *The Limits to Capital* (London; New York: Verso, 2006). By 2010, though Harvey continued to make a case for rent's analytic ability, its canvas had become even grander. Rent's conceptual importance for Harvey now came from the fact that rent and land value integrate geography, space and nature with respect to capitalism. David Harvey, *Enigma of Capital and the Crises of Capitalism* (New York: Oxford University Press, 2010), 183.

88. Johannes Jäger, 'Urban Land Rent Theory: A Regulationist Perspective', *International Journal of Urban and Regional Research* 27, no. 2 (2003); Steven Katz, 'Towards a Sociological Definition of Rent: Notes on David Harvey's The Limits to Capital', *Antipode* 18, no. 1 (1986): 72; Matthew B. Anderson, 'Class Monopoly Rent and the Contemporary Neoliberal City', *Geography Compass* 8, no. 1 (2014).
89. In this context, Rent Gap Theory, proposed by Neil Smith, has been quite dominant. This theory argues that the difference between the current rent and the highest possible rent pushes gentrification. Neil Smith, *New Urban Frontier: Gentrification and the Revanchist City* (London; New York: Routledge, 1996).
90. Marx, *Capital*, vol. 1, 138.
91. I am thankful to Ritajyoti Bandopadhyay for this observation.
92. Sanyal, *Rethinking Capitalist Development*, 61.
93. For a detailed discussion on masculinity in these villages, see Sushmita Pati, 'Anxieties of "Dabanggai": Tales from Delhi's Urban Villages', *Café Dissensus* 35 (2017), special issue on Masculinity/ies in Urban India.
94. I must add here that my experience with Jatav and Balmiki households was very different. They were far more comfortable with me visiting them in their homes.
95. Usually open courtyards, on the outer area of the *haveli*s of rich men that would be exclusively a space for male camaraderie.
96. Madhura Lohokare's work explores the relationship between a female researcher and her male respondents through these terminologies and what burden they possibly come with. Madhura Lohokare, 'Making Men in the City: Articulating Masculinity and Space in Urban India' (PhD diss., Syracuse University, 2016), 213–23.

1

Creating Values of Land
Law, Records and *Kabza*

Munirka ki mahilaon ko Pakistan bhej dena chahiye. Gobar paat paat kar hi adhe Pakistan par kabza kar lengi.[*]

—Local joke

What we call land is an element of nature inextricably interwoven with man's institutions. To isolate it and form a market for it was perhaps the weirdest of all the undertakings of our ancestors.

—Karl Polanyi, *The Great Transformation*

Four hundred square yards of land in Mohammadpur-Munirka,[1] owned by a Murli Manohar and a Gordhan Dass, was set to be acquired around 1989. The brothers decided to put up a fight and file a counter claim under Sections 9 and 10 of the Land Acquisition Act, 1894, of 1 crore rupees as compensation, in addition to solatium and interest. The land acquisition collector knew the drill by then. The formula of coming to a just compensation had evolved to calculating average land prices for the last five years before the land had been notified. According to the collector, most of the land sales had happened in 1984 and the average price was 44 rupees per square yard. No sale was reported during 1985–87. The collector noted, however, that in 1988, one sale had taken place for 1,900 rupees per square yard. On this issue, the collector writes,

> There has been increases in prices of land from time to time but no reliance can be placed on the solitary sale deed executed from the year as the prices would not have jumped so much from Rs. 44 per sq. yard to Rs. 1900 per sq. yard during a span of 4 years.[2]

---

[*] Munirka women must be sent to the border. They will be able to capture half of Pakistan simply by baking dung cakes.

Therefore, 1984 prices of 44 rupees per square yard were held as the baseline for calculating land values in 1989. The brothers were only awarded 39,901 rupees as compensation at the rate of 65 rupees per yard. The hike in 1988 was brushed off as bewildering. The collector saw nothing that could possibly explain why land values could go up so much.

What could possibly have led to such price hikes is anybody's guess. The 1980s was a phenomenal period in Delhi's urbanisation. The 1982 Asian Games, the 1984 Sikh Riots and the construction of a new airport terminal in 1986 presumably created heavy incentives for quick land deals at speculative values in this decade. The land acquisition awards attempted to remain silent on these urban developments. But they give away the fact that they are being drafted by the same bureaucrats who are involved with building the modern and glitzy 'South' Delhi. We see in this case and scores of others how the state attempts to turn a blind eye to the possible levels of speculation. And it helped, because it let the state award far lower rates than the existing market values.

While the case of Murli Manohar and Gordhan Dass may be spectacular because of the extremely high values of compensation claimed, it was not an exceptional case in its nature. Hundreds of counter claims were made under Sections 9 and 10 of the Land Acquisition Act, where landowners demanded a higher price. The method of resolving such disputes also largely remained similar. These high claims were routinely disposed of for not being supported by documentary proof. In cases where there was documentary proof available, they were dismissed for being isolated and inexplicable. A claim filed collectively by a clan group in 1961 demanded 15 rupees per yard for land being acquired for the construction of Ring Road. But it was dismissed on the grounds of fraud.[3] As documentary evidence, the villagers had provided a sale deed where 10 *biswa*s of land was sold at 40 rupees per yard. The collector dismissed the claim because to him a transaction between people of the same village must have been inflated in the light of land acquisition.

Land acquisition represents the state's deceit in the collective memory of the Jat community. Munirka's lands were one of the earliest to get acquired in the late 1950s and early 1960s at dirt-cheap rates even though some of the most important infrastructural developments like the R. K. Puram government colonies and both the Inner and Outer Ring Roads were coming up on these lands as early as the 1960s. Second, as the *lal dora* became the line that differentiated the village from the city, the villagers became increasingly resentful about being squeezed within the *lal dora* with close to no urban amenities, while expensive South Delhi colonies mushroomed all around them.

Furthermore, landowners in villages acquired in the 1980s, like Palam and Mahipalpur, received compensation that was significantly higher. In fact, the Expert Committee on Lal Dora report too alleges that villagers were short-changed for their land, that the land was auctioned off at much higher rates than the compensation amounts.[4] 'Agar private ko hi zameen bechni thi, toh hum khud hi bech dete,'[†] as one young man told me. The Mohammadpur-Munirka villagers thus feel that they got the short end of the stick, because the 'profits' from urbanisation did not trickle down to them.

Land acquisition was meant to be a neat transfer of property from villagers to the state. But that, of course, never happened. Land acquisition by the state and land grabs by people have a long-drawn and overlapping history. Land grab, or *kabza*, as it is locally referred to, has reshaped the urban landscape of Delhi as fundamentally as land acquisition for planned development has. If *kabza* is understood today as unethical forms of possession of land, then land acquisition can always be viewed as large-scale *kabza* by the state. Land acquisition is sometimes even termed 'sarkari kabza' (*kabza* by the government) by people. In other words, land acquisition, though legally sanctioned, remains unethical in the eyes of these villagers. At the same time, there are *kabza*s which are ethical in the eyes of the people but considered illegal under law.

Making Land into Property

Conflicts over value frequently find expression in the friction between communities and state, in court cases and in negotiations over records and documents and legal instruments. As far as the state is concerned, the act of regulating new urban property is fraught with the traffic between the legal and illegal. Given how rampant the issue of unauthorised construction is in Delhi, land grabs are not so unique and unfamiliar. Creation of legal and illegal urban property regimes are often overlapping processes. Legal land acquisition and illegal *kabza*, or land grabs, are thus two sides of the same coin. But while land acquisition introduces one kind of valuation regime, *kabza* introduces an entirely different logic of valuation of property. Once land acquisition converted much of the village land into government-owned property, the process of land grab allowed villagers to reclaim that land, but this time, as private property.

Though private property was not an alien concept to these villagers, the *bhaichara* form of land tenure systems also ensured that private, individuated

---

[†] 'If in the end it was about selling land to private (entities), we could have done it ourselves.'

property was not the only way in which they understood their relationship to land. This brings us to the odd commodity that land is. Unlike nearly every other commodity, land is not a product of human labour. It cannot be valued entirely in monetary terms. It is emotive, even sacred. It is embedded in our social structures. This conversation rests upon a profound question: how can one determine the *value* of land? To understand the evolution of land as a commodity, we would need to go back to a point in history when 'private property' as the norm of possession was taking root in human conscience. In this regard, Karl Polanyi writes about how land transforms into a commodity in the West, however awkwardly.[5]

In some ways, Ranajit Guha, in his magnum opus *A Rule of Property*, shows us how this transformation happened in Bengal. He describes how 'Bengali society was to be fashioned after the image of Whig England'[6] through clear property regimes. The Permanent Settlement introduced notions of private taxable property in 1793 by bringing in *mauza*s of land, of individual farmers under a *zamindar*. Property rights were the pillar of modern society and acted as a stimulus to agriculture and overall economic development. To exercise property law, an effective and privatised land market was essential.[7] Neeladri Bhattacharya's book documents what follows in Punjab, after the Permanent Settlement: a foreign land tenure system is declared a failure. Bhattacharya details the long-drawn process that the colonial administrators undertook—mapping, documentation and categorisation of land—to create a land tenure system based on indigenous land systems; one of them being the *bhaichara* system in northwest India.[8] Bhattacharya writes how diverse forms of possessions and land tenure systems in the region were clubbed together and standardised to allow for a clan-based system of revenue collection. In the spirit of being non-disruptive, the village commons, or the *shamilat deh*, were also mapped and retained as common property in revenue records. This process created a rural property regime, which recorded land revenue documents with details of ownership, cultivation, taxation and, by extension, 'value'.

With land acquisition, rural property ensconced in a particular kind of agrarian political economy of colonial India begins to be written over to create a new regime of urban property. Land acquisition meant that the *bhaichara* land needed to be marked and valued differently. The process was far from being smooth. Often, the determinant of land's value was mediated by factors external to it. In this chapter, we will look at *location* of the tract of land and *time* of its acquisition as crucial arbiters of this value.

Kabza reveals a polar opposite register of valuation, initiated by the people, made effective through instruments like the General Power of Attorney (GPA).

Driven essentially by caste power, it has left its imprint on land revenue documents. The documents, written in a language increasingly becoming extinct, have been interpreted and manipulated in several ways. By going through these records, I explore how land value gets negotiated through both land acquisition and land grabs. As court cases, government awards and land records become arbiters of value, we see value shape up via caste hierarchies and perceptions of injustice, along with free hand of the market. Though this chapter mostly posits value in monetary terms, this monetary valuation is not independent of affective registers of original claims of entitlement. As the status of the land traverses between rural and urban, its monetary value too reflects the same.

Location as the New Marker of Value

Sanjay Chakravorty's book engages our attention on how the Land Acquisition Act, 1894, eventually contributed to creating land markets in colonial India.[9] The postcolonial state as the assessor, buyer as well as the arbiter of land value continued to acquire land at rates that it deemed fit. Colonial revenue documents, once used to collect agricultural tax, have now become the basis of land acquisition awards. The land acquisition papers, therefore, are an incredible source that tells the tale of how the urban land market came to be created. The land acquisition awards reveal their long-lasting impact on both the geography and the social life of the city. Even though the government's award was mostly a conservative one, the land acquisition papers show how land values rose over a period. As land transforms from rural to urban, we see its valuation regime change. Rural land is valued for its own property, its fertility. But urban land is valued much more on attributes that lie outside it—most importantly, location.[10]

The tensions over how to fix values of land were evident right from the start. In order to keep prices low, the state refused to acknowledge that the land in question was already urban. As much as the state may have wanted to believe that it was going to transform pristine rural lands into a modern, planned city, some of these lands had already become a part of the private urban speculation game. The land acquisition award no. 889 of Munirka, dated 10 October 1958, is telling in this regard. Among the villagers who were to receive compensation, there were also names of illustrious politicians, prominent bureaucrats and corporations. Burma Shell Company owned tracts of land here that it had already developed. National Insurance Corporation Limited was another prominent institution to receive compensation under the same award. The chairman of the Rajasthan Public Service Commission, the retired high commissioner for India to Pakistan and even B. R. Ambedkar seemed to have land here. Many among the ones who were compensated had elite addresses like Lodi Estate, Civil Lines and Tughlaq Road in Central Delhi, and even Queen's Road in Bombay and Malleshwaram in Bangalore. Another award noted that during 1958–59, 2,937 *bigha*s of land had changed hands just before that patch was notified for acquisition in 1961.[11] It was evident from all this that rural property had already entered the speculative game of urban property far before the process of land acquisition began.

But as the Murli Manohar and Gordhan Dass story that the chapter began with shows, state officials kept their eyes closed to these variations and decided on a formula for evaluating land purely based on its agrarian value. The aim was to calculate the number and kind of trees, presence of wells and types of soil classified as *barani* (rain fed), *nahari* (canal irrigated) and *chahi* (well irrigated) and the permanent built structure already in place. Compensation value overall would be a sum of land value, value of trees, wells and structures. In addition, 30 per cent of land value as solatium for compulsory acquisition and interest for the period between notification and possession was also to be paid. The first few rounds of compensations were also accompanied by an offer for an alternative Delhi Development Authority (DDA) residential plot of up to 400 square yards at market price.[12] This formula, however, did not free the government of the charge of undervaluation. As is clear, the state was trying extremely hard to feign ignorance that land speculation had already started affecting land prices. The 1958 award document states,

> After the government the government flats came up … the land attracted the attention of the house builders and colonisers for their own houses. It is also possible that some shrewd purchasers might have foreseen the likely importance of the land in question because of the construction of the Ring Road.[13]

But right after acknowledging the possibility of speculative practices that may have been affecting prices, the award document reverted to talking about its soil quality almost immediately, completely negating its previous observation.

> It varies in kinds of soil, productive utility, irrigation facility, advantageous position, special adaptability, or potentiality for building purposes, peculiarity by natural characteristics which need to be taken into consideration. It appears to be necessary to categorise the land in question in blocks of similar quality and type.[14]

The award document decided to apply a flat rate of 3 rupees per square yard for land that it chose to deem 'agricultural'. The compensation value being offered by the state was far lower than what the existing market rates were at the time. To date, not much has changed in the government's methods of undervaluing land meant for acquisition. Even when land has been declared urban, the state refuses to pay commercial rates. In a court case as late as 2010, in *Suresh Prasad alias Hari Kishan vs Union of India,* the plea for increased compensation was dismissed on the grounds that though Masoodabad in Najafgarh had been declared urban, the acquired land in question was still being used for agriculture.[15]

All the same, despite the state's attempts, over time, it became harder for it to justify the acquisition of village land solely based on agrarian valuation. At some point, the state had to come around to taking cognisance of 'location' of the land rather than the 'productivity' of land to calculate compensation awards. As early as 1961, the collector had to begin evaluating the 'correct value' according to the market transactions of nearby land in the last five years, along with the quality of the land for Munirka. This is understandable, considering by 1961 the construction of the Ring Roads had become a tangible reality. The information that both the Ring Roads were to be constructed on these lands had clearly precipitated land speculation, as noted in the award. The shortest link road between the Diplomatic Enclave in Chanakyapuri in South Delhi and the airport (now called Rao Tula Marg) also needed to be constructed through much of what was Munirka's land. Award no. 1133 in 1961 was the first award where location was taken into consideration. The award pegged the value of land at 2.5 rupees per yard on the grounds that though the land in question bore no resemblance to land that it was being compared to, it did have potential value as building sites.

Award no. 1133, readers may recall, is also the one where members of a particular clan were accused of fraud for allegedly producing a fake sale deed. The clan members went to court and got a ruling in their favour. Though we do not know the contents of the case, this judgment seems to have been an important win for the villagers. Later, counter claims for higher compensation based on prevailing market rates cited this court judgment. But they did not necessarily meet with success. One such counter claim filed in 1966 was dismissed on grounds that the land was *rosli* (of inferior quality), and urban development being cited as the reason for higher valuation had only come up post notification.[16]

The land acquisition awards are strewn with such disputes. Every award was invariably followed by a litany of petitions expressing their unhappiness about the proposed value. *Mir Singh*[17] *and Others vs Union of India* case, 1978, is one such case among a host of similar ones filed across the period of land acquisition. The appellants from Mohammadpur-Munirka[18] were trying to prove in court that the piece of land in question could not be deemed agricultural and was in fact worth more in value.[19] The plaintiffs argued that their land lay adjacent to the posh government colony of Moti Bagh (that had come up in the 1960s) and, therefore, needed to be pegged at 12,000 rupees per *bigha*, the same value as land adjoining the Diplomatic Enclave. The court revised the value of their land to 7,500 rupees per *bigha* from 3,750 rupees per *bigha*. Its reasoning was that though the land did deserve a higher compensation because it was not just plain agricultural land, it also did not deserve a compensation of 12,000 rupees per *bigha* because it was not close to any arterial road. This reasoning arose out of the fact that once arterial roads were drawn, 'proximity' to them became an important marker for deciding the value of land. The acknowledgement of location as the primary adjudicator of land value by the state meant that the state had been forced to accept that much of the land it was acquiring was not even rural or 'village' land to begin with. As pointed out earlier, some of these areas had already entered urban land speculation, and the rest did so after their land was notified for acquisition.

Speculation, Urban Property and the Question of Time

Speculation, based on futuristic imaginations and approximations, creates an overlapping notion of value that goes beyond the logics of calculations. Speculation is not new to Delhi's urban economy. Being a city known for its markets and traders, speculation has had a longer presence. New literature on speculation argues that instead of castigating speculation as a moral failure, one should rather view it 'as a range of practices that work with and produce an instability of value'.[20] In fact, Laura Bear et al. argue that financialisation brings speculation from its marginal and illicit position right into the heart of modern economic exchange.[21] Anish Vanaik's work on the land market that emerged in Delhi after 1857 is illuminating in this regard.[22] Joint stock companies, rich landowners and the state had begun to speculate on newly created private property as early as 1857.[23] As land transformed into urban property, it also seamlessly entered the speculative logic through it. Sometimes, speculative windfalls happen after endless waiting. In other moments, speculation is all about quick disposal of the commodity. But mostly, it is about being in the right place at the right time. The moment of land acquisition injected the system with these new land values, where 'time' became a crucial variable.

Apart from location affecting land value as discussed earlier, time also interferes with the process in other ways. It is not uncommon in India for a substantial amount of time to have passed between notification (under Section 4 of the Land Acquisition Act, 1894) and acquisition (under Section 6 of the same). Once land is notified, landowners have the information that their land is to be acquired, but they do not know precisely when. This leaves room for speculation of all kinds. In Munirka itself, the process of land acquisition lasted close to three decades, allowing land value to differ wildly across the village. The owners of tracts of land that were acquired later had by then devised better informational networks and negotiation skills. These factors significantly contributed to the uneven nature of land value. Whether families decided to contest compensation values in court or not and whether they lost or won the case also led to a significant internal difference in land prices.[24] Alternative plots[25] were also offered in the case of at least a few initial rounds of awards. Many of my respondents claim that they either did not know about these offers at the time or did not claim the alternative plots. Some resold the alternative plots to land brokers and some just decided to wait. The effects of land acquisition were anything but uniform.

The information regarding the impending notification had also precipitated a boom in construction in the hope that this may fetch higher compensation for the owners. The earlier one could build something on one's piece of land, the stronger was one's claim that the built structure existed from before the time of acquisition. In this regard, a series of court cases and land award documents make evident how many such claims were dismissed because the built structures in question had come up only after notification. In cases of long years of government inactivity on notified land, shoddy constructions often gave way to semi-permanent or permanent construction, now technically on government land. The promise that these new roads and new colonies held out was too tempting to let go of just because the land had been acquired. Informal markets had quickly mushroomed all along the proposed Ring Road (Figure 1.1). And, as usual, collectors had recorded their disapproval in land acquisition awards regarding the unauthorised construction that had taken place without layout plans.[26]

Figure 1.1 This market area, close to the Ring Road, has existed since the 1960s

Source: Ritambhara Mehta and Dilip Menon.

People had quickly built pucca structures, or local 'colonisers'[27] established ownership over acquired land, cut it up into plots and sold them off as quickly as possible. Many unauthorised colonies in Delhi came up through this subterranean land market created by colonisers. According to the Revenue Department of the Delhi Government, 81 villages house unauthorised colonies within them, which is an outcome of a similar process as the one described earlier. As early as the 1960s, what emerged were rows of markets along the Ring Road. These markets are now a part of the roughly 1,700 'unauthorised colonies' in Delhi.[28]

In another case, 26 *bigha*s of land in Masoodpur had been converted into a modern sports club after its acquisition in 1965.[29] By 1991, this particular establishment came under the scanner because it lay on the new road between Andheria More and the airport that DDA was constructing. A case was filed whereby the plaintiffs, that is the owner of the sports club, argued that the said land be released from acquisition under the provision of Section 48(A) of the Land Acquisition Act. They argued that on the one hand, the government was seeking cooperation from people for development of land into shops, schools, community centres and dispensaries, but on the other, it had no qualms about breaking down a sports complex of such high standards after a gap of 25 years. The Supreme Court, however, refused to entertain the plaintiffs on the grounds that they went ahead with the construction knowing fully well that their possession was unauthorised. The court lamented how people in our country, especially the affluent, flout every municipal and town law and Master Plan without any consideration for the infrastructure of the city and reiterated its stand that the Master Plan must be honoured.

R. P. Kapur vs The State of Punjab, 1960, is another interesting case that shows how fraudulent transactions took place around the time of notification of land.[30] In this case, one Mr R. P. Kapur had bought land from villagers at 5 rupees per square yard in January 1957 in Mohammadpur-Munirka. By March 1957, the land was notified under Sections 4 and 6 and by June that year, the government had acquired the land. Six months later, in January 1958, Kapur sold 2,000 square yards of land that had already been acquired to one Mr Sethi. Kapur promised Sethi that this would make him eligible for compensation and an alternative plot in an upcoming part of South Delhi. For Sethi, it looked like a good opportunity to buy cheap land from a friend and get urban plots in the upcoming DDA colonies as compensation. It soon turned out that the promise was a false one and there was no way Sethi would get an assured plot in return. Consequently, Sethi filed a legal case against Kapur. If this case of fraudulent transfer is any indication, it follows that the information regarding the impending notification of land sometimes resulted in distress sales by landowners in the hope of getting a better price from private players. And as *R. P. Kapur vs The State of Punjab* shows us, the motivation for buying up land could vary a great deal.

Meanwhile, the state, which had a monopoly over planning, was far too slow with whatever little they wanted to do with this acquired land. Planning and its implementation were bureaucratic processes after all. A draft plan made for Munirka in the year 1985, complete with several parks, including a horticultural park, a vegetable market and a hospital, could never be implemented. While these plans were being considered, debated, drawn up and finalised, much of the land under consideration had already become prime property. They were being grabbed and speculated over at a breakneck speed. It was as if a slow-moving bureaucracy was pitted against the lightning swiftness of a speculative market. In effect, when considered against state led capitalism, this informal capital of subterranean land markets appears more flexible, reaching in to plug the gaping holes that state capital leaves behind.

Kabza as Property Making

The process of land grab followed closely on the heels of land acquisition and added further layers to the new property regime. Land acquisition had a differential impact on the three different kinds of land in villages categorised as *bhaichara*, or agricultural land, village *abadi deh* and village *shamilat deh*, or village commons. The *lal dora*, or the red line, had separated the revenue-generating agricultural land from *abadi*, or residential village land, on the revenue map since colonial times. While agricultural land was subject to revenue and taxation, *abadi*, which was merely the residential part of the village, was not a part of the revenue system. As a result, *abadi deh* was never mapped out through the lens of individual property. The third was the village *shamilat deh*, or the commons, that may have been owned by specific clan groups, but the entire village had usufructuary rights over them in some form or the other. While the village land was never mapped for revenue, the *shamilat deh* was understood to be 'wasteland' and designated as such in colonial land records. 'Wastelands' were pieces of land understood by the colonial government as idle and uncultivated, ranging from rocky, sandy barren patches to even forests.[31]

One of my respondents showed me what used to be *shamilat deh* land in Shahpur Jat until almost the 1980s but had become DDA offices now. 'Humse free mein zameen li,'[‡] my respondent exclaimed with anger that has not rusted over all the years gone by. Only in his twenties, he was too young to have witnessed the period of land acquisition, but his feelings of anger and hurt were still palpable. Land worth crores of rupees today was acquired for 'free' and made into state property, and this continues to be perceived both as a personal and communal loss by the inhabitants of the village. For purposes of land acquisition, an insertion was made in the Delhi Land Reforms Act, 1954. According to this new clause, the *gaon sabha* of the village that had ceased to be rural as per Section 507(A) of the Delhi Municipal Corporation Act, 1957, was not only dissolved but all its movable and immovable properties were also vested in the Central government.[32] With the village commons already designated as 'wasteland' with no particular owner, the question of compensation did not arise.

As upset as the Jat villagers may be, the Dalits were hit far harder by this acquisition of the *shamilat deh*. Marginalised communities, especially Dalits, which arrived later, were settled on parts of the *shamilat deh* with the mutual consent of the villagers in order to serve the village society. For a village of settlers, *kabza* or *zameen gherna* were innocent terms. However, Dalits of

---

‡ '(They) took our lands for free.'

Munirka and Shahpur Jat often spoke emotively of their gradual dispossession of the land that their fathers or grandfathers had settled on through *kabza* in the late 19th–early 20th centuries. Once the state acquired the land as 'wasteland', it refused to acknowledge the presence of the homesteads of Dalits. From being commons occupied by the Dalits, now it had become government land, illegally occupied by the Dalits. On the land revenue register, this part of the land is recognised as *hasberasad kabza*, or collectively grabbed land (see Chapter 6).

Kabza did not always carry the pejorative weight it does today. To date, villagers oscillate between both the senses of the term, in the way they use *kabza*. In a village where people came and settled from different parts of the region, *kabza* was a consensual arrangement between the dominant community that already existed and communities that settled in later. Different communities settled in different parts of the village, some with agricultural land, some not, through a process of *kabza*. However, once these lands began to enter more modern categories of property, *kabza* began to acquire the far more pejorative connotation of land grab. *Kabza* was now no longer viewed as a consensual process like before but a severely competitive phenomenon. The race for this new kind of *kabza* ended up in favour of the powerful Jats who could mobilise their social capital, their dominant status strengthened through *bhaichara* and years of colonial law favouring them through the Punjab Land Alienation Act. The meaning of the term *kabza*, as it took me time to realise, thus had to be derived from this complex historical context.[33] But *kabza*'s modern career has also not been any less complex. The chapters to follow could very well be read as a discussion of the diverse effects of *kabza* in the social fabric of these villages.

The village *phirni* land in Munirka was probably the most intensely contested for *kabza* in the 1960s because of its proximity to the Outer Ring Road/Olof Palme Road. *Phirni*, or *gher*, as it was also called, was now in direct contact with the city, and therefore coveted real estate. These became subject to land grab with the emergence of the Ring Road. For example, there is evidence that a full-fledged market called Kartar Market was thriving here as early as 1962.[34] It was acquired in the year 1969. After acquisition, the market soon bounced back and continues to exist to date. The *phirni* areas were part of the village commons, which were traditionally used for storing firewood or even keeping cattle. Some stretches were also occupied by village potters or barbers to run their establishments. But as the *phirni* land began to become more valuable, an intense conflict began whereby families and clans which were powerful began to slowly extend to the vacant parts by tying a cow, storing firewood and even spreading out dung cakes to dry. Drying dung cakes, an activity almost entirely undertaken by women, which requires flat surfaces like walls and therefore a significant surface area, became a common way of surreptitiously making encroachments on land. This form of land grab is akin to the Lockean idea of free and empty land that could be grabbed and possessed by anyone who was able to mark it off as one's own. It was sufficient to lay claim on a particular piece of land if it was 'mixed with one's labour'.[35] Slowly, barbed wires and stick fences came up to claim these as private property.[36] This also led to a far more individually contested process of *kabza* over smaller plots. The fact that both the villages recount similar stories of *kabza* tells us that this must have been a very common way of establishing private 'ownership' over what was common land.

Land acquisition and *kabza* therefore have been caught in a contest of claiming and reclaiming land. A contest that eventually takes place between the state and the community. Urban property of Delhi, therefore, gets created through this jostling between the state and the communities. The entire struggle over legality of land that seems to have choked the courts of Delhi is essentially a reflection of this phenomenon.

The Place of Speculation in Land Records

Kabza does not keep lurking in the shadowy backgrounds. It begins instead to make a partial entry into land record documents, into the black and white world of legal and illegal, creating a 'valid' niche for its greyness. The colonial forms of land documentation for agriculture take on a new life in the postcolonial context. Documents like the *khatauni* or *jamabandi* (ownership register) and the *khasra giradavari* (cultivation register) that were once used to keep a record of landholdings, property relations and details of cultivation in the village were now being used to keep details of urban property. The *khatauni* or *jamabandi* records would change hands via succession, sale and even exchange (an older practice that is not recognised anymore). The *khasra giradavari* enlists names of the owner and cultivator, and information about the land: whether it was self-cultivated or not, its area, what crop was being sown on it and so on. This register has become a key source to track changes like land relations and often bears the imprint of how *kabza* has taken place. The column titled 'cultivator' notes down the name of the 'possessor', the person who 'possesses' the property at the moment but not necessarily 'owns' it. Pages after pages of *khasra giradavari* note the owner as the state, recorded as *sarkar daulatdar*, sometimes even by specific departments like the Central

Public Works Department. But the 'possessor' column would almost invariably have names of individuals who had encroached on the land. The complex status of land has, therefore, allowed for completely different meanings for two terms that are otherwise understood to be synonymous: 'owner' and 'possessor'. The 'owner' and the 'possessor' are often located at opposite ends of the spectrum of legality. In fact, the entry of the 'encroacher' into the register as 'possessor' marks a partial legitimacy of that possession. Rapid construction on already acquired land further deepens the separation between the figure of 'possessor' and that of 'owner'. In the judgment for *Union of India and Another vs Gopal Seth and Others* case, 2011, the Delhi High Court shows precisely such a separation.[37]

These documents do not lend themselves to easy comprehension. Dating back to the times when Persian and Urdu were in circulation for official use, the terminologies and even administrative forms of writing used in these have now become increasingly inaccessible to most. The details and the nuances of the documents remain obfuscated to people not having access to Urdu and Persian. Revenue officers during colonial times would use a specific administrative hand, *shikast*, that complicates the question of access further. The *khasra giradavari* register that I saw was a photocopy of the original document from 1949 to 1950. Since the administrative language was Urdu at that time, the record remains in *shikast*, with various additional details illegibly scribbled in the margins in Hindi. I was told that these documents are supposed to be freshly remade every five years with new changes formally updated, which had not happened in this case. The new information is merely scribbled in the margins to keep track of changes. This has added another, perhaps several more layers of different orders and abbreviated forms. The act of writing is therefore central to much of the politics of land in urban villages and probably even beyond. How the officials write, what they write and how it is interpreted has decisive implications for land control, and this makes these officials key figures in this land politics.

The *tehsildar* and other officials have very little knowledge of *shikast*. The *patwari*[38] I met, Raghubir Shokeen, does not read or write Urdu, while Sushil Verma, his assistant, who has been working in this particular revenue office for years, has equipped himself to understand basic terms and digits, which helps him get by with the documents. With several years of practice, Verma is the only one in the office who can make some sense of these complicated documents to some extent, due to his working knowledge of *shikast*. Knowledge bestows technical authority; but as Michel Foucault would remind us, knowledge also gets produced by technical authority.

Their authority over interpretations of these documents and their limited expertise with regard to these documents creates space for the creation of new knowledge on land. Thus, the practice of land record documentation works entirely on the logic of 'translatability'.[39] It is not only a question of translation from *shikast* to Hindi but also a question of translation of documents from one system of governance to another. It carries within it the dilemma, the limitations and entrapments of translation, that not only can it never be translated precisely but that it is also very much amenable to being intentionally mistranslated.

The revenue office was a busy one. Land brokers and other individuals would always be thronging the office over some land dispute, or in need of confirming the confines of a piece of property and so on. An extremely friendly land broker specialising in big farmlands and institutional spaces was a regular visitor to the office in the days when I was doing my fieldwork there. One day, I found myself peering at the map of a contested piece of land that Verma, the *patwari*'s assistant, had drawn up on the table. Verma would look at the scribblings on the map and then would look up to explain how the conflict could be resolved. The broker, probably guessing my bewilderment at the complicated calculations, remarked, 'Unke apne formula hote hain. Humko woh sab nahi maaloom.'[§] The land documents were just as impervious for him as they were for me. The office of the *patwari* and *tehsildar* have been historically held suspect,[40] and more so in this case, because they are the only people 'able' to understand the language of these documents. As I was sitting in the office and talking to them, Verma exclaimed with exasperation at my state of confusion, 'Aap yeh sab samajhna chahti hain? Yeh sab toh practice se hota hai. Agar kisi ka kaam karna hota hai toh hum kuchh na kuchh dhoondh nikalte hain. Warna "please comment" likh ke file waapas bhej dete hain.'[**] As these land records are now being digitised, and these registers are phased out, it is quite possible that the centrality of the *patwari* and the revenue department officials may just come down significantly. It remains to be seen how these negotiations reshape in the light of new technology.

The 'work' of these lower offices begins to break down the neatness between the state and the villagers. Often from the same social milieu as the villagers, the revenue administrators begin to muddy up the distinction between state and society.[41] For instance, wherever land records are fuzzy, and the

---

[§] 'Now they have their own formulae. We do not know all that.'
[**] 'Do you want to understand all this work? It only happens by practice. If we have to do someone's work, then we find out one solution or the other. Otherwise, we send the file away to someone else saying "please comment".'

access to them is limited, *patwari*s have been instrumental in rendering a property or possession legitimate or illegitimate. Consequently, *kabza*, which makes possible a wide variety of possessions, has made its way into some bureaucratic documents as well. These fuzzy documents and their updating by the revenue officials seem to have made speculation over land possible in unauthorised localities. Documents like *lal dora* certificates, registration and sometimes even electricity bills have enabled various possessions to make their way into the spectrum of legality. And depending on where they are on the spectrum, their value in the speculative land markets has thus been determined.

But it is not enough for land to be possessed. Land, as private property, also needs to be saleable. In the absence of state validation of unauthorised property, new documentary innovations need to be made. This is where the GPA became important. A GPA is ideally supposed to act as an instrument by which a person can nominate one or several people to act on her behalf. However, it has come to act as a modified legal document which may not be a legal sales transfer and yet allows transfer of property rights.[42] The GPA first began to be used to circumvent transfer and sale restrictions placed on leasehold property; there used to be a significant amount of restriction on legally transferring such property.[43] Transfers made through GPA do not invite registration charges and stamp duties associated with legal transfers; thus, its increased use resulted in major losses for the revenue department.[44] Property transfer through GPA is another common practice, which complicates the nature of 'possession': instead of a sale deed, properties are, for all practical purposes, sold through the transfer of power of attorney. Sale of property through GPA was banned in 2012 following a Supreme Court order in 2011.[45] However, due to the overwhelming popularity of GPA, the Delhi Government lifted the ban on registration of property transfers done under it in July 2013.

In the absence of formal land records and documents, the GPA works as an innovation not on the part of the state but rather the people. The presence of the GPA as a document, a sheet of paper, elicits a sense of trust.[46] The *khasra giradawari* and *jamabandi* documents, along with GPAs, create authenticity, however fragile and challengeable, based on precisely the fact that they have been documented on a piece of authoritative 'looking' paper that 'holds' authoritative value. But they perform different functions. If maintenance of land records has created a variegated landscape of property along a spectrum, the GPA has been able to make a market out of it. The value of land in these villages, its production and circulation, thus happens in the shadows through documents like the GPA. At the same time, despite being fired by the fictions of land documents, the practices of accumulation that this community has forged are real. This accumulation takes place in between documents, in between fiction and reality and in between village land and urban real estate. It is negotiated through the power structures of caste, religion and state to produce claims across a wide spectrum of legality. I mention the phrase 'spectrum of legality' because property in these villages did not exist in black and white categories of 'authorised' and 'unauthorised'. In fact, most property in Delhi, even middle-class neighbourhoods and markets, would not fall in the category of 'authorised' property.[47]

How Land Acquisition and *Kabza* Reordered Spaces and Values

Katherine Verdery and Caroline Humphry urge students of property to pay attention to whether the people they study have a property concept and what these concepts amount to.[48] What terms do they use, with what meanings and in what circumstances? For me, the one word that encapsulates the ownership of their property with respect to the rest of the city is *kabza*, in its diverse uses and affects. If legality confers value on land, illegality confers new meaning on the term 'value'.[49] In this chapter, I have attempted to recount the story of how modern forms of property get shaped in different ways. Some enter a system of modern property at the time of land acquisition, others make inroads through violent land grabs and yet others far more subtly, via the manipulation of documents. Different moments of interaction involving state-land acquisition, court cases and revenue office and documents—each of these interactions throws open new complexities. These properties, depending on the kind of interaction they have had, enter the realm of modern property claims in their own circumscribed ways. Sometimes, the property is sold to multiple people using GPA, leading to far more complex claims of ownerships.

Kabza, in the way it is popularly used, has a different inflection than its usage in government revenue documents as well as court documents. Land acquisition erases another level of complexity of the nature of possession of land to create a legible and urban proprietorship of land. Land now had to either belong to the state or to individuals. It could now either be an illegal possession or legal. *Kabza* renders these watertight compartments redundant. The narrative of land grabs, shrinking open spaces, cowsheds converted into commercial buildings, the fluidity of land record documents and newly invented strategies like the GPA tell a story of how spaces metamorphose because of all the 'thinking on one's feet'. Ultimately, it is all about spotting a good opportunity and arriving there first. Any successful businessman will tell you that. And with property, this old adage is even more true.

As the Outer Ring Road in Delhi started becoming a reality, the fringes of Munirka village, now in direct contact with the road, shot up in value. As irony would have it, in traditional village spatial organisation in most of India, the centre of the village has always been the seat of power. The fringes of the village had always been unsafe as they were most prone to attacks by animals and even dacoits. As a result, the Tokas community, which settled in Munirka first, settled other communities and clans around them. When the logic of land values got completely overturned with increasing urbanisation, these fringes adjoining the city became hot property. Fortunes flipped overnight. The Tokas attribute the present prosperity of the Rathis to this 'moment' when the latter became far more well off than the former. Though we follow up with this story in another chapter, it is clear that capital can many a time make an appearance in the city in ways that can be unpredictable. It sometimes even appears as if capital has the ability to undo previous power hierarchies. However, as we have seen, traditional social hierarchies do find a way of reorganising themselves around changed circumstances too. For instance, the Jat clan of Rathis were able to retain their lands, while the Dalits, who had small businesses running on the fringes, could not. In Shahpur Jat, too, the Dalits were dispossessed in a similar fashion (see Chapter 6).

The modern state is invested in an unending project to create legible spaces and citizens, through a continuous process of settling people and creating an entire body of institutional knowledge based on addresses, families and now even fingerprints and biometric information. But just like the career of modernity in India, the career of modern property too has been uneven. If classical liberal political theory believes that property is the mainstay of a modern individual, what kind of citizenship do these inchoate, uneven properties create? In the case of these villages, the state ended up creating spaces for irregular and unclear property regimes in the shape of urban villages and unauthorised colonies in messy and complex ways.

Here, value is made possible purely through exchange.[50] The fuzziness and untranslatability owe themselves to the fact that this kind of land neither remained communal nor could be transformed into the liberal regime of private, exclusive ownership. The vagueness does not lock down value but make it mobile differently. Jean and John Comaroff draw our attention to the aspect of disorder in postcolonial societies where vastly lucrative returns are made possible as new aporias of jurisdiction open up under the neoliberal conditions.[51] Values, therefore, get created and embedded amidst political and bureaucratic uncertainties.

In other words, value begins to have a double life. And with it, the city. Amidst the big, megalomaniac plans of DDA colonies, shopping complexes and flyovers, we see these villages beginning to acquire a new life. And it is not merely a coincidence that this creation of a new kind of circulation of value and the creation of the category of urban villages coincides with each other. Values are not abstracted entities. They are deeply embedded in human relations, exchange and actions. Capital in real estate circulates in built forms through a constant process of abandonment, upgradation or gentrification.[52] As a project of removing blight, these are essentially projects to transform poor neighbourhoods into gentrified localities by transposing a different order of value. But this value is embedded in precisely the fact that these spaces are not gentrified. Value in this informal market is deeply imbricated in the values of kinship and family. Value moves through networks of debt.[53] As the book will go on to show in later chapters, none of this is coincidental. City making and the logic of keeping value chains alive through action, affect and even violence are deeply imbricated into each other. Much of the negotiations over value that define the property market are almost always deep negotiations over the different meanings of the city as well.

If land acquisition is how the state partakes in primitive accumulation, *kabza* becomes the response of the community for the same. The state uses law, documents and courts to gain control over land and the community claims it back by erecting sticks and staves, building colonies and markets, and manipulating local offices. This chapter also goes on to show how the story of land acquisition and *kabza* can both be read through the land record documents that bear the layers of both. While the state's violence of primitive accumulation has been well documented, the violence of *kabza* and similar forms of community land grabs have not been. In the chapters to follow, I would use the analytic of the social history of rent to track in the following chapters how layers of violence shape up in our cities.

Notes

1. Mohammadpur and Munirka were considered as a single revenue village until very recently. They were collectively referred to as Mohammadpur-Munirka in many documents.
2. Department of Revenue, Land Acquisition Award No. 36 (1989–90), dated 30 March 1990.
3. Department of Revenue, Land Acquisition Award No. 1133, dated 21 April 1961.

4. Delhi Development Authority, *Report of the Expert Committee on Lal Dora and Extended Lal Dora* (New Delhi, 2007), 21.
5. Karl Polanyi, *The Great Transformation: The Political and Economic Origins of Our Time* (Boston: Beacon Press, 2001).
6. Ranajit Guha, *A Rule of Property for Bengal: An Essay on the Idea of Permanent Settlement* (Ranikhet: Permanent Black, 2016), 10.
7. Ibid.
8. Neeladri Bhattacharya, *The Agrarian Conquest: The Colonial Reshaping of a Rural World* (Ranikhet: Permanent Black, 2018).
9. Sanjay Chakravorty, *Price of Land: Acquisition, Conflict, Consequence* (New Delhi: Oxford University Press, 2013), xx.
10. Von Thünen's Location Theory makes a case for economic rents rising higher with proximity to urban centres owing to transportation costs. Robert Sinclair, 'Von Thünen and the Urban Sprawl', *Annals of the Association of American Geographers* 57, no. 1 (1967). In fact, Marx's notion of Differential Rent, especially Differential Rent II (where rent arises from more capital investments on the land), speaks back to location as a primary determinant of higher rent. Karl Marx, *Capital: A Critique of Political Economy*, vol. 3, trans. David Fernbach (London: Penguin Classics, 1991), 788–871.
11. Department of Revenue, Land Acquisition Award No. 1133, dated 21 April 1961.
12. Ironically, these residential plots were being developed as layouts by DDA out of the lands that were being acquired from these villages.
13. Department of Revenue, Land Acquisition Award (number blurred), dated 10 October 1958.
14. Department of Revenue, Land Acquisition Award No. 883-PartII (A), date blurred.
15. Delhi High Court, *Suresh Prasad Alias Hari Kishan vs Union of India and Another*, 2012, 2012(129) DRJ 199.
16. Department of Revenue, Land Acquisition Award No. 2122, dated 26 June 1966.
17. Mir Singh will resurface in the last chapter of the book as a major political figure from the village in the 1970s.
18. As mentioned earlier, though Mohammadpur and Munirka are separate villages, they were considered one revenue village for a long time. Locally, as well, Mohammadpur and Munirka are kin villages (therefore, weddings are not possible between families from both villages) because Mohammadpur was settled by a section of the clan who were in Munirka. As a result, most Jats in Mohammadpur are also Tokas.
19. Delhi High Court, *Mir Singh and Others vs Union of India,* 14(1978) DLT 121.

20. Laura Bear, Ritu Birla and Stine Simonsen Puri, 'Speculation: Futures and Capitalism in India', *Comparative Studies of South Asia, Africa and the Middle East* 35, no. 3 (2015): 387.
21. Ibid., 388.
22. Anish Vanaik, *Possessing the City: Property and Politics in Delhi 1911–1947* (Oxford: Oxford University Press, 2020).
23. Ibid.
24. Delhi High Court, *Sarvodaya Cooperative Housing Society vs Union of India and Others*, 2009, MANU/DE/2069/2009. This case was filed in order to waive the conversion charge from leasehold to freehold on the grounds that the society was compensated only 5.64 lakh rupees in 1957 when the cost was 11.70 lakh rupees as per valuation in 1955. Thereafter, the society had existed as a tenant at the rate of 1 rupee per plot as ground rent for ten years, which was liable to revision every 30 years. This case was dismissed by the court.
25. As a part of the compensation deal, villagers were offered alternative plots up to 400 square yards in residential localities of Delhi at a subsidised price.
26. Department of Revenue, Land Acquisition Award No. 1204, dated 28 September 1961.
27. 'Coloniser' refers to people who managed to buy/grab significantly big chunks of land and cut them up into plots to convert them into what can be referred to as 'unauthorised colonies'.
28. PTI, 'Delhi Government Notifies 80% Reduction in Water, Sewer Charges', *DNA*, 28 June 2015, https://www.dnaindia.com/delhi/report-delhi-government-notifies-80-reduction-in-water-sewer-charges-2099707 (accessed 19 April 2016).
29. Supreme Court of India, *Shanti Sports Club and Anr vs Union of India and Ors*, on 25 August 2009, MANU/SC/1505/2009.
30. Supreme Court, *R. P. Kapur vs The State of Punjab*, 1960, 1960 CriLJ 1239.
31. Judith Whitehead, 'John Locke, Accumulation by Dispossession and the Governance of Colonial India', *Journal of Contemporary Asia* 42, no. 1 (2012): 11. Vinay Gidwani urges us to think of the colonial category of 'waste' beyond the lens of revenue. He argues that 'waste' in fact is a much broader cultural and racial marker of value. See Vinay Gidwani, '"Waste" and the Permanent Settlement in Bengal', *Economic and Political Weekly* 27, no. 4 (1992).
32. Sections 150(3) and 3(a) of The Delhi Land Reforms Act. This provision was inserted in 1968 with effect from 7 April 1958 onwards. This reading of the amendment is seen exhibited in Para 20, *Phool Singh vs Gaon Sabha Dhulsiras*, on 30 May 2011. For a detailed study on court cases and

their claims on the Delhi Land Reforms Act, see Radhika Chatterjee, 'Urbanisation in "Unplanned" Mehrauli', (MPhil diss., Jawaharlal Nehru University, 2015), 32–51.

33. Naveeda Khan's work has also looked at the semantics of the term 'qabza', used in the context of politics over mosques in Lahore. In a moment, it could mean an issue of material loss or a sensation of being forcibly bound up; it could also express one's feeling towards matters of Islam as well as one's perceptions of belongingness in Pakistan. *Qabza*, with respect to mosques, could be the basis of strife between sects, between state norms and Islamic principles, between modernity and tradition or simply a claim on the new nation state. Naveeda Khan, *Muslim Becoming: Aspiration and Skepticism in Pakistan* (Durham: Duke University Press, 2012), 21–54.

34. Department of Revenue, Land Acquisition Award No. 11 (1969), dated 26 June 1969.

35. John Locke, a major liberal political theorist from 17th-century England proposed the labour theory of value, which argued that labour is the claim to ownership of property. He claims that previously unowned land can legitimately belong to the person only if the person's labour is 'mixed' into the land. For example, if someone clears up a forest and starts growing crops on the land that was once forested, that person automatically has proprietary claims over that piece of land. See John Locke, *Two Treatises of Government* (London: Everyman's Library, 1993).

36. Nicholas Blomley, 'Making Private Property: Enclosure, Common Right and the Work of Hedges', *Rural History* 18, no. 1 (2007). He discusses the various meanings and significations that hedges acquired during the period of enclosures as markers of private property. He argues how objects like hedges continue to complicate property relations.

37. The case was one of 28 owners of the plots in Sunlight Colony, which were sold during 1952–55 and were a part of Munirka which was acquired; the owners had gone to court and won the case against acquisition. The defendants had filed several letters demanding alternate plots in Masjid Moth in lieu of their land in Sunlight Colony. The judgment, however, notes that they were still in possession of the land in dispute. The defendants had never been dispossessed of this land by the CPWD.

The Delhi High Court notes,

> The only evidence produced on behalf of the defendants, is that possession of this land was taken and transferred to the C.P.W.D. by the Land Acquisition Collector on 8.6.57. No evidence has been produced to prove that the C.P.W.D. was still in possession of this land at the time of the filing of

these suits. It seems legitimate to presume that the defendants so called possession of this land did not go beyond the proceedings of possession held on 8.6.57 and that the C.P.W.D. and other concerned Officers took no subsequent steps to assert their possession.

See Delhi High Court, *Union of India and Another vs Gopal Seth and Others*, 2011, MANU/DE/1541/2011.

38. *Patwari* is a lower-level official in the revenue office who is in charge of most of these land records. Oscar Lewis writes, 'The Patwari system seems to have been established at the time of Akbar in the 16th Century. In former times patwaris were servants of the village and were paid for by the zamindars.'

He goes on to quote Baden-Powell on the Patwari system, saying:

The Patwari is in effect the accountant of the village, both as regards the revenue-payments due to the various co-sharers, the distribution of the profits of the joint-estate, and the accounts of rent payment between landlord and tenant; he is also the registrar of changes in ownership due to succession and transfer.

See Oscar Lewis, *Village Life in Northern India: Studies in a Delhi Village* (Urbana: University of Illinois Press, 1958), 330.

39. Nayanika Mathur, *Paper Tiger: Law, Bureaucracy and the Developmental State in Himalayan India* (New Delhi: Cambridge University Press, 2016).
40. Bhattacharya, *The Agrarian Conquest*; Lewis, *Village Life in Northern India*, 332–36; Khan, *Muslim Becoming*, 31.
41. Akhil Gupta, 'Blurred Boundaries: The Discourse of Corruption, the Culture of Politics', *American Ethnologist* 22, no. 2 (1995); Timothy Mitchell, 'The Limits of the State: Beyond the Statist Approaches and Their Critics', *American Political Science Review* 85, no. 1 (1991). For a historical context, see Bhavani Raman, *Document Raj: Writing and Scribes in Early Colonial South India* (Durham: Duke University Press, 2012). Similar works have also discussed the role of the municipal councillor in negotiating the slippery zone between state and society. See Ward Berenschot, 'Everyday Mediation: The Politics of Public Service Delivery in Gujarat, India', *Development and Change* 41, no. 5 (2010). In a slightly different approach, David A. Ghertner looks at how middle-class neighbourhoods begin to occupy 'new state spaces' that govern cities. See David A. Ghertner, 'Gentrifying the State, Gentrifying Participation:

Elite Governance Programs in Delhi', *International Journal of Urban and Regional Research* 35, no. 3 (2011). Solomon Benjamin and Sudipta Kaviraj, through concepts like 'porous bureaucracy' and 'vernacular state', argue that a series of state spaces have been carved out, outside the domain of formal planning that are attuned to the needs of the underprivileged in society. See Sudipta Kaviraj, 'On State, Society and Discourse in India', *IDS Bulletin* 21, no. 4 (1990); and Solomon Benjamin, 'Urban Land Transformation for Pro-Poor Economies', *Geoforum* 35, no. 2 (2004).

42. Delhi High Court, *Ramesh Chand vs Suresh Chand and Anr*, 2012, 188 (2012) DLT 538 notes that a GPA is not an instrument of transfer in regard to any right, title or interest in an immovable property. The GPA is the creation of an agency whereby the grantor authorises the grantee to do the acts specified therein, on behalf of grantor, which when executed will be binding on the grantor as if done by him (see Section 1A and Section 2 of the Powers of Attorney Act, 1882). It is revocable or terminable at any time unless it is made irrevocable in a manner known to law.

43. For more, see Ranjan Nambiar, 'Conflict, Law and Governance: The Case of Tenure Conversion in New Delhi', (PhD diss., Massachusetts Institute of Technology, 1994).

44. Ibid., 19. Keeping in mind these losses that the state was incurring, in 1989, the government decided to regularise property transferred through GPA with a proof of possession, in return for payment of conversion charge, registration charges and stamp duties. Ibid., 46.

45. Supreme Court of India, *Suraj Lamp and Industries Pvt. Ltd vs State of Haryana and Anr*, on 11 October 2011, SLP (C) 13917/2009.

46. See Shrimoyee Nandini Ghosh, '"Not Worth the Paper It's Written On": Stamp Paper Documents and the Life of Law in India', *Contributions to Indian Sociology* 53, no. 1 (2019).

47. This is the reason ceiling has been such a big issue in Delhi. Post the M. C. Mehta case in 2004, whereby the Supreme Court ordered every unauthorised commercial and industrial unit to shut down, there was utter mayhem. To date, 'ceiling' has been a deeply emotive and unsettling issue for Delhi and has often been an electoral issue, especially for traders. Not only do Delhi's super rich live in completely unauthorised farmhouses and villas in places like Sainik Farms, but even property owners in colonies made by the Delhi Development Authority have encroached, built extra rooms and balconies, rendering even these unauthorised in several ways.

48. Katherine Verdery and Caroline Humphrey, 'Introduction: Raising Questions about Property', in *Property in Question: Value Transformation*

in the Global Economy, ed. Katherine Verdery and Caroline Humphrey (Oxford and New York: Berg, 2004), 12.

49. Nausheen H. Anwer, 'Receding Rurality, Booming Periphery: Value Struggles in Karachi's Agrarian–Urban Frontier', *Economic and Political Weekly* 53, no. 12 (2018): 51.
50. Arjun Appadurai, 'Introduction: Commodities and the Politics of Value', in *The Social Life of Things: Commodities in a Cultural Perspective*, ed. Arjun Appadurai (Cambridge: Cambridge University Press, 1988).
51. Jean Comaroff and John L. Comaroff, *Law and Disorder in the Postcolony* (Chicago: University of Chicago Press, 2006), 5.
52. Rachel Weber, 'Extracting Value from the City: Neoliberalism and Urban Redevelopment', *Antipode* 34, no. 3 (2002): 521; Neil Smith, 'Gentrification and the Rent Gap', *Annals of the Association of American Geographers* 77, no. 3 (1987).
53. David Graeber, *Debt: The First 5000 Years* (New York: Melville House, 2011).

2

From Buying Land, Owning Taxis to Becoming Landlords

The Changing Economic Landscape of Villages

> Political theory is not, or anyway ought not to be, intensely generalised reflection on intensely generalised matters, an imagining of architectures in which no one could live, but should be, rather, an intellectual engagement, mobile, exact, and realistic, with present problems presently clamorous….
> —Clifford Geertz, *Available Light: Anthropological Reflections on Philosophical Topics*

The villagers were not just mute spectators as the city grew around them. Divested of their farmlands, but armed with compensation money, they were now forced to figure out ways in which the money could give them most returns. Stories of the older generation being cavalier with compensation money abound. Some arguably spent their money on alcohol and new possessions. Some were cheated out of their money. Some others made bad financial decisions. But many were clearly trying to make decisions based on available information to make the most of their situation with varying degrees of success. But irrespective of what the villagers did, their fates were intertwined with the fate of the city. This chapter traces what the early period of this transition —from 1960s to 1980s—looked like for these villagers and how they proceeded to create a stake for themselves in the emerging urban economy.

Making use of life histories or rather 'stories they tell themselves about themselves'[1] to narrate an account that spanned generations, of failed endeavours and successful businesses, of pure grit and stray luck, I attempt to tell a story of villages against the backdrop of the urbanising city. Together, the story paints a picture of urban villages, which open up to new businesses, new money and, most crucially, real estate—most of which continue to function in the domain of informality and forge different relationships with the national and global political economy. However, I try to show in this chapter that a process that appears incidental and isolated is deeply linked to a changing political economic landscape of the country.

This story sounds very different from the story of deprivation and dispossession that several other studies have shown. The Jats are able to turn land acquisition into an opportunity, as land acquisition creates an active urban property market. A lot of it has to do with the fact that the creation of the urban village allowed the Jats physical proximity to the city that opened up several entrepreneurial doors for them. Some of it has to do with the fact that they belong to a regional continuum of intermediate classes that had begun to solidify by the 1970s across northern India.

The Jats as an Intermediate Class

A category initially proposed by Michal Kalecki, a Polish economist, the intermediate classes do not depend either on profit or on wage.[2] They may not necessarily be rich but are dispersed across the countryside and at the same time concentrated in terms of their power and influence.[3] As 'a loose coalition of non-monopolistic, regional capital consisting of small landowners, rich and middle peasants, merchants or rural and semi-rural townships, small scale manufacturers and retailers',[4] the Jats in the urban villages of Delhi can be best understood as the intermediate classes.

The 1970s saw an overly insecure state trying to forge a new kind of coalitional politics across the various classes and, more importantly, these intermediate classes.[5] The Green Revolution[6] had, by the 1970s, already reversed the fortunes of several of these classes across the country, more particularly in Punjab and Haryana. Protected with heavy subsidies, these classes were able to forge robust ties with the Indian state. With respect to the phenomenon of rent-seeking in the scholarship around the intermediate classes, Mushtaq Khan and Jomo K. S. argue that in a fragmented clientelism system, redistributive rents in the form of subsidies have been protected by the powerful classes.[7] But quite contrary to the dominant stream, which sees rent-seeking as bad, they claim that in the Global South, rent-seeking may be the only way through which a developmental state can root itself.[8] Craig Jeffrey and Harish Damodaran further demonstrate the unevenness of caste-based rent-seeking by showing how wealthy Jat sugarcane farmers have managed to monopolise those rents by gaining control over the Cane Society.[9]

The Nehruvian command economy had already run into a crisis by the 1960s, and by the 1970s, the economy had begun to move towards liberalisation.[10] Chirashree Das Gupta talks of the period between 1965 and the 1980s as one where the pressures were building on the older dirigiste system and the move towards encouraging private players was becoming established.[11] Both Das Gupta and Harris-White discuss how bank nationalisation, the newly enacted Monopolies and Restrictive Trade Practices Act, the Green Revolution, regimes of price control and licensing provided the intermediate classes like the Jats with a new lease of life.[12] In this period, the intermediate classes, who were mostly landed, seem to have used their agricultural surplus to make investments in diverse channels.

Damodaran shows how this agricultural surplus was then channelled into different industries.[13] The economic relationship of rent—through subsidies and licences that they had been able to forge with the state—allowed the intermediate classes to do so. On the one hand, sugarcane production in this region was increasingly monopolised by the Jats, and on the other, sugar mills also became a popular venture for them to invest money in.[14] Gradually, as political mobilisation in this region emerged in the 1970s and 1980s, it grew in close conversation with this new shift. But besides the rise of the Bharatiya Kisan Union (BKU) around sugarcane growers, Damodaran also shows how rent-seeking reshaped itself to adapt to these new economic relations. The Jats were one of the classes who managed to consolidate their position in manufacturing industries dotting the rural and suburban landscape of Northwest India.[15]

In urban Delhi, this rent-seeking shaped up very differently. Though some Jats of Delhi continued to hold agricultural land both in UP and Haryana, states which lay adjacent to Delhi, their investment in agro-industries was limited. By the 1970s, the Delhi Jats already had a stake in the urban economy and saw little business sense in getting involved with agriculture-related businesses. They had based their investment strategies on compensation and were restricted to petty businesses as opposed to the rich agriculturists riding the tide of the Green Revolution. As different as these strategies were, both rural and urban Jats were dependent on a similar repertoire of rent-seeking methods. The economic transformation of the Jats through new rent-seeking networks serves as a backdrop to how new socio-economic relations were shaping up in the urban landscape as well.

For the Jats of Delhi, land acquisition, in fact, turned into an opportunity for those who had begun to enjoy significant political and economic clout by the 1970s. While buying up property has always been popular with the community, other forms of investments experienced varying degrees of popularity over time. The 1950s and 1960s saw the villagers making their way into the construction business, and from the 1970s onwards, there was a significant move towards the transport business. The collapse of the latter in the 1990s coincided with the rise of the real estate business and the ancillary 'financing' business in the village (Chapter 4). These categories help us see how the transitions from one to the other have a logic and a rhythm. What appears as random at first begins to emerge after a while as patterns. The stories thus become more than mere isolated experiences and struggles and instead bear the imprints of the city's transition. It is with this intent that I tell these tales of property and investments involving individual actors.

The stories, however, were not always easy to come by. Some people I spoke to got hostile, and some others were guarded, not willing to divulge too much information to an outsider like myself—and understandably so. The measure of wealth and how fortunes changed for people is, therefore, tough to establish chronologically. But they more than willingly divulged information about other people and how the latter had managed to accumulate wealth. Information and gossip melded into each other to reveal a picture that is far more layered and complex than one would have imagined earlier.

While the stories themselves may be broken up into acts, actors move across them freely, sometimes even circumventing the structure of the acts. As Marx has famously written, 'Men make their own history, but they do not make it as they please; they do not make it under self-selected circumstances, but under circumstances existing already, given and transmitted from the past.'[16] In presenting these stories as acts, this chapter tries to bring the two narratives—of larger economic transitions and of the Jats of Delhi villages—together to see how they individually and collectively responded to circumstances, particularly to the phenomenon of land acquisition. The narrative that emerges shows how the Jats, with their social and rent-seeking networks, began to find their feet in new businesses in a historically trading city. Unlike the Banias and Punjabi business classes who have counted on their soft skills and shrewd business acumen, the Jats entered businesses where rustic masculinity would find more purchase. While the formal localities of South Delhi were taking shape in accordance with the Master Plan—a document that believed that a modern city could radically modernise its citizens—the same document allowed the Jats of Delhi to be exempt from that modernising impulse. To add to the irony, what also emerges is that the non-urban, rustic masculine forms of sociability of the Jats became central to the execution of the Master Plan.

While a handful of the Jats were wealthy and held significant social capital across villages and sometimes even political influence, this was not true about most of them. Declared a 'martial race' by the British, Jats across Delhi villages had continued to serve in the Indian Army. Their presence in the Delhi Police also became increasingly prominent by the 1960s. Some procured other government jobs because of their excellence in various sports. The sporting culture that many of these villages boast of has for long been a means of social mobility by way of getting government jobs. The Delhi Transport Corporation was another significant employer of Jats, which absorbed them as bus drivers and conductors. The next sections discuss each of these entrepreneurial moves to see how they speak to the changing contours of the city.

Buying Up Property

Despite being from the same larger kinship structure, class differences among Jats from even the same village could sometimes be massive. Often, the affluent ones came from families with very few male heirs across at least four generations. Other families may have started with a similar amount of land as them, but frequent subdivision among several male members across generations had made many far poorer. As a result, *kunba*s with fewer male heirs were able to channelise their concentrated wealth and property into social networks. This handful of families has their fingers in multiple pies to date. Having started factories, brick kilns, dealerships for imported cars, even restaurants and engineering colleges, these few families have set themselves apart as distinct and superior from the average villager whose main source of sustenance remains rent. This distinction was clearly visible during my fieldwork. The rich were almost invariably part of *kunba*s with fewer men. The joint family system had already been on an ebb by the 1960s and had given way to nuclear families even in rural Delhi.[17] But despite the continuous fragmentation of property and households, collective forms of investment, as we will go on to see, were always kept alive.

Socially and historically, land has always been one of the most important ways of accumulation in India. Land's association with social worth has been longstanding. For the Jats, this was even more so. Buying gold, traditionally the other most popular form of investment in India, never had much traction among the Jats. Anish Vanaik notes that Jats have been buying up property in the suburbs of Delhi as far back as the early 20th century, and have consistently used speculation to acquire both wealth and political influence.[18] Therefore, speculation over land was neither new nor was the Jat community entirely alien to the phenomenon of commodification of land.[19]

As land prices began to soar around the news of land acquisition, the landed Jats across rural Delhi began to speculate on land. As compensation awards began to trickle in, some blew up the compensation money initially, while several others were diligent with investments. Given that the period of acquisition was fairly long drawn out in Munirka, spanning at least 30 years, it bought people enough time and information to effect better negotiations and decisions. Ashish Bose and Chaman Singh show that by merely buying agricultural land in rural areas of Haryana, the Jats in one particular Delhi village were able to increase their landholding by 60 per cent while only spending 25 per cent of their compensation money.[20]

As we have already seen, the period of land acquisition had expedited this process of buying and selling of land. Though the rates were measly, the sudden inflow of hard cash compelled people to invest it somewhere. Jwala Singh from Shahpur Jat remembers the time of acquisition when the government offered them 1 rupee per yard or roughly 5,000 rupees per acre. As a part of compensation, they were also offered plots in different localities of urban Delhi: 800 square metres at 16 rupees per yard. Jwala Singh's father could never fathom how these land prices would rise. Also, an alternative plot of land offered on a leasehold basis did not make much sense to him and several others.[21] A larger agricultural plot in rural Delhi or Haryana for the same amount of money seemed like a more lucrative proposition at the time. Some also claim that very few people were aware of the provision of an assured alternative plot to begin with.

Jwala Singh's father, the only male in the family, was a rich agriculturist from Shahpur Jat. At the time of acquisition, he took his friend's advice (the friend was another rich agriculturist from Masjid Moth with a keen business sense), and ended up buying agricultural land in Mehrauli and Fatehpur Beri instead of claiming the alternative plot. The one near Mehrauli has now become a premium wedding venue. Later, in 1967–68, Jwala Singh's family started a brick kiln that his older brother used to look after; this has now become a farmhouse.[22] Jwala Singh's father also bought 60–70 *bigha*s of land from his Masjid Moth friend near Mehrauli in Ladha Sarai[23] for agriculture. Ladha Sarai was acquired by the government much later in the 1980s after being notified in 1965.[24] The last bit of acquisition for the Mehrauli heritage zone happened as late as 2008–09 after being notified in 2004.

Another mode of investing money in land, more so among the Jats of modest means, was the system called *chak*,[25] where a set of people, mostly members of the same *kunba*, would invest in land together. Buying land collectively helped alleviate the uncertainty of doing so in an unfamiliar setting. But even this practice had historical roots as can be seen from a Settlement Report from 1874 from Meerut region, which notes this practice of investment in land: 'A large number of Jats from scattered villages, in no less than three pergunnahs on the Jumna side of their district, clubbed their resources, bought the village, and sent forth a colony to inhabit and cultivate it.'[26] The uncertainty that started with land acquisition precipitated many such collective investments. There were different motivating factors for investing in land. Some just bought agricultural land in order to do what they knew best. Some others had already got a whiff of the speculative potential that land would come to acquire in a few more years. And in most cases, the reasoning just shifted from the former to the latter at some point.

In the 1960s, a significantly high number of villagers from Munirka bought agricultural land in a place around Tauru, in Mewat region, roughly 55 kilometres from Delhi (now Nuh district) as *chak*. When I asked Mange Ram, whose family is in the transport business and whom we will discuss in detail a little later, why Tauru, he had no specific reason to give me. 'We were very tribal minded. Jo ek karta tha, sab karte the'* is the answer I got. The tendency was clearly to do things collectively. He claims that far more fertile land was available in Sonepat and Baghpat at that time. He made their decision sound like a proof of their primitiveness, the lack of acumen that is so obvious in urban people. However, a decision that sounds so illogical today probably made economic sense in the 1960s. Mewat was perhaps as fair a bet as Gurgaon at the time, and there probably was no way then to tell which direction the city would grow in.[27] Many affluent families like Mange Ram's had also ended up making the lousy investment in Tauru, but they had a far higher capacity to absorb financial losses than others. Rawta around Najafgarh, Mukhmelpur on Karnal Road, Khori Kalan, Ambrahi and Dhool Siras are some of the villages where clusters of villagers from Munirka later invested money. The villagers of Hauz Khas, for example, bought agricultural land close to Sonepat and villagers of Shahpur Jat around Jhajjhar Beri. To date, they function as absentee landlords for their agricultural land in Haryana and Rajasthan and travel once in a while to oversee farming. But eventually, everybody was waiting for those land values to go up. Not many moved there. As one of my respondents, who is now a cement dealer, put it, 'Doosre kisi ke gaon mein ja kar rehna, kisi ki biwi hone ke barabar hai.'†

Smaller sets that splintered from the kin group continued to keep buying big and small *chaks* of land in and around Delhi over the next four decades.[28] For families or *kunba*s that bought land close enough to the city, there were soon more speculative opportunities available. Families that had bought *chaks* around the land that would become the Dwarka Expressway or Gurgaon, for instance, found their land values multiplying manifold. Most of these

---

* 'What one would do, the rest would follow in doing.'
† 'To go and live in another village is akin to living like someone's wife.'

investments were being made at the time, however, on the basis of pure speculation about the direction urban development would take in the city. When I spoke to Beenu, the proprietor of a successful financing business in Munirka village, he claimed that Sectors 39–42 of Gurgaon were constructed again on Munirka villagers' land, which many of them had collectively bought as *chak* after their agricultural land had been acquired. This land in Gurgaon was acquired in 1993; Beenu claimed that the land near the HUDA City Centre metro station in Gurgaon was acquired for 6,62,000 rupees per acre, which the government then sold for 14–15 crore rupees per acre. For some other families who had bought land in Rohini, the land was acquired by the government in 1981. Land in Tauru, however, in the depths of Mewat, remained stuck both in time and value.

Clearly, investing in land in times when the nature of land itself was undergoing a massive change, apart from their values, altered lives. If speculation is akin to gambling, foresight and chance are two factors that can turn fortunes on their heads. While getting lucky matters, what is also required is the skill of taking calculated risks. In the case of land speculation, much of this calculated risk is not a question of skill per se but of access to information and, therefore, a function of one's social capital. Thus, the families which moved to Haryana and Uttar Pradesh in the hope of continuing with agriculture as their mainstay occupation lost out on the speculative opportunities that the city began to throw up. On the other hand, the families which bought rural land around Gurgaon, Najafgarh and even Rohini made a windfall as the land in these areas began to be converted to commercial property. In the following sections, we see how different businesses emerged at specific times, reached a crescendo and then ebbed to give way to something else, and how individuals manoeuvred around these varying opportunities to make the most of them while they lasted. Through these stories, we then try and figure out what all of it meant for the rise of this specific kind of intermediate class.

The social and political networks the Jats of these villages inhabited exposed them to information on land values that was crucial. It is also not surprising that most of the established electoral candidates from these villages are from these families. To not get into the ground rent business is a marker of status for them. The upward mobility of these rich families has been independent of the rise of value of the village homestead land. But this chapter is not about them. Though the rich and powerful also make their way into the narrative, this chapter is about scores of middling figures, whose fortunes did not necessarily skyrocket but the ones who fumbled from one business to another and saw more drastic crests and troughs with their smaller businesses. Though their individual journeys may be chaotic, together they reveal something of a pattern.

When the Land Is Gone: Construction-Material Business in the 1960s

'Humne bahot gareebi dekhi hai,'‡ Harpal Tokas tells me, sitting in front of his coal depot in R. K. Puram. Harpal is mostly found seated on a plastic chair outside the coal depot during the daytime. In a quintessential white *kurta-pyjama*, but not necessarily the starched, pristine kind, he looks the part. His father was already in the army by the time land acquisition happened. He remembers that before land acquisition, in the 1950s, people in Munirka used to load *badarpur*[29] on carts and sell it in Meerut, buy jaggery with what they earned and then sell that in Mehrauli. He recalls going to Vasant Vihar, which was under construction at that time, to sell *lassi* made by his mother to the construction workers. The two buffaloes that they owned were significant assets in this regard.

But by the mid-1960s, things began to look up for him. Harpal's father, who had retired from the army in the late 1960s, invested his retirement money in a dairy farm next to the Vasant Vihar bus depot in 1968. It ran into losses within six months and had to be shut down.[30] With the help of an acquaintance, who already had a shop in the R. K. Puram market, they were then able to secure a commercial plot on leasehold. They started a coal depot here, which did roaring business in the 1970s. They also began to stock firewood. As coal distribution was brought into the Public Distribution System (PDS) after the Second Five-Year Plan, its distribution too had become significantly premium.[31] Harpal Singh remembers long queues outside the depot, which sometimes needed manning by Delhi Police constables. While monopolies at the national scale were being broken up, rents through licence-permit *raj* at the fag end of the distribution chains were being constantly recreated by the PDS and other kinds of restrictions on the distribution of several commodities. And if one could enter the distribution chain even at the lowest level, it ensured a stable business.

The late 1960s was also the time when Beenu's father, again an army retiree, invested his money in a brick kiln near Mukhmelpur. Beenu, who had a small transport business in the 1990s, was extremely pleasant and warm and would smile even while talking. His father used the compensation money to

---

‡ 'We have seen a lot of poverty.'

buy agricultural land in Khori Kalan in Gurgaon. Like Harpal, Beenu too recalls how villagers from Munirka were involved in transporting *badarpur* from Pallika Pahar around Chhattarpur to other places. Anita Soni's work on Mehrauli provides some context to the business around construction material that some of these villages were deeply involved in. She shows how quarrying mines in Rangpuri, Masudpur, Mahipalpur, Bhatti Bajri and Rajokri began to support the massive demand for building materials in Delhi in the 1960s and 1970s.[32] The growing demand for granite, sandstone, *badarpur*, and so on made village *panchayat*s open up the village *gram sabha* lands for quarrying operations. This led to village *panchayat*s beginning to act as 'mining contractors'.[33] Munirka or Shahpur Jat never had any quarries of their own. But if Harpal's testimony is anything to go by, many people from Munirka were involved in transporting material like *badarpur* from quarries in other villages.

Beenu has vivid memories of the landscape that is long gone. He describes the terrain around Chhatarpur, starting from Andheria Mor on one end of the Aravalli range to Pallika Pahar, in great detail, including the *johad*, or natural streams, that dotted the landscape and the roaring economy of the quarries of *badarpur* in the area. Since this region is also dominated by Gujjars, the construction business too was mostly controlled by them.[34] But not all building material production require resources like quarries or mines. Brick kilns, though capital intensive, did not need a specific, premium resource and were a fairly common and lucrative business for those with money to sink into a business.

Like Beenu's father, who started his brick kiln around Mukhmelpur, Zile Singh too remembers his father having started a brick kiln in the 1960s. Zile Singh loves to talk. In our first conversation itself, he went on to tell me about his familial investments with a sort of openness that very few others had demonstrated. He recalls his father as having excellent business acumen. His father was the first to start a building material store in Munirka. It was not only the biggest but also extremely well located right along the Ring Road, which got him clients from across the city. Not too many of them were contractors in their own right. To be a contractor was a significantly bigger deal, which required influence and status in much wider networks. I have met only one respondent from Shahpur Jat, Bahadur Singh (who we will meet later in the chapter), who claimed that his father was a rather popular contractor with Central Public Works Department (CPWD) tenders around the 1960s and 1970s; however, he was unable to give me many details.

Construction was probably the biggest business opportunity at that time, which provided immense scope for all these individuals and also some kind of space in the business economy. By the mid-1960s, anyone with a significantly large sum of money was no longer satisfied with investing it all in land like before. As the economy began to move towards a liberalised one, the business opportunities for this intermediate class also began to swell. Unlike in the 1950s when people could possibly not think beyond land, by the 1970s they were able to diversify into other businesses. With the Green Revolution, also in the 1970s, the Jats were in any case beginning to emerge as a strong intermediate class in rural, northwest India. It is therefore not surprising to see them becoming bolder with their economic choices as well. Though the Jats of Delhi were not the direct beneficiaries of the Green Revolution, some of them were certainly part of social networks which included those directly benefiting from the phenomenon.

Becoming civil contractors on their own was rare initially, and therefore most people got into the business as suppliers. With time, however, some people who started their work as suppliers broke ranks and turned into civil contractors themselves. Some started with just transporting building material on their carts across Delhi, others by putting their foot in the door as quarry and brick-kiln owners, or as shop owners who sold building material and hardware. Though brick kilns remained unregulated, construction material like cement was under strict rationing until 1982.[35] The Government of India announced its Industrial Policy in the year 1956, which brought cement under heavy control.[36] The Associated Cement Company Limited (ACC) was brought under the control of the State Trading Corporation (STC) to correct the gap between demand and supply. The supply of cement was organised through a complicated three-tier system between the Centre, the states and then allocation for private consumption.[37] While the supply to large consumers was made directly through the factory, supply to small consumers was done through stockists licenced by the state governments.[38] This made cement an extremely premium commodity, which also led to the emergence of a steady, flourishing black market whereby common people had to pay as much as 200 per cent premium over and above the control price.[39] The 1970s were a tough time for the company, which was working under several constraints and eventually at suboptimal production levels.[40] It was only in 1982 that the industry was partially decontrolled.[41] Today, cement is one of the sectors that allows 100 per cent foreign direct investment.

Kishanchand from Munirka is a tall, lean man with weather-beaten, rugged features. Extremely bitter about land acquisition, he rails against those who had more extensive land holdings and the 'anti-nationals' of Jawaharlal Nehru University[42] who are sitting on the land that once belonged to his family. His grandfather was one of seven brothers, as a result of which the former got a smaller share. He says they claimed their alternative plot from the government much later but were swindled out of it by someone. By the time people began to apply for alternative plots and were being allotted these, 'Bahot broker ghooma karte the gaon mein. Kaafi gaonwaale toh khud hi broker ban gaye the.'§ The cement dealership was awarded to his father by the government after he retired from the Rajputana Rifles in 1975 and since then has been the mainstay of the family's income. Today, he and his two brothers run the business together. It was at an interesting juncture in the larger cement industry that they started this business. Coal was always categorised under the Essential Commodities Act, 1955.[43] In 1977–78, an acute shortage of cement production led to an export ban.[44] All stockists and dealers were to be appointed or licenced by the state governments. The quantity of cement they could sell was also to be limited by the Food and Civil Supplies Department (FCSD). The focal point of the distribution around this time shifted from stockists to the FCSD.[45] This shortage, though, created a parallel black market.

Kishanchand and his brother remember the initial years of starting the business as days of hardship. Unlike Harpal, who looks back fondly at the days of strict rationing as a time of relative comfort, Kishanchand does not seem to harbour any such nostalgia. He and his brother claim that the business picked up pace after the rationing was lifted. Though their father and brothers ran the business, Kishanchand tried to establish himself through other means in the initial years. He worked as a driver for others between 1980 and 1989. In 1989, the family bought their own tempo/pickup van for their cement business, which Kishanchand would drive all around Delhi for collecting and delivering cement. He tried to break away again by 2000, when he began to operate his taxi for the Maurya Sheraton hotel as a tourist vehicle, but that venture had to be shut down in 2003 on a no profit, no loss basis. By 1990, the family's business had finally taken off. They won a big contract for a farmhouse in Dera Mandi, which lasted six years and probably also turned their fortune. Now they hold the dealership for two major cement brands, and they have been able to create a chain of smaller cement dealers whom they are primary suppliers to.

As the breakneck speed at which construction was happening in South Delhi began to slow down, the number of opportunities available here also began to dry up. Beenu's father's brick kiln closed by 1985. New governmental regulations and checks began to be introduced. The overt dominance of two Gujjar brothers who had been major players in the mining business also drove

---

§ 'There were many brokers in the village. A number of villagers themselves had become brokers.'

many smaller brick kilns and stone crushers out of business.[46] One of the last big contracts, that of blasting rocks to make way for Vasant Kunj, was given to 8–10 families, including Beenu's, in Masoodpur, Munirka and Mahipalpur. This work went on between 1982 and 1986. It was far easier to procure dynamite and gunpowder in those days. A small shop in Vasant Kunj used to sell these explosives openly, Beenu recalls. But with the rise of Sikh militancy in the early 1980s, the sale of explosives became more controlled, making this business more expensive and difficult.

For Bahadur Singh Panwar from Shahpur Jat, whose father had become a small-time contractor by bagging some CPWD contracts, that business came to naught by the 1980s because neither Bahadur Singh nor his brother wanted to continue with it. It is possible that by the 1980s, the CPWD contracts also began to dry up. Bahadur Singh was keener on starting a 'financing' business. Today, he owns several commercial properties in Shahpur Jat, a financing business and a cement-supply business which barely runs. A start-up, two designers and two home decor stores run from this particular building among other businesses. A room on the ground floor of one of his commercial buildings functions as Bahadur Singh Panwar's office. The door to his office announces the name of his cement business, but once you enter, it looks too sanitised to be a cement dealership. It is a business that Bahadur Singh no longer bothers about. Or maybe, it just serves as a front. Because in upmarket Shahpur Jat, a cement dealership can no longer make economic sense. The relative success of the construction supply business had indeed run its course for most people by the 1980s. The quarrying business had begun to suffer too by then with increased governmental regulations. Almost three decades after the boom in the 1990s, one such building material shop in Munirka belonging to a local builder is well past its heyday. With the madness over construction within the village plateauing a bit by the 2010s, the demand has shrunk. Though it still does well, building material shop owners do acknowledge that things are not the same for them.

The 1970s and the Rise of the Transport Business

The decline in popularity of the construction business in general coincided with the rise of the transport business. Das Gupta notes that as public investment in roads began to increase exponentially, new chains of private wholesale and retail chains of two-wheelers, buses, trucks and jeeps along with financing corporations began to grow in the 1970s.[47] Stefan Tetzlaff's work on the history of road transport in northwest Uttar Pradesh argues that this process started way earlier. As early as the 1920s, the transport business emerged as one largely controlled by *zamindar*s or *bania*s who were firmly rooted in the villages or small towns.[48] The Great Depression had been as much a challenge as an opportunity with the state promoting their indigenous capitalists.[49] But Tetzlaff argues that by the 1930s, with the onslaught of the Depression, it had begun to profit a class of the rural elite as well. Agriculture had started to move more sharply towards cash crops, owing to which emerged a need for local road transport that could neither be met by animal transport nor the railways. His work traces the emergence of transport in the Meerut district and how this mofussil emerges as an important node because of its proximity to Delhi over the late 1930s. Following the rich Brahmin and Bania owners of such businesses, he looks at how they strove to establish their monopolies over roads. The first castes to have become rural capitalists through transport in the 1930s were either the Brahmins, Banias or Muslim *zamindar*s. The Jat and Rajput ex-army men were only being trained to become drivers and mechanics by the UP government.[50]

As petty entrepreneurships among the Jats grew exponentially in the 1970s, they also began to emerge as transport operators. This trend though may not necessarily have been peculiar either to the Jats or to north India. Harris-White argues that by the 1980s, the bureaucratic system of doling out licences to private bus operators in south India to run on specific routes had already become highly corrupt.[51] Across the country, in fact, the system of permits and licences was twisted to favour of the dominant rent-seeking community. Das Gupta writes that informal markets in finance, by the 1970s, had begun to create the basis for non-banking finance across the country, especially with road networks developing fast.[52] In India, moneylending within communities against collateral like land and gold had been an age-old practice. It automatically led to the emergence of what Das Gupta calls 'rentier' finance, which delinks production from finance by plugging into the asset market. Tetzlaff notes the origins of this system way back in the 1930s when several hire and purchase companies began to emerge as intermediaries providing finance and insurance both in Delhi and UP.[53]

By the 1990s, the landscape of the public transport system in Delhi had begun to change: the Delhi Transport Corporation (DTC), which ran its own buses, had already started giving out permits to private players on a 'per kilometre' basis. Under this new scheme, the parastatal private operator would be paid a fixed amount on a per kilometre basis, but the conductor of the bus had to be a DTC employee whereby the revenue would go straight to DTC.[54] Soon enough, even these regulations were taken off, and transport was almost entirely outsourced to private players. Jagdish Tytler, the Union Minister of Surface Transport, allowed some 2,600 permits for stagecoaches to be given out to private operators for Red Line buses around 1991, whereby bus operators could run independently. This threw open an entire market for small players to jump into. Two huge strikes by DTC employees in 1988 and 1992 over the Fourth Pay Commission led the DTC to formalise the Red Line buses in 1992.[55] Red Line buses provided a unique opportunity to villagers in the 1990s. While earlier, the transport business had meant running buses between towns and cities or having private companies which would rent out buses to schools, for weddings and for religious trips, these permits to run buses within city limits changed the nature of the business entirely.

***

Mange Ram Tokas's uncle had started a transport company in his grandfather's name even before land acquisition. Mange Ram's family had only had one son until his father's generation, which had two brothers, his father and his uncle. Their office was located in Karol Bagh in Central Delhi in the early 1950s, and they would operate buses for several schools in Delhi. This was their primary source of revenue. The business did superbly well and their company's fleet grew to 40–50 buses. Mange Ram claims there were only three—four other transport companies of this scale in all of Delhi at this time. Being a businessman, his grandfather was quite close to some influential Congress leaders of that time. In fact, the Tytler School had come up on land in 1954 that Mange Ram's grandfather had donated to James Douglas Tytler, a Scottish educationist who worked in India. It was his adopted son, Jagdish Tytler, who went on to become the Transport Minister in 1991.[56] Jagdish Tytler's decision to allow private stagecoaches encouraged more individuals and families to simply obtain a permit or even buy it to run a few buses.[57] Several permits were given under the fixed 'graduate quota', 'SC/ST quota' and 'ex-serviceman quota'. It was common practice for these licences to be procured through the permits and then passed on to others, many of them Jats.

As we have seen earlier, the 1960s and 1970s saw some amount of upward mobility in some families owing to the construction material supply business. By the 1970s and 1980s, the transport business began to make its presence felt, until it burst upon the scene in the early 1990s. And finally, post-2000, as neoliberalism sank its teeth into the economy, the rental business took off and with it, the financing business.[58] The remaining brick kiln owners and other construction suppliers, therefore, began to slowly move to the transport business. Beenu, whose brick kiln had shut down by 1975, forayed into transport as well. By the late 1970s, he had purchased two taxis, of which he would drive one himself. He would wait at the airport and drive NRIs from Punjab who arrived with considerable luggage and found it convenient to hire a taxi all the way to the state.

***

The 1980s had begun to usher in a different kind of change. Harpal Tokas's coal depot, which was doing roaring business in the 1970s, had begun to flag by mid-1980s. As LPG began to enter more and more households, including the middle and lower-income groups, cooking coal's demand fell drastically. He and his brother entered the transport business cautiously with some five—six buses which would run on DTC lines soon after. Raman Tokas from Munirka recalls his father buying a taxi in the mid-1970s; he started driving it himself from the R. K. Puram Sector 1 taxi stand. In 1985, they bought their first bus and Raman started driving buses on DTC routes. Slowly, they built up a fleet of 15–16 buses that ran very well for several years until the business ran into rough weather.

The transport sector soon presented tremendous potential for local villagers who had the wherewithal to exploit the opportunity with the loosening up of the permit regime. In 1992, 3,000 permits were given to bus owners with fewer than five buses each to run as Red Line buses.[59] Clearly, the trend for more moneyed landlords owning a fleet of buses was no longer the norm. Anybody with some money to spare for a bus could buy up one or two second-hand buses, paint them and run them on the routes ascribed to them through the permit.

The Fall of the Transport Business

Mange Ram and his brother chose not to continue with the bus transport business by the early 1980s. They had received a decent education, and they did not want to stay associated with 'a business'. As a trained lawyer, he did not feel the need to be in a 'rough' business like transport. Mange Ram also did not succumb to the lure of rental income subsequently. It is only his house in all of Munirka that still retains an old-world, *haveli*-like charm. The doors, the *taak*s or shelves, and the arches have all been carefully preserved. His house is probably a rare one that was not renovated for renting purposes. His was one of the few rare families that did not 'need' to earn from ground rent.[60]

Their *haveli* is a sign of their distinction from the rest. As the transport business became more popular, with every Tom, Dick and Harry calling himself a 'transporter', Mange Ram's distinguished family probably began to see less and less pride in it. The pride with which he would talk of the first model of Chevrolet buses that his family had bought could not be associated with the transport business any longer. The business itself was no longer seen as respectable.

The others, who had jumped into the transport business in the hope of making good money, soon started to see the ugly cracks. Within a year of their launch, cases of accidents, over speeding and misbehaviour began to pile up against Red Line buses.[61] Eventually, they were renamed Blue Line buses and continued to run as stagecoaches. Before the Delhi Metro expanded rapidly, these buses were the primary means of public transport in the city. The demand was steady, but because of competition among the different private operators, these buses were found over speeding and driving recklessly. By the 2000s, the buses were also past their prime with their efficiency levels falling exponentially. Increased environmental controls also meant frequent harassment at the hands of the police. Investing in new buses made little economic sense to the owners and contractors. The introduction of CNG in 2002 imposed an added financial burden on the bus owners, as all the buses needed to be overhauled.[62] But apart from this, as more and more bus operators entered the business, competition escalated significantly. The sheer increase in private transport as well as the Delhi Metro's rapid expansion began to eat into the number of commuters. Bus drivers, under pressure from bus owners, began to drive recklessly to overtake other buses, pick up more passengers and make more trips in a day to maintain profit margins. And once again, quite like the proverbial repeat of history, the Blue Line buses, like the Red Line buses, turned into 'killer buses'. After a spate of accidents by these buses, it was evident that neither courts nor public opinion was in their favour. Harpal tells me dejectedly, 'Hamari line hi badnaam ho gayi.'**
I had spent so much time sitting and talking to him outside his coal depot, but it was only at this moment that I really took notice of the big Blue Line bus parked right opposite the depot. It had Harpal's name written in small font at the back. As the Blue Line buses were phased out in the year 2011, his rickety vehicle was left standing there, abandoned.[63] The image of Harpal in his white kurta-pyjama with black stains of coal, sitting between his spent coal depot and his defunct bus, could not have been more ironic. Even as he continues

---

** 'Our "line" [of work] got a bad name.'

to run a school bus for a private school, Harpal remains hopeful that the coal depot will be converted from leasehold to freehold, so that he might be able to start a different business.

Until 2007–08, Munirka alone contributed 70 buses to the transport system; this number fell steadily over the years. Today, there are close to none. I tried very hard to trace the one person in the village who had reportedly had a thriving business in running the Blue Line buses, but after the business tanked, he had sold all that he could and moved to Haryana. No one seemed to know what he did now. Beenu too shut down his taxi service by the late 1990s and had his house renovated to be able to rent it out. The house, constructed on a 600-yard plot, has 36 'one-room sets', the rent from which is split between him and his brother's family. But all this aside, his main source of income is his financing business, one that he never admitted to me. His land in Jharsa and Mukhmelpur were acquired around 1993, which must have significantly contributed to him becoming a financier.

Varun, whose father had a taxi stand in Shahpur Jat, sold it to a Sikh man in 1985 and started a sweet shop in the early 1990s and a finance company in 1998. Varun recalls that his family had to pool all their money to show 25 lakh rupees in their bank account to start the business legally. But his father is an 'emotional type', he says, and he soon incurred many bad debts. The business had to shut down as they were facing major penalties from the government, he claims. Varun's father probably exemplifies this messy period of uncertainty after the end of a stable business. Varun laughs and says that his father and uncle were a little 'khurafaati'.[††] They would sometimes sell movie tickets in black for a premium for a while. He remembers how at one point, their whole house was stacked up to the ceiling with Limca bottles, in expectation of some windfall profits. Today, Varun's family owns an extremely coveted piece of commercial property in Shahpur Jat. Apart from this, he runs a garment manufacturing unit and a restaurant in the village. People like Kishanchand, who started his business with cement, did not find switching businesses as easy as Varun's father. He struggled with transport but found stability only when their cement business started doing well.

Ground rent income was easy and secure money. Tenants have always flocked to Munirka given its great location and connectivity. It was only by the late 1990s, however, that houses with 'naye design' (new design) began to be built. In 1995, Kishanchand's family had a two-room set house available for rent. In 2002, they converted his house to a series of one-room sets. Harpal and Beenu are not the only ones who started with the transport business and

---

[††] 'Naughty' or 'troublemaker'.

landed up in the renting business. As profits in transport began to fall, many erstwhile transporters began moving to real estate.

Raman Tokas's family too had begun to gradually disband their transport business and move to building floors and financing by the mid-2000s. The larger shifts in business opportunities reflect how the city changed over the decades. The spate of construction work undertaken by the state in the 1960s and 1970s started to ebb by the mid-1980s and early 1990s, and the city began to witness more and more migration into the city. Real estate prices shooting up exponentially also created a vacuum for the lower-middle-class migrant into the city. Thus, renting out property within the villages became the new best form of investment. Older houses needed to be broken down in order to erect multi-storeyed buildings with many one-room sets for the lower-middle-class urban migrant. The rush for this necessitated the consolidation of a group of 'financiers' who could lend money at short notice for people needing credit. It was not that credit was absent in this economy before, but the very scale at which this new business began to take shape made financiers an indispensable node in the economy now.

The Outliers

Not everybody entered the construction business or the transport business. Kamal Panwar from Shahpur Jat feels extreme pride in describing himself as a self-made man. His father, who was a driver employed at the brick kiln of a wealthy Masjid Moth businessman,[64] died of alcoholism in 1976. After he finished school, Kamal did several odd jobs but the pay was hardly regular. He got a job in a manufacturing unit where he earned 150 rupees per month as a helper in the 1980s. He then completed a two-year course where he learnt the skills of a master, cutter and designer while delivering milk in the morning and attending college in the evening. In 1986, he decided to break his *committee*[65] for 30 months to get 6,000 rupees with which he purchased five machines. He started operating out of the three rooms in the house he had just built with his brother. They sold their alternative plot in Safdarjung Development Area, which they had bought for 88,000 rupees in 1982, for 1.75 lakh rupees between 1985 and 1986. They invested the proceeds in rebuilding the house. By 1989, Kamal's business came to a close because he could not retain labour. He claims that the *karigar*s did not see him as a businessman with prospects and fled to better manufacturing units: 'Labour kisi ki sagi nahi hoti.'‡‡ He says this with a hint of drama that is often

---

‡‡ 'Labour is never faithful to anyone.'

accompanied by adages. His own kin members had created trouble for him but he did not care to elaborate on the details. After the unit shut down, a relative of his, who used to work for a big businessman in Jor Bagh, got him work to make cloth bags for the businessman's daughter who was learning fashion designing in London. He was given the contract for 20,000 bags. He spent 1 rupee per bag and earned at the rate of 2 rupees per bag. This was when he earned his first big sum of money: 20,000 rupees. He got it all in cash. 'Aur phir iske baad maine kabhi peeche mud kar nahi dekha,'[§§] he says with considerable pride.

Kamal Panwar started his factory in 1993 after buying a separate unit. This unit is now a five-storeyed building deep inside Shahpur Jat which has 10 hall-like units. He uses four for his factory and six have been rented out. Today, he is a wealthy man. He owns two Delhi Development Authority (DDA) flats in Shahpur Jat and has also booked one commercial property in a new Gurgaon mall. His son runs three commercial units out of Laxmi Nagar in East Delhi with his brother-in-law. The garments manufactured in his factory are sold at those shops. Kamal Panwar's story stands out for two reasons. One, it's the story of a person who arguably built his own fortune. Two, his ascension follows a completely different trajectory of garment manufacture, never truly associated with the Jats. But at the same time, the alternative plot that he could sell, the social network that got him his first big order and the upcoming garment industry in Shahpur Jat speak of his social capital as a Jat.

Zile Singh from Munirka, whose father started both a brick kiln and hardware shop, did not enter the transport business or construction. The hardware shop went to his brother's family while he inherited the commercial building earlier used as their cowshed. By this time, Munirka had already developed into a fully fledged market. Meanwhile, he ran a successful grocery store from Munirka that did thriving business for a reasonable period between the late 1980s and 1990s. Since that shop also doubled up as a telephone booth, it was extremely popular. Its popularity started to wane only in the late 1990s or early 2000s. He flippantly also mentioned having a juice shop and a flour mill, but never elaborated on these. Somewhere around 2002–03, he decided to shut shop and sell the property for 20 lakh rupees. It is unclear why he never went into transport or construction and opened a grocery shop instead. As mentioned already, the building material store went to Zile Singh's brother while the commercial building close to the main road came to him. After selling his commercial property, he took a bank loan of

---

[§§] 'I never looked back after that.'

50 lakh rupees (in the same conversation, he alternately mentioned the figure as 50,000 rupees) and built Parvati Apartments for 80 lakh rupees. Much like many others in the village, after a series of small businesses, it was in real estate in the 1990s that he found redemption.

The real estate boom in the 1990s changed close to everyone's destiny in a big or small way. The entrepreneurs with dwindling businesses quickly moved over to rental property and so did people who had never had any scope of investing in business before and who had clung to the hope of a government job to secure their future. As mentioned before, Raman Tokas and Beenu salvaged their dwindling transport businesses by diverting into buying buildings and going into 'finance'. Varun's family too sold their taxi business to buy prominent real estate in Shahpur Jat, which is now a commercial property. Aspirations had changed and so had imaginations of social mobility. Earlier understandings of stable businesses were now seen to be crumbling. Soon enough, even individuals who had so far depended on government jobs began to enter this business. Rajkamal Rathi, who was in the Delhi Police, for instance, decided to leave his government job to enter the real estate business as a 'builder'. We unpack the rise of this new economy in the next chapter.

Conclusion

What emerges fairly clearly from the previous pages is that the Jat community's negotiation with the changing urban economy was calibrated through kinship relations—of money being lent, of land being bought. And the village, in itself, may or may not have been the unit of such transactions. We see how landowners become transporters, transporters become financiers, construction contractors become educationists and local policemen or ex-army men become builders, in several permutations and combinations at different moments. The curious thing about the decades between the 1950s and 1990s is that these moves and shifts were not necessarily happening intergenerationally, which is usually the more common phenomenon. We see the same family or individuals moving from one business to another or attempting to diversify into other businesses. This gives us a sense of the diverse strategies of accumulation that families and individuals were toying with in the context of the changing urban political economy.

Beenu and Zile Singh started more or less similarly. Both their fathers owned brick kilns. But while Zile Singh went into odd businesses, Beenu went into the transport business and then moved on to becoming a financier in the village. Zile Singh continued with businesses like a grocery shop, or an *atta chakki*, for the longest time and now has finally turned to rent for income. Bahadur Panwar from Shahpur Jat started on a much better footing as his father was a CPWD contractor. Today, he, along with being a financier, is also a big landlord in the village. Raman Tokas and his brothers went from owning a dozen buses to a dozen buildings along with a financing business. Kishanchand Tokas now runs a successful cement business after initial years of difficulty, and after a failed attempt at trying his hand at the transport business, he has also diversified into ground rent.

Not everyone has been equally successful at everything, however. While Beenu, Raman and Bahadur Panwar have jumped from one business to another without too many glitches, Zile Singh and Kishanchand have faced troubled phases where things have not worked out for them at various times. Harpal, as we have seen, has mostly been struggling, apart from the initial success with his coal depot and the years when the Blue Line buses did a roaring business. Today, apart from renting buildings, he is waiting for the leasehold on the coal depot to shift to freehold so that he can put it on the real estate market. Rent and its ancillary financing business are where most people have found some redemption. While the extremely wealthy ones have rejected renting as a 'lowly business', the ones who have been fumbling from one business to another saw the rent business as a godsend. Interestingly, the sections that have taken up the rent business most enthusiastically are mostly people who were never entrepreneurial to begin with. Many of them had petty jobs in the government or the police.

What we have also seen is how this dominant caste, through its army service, managed to bag coveted licences for selling commodities that were at a premium. DTC licences were traded across in such ways that they eventually landed in the hands of the Jats, and the state in the 1970s was able to create its relationship with the intermediate classes through rent. The licence-permit *raj*, the age of state protection, consolidated the position of these classes through these rents. Clearly, by the 1990s, as the licence-permit *raj* was coming to an end, many of these businesses found themselves rudderless. Increasingly, with various state and court orders placing them at immense economic strain, they were left feeling abandoned by the state. The structural adjustment programmes of liberalisation, privatisation and globalisation opened up the economy to free market: the glitzy, glamorous world of global capital. Property was to become real estate, and capital was set to become fictitious. And rent-seeking methods of the licence-permit *raj* were set to disappear.

Notes

1. Clifford Geertz, 'Deep Play: Notes on Balinese Cockfight', in *The Interpretation of Cultures: Selected Essays by Clifford Geertz* (New York: Basic Books, 1973), 448.
2. Barbara Harris-White, quoting Michael Kalecki, in *India Working: Essays on Society and Economy* (Cambridge: Cambridge University Press, 2003), 44.
3. Ibid., 57.
4. Ibid., 43.
5. Francine Frankel, *India's Political Economy 1947–2004* (New Delhi: Oxford University Press, 2006). Sudipta Kaviraj too looks at the period of Indira Gandhi's regime as having evolved into a more centralised but a less effective state. Sudipta Kaviraj, 'Indira Gandhi and Indian Politics', *Economic and Political Weekly* 21, nos. 38–39(1986).
6. The Green Revolution refers to a concerted set of programmes for rapid agricultural modernisation through high-yield variety crops and the use of modern technology; it started around 1965. For more on the Green Revolution, see Francine Frankel, *India's Green Revolution: Economic Gains and Political Costs* (Princeton: Princeton University Press, 1971).
7. Mushtaq H. Khan and Jomo K. S., eds., *Rents, Rent-Seeking and Economic Development: Theory and Evidence in Asia* (Cambridge: Cambridge University Press, 2000), 93.
8. Ibid.
9. Craig Jeffrey, 'Caste, Class, and Clientelism: A Political Economy of Everyday Corruption in Rural North India', *Economic Geography* 78, no. 1 (2002); Harish Damodaran, *India's New Capitalists: Caste, Business and Industry in a Modern Nation* (New Delhi: Palgrave Macmillan, 2008), 33.
10. Atul Kohli, 'Politics of Economic Liberalization in India', *World Development* 17, no. 3 (1989), 308; Stuart Corbridge, 'The Political Economy of Development in India Since Independence', in *Routledge Handbook of South Asian Politics: India, Pakistan, Bangladesh, Sri Lanka, and Nepal*, ed. Paul Brass (London; New York: Routledge, 2010), 305–20.
11. Chirashree Das Gupta, *State and Capital in Independent India: Institutions and Accumulation* (New Delhi: Cambridge University Press, 2016), 178.
12. Because of bank nationalisation, by 1974, 33 per cent of bank advances were directed to 'agriculture, small-scale industry, small transport operators, small business and professional and self-employed persons'. Harris-White, *India Working*, 49.
13. Damodaran, *India's New Capitalists*.
14. Ibid.
15. Harris-White, *India Working*.

16. Karl Marx, *The Eighteenth Brumaire of Louis Bonaparte* (Moscow: Progress Publishers, 1972).
17. Delhi Administration, *Delhi Gazetteer* (New Delhi, 1976), 154.
18. Anish Vanaik, *Possessing the City*, 62.
19. Vanaik draws a much broader scape of property relations across Delhi during colonial times. Apart from traditional landlords, he argues that intermediate classes, local merchants and professionals had entered the property-renting business in addition to their primary vocation. See Anish Vanaik, *Possessing the City*, 67–90.
20. Ashish Bose and Chaman Singh, 'New Rich in Delhi Fringe Village', *Economic and Political Weekly* 4, no. 10 (1969), 465–66. Though this study is based on another unnamed village in the outskirts of Delhi acquired during 1957–67, it can be safely assumed that the same would be true for villages like Munirka and Shahpur Jat, which were acquired roughly in the same time period. Bose and Singh note that the most common form of investing land was that of buying up more agricultural land elsewhere, sometimes without any intentions of developing those tracts of land as agricultural land but merely leasing it out.
21. Later, the land was converted to freehold.
22. The village which really could enter the brick kiln business in a big way, making villagers barons of this enterprise, is Tughlaqabad.
23. Not to be confused with Lado Sarai, also located in the same area.
24. LAC Awards, Land Acquisition Records, Ladha Sarai, South District, Department of Revenue, Delhi Government.
25. *Chak* as a term refers to a diverse range of forms of collective land. The term *chakbandi* is used for land consolidation by the revenue departments. In 1869, a system of *chak* was introduced to settle nomadic pastoralists in Punjab. Bhattacharya, *The Agrarian Conquest*, 350.
26. Friese, 'Peasant Communities and Agrarian Capitalism', A-137.
27. For an exciting discussion around the unpredictability of how and where cities develop, see William Cronon, *Nature's Metropolis: Chicago and the Great West* (New York; London: W. W. Norton and Company, 1991). It discusses how the rise of Chicago was preceded by massive land speculation around where the port city would come up. Eventually, the burgeoning of Chicago led to a massive devaluation in all these other possible locations.
28. Readers may recollect from the introduction that historically, the territorial networks of the Jats across northwest India were created through a similar kind of splintering.
29. *Badarpur* is a reddish building material that is made out of crushed stones, particularly found in the Aravalli region.

30. Dairy was an extremely popular business for several people. The scale of production varied wildly. To date, several of these dairies continue to be functional.
31. FAO, 'Public Distribution System in India: Evolution, Efficacy and Need for Reforms', http://www.fao.org/3/x0172e/x0172e06.htm (accessed 24 November 2019).
32. Anita Soni, 'Urban Conquest of Rural Delhi', in *Delhi: Urban Space and Human Destinies*, ed. Véronique Dupont, Emma Tarlo and Denis Vidal (New Delhi: Manohar, 2000).
33. Ibid.
34. Gujjars around the Tughlaqabad region have benefited immensely from the material supply business and have consequently entered politics.
35. Abha Chaturvedi and Anil Chaturvedi, *ACC: A Corporate Saga* (New Delhi: The Associated Cements Companies Limited, 1997), 384.
36. Ibid., 141.
37. Ibid., 142
38. Ibid., 146. The system of licensing by state governments began only in 1978, when the stockists were completely delinked from the manufacturers. Sales had to be made through a permit system or other systems specified by the state government.
39. Ibid., 206. Cement became such a premium commodity that in 1982, Mr A. R. Antulay, the chief minister of Maharashtra, had to resign after a scandal broke out that he had allegedly received kickbacks for allocating cement to an institution out of turn.
40. Ibid., 217–27.
41. Important commodities like sponge iron and pig iron were also delicenced in the mid-1980s to meet the shortage of this vital product. See Das Gupta, *State and Capital in Independent India*, 210.
42. Jawaharlal Nehru University, which is known for being a centre of leftist politics, was built on the land owned by Munirka. The anger felt by Munirka residents towards JNU was heightened in 2016 when a national controversy broke out after some JNU students were accused of shouting 'anti-India' slogans at a political event.
43. In an interesting parallel, Sai Balakrishnan notes the journey of sugar as an essential commodity and its relationship with the transformation of the agrarian–urban frontier along the Mumbai–Pune Expressway. Balakrishnan, *Shareholder Cities*, 32–92.
44. Chaturvedi and Chaturvedi, *ACC: A Corporate Saga*, 203.
45. Ibid., 204.

46. It is not clear how much truth there is to the claim that the Gujjar brothers drove them out of business, but there are enough news reports naming the brothers as major players in the mining business until the Supreme Court ban in 2009. The brothers also joined politics, both the Indian National Congress (INC) and BJP. They have been known for illegal sand mining from the Aravalli region too.
47. Das Gupta, *State and Capital in Independent India*, 206.
48. Stefan Tetzlaff, 'The Motorisation of the "Mofussil": Automobile Traffic and Social Change in Rural and Small-Town India, c. 1915–1940' (PhD diss., University of Göttingen, 2015), 106–07.
49. Vivek Chibber, *Locked in Place: State-Building and Late Industrialization in India* (New Jersey: Princeton University Press, 2003), 24.
50. Tetzlaff, 'The Motorisation of the "Mofussil"', 93.
51. Harris-White, *India Working*, 70.
52. Das Gupta, *State and Capital in Independent India*, 206. It is telling that the Shriram Group, which had emerged as a major non-banking finance corporation in 1974, owes its origin to chit fund business and a small-scale private lottery scheme.
53. Tetzlaff speaks of a major hire and purchase company, Motor and General Finance Limited, owned by a certain Ved Prakash Gupta in the post-depression era of the 1930s, which had a significant impact on the increase in the penetration of transport in this region. Tetzlaff, 'The Motorisation of the "Mofussil"', 251.
54. D. A. C. Maunder and T. C. Mbara, 'Liberalisation of Urban Public Transport Services: What Are the Implications?' *Indian Journal of Transport Management* 20, no. 2 (1996).
55. Pay Commissions are set up by the Government of India roughly at an interval of 10 years to revise salary structures of government employees. This strike was a massive one with the entire public transport system coming to a grinding halt for close to 20–25 days. Since Delhi's administration was under the Central government at that time, it had to get buses from Haryana, Rajasthan and even Jammu and Kashmir to tide over the crisis.
56. However, Jagadish Tytler is much more infamous for his involvement in the Anti-Sikh Riots in 1984. Despite incriminating evidence and the testimonies of victims, he was not convicted.
57. John Ward Anderson, 'On the Routes of the Killer Buses', *Washington Post*, 26 July 1993, https://www.washingtonpost.com/archive/politics/1993/07/26/on-the-routes-of-the-killer-buses/fb745527-ec07-450e-805b-b68a0301701e/ (accessed 18 March 2016).

58. Though many run hire and lease companies, by 'financing' I mean a local form of moneylending that has emerged in these economies. See Chapter 4.
59. Sundaram, *Pirate Modernity*, 144.
60. Ground rent would refer to rent derived from landed property more specifically.
61. H. M. Mishra, 'Red Line Bus Fleet Wreaks Havoc in Delhi', *India Today*, 15 June 1993, https://www.indiatoday.in/magazine/indiascope/story/19930615-red-line-bus-fleet-wreaks-havoc-in-delhi-811185-1993-06-15 (accessed 17 November 2019).
    The Red Line buses were a predecessor to Delhi's Blue Line buses that shut down in 2011.
62. The environmentalist lawyer M. C. Mehta's PIL in 1985 with respect to air pollution had a long run. Only in 1996 did the Supreme Court pass an order that all government vehicles in the city that ran on diesel and petroleum needed to be converted to a cleaner Compressed Natural Gas or CNG.
63. 'No Blueline Buses in Delhi from Tomorrow', *Times of India*, 30 January 2011. After a series of cases of Blue Line buses running over people, the Delhi government had to respond to the public outrage and a Delhi High Court order by phasing them out.
64. The same businessman who was friends with Jwala Singh's father.
65. A vernacular system of investing money, close to the chit fund form. This has been discussed in detail in Chapter 4.

3
Villages of the City
Ordering Spaces and Aspirations in Neoliberal Times

What is the utility of government and all actions of government in a society where exchange determines the true value of things?
—Michel Foucault, *The Birth of Biopolitics*

M. C. Mehta vs Union of India and Others was a landmark judgement passed in 2004 concerning industrial units in residential areas. It had its roots in a writ petition filed by M. C. Mehta in 1985, an environmentalist and lawyer, on unauthorised land use by stone crushers. Though it was only about the stone crushers, in the wake of the Bhopal Gas Tragedy, this writ acquired a life of its own and stretched across decades. By 2004, this public interest litigation (PIL) had become representative of all manner of unauthorised industrial activities in residential spaces. The judgement noted that close to 93,000 such units were operating out of Delhi and that the Municipal Corporation of Delhi (MCD) had been granting them registrations and licences although they were in clear contravention of the Delhi Master Plan.[1] This case had a far-reaching impact and led to sealing drives extending even to shops, nursing homes and banquet halls across the city.[2] Protests by angry traders eventually led to revisions in the new Master Plan that allowed for more flexible land use. The M. C. Mehta case, therefore, would continue to hold a very important space in the tussle between the state and private players, and concerns of environmentalism and livelihood. The judgement brought the trading community together against the state, but it also brought the extent of unauthorised construction in Delhi out into the open.

M. C. Mehta vs Union of India came after a series of judgements on the fate of slums and unauthorised settlements. *Olga Tellis and Ors vs The Municipal Corporation of Bombay*, 1985, reflects the dilemma of the times. At one level, it acknowledged the right to livelihood of the slum dwellers and took note of the structural inequality of city spaces. But on the other, it settled for rehabilitation for the slum dwellers despite noting the structural injustice.

By the 2000s, this dilemma had evaporated. *Almitra H. Patel and Another vs Union of India* compared slum resettlement to rewarding a pickpocket.[3] The poor were nothing but creatures who led a parasitic existence, and welfare was nothing but a drain on resources. The post–Second World War Keynesian consensus around states ensuring employment, welfare and development had ended. The world had moved stridently towards the market with the emergence of neoliberalism. Assets and enterprises were denationalised, more private players were encouraged, and state bureaucracy and welfare structures were trimmed down. The world had also begun moving towards an economy led by services and finance. With the ideological push that the market was an institution available to all equally and therefore the solution to all problems, the blame for poverty and destitution fell squarely on the poor themselves. They were poor because they were either not hardworking or just plain ignorant.

These two shifts, one economic and the other ideological, were also manifested in the ways in which cities were transforming after the 1990s. Cities now had to compete globally to look like they were part of the neoliberal race—with skyscrapers and new shopping malls boasting global brands and infrastructure considered world-class. Financialisation entered the land game and changed the nature of speculation. Land was now increasingly part of hedge funds and portfolios of major companies or held the promise of immense windfall through widening rent gaps.[4] Special economic zones, ideally meant for manufacturing, began to veer into speculation on real estate values.[5] Neoliberalism also ushered in an urban aesthetic represented by condominiums and shopping malls that appealed to the upper middle class, and the upwardly mobile sections of the population. Simultaneously, it pushed the urban poor further into the margins, that is, the outskirts of the city. The city began to continually reorganise itself along this axis of class and aesthetics. Older, run-down cinema theatres became glitzy multiplexes and dysfunctional cotton mills transformed into shopping malls. But these informal spaces and enterprises continue to thrive. The paradox was that the city had turned increasingly anti-poor and at the same time, it depended on cheap labour to stay on the global map. Gentrification of spaces and the proliferation of informal spaces have undeniably gone hand in hand in most cities of the Global South. PIL encouraged courts to pander to upper-middle-class notions of bourgeoisie environmentalism, which again held the poor responsible for squalor and stench.[6] But at the same time, states also had to look the other way to retain the liminal spaces where the working class continued to live and work. In the case of Gurgaon, this unevenness produced luxury urban development along with expansion in the manufacturing industry.[7] Though most of Gurgaon's population lives in informal settlements and villages, one hardly ever finds anyone associating the city with anything but large condominiums, golf courses and fancy shopping malls. The previous chapter looked at how the urban villages of Delhi evolved from the 1950s–60s until the 1990s. This chapter highlights a different kind of rental economy emerging in these villages after the 1990s and discusses how theories of gentrification and the rent gap theory may not be sufficient to explain our urban realities.

The M. C. Mehta case, as has already been indicated, occupies a central place in the contestations over the city's space. Partly owing to the faulty Delhi Master Plan, and partly to the people disregarding it, currently, as much as 90 per cent of Delhi's buildings fall in the category of unauthorised construction.[8] The judgement, which upheld the Delhi Master Plan as its holy grail, caused mayhem with rampant sealings happening across the city. In the context of *lal dora* villages, the Supreme Court in the M. C. Mehta case noted,

> In respect of the industrial activity in Lal Dora, in the affidavit filed in October 2002 by Chief Town Planner of Municipal Corporation of Delhi it has been stated that the proposal for the withdrawal of exemption notification would be placed before the Corporation. Nothing seems to have been done in that direction. It is not disputed that under the garb of exemption notification dated 24th August 1963, all kinds of buildings have come up in the Lal Dora.[9]

If we wish to understand the evolution of these villages, the 1963 circular is at the heart of it. The circular, in the backdrop of the Delhi Master Plan, had exempted villages of Delhi from building bye-laws. The villagers were expected to carry on with their traditional existence as if they lived in a vacuum. But this exemption became differently useful after the downfall of the licence-permit *raj* and the collapse of the older rent-seeking regime with it. New, small BPOs, training centres and jobs woven around 'soft skills' began to dominate the employment landscape of the city, whose workers started to find homes in these urban villages. Some even turned into manufacturing spaces. It is only ironical that a government circular, in this case, the exemption of 1963, became the basis of irregular urban growth in these villages.

The regime of building exemptions led to the emergence of an alternate system of valuation of property, informal markets and eventually an entirely separate governing logic. A real-estate market, catering to precariat migrant blue-collar workers and manufacturers but under the control of a community of landlords through ground rent, began to emerge at the peak of the neoliberal economy. As we have already seen, this new rent regime came about based on collective ownership of the coveted resource, that is, land. This kind of a real estate market, defined by rent and controlled by a community, not only found ways to exist but also thrive in the age of finance capital. And in doing so, it did not have to melt into neoliberal aesthetics either. On the contrary, as I go on to show, this rent economy becomes crucial precisely because it does not adhere to the neoliberal, upper-middle-class sensibilities.

With the broader political economic shift to neoliberalism, we see two architectural forms that begin to emerge in the urban villages at this time—the 'one-room set' and the *adda*. It is evident that rent increasingly becomes the conduit between the communal ways of living, social control of the landlords and the world of global finance capital. While the community of landlords secured its role of providing housing to workers of the new economy, rent also allowed them to preserve the market within the parameters of their own vocabulary and logic of ownership. These villages thus occupied the margins or frontiers, but always in relation to the centre of the city.

Neoliberalism produces new frictions—of the chasm between legal and illegal, of imaginations of a global city and its realities. And yet, it is not just a relationship of animosity. I explore the physical transformation of these village spaces into real estate of a different kind. I also look at the spectrum of laws, government documents and directives that govern these spaces and their attempt to negotiate their way around these spaces. This shift also signals the change in the attitude of the state. The state first chose to overlook these spaces but over the years realised what could be extracted from them. Increasingly, therefore, we see a state striving to control these spaces. But as this happens, the community's response to the state also transforms. Memories of land acquisition and the decline of Blue Line buses owing to state regulations evoke both anger and hurt directed at the state. But as these villages themselves begin to occupy grey zones between legality and illegality, their anger and hurt find new articulations.

Villages of the City

The 1990s fundamentally changed the physical and economic character of these villages, but the pattern of their physical and economic transformation was vastly different from each other. Bina Ramani, a fashion designer and

Page 3 figure, was arguably the first to foray into Hauz Khas Village to set up her workshop-cum-boutique in the late 1980s. She vividly documents her first impressions of the village when she accidentally 'discovered' it. Written in a tenor that is reminiscent of the orientalist explorer, she describes ruins and tombs and the 'natives' who watch her goggle-eyed. As she leads up to the village, she writes,

> I seemed to have landed in a time warp! Men in white turbans, starched white kurtas and lungis, sat on two charpoys smoking hookahs. Women wearing colourful ghaghras and kurtis, their heads covered with dupattas, were tending to buffalos.... It was obvious that people had rarely seen a car. I was now in the midst of a hidden village, surrounded by a burgeoning metropolitan giant, where time seemed to have stood still. I felt as if I had stepped back by a hundred years or more.[10]

That was the year 1989. As Bina Ramani was revelling in the rustic beauty of Hauz Khas Village, Munirka was already choking with commercial activity. Hauz Khas, tucked away from any major roads, was perfect for Bina Ramani's commercial endeavour. She wanted to handpick designers herself and curate a niche known only to the upper class and expatriates of the city.[11] And it did become so for a while. But in less than 30 years, Hauz Khas Village transformed into a living nightmare susceptible to fire hazards with restaurants, concept stores and pubs with sky-high real estate rates crammed together.[12] As rents have gone up, independent stores have given way to big brands.

In Chapter 1, we saw how land acquisition had not had the same impact for all Delhi villages even if they were acquired at the same time. Different villages, owing to their own specificities and peculiarities, began to respond differently to the loss and the opportunity that came with land acquisition. Understandably, therefore, Shahpur Jat and Munirka, barely five kilometres apart from each other, also evolved in very different ways. With the arterial Ring Roads separating Munirka village from the 12 sectors of R. K. Puram, Munirka entered the throes of urbanisation almost as soon as notification took place, probably even before. Shahpur Jat had had a very different life in the 1960s and 1970s. Sheltered by its distance from arterial roads, it continued to remain agrarian until as late as 1979. People still recall the famous cauliflowers and tobacco that Shahpur Jat used to produce. Unlike Munirka, Shahpur Jat had less, but more fertile, land. Even after Shahpur Jat's land was acquired, the farmers continued to cultivate it in exchange for rent. All of this changed when Delhi witnessed its first mega-event, the

Asian Games in 1982, which precipitated an unprecedented infrastructural development within the city.[13]

Construction began on the Asian Games village and Siri Fort auditorium on the agricultural lands of Shahpur Jat around 1979. Their locations had an immense impact on the urbanisation of this locality. A huge number of construction workers moved to Delhi to meet the construction demand before the Asian Games. Most of them found housing in villages like Shahpur Jat and Munirka.[14] Many low-level government staff also found housing in Munirka. In Shahpur Jat, however, along with the construction workers, some artisans began to share space from the mid-1980s onwards. Tucked away in a quiet corner, these garment factories flourished. While Munirka's local economy became a space for lower-middle-class migrants in the city, Shahpur Jat emerged as a niche hub for fashion designers, and consequently an alternative, bohemian space for artists, newer restaurants, start-ups and so on. The very fact that Shahpur Jat (like Hauz Khas Village) lay hidden and tucked away from arterial roads made it (them) lucrative in the eyes of elite entrepreneurs who wanted to develop these spaces for niche consumption. They were 'pristine', and their rustic rurality could be curated, packaged and sold. As a curated space of consumption, the real estate valuation of this property market rocketed sky-high. The irony is not lost here. Value is erratic and temperamental. One may buy land in the hope that it will appreciate and that may never happen. Another piece of land may remain stuck in a rut for decades, and somehow the same reason that worked against it might become the reason for an exponential increase in its value decades later. Value moves in mysterious ways across these landscapes and ends up creating its own unique order.

One might say that the construction of the Asiad Village to house the players and delegates of the Games and the whole brouhaha around the upcoming Asian Games took away Shahpur Jat's anonymity. Further, a boom in the export–import business in the early 1990s led to Shahpur Jat emerging as a manufacturing space for garments. Scores of small manufacturing units cropped up, and a steady number of migrant garment workers began to live in Shahpur Jat around this time, enabling the village to emerge prominently on the garment manufacturing map in Delhi. As Shahpur Jat quickly rose up the ladder and started to host several fashion boutiques by 2000, its currency in terms of rent, at least in the gentrified sections of the village, went up several notches as opposed to Munirka, which continued to cater to lower-middle-class housing and small businesses. The fringes of Shahpur

Jat have gone up so much in value that the ground-floor properties in the adjoining Delhi Development Authority (DDA) colony of Shahpur Jat have also now been converted into commercial properties. The break that is so clear between Munirka village and the Munirka DDA colony is almost erased in the case of Shahpur Jat. Though this high-end commercial rent business in Shahpur Jat is limited, unlike Munirka where almost every family has been able to convert its property into rental property, it is fast expanding in the case of the former.

Housing for New Labour in the City: The One-Room Set

The 'one-room set' was an interesting innovation to encourage rent (Figure 3.1). As new lower-middle-class employees, mostly young, began to flock to the city, these 'one-room sets' became extremely popular because of their affordability. Rajkamal Rathi, in his 30s, who is now a builder in Munirka, credits himself with coming up with the idea of the one-room sets. 'Mujhe kehna toh nahi chahiye, par yeh sab maine hi shuru kiya,'* he says proudly. Rajkamal had been an international-level swimmer and had represented India in the SAF Games[15] in the early 1990s. He claims that his experience of staying in hotel rooms with an attached bathroom and kitchen when he would attend sports meets gave him the idea for 'one-room sets' or one-room studio apartments. Until the 1990s, the villagers had only rented out parts of their traditional houses to working-class migrants. The common courtyard had turned into a cooking area and the lavatories would be located outside the house. As these villages began to cater to a different class of workers in the city, the need was felt for the housing to mimic a particular middle-class, aspirational life. By the 1990s, the idea of 'flats' had already become normalised in the city as the most desirable form of urban living. The poorer cousin of the flat, the one-room set, became the only space this new migrant labour could seek out to live in.

Most of these multi-storeyed buildings are poorly built matchbox structures with hardly any windows. In a locality jam-packed with houses, windows of one house open up uncomfortably close to windows of others. Not only do these windows have little to contribute to air circulation or light, but they also impinge on the privacy of the homes. Windows also substantially inflate the cost of building houses, so they cannot be a priority. After all, these units are cheaply constructed and just about providing the

---

* 'I should not be saying this. But I began it all.'

Villages of the City

Figure 3.1 Hundreds of buildings like these house the numerous 'one-room sets' in Munirka. Even in broad daylight, these homes and lanes remain dark and dingy.

Source: Ritambhara Mehta and Dilip Menon.

necessary amenities like electricity and water supply. In our conversation, Rajkamal kept emphasising the term *chhote kamre* (small rooms) several times while describing his innovation. Maximisation of rent extraction is based on smallness of the tenements. This architectural form became vital to the current logic of accumulation once it was apparent that the village's real estate boom could only happen by targeting the housing needs of the lower-middle-class migrant.

The 'one-room set' in Munirka can earn the owner a rent between 2,500 rupees and 8,000 rupees. The cheapest are small rooms with a shared bathroom and no kitchen. The rental on a standard one-room set is usually 4,500–5,500 rupees; it usually comes with a small kitchenette with a slab and a fixed kitchen sink. The price moves upwards with better flooring, paint and location. The larger and better-quality ones that get some sunlight and fresh air can fetch a rent up to 8,000 rupees. But a bulk of them is mostly hard to differentiate from one another. As village land started becoming more and more valuable in the 1990s, the stakes increased for many. While several people from Munirka had bought agricultural land in Tauru probably in the hope that it would increase in value, they never saw any. As the rent market began to flourish in Munirka with the arrival of new migrants, many began to sell their agricultural land in order to invest it in the reconstruction of their houses in the urban village. As we have seen already in Chapter 2, the decline of Blue Line buses and failing businesses began to thus give way to this emerging rental business.

Rajkamal Rathi does think of himself as an innovative businessman. He tried to run his construction business along with his Delhi Police job between 1991 and 2005. But then he quit his job and, having reconstructed his share of *dadalayak* (ancestral) property into a series of one-room sets, slowly started taking on building contracts[16] as well as buying up plots. By 2002, he was already earning 2 lakh rupees per month as rent. He only builds in urban villages, however. In a regularised colony, Rajkamal claims, one would have to pay 15 lakh rupees just to get all kinds of clearances, none of which is required for urban villages. When I spoke to him, he did not seem to have any qualms regarding the unauthorised status of his constructions. When I asked him how they negotiated the *lal dora* limits as builders, he told me almost casually, 'Sab risk pe chal raha hai.'† The 'risk' that Rajkamal refers to is a calculated one, which the local villagers attribute to their confidence that an impending threat of demolition will be skirted. They defy almost all principles of architecture to follow just one: maximisation of space.

Shahpur Jat: *Adda* and the Life of Labour

The Asian Games brought in massive changes for Delhi. For Shahpur Jat, it led to an inflow of working-class labour from Rajasthan and Uttar Pradesh, which finally began to converge around an elaborate 'garment factory' ecosystem. Though the outer fringes of the village were converted into stylish boutiques

---

† 'Everything is running on risk.'

and concept stores, Shahpur Jat's innards are full of old-style houses with large rooms and crumbling wooden beams and doors. These spacious, elongated rooms in old-fashioned houses now function as *adda*s or *karkhana*s.

*Karkhana*s are small workshops for different kinds of garment work. *Adda*s are specific types of workshops that specialise in embroidery. The name 'adda' is derived from the big wooden embroidery frame also called by the same name. Today, no one can clearly remember if the garment factories came here first or the artisans, but what is evident is that somewhere around the 1980s, Shahpur Jat slowly began to develop as a garment manufacturing hub. The *karigar*s are mostly Muslims hailing from places like Uluberia, Rishra and other areas in North 24 Parganas in West Bengal. The walls along the narrow lanes of Shahpur Jat are often plastered with handwritten advertisements in Bangla, for tailors, masters and *karigar*s. Shahpur Jat has more shops selling sequins, threads and needles catering to these workshops than any other kind, including grocery; this speaks volumes about the economic character of the village. The *adda* workers remain mostly holed up and working, peering into their frames in the inner lanes of Shahpur Jat. Shops selling all kinds of stitching paraphernalia—threads, needles, sequins, adhesive for fabric and several such embellishments—and small congregations of men at corners around *chaiwalla*s indulging in loud friendly banter make up a manufacturing space organisationally different from the Fordist assembly line spaces. It only goes on to show how deeply entrenched garment manufacturing is in this area. The first such large factory in public memory was called 'Kalamkari'. That factory is now long gone, with no traces of the whereabouts of the owner.

Safiuddin's first job in Delhi was at that factory. He does not clearly remember why it shut down. The history of the factory is somewhat elusive. Few people remember any concrete description of the place, how big it was, who owned it and so on, but the memory of Kalamkari as the first factory remains firmly in place. Safiuddin started his own *karkhana*[17] around 1991, by which time he had already worked as a *karigar* for 7–8 years. Shahpur Jat in those days was geared towards exports and had 8–10 factories. Today, Shahpur Jat is bustling with such *karkhana*s (Figure 3.2). The workshops are of various kinds. Some make generic garments for bulk export or sale, and some are workshops attached to boutiques which customise garments according to orders based on the samples displayed in the shops. Among them, several are sampling units where the designer and the head *karigar* brainstorm and experiment with making a prototype. The prototype is then sent to the *karkhana*s for the lower-level *karigar*s to copy and reproduce. After this rung comes the regular *karkhana*, which can accommodate 7–8 workers and where mass production of clothes takes place. After this, there are a host of *adda*s and *rangrez* (dyers) who operate independently.

Safiuddin today runs such a *karkhana* with six workers. His *karkhana* does embroidery work for cheaper lehengas that sell in Chandni Chowk in Delhi, and Bangalore among other cities. Mostly run by ex-*karigar*s who have moved up a rung and used their networks to become petty businessmen themselves, these work-cum-living spaces reduce establishment costs and also ensure regularity and discipline from the workers. On the other hand, they break down the concept of 'working hours', and the distinction between factory and living space. Safiuddin's *adda* is located in a run-down, visibly old building with electricity wires hanging all around it. In a hall with peeling limestone plaster and wooden beams, a corner of the *adda* is cordoned off with a curtain which has rolled-up mattresses, basic utensils and a gas stove for the workers to cook their meals on. At the end of the working day, the *adda* frames are

Figure 3.2 A regular working day in a garment workshop in Shahpur Jat

Source: Photo by author.

lifted, and the mattresses are rolled out. The ground floor has a courtyard that the workers use for bathing. Safiuddin pays 7,000 rupees for the workshop and 2,000 rupees for electricity at 9 rupees per unit. These *karigar*s occupy the lowest rung in the chain, where their *karigari* is constantly devalued through the piece-rate system.

Shahpur Jat's emergence as one of the most thriving garment 'manufacturing units' in Asia has been gradual. Its development can be called quirky at best with small workshops emerging gradually for a variety of unskilled and specialised processes related to garments. Quite unlike the sound of drills and welding that dominate Munirka, Shahpur Jat's lanes are filled with the dull, monotonous sound of sewing machines, only overpowered at times by loud popular Hindi songs from the 1990s or hugely popular Bangla melodies. Sometimes mixed with the sound of construction work, the songs and sewing machines together create a strange cacophonic tapestry. It is undeniable, however, that Shahpur Jat has earned its name on the global map because of the niche that it has created for itself in the clothing manufacturing market. What started with a few small-scale factories of garment manufacture, and some fashion designers setting up their boutiques, has metamorphosed into an entire locality resembling an elaborate, fragmented factory.[18] A piece of garment travels through the village, undergoing processes such as designing, stitching, dyeing and embroidery in various independent units. The logistics and the movement of these garments are not fixed like in the assembly line. They change direction and speed, and form a dense network of objects, designers, suppliers and labourers who create a web-like space and economy of garment manufacture. Their movement is unpredictable at moments, the workers forever unstable, and smaller boutiques mostly in a state of flux at the end of the chain of what we know as an informal economy.

At the same time, Shahpur Jat has also emerged as a space of consumption in certain parts. This has led to the emergence of a variety of rental possibilities—from spaces for art galleries to offices for start-ups and publishing houses, boutiques and restaurants. By the 2000s, many designers who ran workshops in Shahpur Jat had begun opening their retail stores in the outer lanes of the village. Shahpur Jat is thus fast emerging as one of those alternative places where all kinds of independent cafés, restaurants and hobby groups thrive. The way the village is laid out, visitors to Shahpur Jat can walk unhindered along the prettier, curated and graffitied outer lanes, without realising the dense world of garment production that is alive inside. The narrow inner lanes, teeming with small, dingy units, are occluded from vision, even though they might not be separated from the outer lanes by more than 10 feet. This schism of the visual field splits into two. One showcases the glimmery world of commerce, glamour, of entrepreneurial 'ideas', and the other contains the messy, unkempt and ugly side of the labour and manufacturing that produces the former. Commodities have always needed to invisibilise the social relations of labour that produce them.[19] But in places like Shahpur Jat, where the grimy world of labour and the glitzy world of consumption cohabit, this invisibilisation has to be produced spatially.

Building Aspirations in the World of Risk

For the villagers and some long-term residents in these villages, buying up property and reconstructing their houses became almost the most widely prevalent method of accumulation in the 1990s. Radha, a woman from the Nai caste, became a tenant in Munirka after arriving here with her family from rural Haryana. I met her through her son, a self-proclaimed social activist in the village, Babloo. Her husband, a barber by profession, moved to Delhi in 1987 and after short stints in localities like Azadpur in North Delhi and Nizamuddin in South Delhi, the family finally settled in Munirka in 1992. Radha reminisces that land within the village was quite cheap then. They had considered buying a plot in the mid-1990s for as little as 25,000 rupees, but since it was unauthorised and therefore a risky investment, they decided against it. A couple of years later, having grown more confident about buying unauthorised property, the family decided to buy another plot overlooking a municipal park for 60,000 rupees and fixed a deal with the owner.

On her way back after they had sealed the deal, Radha met an acquaintance whom she told about the plot. According to her, this acquaintance went ahead and bought up the land overnight. The next time, they found a plot of land close to a chowk in the middle of the village for 2.5 lakh rupees. However, once they agreed to buy it, the price was arbitrarily raised to 3 lakh rupees and, therefore, they had to let go of this opportunity as well. In 2000, they finally bought the flat they now live in for 3.5 lakh rupees. Evidently, speculation over land, and quick buying and selling, has been central to the village economy. As the availability of plots began to dry up, flats built by local builders became more popular. Radha's family also managed to buy a plot for 7 lakh rupees by 2007, which they later converted into a four-floor building with multiple 'one-room sets', entirely rented out to several northeastern migrants. Although her family was able to buy two properties, Radha's narrative, when she spoke to me, was filled with remorse and lament: if only she hadn't told her friend about the plot; if only she had dared to buy up that cheap plot that had been offered to her initially; if only she had also bought up the flat next to theirs. Apart from personal ambitions, her narrative also gave me a sense of how land value within these villages was appreciating unprecedentedly in the 1990s, and how Radha and many like her hustled about to buy property. Radha, as a woman with limited means, was acutely aware of the opportunity cost of the decision they had made to invest in property as a means of social mobility. Her younger son was keen to sit for the chartered accountancy examination and had wanted to join coaching classes at the time when Radha and her husband were scouting for land. Owing to a paucity of funds, which meant they could not afford both, they decided to spend the money on buying property. Though the ownership of a piece of property has stabilised the family's economic condition, Radha is filled with remorse that their decision probably denied her younger son opportunities that he deserved. Today, both Babloo and his brother do odd jobs. She detests Babloo's political activism, but that is the subject of another chapter.

By the 2000s, the courtyards had disappeared from both these villages, and so had the *baithak*s. Anything that was considered wastage of space has been done away with the rebuilding of these houses. Munirka had one unnamed *gumbad*, or tomb, from the medieval period, but in the race to construct, not much of it was left intact. The Thanewala Gumbad, in Shahpur Jat, a more prominent historical site, recognised by the Archeological Survey of India, has often been the reason for notices being served. Fauzia, who owns a boutique in the DDA market in Shahpur Jat, recalled that she used to come here in the 1990s to buy material for a small garment company that she used to work for then. Several prominent fashion designers used to have a factory in Shahpur Jat in the early 1990s, which was run from one of the houses.[20] 'It didn't use to be like this. The houses used to be rather far apart,' she recalls. She set up her own factory/studio in 2000 in Balliram Lane[21] of Shahpur Jat and soon added a rack to display her designs as she started noticing interested customers milling around. Fauzia started with paying 10,000 rupees as rent for her space in 2000. In five years, the rent had risen to 25,000 rupees. She complains that the commercial plots have been halved to accommodate more tenants. That was one of the easiest ways in which the local inhabitants could double their income. Splitting one commercial unit into two automatically brought in much higher volumes of rent without necessarily significantly cutting down on the rent amount. Lalita, a landlady, and also one of the early entrants in the property business in the village, speaks proudly of the numerous innovations she introduced to increase rents over time—constructing basements, erecting partitions, changing the entrances. 'Na jaane kitne baar renovate kiya,'‡ she says nostalgically, looking at her house.

Dharampal Panwar's grandfather built house no. 160 here in 1907. It still stands with its traditional arches and old-fashioned wooden doors in a narrow lane around the Purana Chaupal (Old Community Centre), which is filled with the constant din of sewing machines from neighbouring houses. A notice hanging by the main door of Dharampal's house, reads: 'This is a heritage property. This property was build [*sic*] during the Mughal emperor rule.' Along with another notice stating the requirement for a 'master tailor', a board hangs outside the door, which reads: 'Only interested in giving to foreigner [*sic*] for rent.' The term 'Mughal' in the first notice stands merely as a marker of the house being old rather than denoting an authentic timeline. Wanting to promote this particular house as a 'heritage' property, Dharampal wanted to increase the valuation of the building by getting 'foreigner' tenants who might want to spruce it up and turn it into an exotic boutique. But situated deep inside the village, with noisy *karkhana*s all around, it could not be sold or rented out as a boutique.

Be it Rajakamal, Radha, Dharampal or Lalita, they do think of themselves as individuated economic actors who were capable of innovation, who could take supposed 'risks'. Their victory is important to them because they succeeded in an extremely competitive affair. Rajkamal Rathi feels tremendous pride in his endeavour as a builder. He thinks of himself as an entrepreneur who thought up the innovation of one-room sets and dared to take the risk of building them. Lalita Panwar, from Shahpur Jat, who was widowed rather early, spoke with nostalgia about having gone against the family's tradition and worked hard to constantly renovate her property. Both Radha and Lalita speak of prices that they have paid. Their risk-taking abilities and innovative capabilities give them a self-perception of being entrepreneurs, that is, someone with a sense of endeavour, adventure and abilities, and in control of uncertainties.[22]

Though all of them operate in the domain of ground rent, their testimonies defy that association. Rent minimises risk: the hallmark of financial capital. Arjun Appadurai makes the important observation that with finance capital, the 'spirit of capitalism' had moved away from being embodied in an austere, protestant Christian who found virtue in hard work to a far more maverick, adventurous, risk-taker figure.[23] It is not surprising, thus, that several landlords want to think of themselves as entrepreneurs. Many would not want to identify

---

‡ 'Don't remember how many times I have renovated this.'

with being a rentier alone—a rustic, idle villager who does nothing apart from rebuilding his property. Rent provides a world where there are no successes or failures. But living in the world defined by capital, which celebrates 'self-made men' and 'risk-taking individuals', many landlords, too, see themselves in the same image. The 'risk' that they often refer to does not arise from the vagaries of the market, but rather from the threat of demolitions from the state. Though they often use 'risk' to distinguish themselves from the rest, their testimonies obfuscate the fact that they are beneficiaries of a uniform possession of a resource; the risk is posed by the state trying to break it.

Demolitions and the State

The careers of cities have been historically made possible through demolitions, and Delhi's story is no different.[24] The massive demolition drives around the Yamuna Pushta squatter settlements in 2004 in preparation for the 2010 Commonwealth Games is one episode in the capital's history in this regard. As evident in the M. C. Mehta case as well, demolitions have, for long, been the most accepted method of the state for regulating spaces. By razing a built structure to the ground, the space is freed up to rebuild it as per law. It is also a way of penalising the ones who break the law. But demolitions, when looked at closely, tell us something vital about the relationship between governance, citizenship and political power. Demolitions are in fact an important field for studying the constitution of these interrelationships. There are reasons why orders like that of M. C. Mehta have created immense stir, but have seldom succeeded.

The only massive demolition drive that took place in Munirka was in 1985 (to be discussed in Chapter 6). This demolition became intensely controversial, so much so that even the Union Minister of Urban Development at the time, Abdul Ghafoor, had to field questions regarding the Ministry's legitimacy and rehabilitation policy in the lower house of the Indian Parliament, the Lok Sabha. The following was Mr Ghafoor's reply:

> In Delhi and elsewhere there are land grabbers who have made it a profession to grab land and they let it out to other people on payment. Currently, their market rate is Rs. 5,000 to Rs. 6,000. They include the people who are tenants elsewhere, live at other places, but had opened a shop on such land. Therefore, it is not like this that only those persons had been removed who had no other place to live. They included all types of people. The second point is that they erected pucca or semi pucca jhuggis on the DDA land which had been earmarked for some school, park or a higher secondary school. How far can we allow them to

encroach upon DDA land in such a situation? You have mentioned the case of Munirka in your question; demolition was done there in 1983–84 too, but those people again occupied the land and put up constructions. These constructions were again demolished but they again built up dwellings. This has happened for the third time. Of them, some people are such as prompt the people to resist the demolition operation. Now, you tell me how can work go on smoothly if they are not removed?[25]

This statement by the Urban Development Minister that betrays his sense of helplessness probably encompasses the story of demolition drives in India. More often than not, they are rendered useless by new informal settlements that crop up almost immediately after. In the contemporary cases of demolitions that I 'witnessed', demolitions had begun to look very different. For the lower bureaucracy in charge of them, 'proof' of demolition effectively translates into breaking a few sections that can be repaired easily. Rambir Singh, in his 70s, can be found sitting outside his massive commercial property of five floors in Shahpur Jat smoking his *hukka* on most days. While it is partly used for residential purposes, several floors of the building are let out to start-ups, firms and chartered accountant offices. Although the building is located along a commercial road, Rambir Singh claims they do not pay any house tax or conversion charge.[26] 'Yahan koi nahi dekhta,'[§] he says. On asking him about the threat of the MCD wanting to demolish his property, he says nonchalantly, 'Yahan koi kabhi kisi ko kuchh todne nahi deta. Agar kabhi aisi naubat aa jaaye, toh poora gaon saath mein khada ho jata hai.'[**] Singh's comment is reminiscent of an incident in 1997, when demolitions ordered by the then South Delhi Deputy Municipal Commissioner, Chetan Sanghi, led the residents of Shahpur Jat to congregate outside the MCD office with sticks and rods.[27]

When I was carrying out my research in Shahpur Jat, one of my respondents happened to mention that a house had been demolished just the day before in the village. I had been in the village the previous day as well, but had barely caught a whiff of this. Curious, I asked him which house it was, as I wanted to see for myself what had happened. On finding that house number,[28] I stood there utterly confused. The house, a three-storeyed one, with plush interiors, looked intact. As the door was open, I could see four—five men seated around a table in the lobby of the house. Those men were by now all looking at me

---

[§] 'Nobody really looks here.'
[**] 'Nobody really allows them to break anything. If it comes to that then the entire village comes together.'

with suspicion. Standing there, peering at the house, looking up and down, I am not surprised I came across as suspicious. I decided to clear the air by asking if I was at the right house. One of them said yes and asked what I wanted. As I explained my research to them and said that I was there because I had heard of the demolition, I could see their suspicion rapidly transforming into hostility. The person I was speaking to responded rudely that no such thing had happened. His body language made it evident that the conversation had reached its end. I quietly walked away.

As most properties in these villages are unauthorised, the local councillors are crucial for preventing any demolitions from happening. Also, a demolition drive is different from an isolated demolition. Of late, most cases of demolition have been of individual properties as a consequence of complaints and accusations by neighbours. Rajinder, a property dealer who exclusively deals in disputed properties, took it upon himself to explain to me the legal-administrative status of these urban villages. 'Upar se neeche tak sab inhi ke log hain!'†† he says with a smirk on his face. He is not entirely wrong. The South Delhi Municipal Corporation has a significant number of Jats in hugely influential positions, many of whom own property in such disputed urban villages. A complex system that involves the MCD, the local councillor and the clout that these villages enjoy determines the nature of the demolition. It might even be said that the vague laws and rules that the state once deliberately maintained do not seem to be working in favour of the state anymore.

The state is not unaware of all this. It realises that demolitions are a rather ineffective way of ensuring compliance. Not only do the unauthorised structures return but demolitions also add huge expenses to the state's exchequer. The M. C. Mehta judgment and what followed exposed the sheer impracticability of such a policy. On the one hand, demolitions have not solved the problem of unauthorised construction, and on the other, their unauthorised status then precludes the state from staking a claim in the share of the revenue pie. The one strategy that enables the state to claim its revenue is regularisation. This is probably one of the reasons why, of late, we have been hearing the state beginning to emphasise on regularisation.[29] It helps the state in mapping these localities, making them governable and opening them up to real-estate markets. It also allows taxes to be drawn from them more legibly, something the state has not been able to do successfully so far. Understandably, for a cash-strapped South Delhi Municipal Corporation,[30] property tax, circle rates and conversion charges from these villages would be

---

†† 'From top to bottom, they have their people!'

an important source of revenue. For ruling governments of the capital as well, meeting the longstanding demand for regularisation of unauthorised colonies brings in electoral gains.[31] With regularisation, however, the state also formally came around to accepting that a city like Delhi will be inhabited by a far different aesthetic than what the Ford Foundation had conceptualised with the Delhi Master Plan.

This shift in the state's attitude towards these villages has been taking place over a couple of decades. With respect to urban villages, the Mini Master Plan 1985 had suggested that the earlier privileges which were accorded to villages as exemptions to building bye-laws must end and that building plans have to be sanctioned by either the DDA or MCD.[32] After two editions of the Delhi Master Plan refused to even mention urban villages, the Delhi Master Plan 2021 ruled that urban villages would be governed by special regulations like the walled city, while leaving immense scope for authorities yet again. Furthermore, digitising land records has been one of the core mandates of the Jawaharlal Nehru National Urban Regeneration Programme. The final step of the transformation, however, came in the year 2011 in the form of a rejoinder to the circular in 1963, saying that the exemptions given to villages were only applicable to rural villages and not to urban ones. In this version of the state's articulation, the exemption never existed at all. The 2011 circular, by ending all ambiguity over the *lal dora* for urban villages, now staked a claim on the new kinds of value increasingly embedded in these villages. What had happened in effect was that the postcolonial state had finally taken cognisance of these spaces as ones of value and it now needed to organise them into grids of property and taxation. By making these villages equivalent to unauthorised colonies, the administration attempted to end the ambiguity over the status of *lal dora* areas and made the villages subject to 'law'. From a time when it turned a blind eye to the fluidity of land records and the illegalities that surrounded land ownership in *lal dora* areas, the state now attempts to wrest control over these spaces and constantly strives to bring in regulations. In doing so, it is trying to generate a newer kind of 'formalised' documentation through circulars and directives. The state has thus come full circle.

Even as the state is possibly moving from demolitions to regularisation as a method of staking claims in these unmapped localities, regularisation continues to be looked upon with suspicion by the landlords in the villages.[33] They have lived outside the state's purview for long and have figured out networks that have allowed them to create a vernacular economic system.

They are well aware that regularisation would subject them to state regulations, various taxations and charges. The contradiction therefore is this: the state that once 'forgot' these villages and allowed these illegible forms of ownerships to proliferate now increasingly intends to bring them into the fold of regulation. The villages, on the other hand, which have discovered the advantages of being unregulated, want to continue to remain outside the 'gaze' of the state. While the unauthorised colonies have been clamouring for regularisation, these villages have never really responded to such promises by the state. Not new to rent on the basis of social capital, this community, as owners of urban real estate, now has to figure out how it can protect its own interests—social and economic. The tussle between the state and the villagers is mediated through various governmental directives and notifications, court cases, demolition drives and the gaps and contestations they create. And the contentious *lal dora* has in effect become the frontier between the state and the community.

The villagers, as a result, continue to hold on to the *lal dora* as a source of and claim to legitimacy. They often complain that their *lal dora* should have been extended like it was for rural villages. The attempt to make the villagers fall in line, follow building bye-laws and pay taxes is only met with scepticism and defiance. Anger on the grounds of low compensation and poor infrastructure is used to validate this non-compliance. Anger and a feeling of injustice are therefore at the heart of the villagers' relationship with the state. But there is more than anger at play. The rejection of modern property regimes, dominated by regulations and clear land titles, is central to this rent economy.[34] While residents of unauthorised colonies feel vulnerable about the status of their property, the villagers seemed to have learnt that the label of 'illegal' does not threaten the security of their ownerships. In fact, it might work in their favour. On the other hand, regularisation would subject them to the state through a regime of taxation and laws, and need them to produce papers and documents to prove their possession of property. It will also subject them to laws and regulations that may weaken their communal control over the real estate markets in such places.

Property is not merely a claim to right to a piece of land. Property has been central to liberal political philosophy's understanding of citizenship.[35] In the case of a fuzzy property regime, what kind of citizens does it go on to produce? When slum dwellers ask for regularisation of their slums, it is fundamentally a claim of citizenship that they make. In the case of the two urban villages we are looking at, what we come across is a form of an alternate system, a parallel logic of governance by non-state actors that comes into existence in the cracks of governance and law. It also begets the question of political authority. If property and citizenship constitute political authority as much as political authority constitutes property and citizenship,[36] then it becomes an important matter to ask how the state figures here. Christian Lund argues how production and rearrangement of property and citizenship have consolidated, challenged and even fragmented political authority.[37] But instead of understanding the state simply as 'weak' or 'fragile', Lund argues it would be productive to understand a far more complex relationship between political authority and alternative claims over property rights. These alternate property claims, arranged all along a spectrum of legality, have engendered a range of political authority that oscillates between institutions like *panchayat*s, resident welfare associations (RWAs) and municipal corporations (Chapter 4).

Negotiating with the State through Anger and Hurt

Hurt and anger, historically, have been powerful tools for political organisation.[38] The particular discourse of hurt that is used by the villagers has been an important affect through which they relate to the city. It does two things: it evokes the greater injustice done to the villagers in the name of development and becomes the basis for an appeal to the state to continue with the exemptions earlier available to them. Anger and hurt, therefore, also go on to become the affect that constitute the villagers as a community in opposition to the urban citizens. However, the deployment of this discourse of hurt has changed considerably. In this section, we examine how hurt and anger have been deployed in opposition to the state at various moments in the case of the two urban villages we are interested in.

A steady number of elected members being from Delhi villages allowed some of these contradictions and sore points to find a voice in state institutions. Fateh Singh, a senior member of the 1967 Metropolitan Council who hailed from Jagatpur village, had brought it to the notice of the council that land acquired from villages for 50 paise per yard was being sold by the DDA after minimal redevelopment for 100 rupees per yard. Citing the example of villages that were acquired in 1911, Fateh Singh had argued,

> If you see their state today, they are filled with lavish houses and the villagers live by digging grass for their lawns…. If you want all of Delhi's villages to be reduced to this state and Delhi's population keeps increasing exponentially, you totally can but you must know that Delhi's problem would not be solved like that.[39]

Fateh Singh had evidently felt that the only way to save the villages of Delhi was to stop overpopulation within the city. In the early years, rural members of the council had made angry demands, ranging from alternative plots in rural areas for continuing farming[40] to acquisition of only infertile land[41] to crop insurance.[42] It seemed like their first impulse was to keep the agrarian question alive in an urbanising context. The point they were trying to make about unfairness found expression through demands for extending the *lal dora*, or a rhetoric about the lack of services in the mid-1970s and 1980s.

Slowly, however, their anger began to veer towards the issues of charges and taxation around construction. The injustice of unfair land acquisition was clubbed with the unfairness around house tax, development charges and even with demands to authorise property. On the question of house tax, for example, Shishpal Bidhuri, a Gujjar leader from Tughlaqabad, argues emotively,

> Un logon ne jinki kauriyon ke bhaav zameen acquire kar li gayi, un logon ko jinka rozgaar pashu paalne ka tha, woh dilli sarkar dvara band kar diye gaye, jin logon ne dilli develop karne ke liye zameen zaydaad de di, un logon ka house tax maaf nahi kiya gaya.‡‡

The speculative tendencies that had entered the discourse in the interim are quite evident now. In the 2012 legislative assembly debates, a minister argued, 'Aap kya chahte hain, hum zindagi bhar hal jot kar aapko sabzi bo kar khilate rahein? Aap Janakpuri ki kothiyon mein rehte ho. Kya kisaan ke bete ko kothi mein rehne ka haq nahi hai? ... Kya kisaan ke bete ko builder banne ka haq nahi hai?'§§ Dharamdev Solanki, a member of the 2012 legislative assembly from Palam, raised the issue of regularisation of unauthorised colonies in conjunction with the question of injustice meted out to the villagers. Solanki raised the problem of poor hardworking migrants who bought property in these unauthorised colonies and the hapless villagers who lost out in the process together. In order to end the precarity of both groups, Solanki demanded that 81A of the Delhi Land Reforms Act, which prohibits landowners to use their land for any other purpose apart from agriculture, be scrapped.[43]

---

‡‡ 'The people whose lands were acquired for peanuts, the people for whom animal husbandry was a source of income, they were stopped by the Delhi Government. The people who gave up their land for Delhi's development, their house tax was not waived.' Shishpal Bidhuri, *Legislative Assembly Debates*, 19 March 1996, 135.

§§ 'Do you want that we plough our fields for life to feed you vegetables? ... You live in bungalows of Janakpuri. Doesn't a farmer's son have the right to live in a bungalow as well? Doesn't a farmer's son have the right to become a builder?' Mukesh Sharma, *Legislative Assembly Debates*, 29 May 2012, 248.

'Jahan par 81A ka notice jo adhyaksh ji keh rahe hain. Unko uski copy mangakar use khatam karke unko private land maankar un colonies ko pass kar do. Usme zyada chakkar mein mat pado. Woh gareeb log hain. Bhale hi paise aa gayein hon.'[****] Though rarely stated upfront, the implicit demand was only that the exemptions from bye-laws should be retained.

The anguish and hurt are real. The feeling that they have been short-changed by the state with regard to compensation money is a living wound. When they could have been owners of prime property of Delhi, they are instead reduced to protecting a few buildings in and around the village. But that anguish and hurt is also to some extent instrumentally deployed to keep the exemptions going. The discourse has clearly witnessed a shift as real estate has become a far more lucrative option than agriculture. But one thing that has stayed constant is the claim of being different from 'city people'. The accusation that Delhi has accorded them stepmotherly treatment is a constant. Speaking of themselves as *bhole bhaale*, or simple, gullible people, at the time of land acquisition, the lament of having very little bargaining power comes up time and again. The slow disappearance of cattle from their environment generates a deep sense of loss for their pure, unadulterated worlds. This account of the state's injustice is still alive in the collective memory of these villages and conversations often lead to it. Though often exaggerated, these memories hark back to the originary injustice meted out to the naïve and gullible villagers in the face of a powerful law. Having witnessed the real estate boom around them in a decade or more, whereby their agricultural land slowly transformed into upper-middle-class localities, the villagers continue to begrudge the loss of their land at a pittance.

This sense of hurt, anguish and loss creates an interesting opposition between the state and the villagers. The landlords have identified this space of exemption, of informality, where the state almost ceased to exist, as a space where their interests could be maximised. I have argued elsewhere that when demolitions are stopped through public action or effort, it somehow distorts the typical image of sovereign as Leviathan.[44] The Leviathan seems to be lumbering along in these spaces where it finds its power interrupted. The people who constitute the body of the Leviathan step out of it to challenge the sovereignty of the state, which may not require the state to react with

---

[****] 'The notices given out for 81A for colonies that Mr Chairman is referring to, you must order that copy, abrogate it, and consider it as private land. Don't bother too much about it. They are poor people. Even if they have got money now.' *Legislative Assembly Debates*, 11 December 2012, 260.

violent repression, but where the state finds itself outwitted. The Comaroffs summarise the situation quite aptly:

> Postcolonies tend not to be organised under a single, vertically integrated sovereignty sustained by a highly centralised state. Rather, they consist in a horizontally woven tapestry of partial sovereignties: sovereignties over terrains and their inhabitants, over aggregates of people conjoined in faith or culture, over transactional spheres, over networks of relation, regimes of property, domains of practice, and, quite often, over various combinations of things; sovereignties longer or shorter lived, protected to a greater or lesser degree by the capacity to exercise compulsion, always incomplete.[45]

It is not surprising, therefore, that in none of the protests and petitions has the rancour been directed at clarifying property ownership in the *lal dora* or to digitise or formalise land ownership. They may have mastered their own version of the 'art of not being governed' but are far from the Zomia lands that James Scott discusses—pristine, untouched by state and capital.[46] They may have learnt how to keep the state at bay, but they are absolutely clued into the webs of capital. As we examine more clearly in the next chapter, the landlords of these villages find informality to be the only avenue to further their interests. It becomes imperative for them to organise themselves as effective cartels and vernacular joint stock companies outside the purview of law. The subterranean land market created through inconsistent land records and the General Power of Attorney begins to get regulated by these informal institutions. Informality is not an impediment; instead, it is an opportunity. Thus, being subsumed into modern, legible forms of property is not an aspiration the landlords have.

Conclusion

The pace at which these villages have grown is incredible to say the least. But these transformations are not without their ironies. Amidst all of this mayhem of traffic and construction, there are also donkeys. You see a retinue of donkeys walking in a line, loaded with building material to carry them into the depths of the village. As trucks and minivans cannot enter many of these lanes, the donkeys become the only means of transporting building material once inside the village. Donkeys laden with bricks and cement are visual metaphors for all that is going on in these villages. It is not the glittery, phantasmagorical world of capital that creates a culture and a space in sync with what is understood as global. This capital is locally embedded, slowly but steadily tottering into spaces—much like the donkey. It is also internally mobilised, imbued with local sensibilities and stealthy when needed. This is the other side of global capital that transforms from being agrarian capital to real estate through its vernacular methods.

The modernist project of city making in the 1960s often created spaces that the state did not know how to govern. Quite ironically, the period of Nehruvian command economy, which is known for the state reaching out to order and regulate as much as it could, turns out to be the period when the state leaves these villages to fend for themselves. On the other hand, in the period of neoliberalism, which is theorised increasingly in terms of the 'rollback of the state', we see the state wanting to regulate and order them. Monetisation of land in the Global South, through massive real estate projects, has happened through sustained state intervention.[47] But more importantly, Aihwa Ong shows us that neoliberalism is essentially 'a new relationship between government and knowledge through which governing activities are recast as nonpolitical and nonideological problems that need technical solutions.'[48] The state couches its interest in value extraction as merely a dispassionate techno-managerial exercise. The villagers, in return, counter this more emotively, evoking other notions of value like justice, articulated through anger and hurt.

Anthropological theories of the state argue that the state and its practices are constantly produced by the 'margins'.[49] Margins for Veena Das and Deborah Poole are peripheries or territories in which the state is yet to penetrate but at the same time where the state is continually experienced and undone through the illegibility of its own practices. The urban villages at the margins of the city constitute the life of the city in myriad ways, and seem to have a similar relationship with the state. Their illegibility in the eyes of the state has been turned into an administrative exception. And yet they occupy a rather central role in producing life in the city. Despite the marginality of their appearance, they are at the heart of the political economy of the city. Affects of anger and hurt are also not untouched by the effects of these larger transformations. The 1990s economic reforms have changed how the villages and their residents relate to the city and the state. As these villages keep reinventing themselves, so does the discourse of anger. The struggle is now over the question of 'exemption'. Exemption means far more to the villagers than just an administrative relief now. It is a struggle over identity, over local control and a stake in the everchanging life of the city.

Notes

1. Supreme Court, *M. C. Mehta and Others vs Union of India*, 2004.
2. Diya Mehra, 'Protesting Publics in Indian Cities: The 2006 Sealing Drive and Delhi's Traders', *Economic and Political Weekly* 47, no. 30 (2012).
3. Usha Ramanathan, 'Demolition Drive', *Economic and Political Weekly* 40, no. 27 (2005): 2908.
4. The rent gap theory put forward by Neil Smith summarises the speculative potential of land as the difference between capitalised ground rent and the potential ground rent if the land is put to its monetarily best use. Neil Smith, 'Gentrification and the Rent Gap', *Annals of the Association of American Geographers* 77, no. 3 (1987).
5. Michael Levien, *Dispossession without Development: Land Grabs in Neoliberal India* (New York: Oxford University Press, 2018).
6. Amita Baviskar, 'Cows, Cars and Cycle-Rickshaws: Bourgeois Environmentalists and the Battle for Delhi's Streets', in *Elite and Everyman: The Cultural Politics of the Indian Middle Classes*, ed. Amita Baviskar and Raka Ray (New York: Routledge, 2011); Anuj Bhuwania, *Courting the People: Public Interest Litigation in Post-Emergency India* (New Delhi: Cambridge University Press, 2016).
7. Tom Cowan, 'The Village as Urban Infrastructure: Social Reproduction, Agrarian Repair and Uneven Urbanisation', *Environment and Planning E: Nature and Space* 4, no. 3 (2021).
8. A three-member expert panel set up by the High Court of Delhi concluded, 'It can safely be said that at least 90 per cent carry one kind of violation of the extant building bylaws or another.' See PTI, '90% Buildings in Delhi Illegal, Panel Tells HC', *Pioneer*, 5 October 2017, https://www.dailypioneer.com/2017/page1/90-buildings-in-delhi--illegal-panel-tells-hc.html (accessed 7 November 2018).
9. *M. C. Mehta and Others vs Union of India*, 2004.
10. Bina Ramani, *Bird in the Banyan Tree: My Story* (New Delhi: Rupa Publications, 2013), 222–23. Taking the Pradhan into confidence, she develops Hauz Khas as a niche and quaint market for the rich and expatriates of Delhi.
11. Sudev Sheth, 'Historical Transformations in Boundary and Land Use in New Delhi's Urban Villages', *Economic and Political Weekly* 52, no. 5 (2017). Also see Emma Tarlo, 'Fashion Fables of an Urban Village', in *Clothing Matters: Dress and Identity in India* (London: Hurst and Company, 1996) for a longer discussion on the creation of 'ethnic chic' in the backdrop of a rapidly transforming village.

12. A PIL that raised concerns over poor compliance by close to 120 restaurants in Hauz Khas Village with respect to fire hazards, waste and sewage regulations and in some cases even without NOCs from various departments pushed the Delhi High Court to call Hauz Khas a 'ticking time bomb'. PTI, 'Hauz Khas Village Is a Ticking Time Bomb: High Court', *Economic Times*, 15 September 2017, https://economictimes.indiatimes.com/news/politics-and-nation/hauz-khas-village-is-ticking-time-bomb-high-court/articleshow/60517338.cms (accessed 20 March 2018).
13. Sporting events have been crucial for an infrastructure-heavy, speedy urban growth. With respect to the Commonwealth Games held in Delhi, see Amita Baviskar, 'Dreaming Big: Spectacular Events and the "World-Class" City: The Commonwealth Games in Delhi', in *Leveraging Legacies from Sports Mega-Events: Concepts and Cases*, ed. Jonathan Grix (London: Palgrave Macmillan, 2014). Gautam Bhan and Kalyani Menon-Sen speak of the unprecedented violence of Commonwealth Games with respect to the widespread demolitions in Yamuna Pushta. See Gautam Bhan and Kalyani Menon-Sen, *Swept off the Map: Surviving Eviction and Resettlement in Delhi* (New Delhi: Yoda Press, 2008). The Asian Games is far sparsely accounted for, but even that radicalised the presence of infrastructure in the city. Apart from the Games Village, stadia, new luxury hotels, a new international airport terminal, several flyovers and underpasses had to be built before the Asian Games took off.
14. By one estimate, close to 150,000 migrant workers were already employed in construction projects linked to the Asian Games. The largest number of workers came from either Bihar or Orissa. See Sharat G. Lin and Nageshwar Patnaik, 'Migrant Labor at ASIAD '82 Construction Sites in New Delhi', *Bulletin of Concerned Asian Scholars* 14, no. 3 (1982).
15. Stands for South Asian Federation Games. Now renamed as South Asian Games.
16. Since most people construct their own building, his clientele is mostly salaried people or people with lesser property. The share between the owner and the builder depends mostly on location. If it is located on the outside of the village, it is mostly struck at a 50:50 ratio. But if it is on the inside, which entails higher construction costs as donkeys are needed to ferry construction material inside, the deal is struck at 60:40. But mostly, people choose to build themselves with the help of a *mistri*.
17. Many a time, the words *adda* and *karkhana* are used interchangeably. Safiuddin runs an *adda*.
18. I am not the first one to be calling these spaces 'factories'. Solomon Benjamin, 'Neighbourhood as Factory: The Influence of Land Development

and Civic Politics on an Industrial Cluster in Delhi, India', (PhD diss., Massachusetts Institute of Technology, 1996) discusses the transformation of a neighbourhood into a factory. Sharad Chari also compares Tiruppur town to a decentralised factory. Sharad Chari, *Fraternal Capital: Peasant Workers, Self-Made Men and Globalisation in Provincial India* (New Delhi: Permanent Black, 2004).
19. Marx, *Capital: A Critique*, 163–77.
20. Many famous designers like Suneet Varma and Manish Arora used to have huge factories in Shahpur Jat when they started their careers. As rent started escalating, these bigger factories have now moved to Noida.
21. It is one of the most expensive real estate within Shahpur Jat today. It will be discussed at length in the next chapter.
22. Arjun Appadurai, 'The Ghost in the Finance Machine', *Public Culture* 23, no. 3 (2011).
23. Ibid.
24. Here I am referring to the creation of cities like Paris and New York under urban planners like Baron Haussmann and Robert Moses who were able to create a new identity for these cities through a spate of merciless demolitions. For more, see David Harvey, *Paris: Capital of Modernity* (New York, London: Routledge, 2003); and Robert Caro, *The Power Broker: Robert Moses and the Fall of New York* (New York: Knopf, 1974). In Delhi, that attempt was made by someone like Jagmohan, particularly during the Emergency. Sushmita Pati, 'Jagmohan: The Master Planner and the "Rebuilding' of Delhi"', *Economic and Political Weekly* 49, no. 36 (2014).
25. Oral Answers, *Lok Sabha*, IVth Session, VIIIth Lok Sabha, 25 November 1985.
26. Conversion charge is a charge claimed by the MCD to convert land use of a property from residential to mixed or commercial. It must be noted that though most of these properties are considered unauthorised, they are still liable to pay house tax. In the absence of proper land records, however, the payment of tax is a voluntary activity. Conversion charge, a one-time payable charge to change the land use of a property, is considered to be high
27. N. Vidyasagar, 'Demolition Man', *Times of India*, 22 June 1997.
28. Shahpur Jat has a far neater sense of house numbers.
29. Regularisation is not a dominant strategy that has been fully adopted by the Delhi government yet, but definitely something that it is toying with. Mukta Naik and Manish, 'BJP and AAP Know Regularising Delhi Colonies is Smart Policy, But It's an Incomplete Plan', *The Print*, 26 January 2020, https://theprint.in/opinion/bjp-aap-know-regularising-delhi-colonies-is-smart-policy-but-incomplete-plan/354709/ (accessed 15 April 2020).

30. Express News Service, 'Levy Higher Property Tax on Those with More than Two Kids: Delhi Councillor', *Indian Express*, 3 December 2019, https://indianexpress.com/article/delhi/levy-higher-property-tax-on-those-with-more-than-two-kids-councillor-6147529/ (accessed 7 January 2020).
31. The BJP government announced the regularisation of unauthorised colonies in Delhi right before the 2020 legislative assembly elections.
32. DDA, *Mini Master Plan: Integrated Development of Urban and Rural Villages of Delhi* (New Delhi, 1985), 5.
33. This is of course not the first time regularization has been introduced as a policy. It has existed since 1962. But it has been implemented very sparingly. See Banashree Banerjee, 'Security of Tenure in Indian Cities', in *Holding Their Ground: Secure Land Tenure for the Urban Poor in Developing Countries*, ed. Alain Durand-Lasserve and Lauren Royston (London: Earthscan Publications, 2002), 52.
34. This seems to be the practice in most of the urban villages. Surajit Chakravarty, 'Mahipalpur Village as an Entrepreneurial Space', in *Space, Planning and Everyday Contestations in Delhi*, ed. Surajit Chakravarty and Rohit Negi (New Delhi: Springer, 2016), 129.
35. Christian Lund, 'Property and Citizenship: Conceptually Connecting Land Rights and Belonging in Africa', *Africa Spectrum* 46, no. 3 (2011): 71–75.
36. Christian Lund, 'Rule and Rupture: State Formation through the Production of Property and Citizenship', *Development and Change* 47, no. 6 (2016).
37. Ibid., 1218.
38. Wendy Brown, *States of Injury: Power and Freedom in Late Modernity* (New Jersey: Princeton University Press, 1995).
39. Fateh Singh, *Metropolitan Council Debates*, 17 October 1967, 68–69.
40. Bhagwan Das, *Metropolitan Council Debates*, 14 October 1966, 84.
41. Bharat Singh, *Metropolitan Council Debates*, 16 October 1967, 5–6.
42. Shanti Swaroop Tyagi, *Metropolitan Council Debates*, October 17, 1966, 47–67.
43. Section 81 of the Delhi Land Reforms Act states,

> A Bhumidhar or an Asami shall be liable to ejectment on the suit of the Gaon Sabha or the land holder, as the case may be, for using land for any purpose other than a purpose connected with agriculture, horticulture or animal husbandry, which includes pisciculture and poultry farming, and also pay damages equivalent to the cost of works which may be required to render the land capable of use for the said purposes.

In a Delhi High Court case, a special bench refused to stay the order of demolition of shopping malls built on the Mehrauli–Gurgaon Road on the grounds that *lal dora* is meant for villagers and not shopping malls, hotels and restaurants. The case, filed by high profile international brands like Rohit Bal, to stay the demolition order argued that the construction had taken place prior to the year 2000. The court however noted that irrespective of the year it was constructed, *lal dora* land was not meant for commercial purposes. PTI, 'HC Refuses to Stay 1, MG Road Demolitions', *Outlook*, 2 February 2006, https://www.hindustantimes.com/india/hc-refuses-to-stay-delhi-s-mg-road-demolitions/story-EPCB8ngjp1EW66b01MP1uK.html (accessed 29 December 2015). This order caused demolitions in villages like Ghitorni, New Manglapuri and Sultanpur. Of late, however, similar high-end stores have again begun to crop up in the same spots. Ambika Pandit and Paras Singh, '12 Years after Bulldozers Ended Dream Run of MG Road, New Malls Rising Again', *Times of India*, 10 May 2018, https://timesofindia.indiatimes.com/city/delhi/12-years-after-bulldozers-ended-dream-run-of-mg-road-new-malls-rising-again/articleshow/64101807.cms (accessed 27 November 2020).

44. Sushmita Pati, 'The Productive Fuzziness of Land Documents: The State and Processes of Accumulation in Urban Villages of Delhi', *Contributions to Indian Sociology* 53, no. 2 (2019).

45. Jean Comaroff and John L. Comaroff, 'Law and Disorder in the Postcolony: An Introduction', in *Law and Disorder in the Postcolony* (Chicago: University of Chicago Press, 2006), 35.

46. James C. Scott, *The Art of Not Being Governed: An Anarchist History of Upland Southeast Asia* (New Delhi: Orient Blackswan, 2010).

47. This is evident in the case of special economic zone (SEZ) projects in India. Gavin Shatkin shows this as a stable phenomenon across several cities in the Global South. See Gavin Shatkin, *Cities for Profit: The Real Estate Turn in Asia's Urban Politics* (Ithaca; London: Cornell University Press, 2017).

48. Aihwa Ong, *Neoliberalism as Exception: Mutations in Citizenship and Sovereignty* (Durham, London: Duke University Press), 3.

49. Veena Das and Deborah Poole, 'Introduction: State and Its Margins: Comparative Ethnographies', in *Anthropology at the Margins of the State*, ed. Veena Das and Deborah Poole (Santa Fe: School of American Research Press, 2004).

4

In the Shadows of the State
Community as a Mode of Political and Economic Organisation

Old modes of honour and dignity do not die; instead, they get incorporated into the market, take on price tags, gain a new life as commodities.
— Marshall Berman, *All That Is Solid Melts in the Air*

The villages, as noted in the previous chapter, rapidly changed into spaces that defied terminologies. They were not slums, nor were they apartment-style neighbourhoods. Instead, they emerged as one of the several forms of spaces that the precariat labour in big cities inhabit. But the 1963 exemption had not just changed the village physically. In the absence of the state following the exemption, the village community banked on its own informal set of institutions to fill the vacuum. In this chapter, I explore two such community institutions—the *panchayat* and the *kunba*, which work as economic institutions; and two economic institutions—committees and 'financing', which in turn function as social institutions. The *bhaichara* form of social cohesion, deeply ingrained in the *panchayat* and *kunba* relations and even in the ethos of the local financing forms since the 1960s, was further strengthened in the absence of the state. In the shadows of the state and its laws, these institutions flourished and became dynamic entities that could respond to the changing political economy of the city surrounding the villages.

In the next pages, we examine how these institutions were able to interweave their community and economic interests. One functioned like a cartel, another like a joint-stock company and the committees work like localised banks. These new solidarities allowed them to oppose the state during demolitions, consolidate their economic interests, manage the circulation of money and assert themselves as a social group in changing times. As we have seen in the previous chapter, the modern state finds itself co-opted and even interrupted in these spaces where new kinds of sociabilities emerge to sometimes collude with the state and at other times to oppose it. In this chapter, we delve into how a specific kind of accumulation, a vernacular kind, based on the ownership of land, begins to forge itself on the lines of community solidarity. The *kunba*, the *panchayat* and the committees, piggybacking on the strength of the community, managed to consolidate the real estate market, create channels of credit networks as well as prevent demolitions. The vernacular market of renting out property was forged through old institutional networks. The cartel, the vernacular joint-stock company and the local forms of financing became their mode for carving out their niche in the world of global capital.

Caste, Community and the Nature of Vernacular Forms of Capitalism[1]

The relationship between caste and economy has been fairly well established in academic scholarship by now. Caste refuses to be a stable category and is yet one of the stickiest identities that one can encounter in India. It has been the basis of extreme degradation of human life, and also the basis for people to organise and demand both dignity and equality of resources. Caste has been defined as endogamy, hereditary membership, sometimes associated with a particular occupation, but it has also been an extremely volatile institution. M. N. Srinivas's sociological study also alerted us early on that the nature of hierarchy is barely stable across a region and that if caste hierarchy has to be understood in India, it has to be understood through the category of the dominant caste.[2] The term 'dominant caste' could vary from context to context but is conceptually used to describe a caste group that wields social, economic and political power locally. The strong corroboration that these castes have with class in feudalism has in many ways been reorganised by capitalism.[3]

In the context of India, caste and community have mostly been used interchangeably. Caste groups tied together by everyday practices, rituals, the use of specific symbols and myths function like a community. It is also not unknown for caste groups to assert themselves as civil society organisations in the form of caste *sabha*s and *samaj*.[4] Caste groups perform as communities in different ways in the context of modern politics. Expressions of community are differently deployed to demand protective discrimination, assert themselves as modern citizens[5] or even articulate their alternative imaginations of the nation state.[6] It is, therefore, of utmost importance to understand how different caste groups choose to make themselves visible. It is not difficult to see why Dalits across castes emerged as a community by way of identity politics stemming from a shared experience of humiliation, or why Marwaris assert themselves as communities through civil society activities and religious activities like temple building. Caste becomes a modern institution, one that is a constant presence in almost all social phenomena in India. It is the social hinge for social capital, for networks, for access to institutions and even electoral politics. But simultaneously, caste is also a platform for competition. As we see communities coagulating around economic interests, we also see how these social formations of community and caste speak back to these larger economic processes. And we witness how communities emerge stronger in the world of capital.

In the case of Jats also, the community coalesced around the idiom of *bhaichara* during colonial times each time they faced opposition from a harsh state or natural calamities.[7] The most militant activism of *khap panchayat*s was seen in relation to taxes in the 16th century, and has now progressively moved on to claiming a share of resources in the global economy.[8] That solidarity remobilised itself into the language of modern politics through political parties like the Bharatiya Kisan Union and the Lok Dal and organisations like the All India Jat Mahasabha. In this chapter, I discuss how Jats, the dominant caste in these two villages, emerge as a community of a particular kind owing to their economic interests in the growing real estate values. The solidarity of *bhaichara* ownership of land finds its way into the neoliberal real estate market through a community of property holders. This solidarity is as much about drawing one's strength from the collectivity as it is about competition and rivalries. It is as much about community assertion as it is about one's self-interest and self-preservation. I show how the community form remains a malleable one, which keeps responding to its political and economic environment. A sociological, kinship-bound community also begins to morph itself to become a community bound by the 'politics of the governed'.[9]

As mentioned earlier, since the 1960s, partly abetted by land acquisition, joint families were giving way to nuclear ones across rural Delhi. Though the older modes of associations like the joint family system were feeling considerable strain, notions of community evolved very differently. As the city moved towards a liberalised economy, the relationship that the community had forged with the city and the state also had to reinvent itself. As the developmental welfare state declined so did the rent-seeking networks with it. Rent now began to be reoriented to collectively manage private property.

I argue that the nature of a community and the way it controls both money and the rental market allows for a vernacular form of capitalism, within the ambit of neoliberal capital. The creation of a real estate market now required the reorganisation of these community forms to exercise control on this new form of economy. This new mode of economic organisation based on community forms was required for two reasons. First, unlike the 1970s, when they had to lobby with the state to tap into patronage links of the state to get exclusive licences and permits: this time around, they were themselves the owners of this resource called land. Second, the real-estatification of village land had ensured the democratisation of the category of rentiers. An activity that was limited to a few families with social capital in the 1970s, like we see in Chapter 2, was now open and available to almost everyone. Everyone owned their homestead land that now held immense value. The exemption made sure that the institutions that would moderate this real estate market now could only be an internal community issue. In effect, looking at the transformation of *panchayat*s, *kunba*s and committees into new forms of community associations allows us to see how the Jats negotiated with the state in a neoliberalising city.

I am calling this economy vernacular for two reasons. First, vernacular forms of capitalism have predated neoliberalism. These village societies had been a part of agrarian capital for long, and these older village institutions like the *panchayat* and *kunba*s in time rapidly transformed themselves to perform relatively modern economic functions. Second, these institutions were able to keep money in hard cash and within closed networks of trust. Financialised modes of capitalism constantly strive to grow by fragmenting ownership, by making commodities out of debt, by introducing mortgages for quick selling and buying. But these vernacular forms are designed to do just the obverse. In the face of a new economy, where value is created through fictitious means and multiplied through dispersed ownerships, this vernacular form of capitalism is managed by holding it together. It refused to move to fictitious forms of capital and refused to loosen ownerships. And that, I argue, is specific to how rent works as a mode of accumulation through community in these spaces.

Community in the Time of Neoliberal Individualism

With the boom in the 1990s, when almost anyone could become a landlord and earn money by renting property, it became sensible to invest in the housing rental market. The rent-seeking possibilities that had been limited in the 1960s and 1970s to a few families with social capital had exploded. The previous chapter dwells on how several landlords think of themselves as individuated, entrepreneurial actors. While the new economy was a source of immense confidence, at the same time, it also led to considerable anxiety with regard to a loss of community. On the one hand, it intensified competition and allowed more people to think of themselves as individuated economic actors who were capable of innovation and who could take supposed risks in their business. And on the other, it also made the Jats increasingly protective about their own turf: their culture, identity and spaces. Though, one can always argue that this is misplaced: first, the affective community that people feel nostalgic for never really existed in the ways in which it was often romanticised, and second, older institutions did not disappear but reinvented themselves to find a place in the new economy. This new-found economy heightened such contradictions among these communities. A cultural ethos, deeply imbricated in an agricultural, rural lifestyle, has become an entity to be protected in the face of the urban onslaught. Suspicion has been mutual in this regard. While the upwardly mobile middle class that settled in the posh colonies of South Delhi saw the Jat landlords as uncouth and uncivilised, the villagers saw the city dwellers as a morally corrupt force.

In 1999, the newly formed resident welfare association (RWA) in Munirka, under the leadership of Chaudhari Mahendra Singh Tokas, brought out a village directory with prints of hand-drawn maps of various clusters of houses in the village intact with names of *mohalla*s and *pana*s. He also took the effort to number houses across the village so that there could be a standardised address that was not there before. A directory was printed and circulated with freshly indexed house numbers, each with names of 'head of the family'. But soon enough, these house numbers were rendered ineffective. The process of construction never stopped. New houses kept cropping up, new property divisions kept taking place and the local geography remained fluid. Today, the *pana*s or *mohalla*s have merged seamlessly into each other, other landmarks like chowks and wells have simply disappeared and the house numbers have no bearing on their location. However, people continue to use the names of these invisible *mohalla*s and chowks although they have been rendered nondescript. Along with the village directory, Mahendra Tokas published a few more such booklets. One of them was a booklet on the social history of the village, complete with family trees defined by the male lineage of all the villagers in Munirka and details of their social customs and practices. Another booklet documented the Haryanvi idioms and phrases commonly used in the villages of Delhi. In the maelstrom of development and transformation, Tokas had felt the need to painstakingly archive names of forefathers and provide a detailed description of social customs, or *reeti-rivaaz*, around festivals and kin structures. When examined closely, it is clear that this is anything but a coincidence. The city by the 1990s had finally closed in on the village. The old ways of living were changing rapidly. It made sense to document in writing all the social practices that Tokas feared may get lost in time.

Being hopeful as well as suspicious of what the future holds for them, the Jat villagers have negotiated their way into urban life while romanticising their past. There is a great desire to preserve their language, their sporting cultures through *dangal*s, and that one attribute that is central to their cultural worlds—deference to elders. Smoking the *hukka*, especially by the older generation, remains a communal activity, and there are distinctive societal protocols that govern that act. There is also a gnawing discomfort that their community fabric may be slipping out of their hands. This fear or discomfort is not unique to the Jats alone. This language of fear of other marauding communities, and anxiety with respect to their own disintegrating one, has been central to all violent and majoritarian expressions across the world.

In this chapter, we focus on understanding three associational forms and how they adapt themselves to the changing times and begin to function as quasi-social, quasi-economic bodies in the villages. We discuss the *panchayat* as the cartel, the *kunba* as the joint-stock company and the committees as financial institutions, and how each of them negotiates its social worlds and the changing economic realities to collectively create their own, unique vernacular form of capitalism.

The *Panchayat* as a Cartel

The 1960s and later the 1990s were a messy time for Munirka. Though buying and selling of land has always been a part of life in an urban village, these two decades saw intense hustling around property claims. Partly because the state was not concerned about the villages, and partly because of the villagers' reluctance in approaching formal institutions, it was the caste *panchayat*s[10] of the village which mediated several of the ensuing conflicts between different landlords. But these *panchayat*s never received any formal recognition. These villages were formally incorporated under the Municipal Corporation of Delhi (MCD), but, by the 1990s, the village caste *panchayat* began to feel the need for some legal recognition as well. It became clear that the *panchayat*, which had been a local and informal body so far, had to grow beyond its traditional limits and engage with state institutions.

In 1997, Mahendra Singh Tokas, Pradhan of the Munirka *panchayat*, took the initiative to register the RWA with himself as the new chairperson. Conflicts over land and property among villagers were on the rise and not being a recognised body by the state was not helping. The RWA was supposed to be a new institution, but it continued as an extension of the *panchayat*. Informality allowed the *panchayat*s of these urban villages to transform and transmute in ways different from *panchayat*s elsewhere. As an RWA, the organisation became visible in the public sphere of the city. But at the same time, it continued its double life as the informal *panchayat* that allowed it to do just the opposite—to remain invisible from the eyes of the state. The *panchayat* is able to function and intervene in the social and political life of the village in ways that no modern political system would allow it to. Its existence as the *panchayat*, though quite different from its pre-colonial variant, allows it flexibility and informality that lets it intervene in the economic organisation of the village and in the real estate market.

As carry-overs of an older, more extended form of territorial consolidation among the Jats, *khap panchayat*s have been in existence as early as 1556.[11] Historically, apart from adjudicating on community matters, they have also played a significant role in making political demands.[12] *Khap panchayat*s have earned infamy in more recent times owing to their involvement in honour killings in Uttar Pradesh and Haryana. But unlike the *khap panchayat*s that exist in the hinterlands of Haryana and Uttar Pradesh, the *panchayat*s in these urban villages do not, or rather cannot, operate in the same fashion.[13] The historical association of the Jats across northwest India had anyway gotten ruptured by the territoriality of the modern state. Being a part of the Palam 360 unit,[14] with most other Delhi villages, the *panchayat*s have greatly diversified owing to their urban location. And yet, despite having come into the urban fold, they continue to hold on to their rural networks. In places like Munirka, for instance, the RWA doubles up as a traditional *panchayat* and a modern, rational institution, showing us the malleability and the precise form of modernity that these villages and institutions therein inhabit.

The *panchayat* registered itself as an RWA but, from the outset, overstepped the usual scope of functions of RWAs.[15] The mandate of RWAs is to facilitate civic amenities and organise social events within their communities. The village directory brought out by the new RWA emphasised the role of village elders, the need for the community to come together to organise daughters' weddings as well as to hold mediations for property feuds. These meetings could only be attended by those who were 'permanent' male residents of the village. Women, until very recently, were not allowed to vote in RWA elections. Eventually, *panchayat*s or RWAs in Munirka emerged as economic cartels or as associations of landlords. Cartels are the final stage of development of monopoly capital, which is possible only after a high degree of centralisation.[16] As the 'one-room sets' begin to proliferate through the village as units for renting out, the property units also begin to lend themselves to a high degree of standardisation. Cartelisation works best in such a case as it is a market of uniform one-room sets, with little distinction. The *panchayat*s or RWAs are, in effect, associations of individual actors who need a platform to create a monopoly, to be able to control the market. The emergence of this kind of a *panchayat* or RWA can be traced back to the competition that was unleashed by increasing land values, which had to be replaced by some semblance of solidarity among the villagers.

A 'one-room set' in Munirka started being rented out for around 2,000–2,500 rupees in the early 2000s. Currently, the rent they command varies around 6,000–7,500 rupees. Though attempts towards gentrification are not unknown, most landlords refuse to spend money on the upkeep of these properties. But despite being run down, they remain highly in demand. Given that these rental spaces are targeted at the precariat working class and young students, the rent rates have been relatively stable. This is understandable because rent hikes beyond a point would drive these tenants outside the village. The landlords, however, are merciless with the timeliness of payment of rent. Any kind of delay in payments, some tenants allege, usually end up in threats, altercations and even violence. Some tenant families also offer services for free to keep their rents stable. They take responsibility of overseeing matters such as general cleanliness, managing the water pump and locking the front gates of their buildings. The ones with bigger buildings many a time employ a 'caretaker' who looks after these responsibilities and also collects rent.

Manoj, an autorickshaw driver, has been living in the same one-room set for the last four years with his wife and their eight-year-old son. I had gone to see him on his off-duty day. Located in a regular multi-storeyed building, his one-room set, on the second floor, unusually had a balcony. However, the balcony was completely blocked off by another building. There was no possibility of even a sliver of sunlight entering the house. The one-room set was methodically organised to contain the basic necessities of a family of three. A fridge right next to the door and a bed jammed against the wall left a narrow passage for one to access both the balcony and the kitchen on either end of the room. A shelf next to the table had neatly arranged photos of deities and older family members as well as the child's books. A small folding table that almost blocked the entrance to the kitchen held the child's school bag and a few books. Manoj's rent had been stable at 5,500 rupees for three years and then hiked to 6,500 rupees the previous year. But more than the rent, it is the electricity bill that pinches him. At an arbitrary rate of 9 rupees per unit, it comes close to 1,200 rupees a month.[17] Apart from this, water charges are an additional 200 rupees a month, and then there is the expense to keep the common areas clean. Landlords, including Manoj's, never show electricity bills, even to be used as address proof, because that would reveal the amount they pay. At the time of vacating the premises, it is common for landlords to cite fictitious damages so that they do not have to return the security deposit they received from the tenant at the time of renting. When the situation escalates, landlords have been accused of confiscating belongings as well. The presence of a cartel means that the norms that govern such negotiations are managed efficiently, and certain practices are normalised due to the landlords' monopolised control over cheap housing. It would not be too misplaced to argue that rent markets across major cities in India require some form of cartelisation or other.

The *Kunba* as the Joint-Stock Company

While the workshops that run inside the belly of Shahpur Jat resemble ill-maintained, standard, airless coupes, the ushering in of fancy boutiques has changed the landscape there significantly. Unlike in the case of Munirka, in Shahpur Jat, gentrification has fragmented the land market. Indeed, in Shahpur Jat it pays to gentrify your property. But then, it is not enough to just gentrify your own. Stretches of the village have to gentrify together to be able to make a dent in the property market. The curation of these lanes, therefore, becomes a collective effort of a different sort. In this case, extended families organised through the kinship group of the *kunba*, which are spatially organised, have been found to be most effective. *Kunba*s are central to the social capital of most Jat villages. Usually, bigger and well-knit *kunba*s are a function of wealthy and influential families. And much of the social capital is exhibited and performed through the *kunba* itself, by staying together. In this case, the *kunba* becomes that social institution which organically begins to organise the gentrification efforts of their collective property.

Chaudhary Balliram, a powerful landlord from Shahpur Jat, reconstructed his large homestead to build *haveli*s for his five sons probably around the 1970s. Today, his sons and grandsons are owners of this stretch of property. Though their endeavours were individual to begin with, at some point, the family realised that collective upkeep of their property would fetch them far higher rent. Lalita, mentioned in the previous chapter, is a daughter-in-law of this family. Her husband had first started to rent part of their property to a leather factory coming up in their premises. She vividly remembers how many in the family looked down upon them. After her husband's premature death in an accident in the year 1998, she took on the mantle and began to handle the rental business. She speaks of her struggle and her determination to make the business work all by herself before other members of the family also joined the bandwagon. Soon, the five *haveli*s, which had a private back lane running between the houses, began to realise the potential the rental market held. The *haveli*s were quickly torn down and new modern buildings erected; this time, the buildings faced inwards, and the private lane that ran between the houses became a major commercial lane in the village. However, it continues to be a 'private road', which is governed by private rules. A laminated list of dos and don'ts hangs by both the gates that man Balliram Lane. Money has been poured into the upkeep of the lane by the family, by either paving it or installing stylish street lamps to make it look more exclusive. As a result, this familial property fetches a far higher rent than any other in the village, proving to be a rather profitable investment for the family.

Shahpur Jat's increasing reputation in the high-end fashion clientele has also added to the swelling fame of this private lane. It is today a conglomerate of over a hundred stakeholders. Keeping the family together is not easy. Mired in jealousies, ego clashes and conflicts, these *kunba*s seem fragile at times. Two young grandsons of Chaudhary Balliram, after having experimented with different kinds of businesses, have now come around to managing their collective property. They speak of having worked hard to bring a somewhat fragmented and quarrelling family together by making people talk to each other. They have organised family lunches, dinners and even parties for cousins to be able to bond with each other. Initially, these meetups would end up in brawls and arguments, but slowly, they report, everyone began to come around. Despite all the internal fractures, as an economic unit, the *kunba* is working quite successfully. Investments for upgradation of their property are collectively made. The *kunba* makes it a point to present a collective face to outsiders. The family makes joint contributions to social functions and festivals to appear as a single institution.

In many ways, the *kunba* thus works like a joint-stock company. It has different stakeholders with varying degrees of ownership coming together to form a corporate identity. A joint-stock company, by being consolidated through stocks and shares, is able to bring together a significantly diverse and anonymous body of stakeholders together. In effect, it becomes akin to a 'legal person'. The stakeholders are also a transient body of people with stocks and shares being constantly bought and sold. In the case of the village, however, the *kunba* form controls the profile of the stakeholders. The joint-stock company model seems to have been appropriated and adapted to work for this mode of vernacular capitalism. Ownership in rent-seeking stakes, though professionalised, becomes the mode of accumulation. The *kunba* adopts and closely resembles the form of a joint-stock company in order to function as an economic unit so that it can generate profits for all stakeholders. But, unlike a regular joint-stock company, control over membership is crucial.

In response to a *kunba* like the Balliram family, some other landowners, and economically weaker and fragmented sections, are trying to consolidate themselves as RWAs. Since they do not have a strong *kunba*, some other young people have now begun to emulate the *kunba*-joint-stock model to run their rental market collectively under the aegis of an RWA. As a result, unlike Munirka, Shahpur Jat has several RWAs, all of which consider each other to be competition. Supported by active WhatsApp groups and regular meetings in their various 'offices', these networks are consistently worked upon and strengthened. Men with any amount of importance, or wanting to acquire some, have something called an 'office' in these villages. As *baithak*s evaporated from the social life of these villages, with houses getting remodelled to economise space for the accommodation of maximum number of tenants, the void to some extent is being filled by these 'offices'. Landlords sometimes reserve a one-room set in a building they own, sometimes a lobby of that building or sometimes basements of their homes as their 'offices'. Offices are thus spaces of male camaraderie that have replaced *baithak*s. Gossip around land, money deals and politics happen here. Therefore, what could have been a rich space for understanding these spaces of sociabilities of some important and not so important men through participant observation was precluded for me because of my gender.

The first project of the RWA that I got in touch with was to paint the houses on that street in a uniform colour. After much wrangling, around 40–50 households contributed 6,000 rupees each towards this effort. The households which did not contribute were left out, leaving bland gaps in the middle. Painting the houses in one uniform orange has hardly been able to hide the dreariness of these streets. Still lined with small grocery stores, *atta chakki*s (flour mills) and barber saloons interspersed by some speciality stores, it might still not be easy for this lane to escalate the property values of its rental units. 'If you have to get the showrooms here, it is important to get "class",' the young man heading the RWA says to me. 'Class' for him is not a sociological category defined by income. 'Class' would refer to an amorphous sense of aesthetic that the masses are not privy to.

It goes without saying that landlords in Shahpur Jat are in constant competition with each other to please potential high-net-worth clientele. But despite all their attempts to attract such clientele, they have figured out that they cannot afford to allow the tenants to unite. Some designers who had their boutiques on this lane were excited about joining the RWA. The landlords, however, maintained that the tenants would not be allowed to do so, and with time the designers lost interest and only contributed to the new hoardings and flex banners that hang from the two ends of the streets. Similarly, the list of instructions that hangs by the gates of Balliram Lane specifies the size of banners and prescribes how they should be installed. The list also disallows pets, and reiterates that rights to admission are strictly reserved, making it quite clear that the controls remain in the hands of the landlords. At one point, the commercial tenants of Shahpur Jat had tried to form an association to protect their interests. The landlords did not take to this kindly and blocked the parking lot. As a result, the association had to be disbanded soon after.

There is a tacit understanding among the villagers that the 'development' of the village, its commercialisation and the control over its infrastructure have to remain controlled by the villagers. Both the cartel-like *panchayat*s and joint-stock-company-like *kunba*s are at the service of new kinds of collaborations, competitions, rivalries and jealousies aimed at maximising profits. But despite brothers not talking to each other, neighbours having daggers drawn on each other, and countless cases of cheating and betrayal, these kinds of collectivities work in opposition to an 'outsider' figure, be it the state, tenant or the city itself.

Matters of Money, Instruments of Finance

A vernacular form of capitalism in a localised economy is not possible only through control over property. The control that the *kunba* and the *panchayat* exert has to be replicated within networks of investments as well. As more and more people began to convert their houses into rental property, the popularity of this method of both borrowing and investing exploded. Their money runs through the wiry, sinewy capillaries of local credit networks. This form of accumulation is operationalised through control, of money and of resources. After all, no matter how small or vernacular an economy, it cannot run without control over channels of money. As Chapter 2 indicates, the traditional methods of buying land together, such as army men pooling in money, or conventional forms of moneylending formed the edifice of the credit networks of such an economy. The period of land acquisition provided a further fillip to this form of business because it immediately pumped liquid cash into the economy for circulation. The sudden boom in investments in real estate in the 1990s also created a demand for the flow of credit. Although credit or demand for credit was nothing new, the 1990s ensured a scramble for both land and liquid cash for construction purposes; the volume of people looking for both was also much larger than before. The availability of liquid cash and its circulation became so crucial for the economy at this point that older methods of moneylending were no longer sufficient. Forms of lending and borrowing thus underwent innovations to keep pace with the market.[18]

In the absence of clear titles, home loans from banks were out of the question. The property boom in the 1990s, which pushed everyone to get involved in the renting business, required unprecedented access to/demand for flow of money in the local economy. Additionally, the brand new rent economy, most of which is based on liquid cash, needed a local circuit where such money could also be reinvested. The absence of the involvement of the state, or of formal banking options in these villages, made it necessary for these communities to come together and create their channels. Despite countless stories of people losing money or being betrayed by fellow villagers, circles of trust have emerged with overlapping circuits of cash moving across them. Many argue that global finance has a violent tendency to penetrate and subsume economic activity and social life as a whole.[19] Jean and John Comaroff argue how local economies are not very different from the speculative world of global finance. Gambling, for instance, a truly local sport, is essentially the force behind financial capitalism and speculation.[20] They write,

> Insofar as the growth of globalised market, electronic media, and finance capital have opened up the potential for venture enterprise, the gaming room has actually become the iconic of capital: of its natural capacity to yield value without human input, to grow and expand of its own accord, to reward speculation.[21]

Ritu Birla's historical work looks at how indigenous speculative and future trading practices like *satta* and *hundi* were rendered illegal by the colonial state, despite being similar to practices pursued by the British themselves.[22]

The vernacular form of capitalism focused on rent, however, is based on its very difference from the world of speculative capital. The essential difference that I am trying to highlight here is that between 'finance' and 'money'. Finance runs on the principle of fictitious capital and speculation, and straddles both the world of stock markets as well as the world of *satta*s and Ponzi schemes which go bust. Finance inhabits the heady world of risk, where risk-taking becomes the symbol of one's manliness.[23] But like we discussed previously, 'risk' that has become synonymous with capital accumulation[24] seems relatively absent in the rent economy. Unlike other businesses, which require business acumen and the ability to run risks, renting out property is fuelled by demand with close to zero risk. RWAs also work at mitigating the risks that come with *kabza*. This is possible because the economy is structured through 'money'. Money retains control within networks through which hard cash flows. 'Money', unlike finance, does not grow by loosening ownership, by quick buying and selling. 'Money' grows by keeping it contained within dense networks of trusted people. This form of circulation of money runs entirely in hard cash and leaves no room for fictitious, speculative capital. The logic of how this money grows is sharply different from that of speculative capital. Two local forms in which 'money' proliferates within these localised channels in the two urban villages within our purview are *committees* and *financing*. It is not a coincidence that both these terms are English words but do not necessarily correspond to the meanings they convey in the English-speaking world.

Committees

Committees, or *kameti*s, as they are called, are not unique to these villages, nor are they a recent innovation. Committees have been fairly popular all across northern India, in small towns and big cities, as local means of investing money over generations. They have also been popular with women as a mode of investment. Chapter 2 discusses how Jats would often pool resources together to buy land together as *chak*. Jat men in the army often pooled money as well to send home to buy land, cattle or even repair houses. A form of collective investments, by way of buying land or even pooling money, therefore, had been well in place. But they slowly evolved as a self-sufficient mode of investment over time. This form of channels of money has been thriving in the last few decades, and yet there is little clarity regarding the reach of this economy. Committees are run by individuals or 'organisers' who put people in groups, pooling equal sums of money from members of the groups.[25] There are numerous instances of committee organisers having taken off with the money that had been collected or refusing to shell out the money for the purpose for which it was collected. However, that has not deterred this form of investment.

Committees today are mostly diverse groups, wherein some individuals might not even know each other; however, everyone is known to the organiser in some way or the other as the group comes into being at the discretion of the organiser. The credibility of the organiser as a trustworthy person with significant stakes in the local economy is key to the formation of the committee. Committees of different sizes exist. There are scores of small committees run by professional organisers which pool in a few thousand rupees each month from each member. These smaller ones are popular with working-class people, people running minor businesses or individuals in small-time jobs who pool their savings in these networks. Many people who earn in cash, and are uncomfortable with bank accounts, also gravitate towards these kinds of smaller committees. There are also, however, committees that have individual contributions of several lakhs from each member; these are usually maintained among a very closed group of trusted friends or relatives to establish a bigger pool of liquid cash. As these committees are not registered, and the money that circulates within them is only internally managed, they do not follow the rules that formally recognised methods of investments do, and also do not fall within the purview of taxation. As a fieldworker, I could only get a sense of the thick networks of committees of hard cash that criss-crossed these villages and even beyond.

Committees in this context seem to be rather an effective form of investing money. For people who are involved in frequent and rapid transactions, they are particularly crucial. For more safe players, it is a good investment, as even without making a bid one can end up with a significant amount of interest earned out of simply pooling their money with that of others. Though this form of finance and credit is not regulated by the government, unlike the chit fund, it has its internal mechanisms of ensuring compliance. It works like a pool whereby keeping a certain amount of money gives one access to a larger sum of money at short notice, without much bureaucratic hassle, while continuing to earn interest and not being taxed for it. These unregulated financial schemes are often hugely popular among the weaker sections of society, which also makes them susceptible to fraud and irregularities.[26] In the urban villages, though, this is only partially true. While small-business people and migrant workers also invest in committees, the committees of the rich and landed, with much larger sums of money, are organised within really thick and close networks of kinship and are often tightly closed.

Moneylending to *Financing*

Shakti Tokas from Munirka told me the story of his first tenant who had rented the ground floor and courtyard of his house to open a garment shop in the early 1960s. He paid a rent of 10 rupees a month for the courtyard. The tenant was a genial, well-spoken man from Mehrauli who instantly gained the local people's trust; the latter soon began to buy cloth from him. Soon after, the trader started borrowing money from villagers on interest which he would dutifully pay back, sometimes even before time. In time, he garnered a reputation for being reliable and honest. The early 1960s being a period when villagers had more liquid cash to dispose of than usual, lending money was a lucrative business at the time. More and more villagers began to lend money to the cloth seller with the assurance that their money was safe. One day, however, he simply disappeared into thin air, just as he had once appeared from nowhere, leaving behind all his stock in the shop, never to return.

When land acquisition started, which immediately increased the circulation of money in the local economy, a large number of villagers became moneylenders, sometimes to each other and sometimes to their tenants. The scramble around the 1990s, which sent everyone into a tizzy to build, seems to have been the moment when moneylending began to become more organised.[27] Financing, therefore, emerged as a locally evolved form of moneylending. This financing has little to do with the global financial economy fuelled by speculation; it runs on hard cash. With the changes in the economy, the moneylending business had to become more dynamic, allowing liquid capital to flow much faster in the local economy than ever before. Financing started working with the idea of 'daily collections': instead of waiting for interest to be paid along with the principal amount at the end of the loan period like in a standard moneylending business, the interest and the principal amount are broken up into a daily amount and then collected every day. This way, the financier has more liquid cash to keep in circulation. This transition of moneylending into financing makes evident how sharp and fast the flow of money needed to be in the context of an emerging rent economy in the villages after the 1990s. Second, this new form of providing credit also allowed scope for profit, leading moneylending to emerge as a full-fledged profession for many, rather than something that they did on the side.

At the time he was looking to reconstruct his house in the late 1990s, Beenu says that he had enough money to build only one storey. A 'gaon ke chacha' (an uncle from the village) told him that if Beenu wished to build five storeys, he could lend him money for him to do so at 2 per cent interest. He claims that he was charged a nominal interest because he had been nice to people, and so, people were nice to him in return. 'But then why charge interest at all?' I asked. He explained to me quite matter-of-factly that if one takes a loan to tide over a personal crisis like a wedding or sickness, it is one thing. But if one is borrowing money to build a house for business, it only makes sense that the lender also earns some interest on it. The logic was infallible. If rent needs to be kept within local networks, then it is equally important to create networks for financing that are controlled locally. And it is only fair to share those profits. Only much later did someone else tell me that Beenu was a financier himself.

As we have seen in Chapter 2, Raman Tokas and his brother from Munirka also shut down their transport business and diverted their investments into rental property. Together, they owned 12–13 buildings in 2014. Another builder from Neb Sarai, who was trying to make inroads into Munirka's construction business, alleged that Raman Tokas forced him to sell three flats to the former in a building that he had constructed on a local's property. Raman Tokas, I was told, was also involved in the financing business in the village, but, predictably, he denied it. In my naiveté, I had put the question to him rather bluntly, which made him defensive. He claimed that the finance company was a registered one and that he had shut it down a long time back. 'Woh koi kam nahi hota. Woh toh chor bazaari hai. Usme toh har sham ko dukandaron ke paas paise mangne ka kaam hai. Ladke lagte hain ki, paise de varna maar denge.'* *Financing* of this kind is mostly carried out by individuals informally. 'Financing companies' are few. The first time I heard the term 'leasing company' was from Bahadur Singh Panwar in Shahpur Jat (mentioned in Chapter 2).[28] Through his company, he has lent money to shopkeepers in Lajpat Nagar, Kalkaji, Defence Colony and Shahpur Jat. His father's cement shop still exists but it does not look like any cement is ever sold out of there. Bahadur Singh Panwar concentrates his time and energy on his financing business and in managing his commercial property.

As mentioned at the beginning of this chapter, the difference between 'money' and 'finance' is a crucial one. They grow in different directions and in different circuits, both of which plug back into the global capital in different ways. The circuits of 'money', in this case, ordered through *committees* and *financing*, do not subsume themselves into the channels of high finance and yet maintain their stakes in global capital. Institutions like the World Bank have frequently suggested giving people property rights, which would immediately allow people to release money through mortgages.[29] What these institutions fail to understand is that the need for property rights in the Global South is not linked to unlocking value through mortgages. Instead, there exists a somewhat practical and effective way of unlocking value through circuits of money. But this relationship between the world of finance and the world of money is a tenuous one.

On 8 November 2016, the Government of India banned all 1,000 rupees and 500 rupees banknotes on the grounds that those were the most counterfeited banknotes in the country. Given that around 86 per cent of the bulk of

---

* 'That isn't work. It's work that involves going to shopkeepers every evening to ask for money. It requires men. To say, give me money or I will hit you.'

currency in circulation was in 1000 rupees and 500 rupees banknotes, demonetisation created a massive crunch in the shadow economies that ran on circuits of money. Demonetisation was supposed to be the blitzkrieg that would kill these shadow economies[30] and plug the money back into formal channels, but that was far from what happened. Though demonetisation adversely affected the entire chain of economy, the shadow economies tottered back into action in time. If regularisation has been an attempt to make their spaces legible, demonetisation was an attempt to make their money legible. However, just as regularisation, as we have seen already, had been thwarted, demonetisation too failed massively in achieving its avowed goals.

Rent, Control and Security

Control is essential to a rent economy. But control manifests differently in the two villages that we are looking at. While Munirka works in a somewhat subliminal housing market, Shahpur Jat rests at the fag end of the global garment industry. Trying hard to gentrify and appeal to a clientele composed of upper-class Delhi elite, the villagers in Shahpur Jat are a different deal. The younger generation here attempts to break out of the image that their grandfathers are associated with. 'Once my grandfather had slapped a guy found kissing someone in the lane,' Brajesh, one of the stakeholders of Balliram Lane in Shahpur Jat, laughs and tells me, indicating to me his disassociation from his grandfather. The landlords here are overeager to please their tenants. And coming across as 'polished' and 'well mannered' is the least they can do to keep the control in their hands. When Shekhar, an entrepreneur who runs a restaurant with his wife here, complained to his landlord about brawls breaking out on the streets outside among villagers and of locals staring at his customers from their balconies, his landlord immediately took care of it.

The nature of security has also changed the spatial contours of the village. The lane would earlier be the common space for the elderly members of the family to spend time and also keep a watch over their properties, and to look out for trespassers or other unwanted characters. Now the lane is monitored by professional private guards. The social control that has loosened up towards the village's high profile tenants has moved elsewhere. The Bengali Muslim *karigars* who live and work in the depths of the village remain invisiblised in every sense of the term. Clanking away at their sewing machines or peering into the *adda* frames with their needles, their presence is mostly manifested in the presence of innumerable handwritten posters announcing the requirement of *karigar*s in Bangla. The fact that they blend into the environment so unobtrusively strikes one as odd if one knows a little about the spaces of industrial labour in the city. Not too far away from Shahpur Jat, Okhla, an industrial area with its dirt and grime, smoke and noise, simmers with labour unrest and strikes.[31] But the working class seems curiously docile in Shahpur Jat. The landlords not only make sure that the property is well maintained and looked after, but they also take care of municipal problems, local disturbances and even labour unrest. Women fashion designers often do not mind paying higher rent to landlords for the 'safety' that some landlords ensure them from their male *karigar*s. The landlords may not be slapping visitors any more, but most of them also double up as male authority figures to ensure that the labourers are well behaved. The value of a 'good landlord' often translates into values of property as well.

Indeed, 'security' becomes the logic of governing these spaces. While in Munirka, it is done by cultivating a culture of fear and suspicion (more about this in Chapter 5), in Shahpur Jat the landlords try to outdo each other in becoming providers of security. Shahpur Jat's connectedness to global capital through the garment industry being more direct, there is a constant emphasis to underplay the racism and violence that exists there, unlike in Munirka. The cartel form or joint-stock-company form works through the limitations and possibilities of the local conditions to shape its own relationship with capital. Rent not only allows a certain kind of accumulation but also a specific kind of expression of social anxiety through violence in a way that the question of anxiety and the forces of accumulation become inseparable. Rent also allows economic control in a situation where the urban Jats find themselves completely inundated in the throes of urbanisation.

As the landlords of Shahpur Jat realise this, they probably feel the need to be pliant towards high commerce. Unlike Munirka, which has developed a fair amount of confidence in renting to a particular class, Shahpur Jat is in the throes of gentrification and knows it can get more rent if it plays its cards right. 'Getting a bad name' is the last thing they want. The logic of accumulation demands that Shahpur Jat present itself as a safe, secure and a well-curated space with an 'edge' that only it can provide. However, one must also keep in mind that whenever tenants have wanted to exert pressure collectively, the structure of control otherwise kept muted shows up in full ferocity.

The commercial tenants of Shahpur Jat, mostly designers who had started renting here in large numbers around early 2000, had formed an association in 2002 to raise their concerns with the MCD. Though it was never floated to ostensibly organise themselves against the landlords, the landlords did not respond too well to this development. As was mentioned earlier in this chapter, as a reaction, the landlords restricted the tenants' and their customers' access to parking space in the village, which had always been at a premium. The commercial tenants decided it was not worth the trouble and disbanded the organisation within six months of starting it. The families that are able to collectively invest in property have a far higher control over their tenants. They have been able to establish rules that their tenants are expected to follow. 'We see to it that the tenants do not get united,' Brajesh told me. Even the RWAs, which are struggling to gentrify their properties collectively, dither from including commercial tenants as members despite the latter's willingness. Historically, the villagers know what collectivities can do. Their tenants organising themselves, thus, is the last thing they want.

Rent and the Place of Vernacular Capitalism

The hallmark of these localised institutions, be it the RWA, *panchayat* or the *kunba*s, is that they are elastic. They sometimes work as a village development committee, or an organisation of landlords, as an organisation of struggling entrepreneurs and other such formations, depending on what the need is. The RWA form comes across as exceptionally flexible. In the garb of a civic association, it can take up the form of both a cartel and a joint-stock company as the need arises. Their strength lies in this elasticity. The RWA, *kunba* and the *panchayat* may not make up the totality of vernacular institutions that exist in these localities, but they effectively represent locally mutated formations within the city. Working on the premise that economic transactions are fundamentally social interactions, these institutions of vernacular capitalism go beyond markets and firms to domains of intimate spaces, families, kinship and communities to understand the nature of constitution of the two. Thus, kinship and family networks in the context of emerging rent economies become the basis of forging new kinds of economic relations with others. In effect, what the Organisation of the Petroleum Exporting Countries (OPEC) makes possible at the level of controlling an international market of crude oil, the Jat landlords do in the case of the housing market with these vernacular institutions. While discussing Venezuela as an oil-producing state, Fernando Coronil argues that in societies where revenues derive predominantly from rent, the dominant tendency of maximising rent and increasing access to rent's distribution is different from an economy based on the logic of production.[32] In the case of our urban villages, this maximisation and increased access to rent is made possible through the community networks.

But these economic relations do not float in a vacuum. These new economic relations are a part of the city's neoliberal economy. These unregulated spaces, which have emerged as spaces of manufacture as well as living spaces for the precariat working class of the city, are crucial to both the state and to neoliberal capital. Urban villages are not the only spaces to offer such possibilities. Several residential colonies that house unregistered factories, with poor infrastructure and no safety regulations, have constantly been in the news for being a death trap for workers.[33]

The urban villages, be it for residential purposes or for manufacturing, are therefore nestled in the space between rent and capital. While rent allows these villages to maintain their social cohesion, capital allows them to enter the circuits of value creation. The relationship between this vernacular and global economy is different from any other, if not more complex. They sit uneasily together, snubbing each other frequently. Rent is defined essentially by control that comes from ownership and possession. Capital, on the other hand, is defined through devising ingenious ways of multiplying it, even if it means fragmenting ownership. Stocks and shares and similar financial instruments are ways of making ownership extremely tenuous and fluid, which contributes to erratic and heady market fluctuations. In the case of rent, ownership and control over the resource becomes the defining feature, and in the case of the urban villages, as we have seen, this control has to be communally charged. If the relationship of the city and this village community has to be understood, it cannot be done without understanding how rent shapes them both. The landlords are suspicious of fictitious global capital, knowing that its force would decimate their belongingness and the control they exert in these villages. Regularisation and formalisation are suspect not just because they pave the way for the state, but because they also pave the way for finance capital. Similarly, global capital too is cautious about incorporating a Jat landlord's money in its portfolio.

Sanchit, who runs a start-up from Shahpur Jat, had accepted 30 lakh rupees from his landlord, Bahadur Panwar, a cement dealer-turned-financier. Panwar, worried about his unmarried son who was not finding a match because he was unemployed, was keen on inserting his son's name as a stakeholder in a business to signal to prospective *rishta*s (marital prospects) that his son was a businessman. Bahadur Panwar's son ended up becoming an 'angel funder' at a time when Sanchit was in dire need of money. In a year, when the latter approached international venture capitalists to raise money, they put in a condition that he would have to remove his landlord as a partner because he was a 'dormant' partner and was not adding any 'value' to the company.

Evidently, the Jat landlord, with his access to money through localised channels, is looked upon with suspicion and disdain in the world of global speculative capital. It is fairly common for local manufacturing units or entrepreneurs to seek loans from within these local channels, but having them as funders is a different ballgame altogether. The Jat landlords and their 'money' evidently do not evoke trust. He is seen as being stuck in time, with no understanding of the world of finance and, therefore, a plain liability.

And here, we come back to the question of value. Value, as amorphous a term it may be, reflected in possessions, in cultures, in attitudes where at times one sensibility rubs off on the other, and at other times, they stand at loggerheads. But notions of value also work in very neat ways, in exclusive worlds. Lilly Irani's work shows us how innovators of the finance capital world look to create 'value' in global value chains as consultants and entrepreneurs.[34] They added value to themselves, to their clients and to the nation.[35] Value was a way for them to exhibit creative autonomy, and terms on which they negotiate with their clients in the world of 'finance capital'. This notion of value has no resonance in the world of 'money'. Though some villagers see themselves as entrepreneurs and wish to inhabit the masculine world of 'risk' instead of the world of lazy rent, they have no pretence of contributing to nation-building or a sense of adding 'value' to the global commodity chain. If the world of finance values risk and innovation, the world of money values loyalty and kinship. This value enters the subterranean world of money, of committees and financing, only to be fuelled back into the housing and property market largely.

Harvey writes that in an urbanised world, the distinction between capitalist and landlord has blurred with the blurring of the distinction between land and capital.[36] In places like Munirka and Shahpur Jat, which are constantly in a state of being constructed, broken down and then reconstructed, buildings are often not *produced* (read: 'built') for a long term, but probably as commodities that need to be consumed and then reconstructed to meet newer demands. Clearly, capital and rent have overlapping realities that become difficult to segregate at times. But if we were to subsume our understanding of rent within that of capital, we would be unable to grasp the essential ways in which power works here. The reason this economy is so closely guarded by the locals is because of the power that extraction gives them as a community. That control, the villagers know very well, will not be possible in the realm of finance capital. And that control is non-negotiable for their own sense of being a community. At the same time, rent shapes more than just the process of accumulation. Rent shapes cities. It creates new subjectivities and hierarchies and mediates the way in which the villagers relate to the city, as landlords to urban migrants and entrepreneurs. Rent shapes the physical space of these villages and appears to be the only common 'asset' which unites them socially and economically. It makes them 'brothers' in a city. It makes the community in these villages powerful and yet vulnerable to the changing demography of the city.

Conclusion

In the previous pages, we have tried to examine how the consolidation of an economic form takes place through kinship. The 1963 exemption that was supposed to be an administrative one with regard to building bye-laws spawned an extremely well-networked form of local economy that has made the state close to redundant. No wonder then that the removal of the exemption was met with suspicion. The exemption allowed the older, traditional way of the *panchayat* to travel into the urban realm to create a platform for organising the community's interest in the real estate market. Families could rebuild, reconstruct and gentrify collective property for the same reason. In the absence of formal avenues of lending, the local and informal channels of lending became far stronger and better knit. The community was able to create an extremely localised form of real estate market in the absence of any clarity in the law.

Furthermore, at the margins of the law, these spaces are continually reshaping the idea of life in the city. One way to look at such seemingly primitive modes of investment is to attribute it to their ruralness, to the possibility of financial capital being inaccessible to the Jat villagers. The other explanation could be that the localised, tightly held economy based on kinship networks, far from the world of 'risk' and abstraction, is where they find their community strength. The village 'cartels' and 'joint-stock companies' that we have looked at might appear fractured and contested at times. The collective interest in the market allows social capital to intervene in ways where autochthony, kinship, belongingness can mutate with market forms to create effective market control. It might be fruitful to understand them as a flexible form, but one that is here to stay, which can legitimately be studied as a form of capitalism. I would also not suggest that we see these communities as fixed, ahistorical entities, but rather understand their formations and transformations as profoundly modern and flexible to adapt to the market. What is clear then is that capital is not the only force that radically transforms our landscape.

Notes

1. Dipesh Chakrabarty's 'Two Histories of Capital' has been central in pushing social scientists to articulate divergent trajectories of capital in postcolonial societies. See Dipesh Chakrabarty, *Provincializing Europe: Postcolonial Thought and Historical Difference* (New Jersey: Princeton University Press, 2000). Kalyan Sanyal and Iman Mitra et al. have used the term 'postcolonial capitalism' to understand forms of capitalism in postcolonial societies. See Sanyal, *Rethinking Capitalist Development*; and Iman Mitra, Ranabir Samaddar and Samita Sen, eds., *Accumulation in Postcolonial Capitalism* (Singapore: Springer, 2016). I would however use the term vernacular capitalism as a more specific subset of postcolonial capitalism, as I show the constant attempt to draw capital to speak to vernacular forms for accumulation in postcolonial spaces, which work on very different logics than that of capital. Ritu Birla has used the term vernacular capitalism as well to describe the Marwari community's transition to becoming capitalists. See Birla, *Stages of Capital*. I, however, see this vernacular capitalism as a frictional relationship between rent and capital.
2. M. N. Srinivas, 'The Dominant Caste in Rampura', *American Anthropologist* 61, no. 1 (1959).
3. Balmurali Natrajan, 'Caste, Class, and Community in India: An Ethnographic Approach', *Ethnology* 44, no. 3 (2005); Carol Upadhya, 'Social and Cultural Strategies of Class Formation in Coastal Andhra Pradesh', *Contributions to Indian Sociology* 31, no. 2 (1997).
4. Balmurali Natrajan, 'From Jati to Samaj', *Seminar* 633 (2012).
5. Akshaya Mukul, *Gita Press and the Making of Hindu India* (New Delhi: Harper Collins, 2016).
6. Assa Doron, 'Caste Away? Subaltern Engagement with the Modern Indian State', *Modern Asian Studies* 44, no. 4 (2010).
7. Eric Stokes, 'Agrarian Society and Pax Britannica', quoted in Sumit Guha, *Beyond Caste: Identity and Power in South Asia Past and Present* (Ranikhet: Permanent Black, 2016), 109.
8. Guha, *Beyond Caste*, 250.
9. Partha Chatterjee, *The Politics of the Governed: Reflections on Popular Politics in Most of the World* (New York: Columbia University Press, 2004).
10. At no point should these *panchayat*s be equated with the formal village *panchayati raj* system that was formalised through the 73rd Amendment. These are caste-based, hierarchical *panchayat*s that have had a social legitimacy since pre-colonial times in this region.
11. The villages inhabited by a clan are organised into a clan council, and the area under its jurisdiction is called the *khap*. See M. C. Pradhan, 'The Jats of

Northern India: Their Traditional Political System', *Economic and Political Weekly* 17, no. 50 (1965): 1821.
12. M. C. Pradhan writes, 'Several instances from the historical records of the khap Panchayat of Baliyan and from the minutes of the Panchayat meetings can be cited where certain rules of conduct for inter-personal, inter-group, and inter-caste relations, rules guiding land revenue collection, and general policies of social welfare for the people, were framed and executed by the khap Panchayat.' See M. C. Pradhan, 'The Jats of Northern India: Their Traditional Political System—II', *Economic and Political Weekly* 17, no. 51 (1965): 1855.
13. It needs to be kept in mind that the *panchayati raj* system that was brought in within Directive Principles and then introduced through the 73rd Constitutional Amendment in 1992 is very different in its structure and form and should not be confused with *khap panchayats*. For *khap panchayats* and their role in honour killings, see Prem Chowdhry, 'Caste Panchayats and the Policing of Marriage in Haryana: Enforcing Kinship and Territorial Exogamy', *Contributions to Indian Sociology* 38, nos. 1–2 (2004). Regarding their complicity in riots against Muslims, see Virendra Nath Bhatt, 'What Led to the Muzaffarnagar Communal Riots', *Tehelka*, 8 September 2013, http://old.tehelka.com/what-led-to-the-muzaffarnagar-communal-riots/ (accessed 16 November 2015). Also, see Mohan Rao et al., *Communalism and the Role of the State: An Investigation into the Communal Violence in Muzaffarnagar and Its Aftermath: A Report*, December 2013. The documentary films by director Nakul Singh Sawhney, *Izzatnagari Ki Asabhya Betiyaan* (2012) and *Muzaffarnagar Baaqi Hai* (2015) extensively cover the issue of honour killings and communal violence respectively.
14. The *khap panchayat* is a tiered structure, with clusters of villages forming up as regional units.
15. The Bhagidari scheme of the Delhi Government from CM Sheila Dikshit's time, which only includes RWAs in middle-class and legal colonies, has been trying to attain citizen participation in matters of civic infrastructure. Stephanie Tawa Lama-Rewal argues that RWAs have been largely undemocratic and seem to have no clear overall charter to adhere to, which allows every RWA to formulate its own. See Stephanie Tawa Lama-Rewal, 'Neighbourhood Associations and Local Democracy: Delhi Municipal Elections 2007', *Economic and Political Weekly* 42, no. 47 (2007): 51–60. For a detailed description of the nature of the RWA's politics in upper-middle-class colonies, see Sanjay Srivastava, *Entangled Urbanism: Slum, Gated Community, and Shopping Mall in Delhi and Gurgaon*, (New Delhi: Oxford University Press, 2014), 85–111, 172–82; and Ghertner, 'Gentrifying the

State, Gentrifying Participation'. This book, however, considers the politics of the RWAs at the level of the state and such governance mechanisms beyond its scope.

16. Paul M. Sweezy, *The Theory of Capitalist Development: Principles of Marxian Political Economy* (New York; London: Modern Reader Paperbacks, 1968), 262–65.
17. The electricity rates have fallen further with Arvind Kejriwal's populist measures of slashing electricity rates in the city.
18. For a detailed discussion on how property construction is linked with the rise of local financial actors, see Mukta Naik and Eesha Kunduri, 'The Role of Housing Finance Actors in Regenerating Delhi's Unauthorised Colonies: An Examination of State–Citizen–Market Boundaries', *Urbanisation* 5, no. 2 (2020).
19. Sandro Mezzadra and Brett Neilson, 'Operations of Capital', *South Atlantic Quarterly* 114, no. 1 (2015): 2.
20. Jean Comaroff and John L. Comaroff, 'Millennial Capitalism: First Thoughts on Second Coming', in *Millennial Capitalism and the Culture of Neoliberalism*, ed. Jean Comaroff and John L. Comaroff (Durham; London: Duke University Press, 2001), 6.
21. Ibid., 7.
22. Birla, *Stages of Capital*, 143–98.
23. Imre Szeman, 'Entrepreneurship as the New Common Sense', *South Atlantic Quarterly* 114, no. 3 (2015).
24. Geeta Patel, 'Risky Subjects: Insurance, Sexuality, and Capital', *Social Text* 24, no. 4 (89) (2006).
25. Committees are a variation of chit funds, but qualitatively different from them. Solomon Benjamin in his analysis discusses what makes committees more popular than chit funds in such economies. Chit funds are a formally recognised form of investment, which bring them under the purview of a number of governmental checks and balances including taxation. See Solomon Benjamin, 'Neighbourhood as Factory'. Committees, though run on the same principles, on the other hand, are mostly informal. They are mostly run among a group of 20 people, for an average duration of 10 months through an 'organiser' who organises the committee. If the committee is for 20 lakh rupees, for instance, every member is expected to pool in 10,000 rupees in the first month. The members meet on a particular date and time, which is pre-decided every month and people call for a 'bid', or a *boli*. There is an upper limit to the *boli*, which is mostly 40 per cent of the pool's collection. So as the first month creates a pool of 2 lakh rupees, a bid for up to 80,000 rupees can be made in that month. The *boli* is always on the basis of the deductions that the bidder is willing to take. For example, Bidder

A can bid that she would be willing to take a hit (technically called a discount in chit funds) of 20,000 rupees for a bid for 80,000 rupees, which means that A will get to borrow only 60,000 rupees while 20,000 rupees will be distributed among the other 19 members, so that every member gets 1,052 rupees as a part of the interest. In case of multiple contenders for a bid, the person who is willing to take a bigger hit wins the bid. The organiser gets to claim the entire bid of the second round as remuneration. It continues in the same cycle for 10 months when the committee is dissolved and the money in the pool is equally distributed among all the members.

26. Dinesh Unnikrishnan, 'Regulations Yet to Catch Up with India's Illegal Chit Fund Industry', *Mint*, 24 May 2016, https://www.livemint.com/Money/PYvp2nBSpJJZ2IK9vsJwNP/Regulations-yet-to-catch-up-with-Indias-illegal-chit-fund-i.html (accessed 19 August 2016).
27. If David Graeber's thesis of debt being the primary driver of economy and not really exchange has to be taken seriously, the historical relationship that Jats have had with moneylending as a form is important. See Graeber, *Debt: First 5000 Years*.
28. Though there are a few registered finance companies, it does not mean that every time someone says finance company or leasing company, they really mean a company. Many a time the use of the term 'company' is merely colloquial.
29. Hernando de Soto, *The Mystery of Capital: Why Capitalism Triumphs in the West and Fails Everywhere Else* (New York: Basic Books, 2003).
30. These 'shadow economies' need to be understood in the light of shadowy institutions that are created within the financial capital itself. Maria Mazzucato throws light on 'shadow banking'—a term increasingly popular after 2007 to describe a diverse set of financial intermediaries like payday lenders, mortgage lenders, investment banks, mobile payment systems. See Mazzucato, *The Value of Everything*, 135.
31. Sunalini Kumar, 'Chronicles of a Death Untold: The Lethal Geographies of Delhi's Peripheries', in *Critical Studies in Politics: Exploring Sites, Selves and Power*, ed. Aditya Nigam, Nivedita Menon and Sanjay Palshikar (New Delhi: Orient Blackswan, 2013).
32. Coronil, *The Magical State*, 32.
33. The Anaj Mandi fire, which broke out in December 2019 in an unregistered bag factory killed 43 workers and injured close to 100 who were sleeping inside, spoke volumes of the precarious conditions in which the working class both lives and works. Many of those injured or killed were said to be between 15 and 20 years of age. Anaj Mandi, though a residential area on paper, has been known for its narrow lanes dotted with scores of similar

small-scale factories. 'Lethal Misgovernance: On Anaj Mandi Fire Tragedy', *Hindu*, 10 December 2019, https://www.thehindu.com/opinion/editorial/lethal-misgovernance/article30259827.ece (accessed 10 December 2019); also Krantikari Naujawan Sabha, 'Rise in Rage Against Massive Factory, Fire in Anaj Mandi, New Delhi: A Report,' pamphlet, 2019.
34. Lilly Irani, *Chasing Innovation: Making Entrepreneurial Citizens in Modern India* (New Jersey: Princeton University Press, 2019).
35. Ibid., 85.
36. David Harvey, *Urbanization of Capital* (Baltimore: Johns Hopkins University Press, 1985), 65.

5

Culture, Gender and Belongingness?
City and the Violence of Rent

Kaun hain hum? Humara kya pata hai? Kya parichay hai hamara? Hum woh kisaan hain jinhone Dilli ki pragati ke liye sabse pehle apni bhoomi di.*

—Youth Brigade, Munirka

We have to interpret the war that is going on beneath peace; peace itself is coded war. We are therefore at war with one another; a battlefront runs through the whole society, continuously and permanently, and it is this battlefront that puts us all on one side or the other. There is no such thing as a neutral subject. We are all inevitably someone's adversary.

—Michel Foucault, *Society Must be Defended*

Beenu was an affable man, and rather quick witted. Since he had seen his father run a brick kiln, and dabbled in the transport business, real estate and local *financing* himself, I asked him to tell me what the experience of seeing things changing so drastically right before his eyes had been like. He responded with a smile,

> Aapne woh kauue ki kahani suni hai? Ek kauua tha jisko mor banna tha. Toh woh apne upar kuchh mor ke pankkh laga kar moron ke saath rehne chala gaya. Moron ko pata chal gaya ki who kauua hai toh use nikaal diya. Woh waapas kauuon ke beech aaya toh use kauuon ne nikaal diya ki woh kauuon ke saath rehna nahi chahta. Hum bilkul us kauue ki tarah hain.'†

The contradiction that Beenu had drawn was not merely a spatial one. There is a world of difference between the city and the village. People of South Delhi

---

* 'Who are we? What is our identity? We are those farmers who first gave up our land for Delhi's development.'

† 'Have you heard the story of the crow? So this crow wanted to be a peacock so he finds some peacock feathers, attaches them to his own body and goes amongst the peacocks. The peacocks realised he was a crow and turned him away. When he came back to the crows, the crows excommunicated him since he had left them to live with the peacocks. We are just like that crow.'

belong to the upper middle class and might even be considered the city's elite. Businessmen to government officials to members of the cultural and intellectual elite inhabit the many localities of South Delhi—all built on the agricultural lands of these villages. The villagers, however, may have money, but they do not embody the cultural capital that defines South Delhi. Both the city and the village have become cosmopolitan spaces, with aspirations that are quite 'urban', with inhabitants moving in and out of them seamlessly. This blurs the conceptual borders between urban and rural without erasing them, while also producing differences and hierarchies spatially. It also messes up identities. Proud Jat men find themselves derided in an urbanised world. But feudal hierarchy has taught us that the only way pride can be salvaged is by looking for someone else to belittle.

A series of urban historiographic work based in South Asia has argued how urban neighbourhoods reproduce the logics of exclusion based on caste, religion and race. Ghettos in urban spaces are products of this form of segregation. Urban villages, however, have not been based on such logics of exclusion. Since cheap housing is the mainstay of this economy, the villagers do not have the luxury of denying housing to anyone. As a result, many of these villages have emerged as deeply multicultural and heterogeneous spaces. The villages have slowly become home to the LGBTQ community, young live-in couples, migrants from the northeast of the country and from African countries and many more.[1] The migrants too, having lived in these villages for long, have managed to create social networks that give them a sense of community. Local businesses like grocery shops, with very specialised items needed for the northeast style of cooking, braiding services for African migrants and restaurants serving Naga and Manipuri food have emerged all over these villages (Figure 5.1). Despite this openness, however, these villages have also been sites of discrimination. This seeming contradiction between openness and discrimination has been the reality of the urban experience in a city like Delhi.

The rise of the globalised service industry created a massive demand for jobs that required the performance of emotional and immaterial labour, which was mostly gendered. The growing service industry since the 1990s led to the creation of jobs where 'femininity is produced, repetitively, in the specific circumstances where it is performed as a normative requirement of the job'.[2] Literature around these new forms of labour has consistently pointed out the blurring of lines between commodity and labour, and between production and consumption.[3] Most of these new kinds of jobs have therefore emerged around particular notions of behaviour, fluency in English, particular modes of

Figure 5.1 A shop selling 'Northeast items' and 'Himalayan Chinese' food in Munirka

Source: Ritambhara Mehta and Dilip Menon.

dressing, make-up and such. Carla Freeman's work with respect to the rise of the 'pink collar' economy in Barbados shows how the informatics industry does not just employ more women, but the nature of work has progressively become more feminised.[4] Freeman also points out that demands of professional fashion from workplaces reproduce these pink-collar workers as different kinds of consumers as well. Though men are not necessarily excluded from jobs at mall stores, high-end salons and as fashion models and lifestyle managers, women who fit the global notions of 'smart and good looking'[5] are high in demand.

In this scenario, women from the northeastern parts of the country are in great demand as part of this globalised labouring class. Their influx into Delhi since the late 1990s converges with the rise of a neoliberal Delhi.[6] Keya Bardalai's work shows how human resource departments of several corporations prefer northeastern workers because they 'have the right look', are 'well dressed', have 'fit and athletic bodies', 'fair skin' and are 'already well groomed and hygienic'.[7] In other words, they are sought after in the labour market because of their appearance, which is fetishised in the global economy, their ability to speak fluent English, as well as their comfort with western attire. But as Bardalai shows, the same look and bodily comportment that gets them decent jobs in the neoliberal market renders them susceptible to perceptions of being 'immoral' and 'fast'.[8] Sometimes garbed as humour, at other times as affront, the intensity of the violence these women face varies. The overarching threat of violence that women invariably face for accessing public spaces gets doubly accentuated when women are read to be 'loose and immoral'.[9] Data has it that 50 per cent of all sexual violence in Delhi is committed on women from the northeastern states.[10]

In the case of the urban villages, this contradiction takes the shape of the northeast tenants becoming coveted tenants because of their 'ability' to pay higher rents even as their cultural and ethnic differences mark their bodies as polluting. Duncan McDuie-Ra discusses how some urban villages have emerged as hubs for the new arrivals from the northeast.[11] Among the two villages of interest to us, Munirka continues to be a popular place for new migrants from the northeast. The racial hostility they face here is offset by the attractions and security of a concentrated population of people from 'home'. Tenants in Munirka, a large number of whom are from the northeast, outnumber the villagers themselves now. The high concentration of racially and culturally different communities disrupts the 'order of the sensible' in these villages, which in turn stokes deep anxieties.[12] In examining the neighbourhoods in Delhi with prominent northeast subcultures, McDuie-Ra highlights a different kind of social and emotional geography that the migrants from the northeast delineate to create their own sense of community.

The northeast community is hardly an undulated one. It works with its own set of complex relationships with regard to different tribes and states. The economic location that the migrants come from also varies vastly. While fancy blue-collar jobs do privilege women and men from the northeast, it would be grossly misleading to assume that all of the migrants from there get absorbed in these jobs. Migrants from the northeast who are poorer and hail from politically disturbed areas end up doing menial jobs and running minor businesses like making and selling *momo*s, cooking 'Chinese' food in small food joints or stalls or waiting tables. Otherwise considered a reasonably open and equal society, the women from the northeast are also subject to an intimate form of violence and control in a city like Delhi. McDuie-Ra writes that northeastern women perform far better academically and have a far higher chance of landing better jobs than their male counterparts. This in turn has shaken the masculinity of the men of the community who were earlier comfortably ensconced in 'warrior' tropes or that of being 'protectors' of their community from *mayang*s, or 'outsiders'.[13]

McDuie-Ra notes that the most profound experiences of racism and discrimination take place when it comes to housing.[14] As most migrants find housing in these urban villages, it becomes essential to see how discrimination of the racial other and anxiety around the body of the 'pure self' get constituted spatially. In the next few pages, we delve into this co-constitution—of racial violence and cultural anxiety, and how these are woven into the form of everyday life, through surveillance, YouTube videos and community meetings. As we will see, violence and the anxieties produced by rent are crucially different from those produced by capital and yet, like all things contradictory between urban and rural, the violence of rent and that of capital also coexist and feed into each other.

Rent in the World of *Majboori*

Indian cities have had a history of being reproduced through prejudices. Non-vegetarians find it hard to rent places in Bangalore, single women do not find houses to rent in Chennai and Muslims do not find housing anywhere. The concept of gated communities—with private security guards, boundary walls and now even security apps—have normalised the hierarchies between insider and outsider, resident and alleged trespasser.[15] After all, internationally, too, walls, fortification and surveillance cameras have become the modes through which hierarchies manifest in cities, whether in Sao Paolo or Cape Town or even London.

In the case of the urban villages of Delhi, these hierarchies need to be reproduced in a situation where everyone lives cheek by jowl with each other. Unlike in the city outside, here hierarchies are not maintained by denying housing to people from suspect communities, because the 'other' is also a source of income. The fact that they are the 'other', the fact that they are vulnerable in the city, as this chapter will go on to show, makes it easier to extract higher rents from them. Furthermore, an average family in the village, who might be in debt to local financiers and whose primary source of income is rent, cannot afford to not rent out to the same communities that they might look down upon.

As a result, if communal social control, through *panchayat*s and *kunba*s, defines the structure of rent, as we see in the previous chapter, *majboori*, or compulsion, defines its social life. The story of rent is not subsumed by control alone. It is also a matter of compulsion that the community has to rent out their properties, and that too to people whom they perceive as polluting their society. They suffer from the guilt of having 'sold out' and feel anxious about losing any remaining engagement with their culture. Their feeling of being persecuted by city dwellers and the state only heightens this sense of injury. For an average landlord, the hubris of influence and macho pride only exists within the bubble of relationships with their tenants. These are not the Jat men with Land Rovers zipping through Delhi streets. Devoid of the cultural capital of an urbane life, their alienation cannot be solved by throwing money at it, the availability of which is anyway quite limited. Behind the veneer of masculine pride exists a far more entrenched fear of being emasculated.

The discourse about the 'polluting other' therefore becomes directly proportional to their own feeling of *majboori*. The talk of 'difference'—what they eat, the clothes they wear and how they socialise—helps portray the northeast migrants as 'antisocial'.[16] Rent fixes itself in urban villages in a very different way from capital. This does not mean that categories of race, gender and caste stop mattering, but that they reproduce themselves differently. Rent, while having generated a mode of largely risk-free wealth generation, has, in the case of these urban villages, produced a sense of both control and loss. With the demand for tenement housing in urban villages having grown manifold, immense insecurities have simultaneously been produced by the changing demographics. The new 'cosmopolitanism' of many in these villages and the diverse cultural and lifestyle practices, especially of the younger migrant population, chafe at the cultural ethos of the villagers.

I organise this chapter into three expositions of relationships between anxiety and violence. First, as a significantly high number of tenants in Munirka are from the northeastern part of India and from African countries, the discourse of cultural preservation quickly takes on a racial overtone. Second, the discourse on cultural preservation has rested traditionally on the bodies of women, around their honour—an ethos shared across the subcontinent.[17] In the villages, too, patriarchal control, especially over younger, unmarried Jat women, has been significant. Third, the presence of different kinds of racial bodies has produced anxiety over the state of the Jat male body itself. The sense of collective loss comes from the acknowledgement that they have allowed their villages to get ruined, subjected their women to the possibility of getting defiled and their bodies to be degenerated by the urban lifestyle. A constant lament about how they have allowed their own greed to wreck their idyllic, romanticised village life of the past, where everyone looked out for one another, exists alongside the pride and confidence that comes with money. At other times, the lament is overtaken by distrust towards the outsiders, that is, the tenants.

Renting to the Other?

Rajkamal Rathi, a man in his mid-30s, is a successful builder from Munirka (discussed at length in Chapter 3). Like many other affluent people from the village who have moved to middle-class localities of Delhi, he continues to hold significant economic stakes in the village real estate. As a builder, he not only reconstructed his property in Munirka but also bought more land on the fringes of other villages, such as Masoodpur, which are located across from middle-class localities. His building in Masoodpur village, a plusher variation of the 'one-room set' and more akin to a serviced apartment, has been constructed keeping in mind short-term foreign visitors to Delhi. The lobby on the ground floor of his four-storeyed building, what he calls his 'office', is where I met him. He had warned me beforehand that our conversation would get interrupted as he would have to speak to an Iraqi man—a potential tenant. He told me categorically that he does not rent out to blacks or Muslims owing to their 'dubious characters'. When the Iraqi national arrived with the property dealer, an unconvinced Rathi questioned and cross-questioned him. Rathi kept fiddling with the man's passport and peering at the visa stamp from all angles. He even held it up against the light as if he could tell that the passport was forged. The accompanying property dealer kept insisting on the validity of the passport with its Government of India stamp. Ultimately, Rathi seemed to give in and asked the tenant to move in at a particular rent. As the Iraqi national made an attempt to object, saying the rent was too high, he was reprimanded by the property dealer who indicated to Rathi and exclaimed, 'This is a multi-millionaire!' The deal was finally struck at 13,000 rupees a month. It did not seem to me like Rathi ever wanted to deny the man accommodation. But by peering at his passport, asking him all sorts of questions and generally acting reluctant, he created a situation where the Iraqi national was not in a position to bargain further; rather, he was probably thankful that he had found a place to live in. If it is within one's means, paying a couple of thousand more than the market price is not such a bad deal when you are afraid you might not find shelter in an unfamiliar city because of your identity.

The same applies to the northeastern tenants of Munirka as well. The one-room set that is otherwise rented out for 5,500–6,500 rupees per month is rented to them at 8,000–10,000 rupees, the extra being a racial surcharge. Despite the racial surcharge on the rent, however, racial discrimination does not disappear. Northeastern women are seen as having dubious moral standards, their way of dressing is considered improper and their food is considered putrid. In most cases, the poorest migrants from these communities live in the worst kind of properties. They live in the dingiest of lanes with poor ventilation because of the inflated rents they have to pay. The violence becomes far more accentuated in these pockets. Several of these young northeastern men get trapped in circuits of unemployment, and form gangs or groups to seek validation from each other in a city that is especially harsh to them. When the influx first started, many villagers thought the northeast migrants belonged to a foreign country because of their paler complexion, and that they were financially better off because of their westernised attire. They were, as a result, quoted higher rents than usual. Munirka, over the years, has come to have designated lanes run by people of the northeast for a specialised northeastern clientele with shops selling vegetables and perishable food items from the northeast, small eateries serving local northeastern food, even western clothes flown in from Bangkok, as well as specialised travel agencies.

Binod runs a small grocery store here which sells leafy vegetables and mushrooms used in Manipuri cuisine along with bamboo shoot, chillies and dry meat. Binod came to Delhi in 2004 for the civil services examinations. He used to stay in North Delhi at that time. He shifted to Munirka once he decided to open a shop after not having succeeded at the exams. The fresh vegetables he sells are shipped daily from Manipur and other parts of the northeast through airline cargo. I asked him if he had had any problems while convincing the landlord to rent the place to him. He replied in a softer voice, 'Yeah you know, he asked me the usual questions like if I am going to sell smelly stuff and things. But then he agreed.' Binod says he did not face any trouble after that. As I asked him more questions, he got uncomfortable and asked me why I need to know all this. I noticed that his wife, who was working in the shop, was also visibly uncomfortable, and decided not to probe further.

Migrants from African countries are also subjected to a similar register of stereotypes, albeit different in specifics.[18] They are often called *habshi*s[19] and thought to be loud and aggressive. Like in the case of men and women of the northeast, men from African countries are seen as being prone to addictions or as being drug peddlers, and the women as being involved in sex work. Race is not a fixed entity, and in keeping with this, racism too acquires different layers and connotations. Racial stereotypes and connotations are far more charged in villages where there are a significant number of African tenants. In the case of Munirka, where African tenants are few, the stereotypes associated with northeastern tenants are foisted on African tenants as well. Although close to 85 per cent of the northeastern tenants in Munirka are Manipuris, for the landlords, the differences between people from different regions of the northeast, different tribes and classes hardly matter. For the locals and tenants from the mainland alike, the source of the problem is the 'people from the northeast'. 'Saare bure kaam yahi karte hain,'‡ respondent after respondent said to me. At the same time, they also mentioned in the same breath, 'Saare ek jaise nahi hote.'§ In fact, their ability to stereotype gets severely constrained by their lack of knowledge of people whom they call 'chinky'. Racial strife between African and northeastern migrants, especially over women, is also not unknown.[20] Racial hierarchies and conflicts between groups representing different tribes of the northeast exist as well. YouTube is teeming with videos of fights breaking out among northeastern migrant communities and locals trying to mediate between them. The comments posted below such videos are often a slugfest where people from the northeast are seen debating the ethnicity of the people involved. It is also quite common among several communities from the northeast to refer to mainlanders as *mayang*, which has racist connotations of its own kind.[21]

Suspicion and surveillance are ordered spatially in the village. Most landlords live on the topmost floor of their buildings because of the view this vantage provides. 'Makaanmalik agar upar rahega toh use dikhega ki neeche kya ho raha hai. Neeche aane jaane se pata chalta hai ki kya chal raha hai. Agar neeche rahoge toh upar aane ka koi kaaran hi nahi hai, toh phir kirayedaar jo marzi karte hain.'** The locals have also pooled in money to instal closed-circuit television (CCTV) cameras throughout the village.

---

‡ 'They are the ones who do all the bad things.'
§ 'Not everyone is like that.'
** 'If the landlord lives above, she can see what is happening downstairs. Because you use the staircase, you know what is happening. If you live downstairs, then there is no reason for you to go up. Then the tenants do whatever they please.'

As the tenants complain of discrimination, the villagers complain of northeastern tenants spreading *aatank*, or terror, across the village. They allege that the northeastern tenants are often found drinking in the open, screaming loudly and getting into brawls late into the night. Furthermore, according to the villagers, women from the northeast solicit sex on the streets late into the night. Here, racial difference, mixed with suspicion and a deepening sense of othering, which works within both communities, becomes even more complicated by the mutual interdependence of landlords and tenants. For our purposes here, it is important to note that the nature of violence, and the racialised interaction between the communities, as evident from a series of YouTube videos, takes on a unique form which, I argue, further aids accumulation.

Youth Activism and the Politics of Loss

Jab apne ghar se bahar dekhta hoon gagan ka seena cheerta hua 8 manzila makaan dekhta hoon,
Prayatn karta hoon ki woh bachpan wala ugta sooraj dikh jaaye jo purab se mere aangan ko dekhta tha,
parantu ab toh bas un imaraton ke peeche se dabe paanv bhaag jaate dekhta hoon,
Nahi woh goolar ke pedh par panchhi, saath waale aangan ka neem, peepul par chadhi gilahri dekhta hoon,
Main toh bas ek manzil aur thoda sa chhajja badh jaaye kehte hue logon ko zameen aur aasman gherte dekhta hoon. ††

This is a poem written by one of my respondents, Shashi. A Jatav by caste and landlord by profession, his lament for the lost world is quite apparent in the verses above. Despite having done well economically, Shashi feels the irretrievable loss of the village of his childhood in the rush to build more. This poem, however, also alludes to the fragmentation of a community. As the sense of individualised private property intensified, property feuds and stealthy land grabs became the norm, changing the village irreversibly, both spatially and socially.

---

†† *When I look out of my house, I see the sky getting split across by an eight-storeyed building,*
I try to see the rising sun of my childhood, but I see it running away stealthily from behind these buildings,
I do not see the birds on the fig trees or squirrels on the neem and peepul,
People wishing to increase one storey or extending their eaves, I see them occupying earth and the sky

This feeling of loss is pivotal to the internal discourse of the villages. The villagers often speak of how they were disunited by selfish interests. Anthropologists studying kinship and village societies have argued through the ages that no community solidarity exists without competition and rivalry.[22] But for the villagers, there is a clear break in their imagination. The past is coloured with nostalgia; the present is only about selfish, narrow interest. They lament that with urbanisation, many do not see much value in sustaining their community ties. While this may be partially true, the fear of a disintegrating community seems unfounded given how the economic interests of the village are embedded in their social relationships. To fill this gap, local associations have often emerged to address the issue of their fragmenting social ties. Youth associations have been formed to work on cleanliness and gentrification. One such youth group called 'Commando' has now beautified an old dysfunctional well in Munirka. They have also posted notices about streamlining parking as well as made appeals to keep their neighbourhood clean, with the name of their group at the bottom of each such notice.

Formed in 2013, Youth Brigade Munirka (YBM) was initiated by a young Nitin Tokas; its main agenda was to address the local concern of lack of 'unity' and 'brotherhood' within the community or village in contemporary times. Initially, it was most concerned with raising local issues that affected the village and sort them out collectively. However, who constituted 'locals' kept shifting—from Jats to local villagers to anybody who lives in these villages; this idea of who is an 'insider' has been fraught with contradictions. Having begun its career aiming to promote Jat solidarity in the village, the first few meetings of YBM were rife with anxiety about the northeastern tenants. In one of the early meetings called by Nitin Tokas, it was unanimously agreed that shops would shut by 11 p.m., which would discourage tenants from roaming the streets at night. It was also decided that there should be gates at the entry points of Munirka to restrict entry after 'civil hours'. This was directed against the young northeastern tenants, who constitute more than half of all the tenants who live here and often stay out late. The demand to ensure a curfew time at 11 p.m. has, however, not found significant resonance. The gates also never materialised.

One of the pamphlets disseminated by YBM carried Nitin Tokas's poem:

Arre sambhalja ho ja chokas,
Kya kya na tune gawaya Tokas,

Culture, Gender and Belongingness?

> *Na gaaon, na peepal, na koi chaubara,*
> *Flat, makaan aur jhod bechara.*
> *Na dada, na dadi na koi kahani.*
> *Main mera gurur aur bas beimani.*
> *Parvat jo kaate toh tu basa hai,*
> *Phir bhi aapas mein kyon itna bataa hai?*[23]

> *Become wary and get in control,*
> *What all have you lost, o Tokas!*

> *No village, no trees, no sheds.*
> *Only flats, houses and the poor village pond*
> *No grandparents or their stories to tell*
> *Just me and my egotism and all the deceit*
> *You have settled after cutting through mountains*
> *Then why are you so split amongst yourselves?*

YBM's emotive plea called out landlords for their complacency, which arises from easy money like house rent. The association was initially a response to this parable of insecurity that leads to Jats being scattered and fighting with each other in the face of an impending social crisis, which threatens their existence. YBM's pamphlet alludes to the 'danger' posed both by the state and the tenants. The rhetoric of unity in the face of this 'danger' is evoked to oppose the state's tactic of trying to make the villagers legible, taxable and hence accountable (Chapter 1). It is also evoked by invoking the 'fear of numbers'[24] of tenants in general and of the northeastern tenants in particular. At the same time, however, the pamphlet and this view led to other discomforts. Men from the Jatav and Nai communities felt uncomfortable at the issue being portrayed as a Jat issue alone. For instance, Babloo, a youth activist from the Nai community whom I spoke to and whose family owns rental property in the village, was upset with Nitin Tokas for making it into a Jat issue.

Babloo eventually started his own NGO called Adhikar Darshan Manch, which wished to take up the issue of landlords' rights in response to unruly tenants. Its first campaign was an initiative around police verification of tenants. The pamphlet distributed to create awareness about this listed the rights of landlords. It opened with the fairly provocative line: 'Kirayedaar rakh rahe hain ya pangebaaz?'‡‡ (see Figure 5.2) The idea was to facilitate the process of police verification and maintain a register of tenants and their details across the village; however, it was an impossible campaign to pull off.

---

‡‡ 'Are you keeping a tenant or a troublemaker?'

After the very first meeting with the station house officer (SHO) at the local police station, who raised a few basic logistical questions, the idea fell through. Adhikar Darshan Manch also died a somewhat premature death.

Discourses on communalism, xenophobia and homophobia are mainly built around cultures of fear and narratives of pollution. The case of urban villages in that sense is not isolated. While new-found wealth has given landlords a sense of confidence, the fact that they have no choice but to rent their property

Figure 5.2 The pamphlet issued by Adhikar Darshan Manch

Source: Photo by author.

to the same people they consider depraved and dirty also generates a sense of shame. It has left them with a feeling of having compromised with their cultural ethos to make money. The landlords frequently lament how Munirka has become a den for all kinds of crime and feel helpless about not being able to control the situation. The president of the resident welfare association (RWA) and several residents claim that despite repeated complaints to the police, nothing has been done from the administration's side to control such activities. As a researcher who would conduct most of her interviews during the day, I only heard stories of what goes on in the night. How certain lanes completely transform at night with women soliciting sex and *habshi*s, or 'negros', selling drugs openly. Despite the fact that prostitution is an open secret, it only occasionally finds place in news reports of a police raid[25] or some vigilante exposé uploaded on YouTube.

The relationship between race and prostitution has historically not been a weak one. Racial difference is predicated upon sexual difference, and the history of slavery reveals just that.[26] Sexual transactions increasingly begin to sustain a region in the face of inequalities created by global and colonial forms of capitalism.[27] Migration reinforces these inequalities in different locations differently. This spate of migration also coincides with the global revaluation of skin colours and racial hierarchies within the global image market, much of which begins to find resonance within the sex market as well. Kimberley Hoang shows how Vietnamese sex workers began to copy the make-up and attire of Korean and Japanese women and not white women, for they had come to realise the value of their skin colour and facial features in the new economy.[28] Hoang shows that apart from their physical features being valorised, Vietnamese sex workers are also expected to display submissive behaviour with their clients, especially the western ones. These global images and forms of valorisation work their way into Delhi as well. Demand for women with Mongoloid features keep shooting up in the sex market, but the demand comes laced with all kinds of racialised, neo-colonial hierarchies between mainland India and the northeast.

By blaming the migrants for all the 'filth' in their society, however, the villagers neatly paper over their own complicity. An enterprise like prostitution cannot run without the knowledge of the landlords. Once you scratch the surface, out come several stories of how some landlords are indeed complicit.[29] Furthermore, locals who have moved out of the village seem to retain little stake in the village apart from collecting rent. One of my respondents tells me,

Humne kai baar jaake un makaanmalikon se baat ki, unko bataya ki unke makaan mein kya ho raha hai. Par woh kuchh nahi karte. Kehte hain hi unke upar bahot loan hai. Unko gaon ke mahaul se koi matlab nahi hai. Agar ek-ek kamre ka 25,000 rupya mile toh who humari baat kyun sunenge?§§

The involvement of locals is a public secret, but in the public discourse, the blame is squarely placed on the tenants from specific ethnic backgrounds. Apart from the racial surcharge that the northeastern tenants pay over and above their rent, prostitution becomes another way in which living labour is extracted from the racialised and sexualised body of a migrant.[30]

Masculinity at Stake

Critical race theory has consistently argued that race is not biological but rather a socially constructed phenomenon. Notions of race are associated with bodily and cultural attributes and get embodied as performances of the self. 'Koi bhi aapse baat nahi karega. Yahan sab jaat khopdi hain. Jaat khopdi samajhti hain aap?'*** a Brahmin villager had asked me when I had explained my project to him, evading the fact that they are no different as landlords. Jat men have for long been associated with an intensely masculine expression of aggression. This aggression, however, has been both a reason for derision as well as a source of their identity. For Jat men, *dabangg*—a masculine body language which evinces both pride as well as associations with power—has been both a source of fear and admiration. A village elder once explained to me what Jat pride means. 'Hum sahi kaam karne se nahi darte. Jo sahi hota hai wahi karte hain. Varna madam, kanoon todne mein humein ek minute nahi lagta.'††† *Dabangg* is essentially about power derived from one's social location, which allows one to assert oneself physically. *Dabangg* is not an attribute a poor Jat may exhibit. It is a function of power derived from wealth and social capital.

Racialised discrimination and violence is not unidirectional. The anxiety over the presence of northeastern tenants with 'loose morals' has also deeply

---

§§ 'We have gone to these landlords several times to talk, we have told them what goes on in their buildings. But they do nothing. They say they have a lot of loans to pay. They don't care about the environment of the village. If they are getting 25,000 rupees for each room, why should they listen to us?'

*** 'Nobody will talk to you. Here, everybody is "Jat headed". Do you even understand Jat headed?'

††† 'We are never scared of doing the right thing. We do what we think is right. Otherwise, Madam, we don't really take time to break the law.'

complicated the Jats' own sense of the racialised body. Therefore, *dabangg* as a term evokes these racial assertions. Apart from wealth and social capital, physical prowess is an important component of being *dabangg*. The culture of sports has now taken a backseat among the Jat youth with increased incomes, as a result of which they no longer feel they need to have jobs. Wealth is thus perceived as having harmed their physical prowess. There have been cases where groups of young Jat and northeastern men have clashed, and the Jat men have been severely thrashed. This has also added to the anxiety of their own *nasl* (breed) having degenerated. The older men, while talking about such confrontations, pooh-pooh the younger ones for having become weaker. They say, 'Hum toh apne zamane mein do-do kilo ghee roz khaate the. Inse toh 200 gram bhi nahi pachega.'††† For them, the city is also a place that has led to the degeneration of their own children. The younger ones, spoilt with excess, have now become wastrels and lack the discipline that is required to maintain strong bodies. As much as they find other racial bodies reprehensible, they are acutely aware of the decline of their own. The pursuit of money, despite its allure, is thus seen as a corrupting force in this regard as well.

The gendered aspect of this masculinity is also drawn on racial lines. The women from the northeast are as much objects of desire as they are of reprehension for the Jat men. Desire and reprehension mixed together creates its own set of insecurities about morality and the purity of their own race. Ram Pratap Tokas, a local landlord active in Congress politics, says,

> Unka pehnawa alag hai. Ab main makaan malik hoon, main unko kapdon ke liye nahi bol sakta. Aur unke culture mein hai. Hamare culture mein nahi hai. Toh kahin na kahin logon ki nazar jaati hai. Ab aap bataiye, aap itne dino se gaon mein ghoom rahi hain, aap ko kisi ne dekha?§§§

'Nazar jaana', which roughly translates into 'the eye wanders', is an interesting choice of words as opposed to the more regularly used term 'dekhna', which means 'to see'. *Nazar jaana* is a passive form, as opposed to *dekhna*, which is an active form. The responsibility of *nazar jaana*, therefore, is squarely put on the body of a woman from the northeast, and the 'eye' of the helpless Jat men is 'compelled to wander' after the body of the northeastern woman.

---

††† 'In our time, we could easily eat two kilos of clarified butter every day. These kids cannot even digest 200 grams of it.'

§§§ 'They dress differently. Now I am a landlord, I cannot tell them anything about clothes. It is in their culture, not in ours. So somehow or the other, you do end up looking. Now you tell me, you have been moving around the village for so many days. Has anybody even stared at you?'

However, barely five kilometres away from Munirka, the villagers of Shahpur Jat do not bat an eyelid at the fashion designers and their clients, often dressed in clothes that are seen as improper in Munirka. The entire narrative of moral corruption among the northeastern tenants that is rampant in Munirka breaks down in Shahpur Jat. The lifestyle that is seen as degenerate in Munirka is created and celebrated as an object of consumption in Shahpur Jat. Neither can one deny the racial underpinnings of these attitudes, nor the economic logic which is operating in the backdrop.

The Value of Daughters

'Value' as a term doubles up to not only mean something that is tied to the notion of the market, but also something that is defined by its opposition to the market. That is probably the reason anthropologists have spent so much time thinking about the two registers the term 'value' operates on. If land's value comes from the market, family values derive their importance from being outside it. 'The value of "values" in contrast lies precisely in their lack of equivalence; they are seen as unique, crystallised forms. They cannot or should not be converted into money. Nor can they be precisely compared with one another.'[31] And despite this opposition, David Graeber tells us, the term 'value' applies to both. But because value etymologically lends itself to two diametrically opposite meanings, anthropologists have been concerned with it for decades. Like economists, anthropologists too have completely ignored rent. But, I argue, rent also lends itself to diametrically opposite sensibilities, which produces its own set of conflicts.

Throughout my fieldwork, I had little access to the private spaces of the people living in Munirka and Shahpur Jat, especially those of the Jat families. As an unmarried, PhD student from JNU, already approaching her 30s, I was a threat. I had managed to meet one young woman, Rajani, who was pursuing her undergraduate studies, through one of my respondents. Chirpy and vivacious, in tight-fitting jeans and a top, she was every bit of a regular college-going kid. Families in the villages had started allowing girls to finish graduation only recently. However, these young women are mostly never allowed out unless accompanied by an older family member. Once, a boy Rajani knew in the village had offered her a lift, and that same evening, someone had come home and complained to her father that she had been seen with a boy. At the same time, however, Rajani's best friend is a boy, but she would never tell her family this because they would not understand. Daughters are protected virulently.

Culture, Gender and Belongingness? 161

But Rajani is not a coy, shy girl. She, like many other girls in the village, has been active in sports like swimming and even boxing. 'Papa ne mujhe koi chup si ladki nahi banaya.'†††† The contradiction is not entirely lost on her, however. She laughs and says, 'Korea (for sports tournaments) tak akele bhej denge, par yahan bagal mein akele nahi jaane denge.'††††

This is probably the nature of patriarchal control. It completely normalises what it cannot control, but what it can, mostly the domestic, it controls with absolute impunity. It is also the transgression of the domestic that is considered the most humiliating. The proximity of young tenants who live far from parental control, who wear clothes that they wish and date freely comes dangerously close to disrupting what the local community has held on to so tightly so far: the status quo of their women. Though the community has had to offer some concessions to the young women, their bodies continue to be the site where both culture and honour are preserved and displayed. These contradictions do nothing but reveal conflict. Sunil Khanna, in the context of the urban villages of Delhi, writes of a 'shehri Jat and dehati Jatni'—an urbanised Jat man who has access to the public as opposed to a ruralised Jat woman who is restricted to the domestic sphere.³² Radhika Govinda disagrees with this neat divide between the 'shehri Jat' and 'dehati jatni' and opts for a far more complex picture of the upward mobility of women. She argues that while women have received an education, and some of them have started working as well, they are still subject to a form of patriarchal control in the garb of 'protecting' culture.³³ She points out the tension between claiming to be 'urban' and wanting to retain their cultural ways of life across both the genders.³⁴

My conversation with Rajani was enlightening in this regard. Being her lively self, she insisted that I go with her to meet her family in our first meeting itself. I jumped at the offer. This was that rare opportunity where someone had invited me over to their home. I met her mother who was campaigning for the Bhartiya Janata Party (BJP) in the upcoming Delhi legislative assembly elections in 2015. I asked them how and when they had built their five-storeyed building and how their big *kunba* of five brothers functioned. Rajani started telling me how around the time of the property division in the late 1990s, there were a lot of fights in the family. However, her mother did not let her finish what she was saying and ended the discussion with

---

†††† 'My father has not brought me up as a quiet girl.'
†††† 'They will let you go alone all the way to Korea but won't let you go alone to a nearby place.'

'Par humme pyaar bahot hai. Humme kabhi utna man mutaav nahi hua.'‡‡‡‡ She asked me who I was going to vote for, and I responded that I would probably vote for Aam Aadmi Party (AAP). She looked disappointed and said, 'Kya faayda hua itna padh ke agar Modi, jo itna vikaas kar raha hai, uska saath na do toh?'§§§§ Her daughter cheerfully quipped at this point that JNU students would never vote for Modi because Modi does not like Muslims. Her mother's look suddenly hardened, and she asked me sternly, 'Tu ke hai?'***** Partly rattled by this sudden change in tenor, I ended up mumbling that I am a Hindu. The tension in that room was palpable by now. She smiled at me then and said to her sister-in-law, 'Mhare laga mulli hyagi.'††††† At this point, Rajani muttered to me in English, sounding embarrassed, 'This is why I do not bring my friends here.' I returned from their home shaken but fairly enthused, wanting to know more. I called Rajani later, wanting to meet up, but she told me she had exams. I called her again a few days later, and she said she was busy and that she would call me back. I phoned her back again after a few days, and this time she just did not pick up. Finally, I got the message.

The Crisis

In the years 2014 and 2015, the racial dimension that festered under the surface in these villages in everyday interactions suddenly flared up. Almost as a domino effect, in quick succession, news of racial violence in Delhi's urban villages began to make headlines. One of the most talked-about cases involved Somnath Bharti, law minister in the Delhi government at the time, who disregarded all legal procedures and raided the house of some Ugandan women in Khirki village on the charge that they had been running a prostitution racket.[35] What ensued was a high-voltage drama with the Chief Minister Arvind Kejriwal holding a *dharna* outside the Rail Bhawan in support of Somnath Bharti, a member of his cabinet. Kejriwal defended Bharti and made it a case in point to demand that police be brought under the purview of the state government. Several cases of violence against racially different migrant communities occurred around the same time. A 20-year-old man from Arunachal Pradesh, Nido Tania, was beaten to death in Lajpat

---

‡‡‡‡ 'But we share a very loving relationship. We have never had bad blood between us.'

§§§§ 'What was the point of studying so much if you don't support Modi who is doing so much development?'

***** Usually it translates into 'who' are you. But in the given context, it should be read as 'what' are you.

††††† I thought she was a Muslim.

Nagar in January 2014, which led to widespread protests across Delhi.³⁶ Locals attacked another Nigerian woman at a grocery shop in Munirka in 2014.³⁷ This was followed by another terrible incident where a young Congolese man was beaten to death in another urban village called Kishangarh in May 2016.³⁸

In this spate of violent incidents against migrants from African countries and the northeast in early 2014, there was also a case of rape of a minor Manipuri girl by a landlord's son that hit Munirka hard. In an already vitiated atmosphere, the news travelled like wildfire and led to an escalation of animosity between the Jats and the northeastern communities. Institutionalised racism, the sense of loss and a crisis of masculinity all converged at this moment of standoff. After a few days, the village RWA called a *panchayat* to discuss the 'northeast problem'. Rumours started running rife about how the *panchayat* had decided to evict the northeastern tenants and this led to a heightened sense of fear and insecurity among the latter.³⁹ Social media became instrumental in spreading both rumours and racial vitriol around this time. The northeastern tenants, deeply alarmed at the reports that the *khap panchayat* in the village had decided to throw out all of them, took the matter up with higher state officials and the police.⁴⁰ The representatives of the local RWA, however, kept denying that such a meeting had been held at all. They said it was a regular meeting where it had been decided that all shops should be shut by 11 p.m. and that CCTV cameras needed to be installed in the locality. However, there were reports in some newspapers that the villagers did indeed have a meeting where a unanimous decision was taken that those tenants who stayed out till late at night should be evicted.⁴¹ Ultimately, the matter required police intervention to engage the village representatives and the northeastern tenants in a discussion and to elicit an assurance from the villagers that they would not be evicted.

It must be kept in mind that there were people from more than one community in the *panchayat*, which unanimously passed the dictum against the northeastern residents. Even the vocal Dalits of the village, who quote Ambedkar and M. N. Srinivas in the same breath, will tell you how the 'chinky log' are morally degenerate and eat extremely foul-smelling things. They seemed to be oblivious to the irony that Dalits have historically been castigated for what they eat. Notions of 'pollution' that are the basis of caste discrimination get reinforced by the Dalits themselves here with respect to the people from the northeast. Quite predictably though, the incident of rape did not come up in any of the fieldwork conversations I conducted through the crisis. Or it was simply avoided when I did try to bring it up. The villagers argued that it was not a *khap panchayat* that had been held; going strictly by the facts, they were not wrong. In their defence, they argued that they usually refer to any community meeting as a *panchayat*. Some young men from the village were outraged by the way the news of the meeting was splashed all over the media as a *khap panchayat* and saw it as a way of maligning them. 'Hum apni sanskriti ki baat karein toh hum khap panchayati ho jaate hain,'[####] many argued. This moment of conflagration brought to the fore the slipperiness between the two institutions of *panchayat* and the RWA, where one can seamlessly transition to another, as discussed in the previous chapter. In a pamphlet circulated by the YBM, to clarify that it was not a *khap panchayat* meeting but a regular RWA meeting, an emotive statement was made about the locals being sidelined in the process of development where they have remained a semi-urban, semi-rural populace:

> Hum woh log hain jinhone sadiyon se aravali ke is kathor vaksh ko cheer kar usme apna pranad kiya … humne aapko apni bhoomi di aapke sapnon ko poora karne lie liye. Humne aapko ashray diya…. Hamari aane waali peedhi poornatah nagariya ho jayengi jisse nagaron mein hamari sanskriti ka koi chinh shesh nahi rahega, kyunki nagaron mein hamari deshbhakti ne humein alpsankhyak bana diya hai…. Is dilli ke ab hum nivasi nahi rahe. Shasan mein baithe logon ki dilli yahan ke moolnivasiyon ki nahi hai.[§§§§§]

The use of the term 'mulnivasi' is an interesting one. Translated as 'original inhabitant', the term 'mulnivasi' has been used in recent times for political mobilisation by both tribal and Dalit communities as part of their claim of being indigenous people. Though the term never really finds a place in the everyday discourse of the Jat urban villagers, its usage in the pamphlet is interesting. The emotive allegations of total annihilation at the hands of the city, of having been made into a minority and of having no representation in electoral politics are mostly rhetorical hyperbolic devices which are not factually correct. But the anger in the pamphlet was real, and it articulated the pain of being dismissed as unbecoming of the city. Jats are quite frequently derided as 'uncouth' and 'rustic' by the upper middle classes of South Delhi.

[####] 'If we speak about our culture, we become *khap panchayati*s.'
[§§§§§] 'We are those people who have for centuries been tearing apart the hard chest of the Aravalli and infusing it with our lifeblood. We have given you our land so that you could fulfil your dreams. We have sheltered you … our forthcoming generations will become entirely urban, and there will be no trace of our culture, because in the cities our patriotism has turned us into minority…. We are no longer the *mulnivasi* of Delhi. Delhi belongs to the ones sitting in power, not to the *mulnivasi*.'

Their language, their popular culture has been an object of sneer and mockery as no amount of wealth can actually replace the power of cultural capital. This claim of indigeneity could be read as a response to this kind of derision that they face.

It is interesting that 'development' and 'urbanisation' were not attacked in the pamphlet for being an economic onslaught, but a cultural one. The community's discrimination at the hands of the state seamlessly merged with how they needed to protect their 'culture' in the face of their tenants. The use of the 'indigenous argument', of being the rightful inheritors of the resources of the city and the abuse at the hands of urbanisation was their defence against allegations of racism. This feeling of victimhood mixed with the son-of-the-soil rhetoric thus became their instruments to lay claim to the city.[42] The pamphlet went on to argue, albeit without naming particular communities: 'Hum un asamajik tatvon ke ghor virodhi hain jo madyapaan ke uparaant sadakon par rakt-ranjit hinsa, yaun durachar tatha ashanti ko niyamit roop se prasarit karte hain.'[******] But drinking is not so uncommon among the villagers either. When I asked the landlords about this, one of them gruffly replied that they only drink inside their homes. Problems of alcoholism, drug abuse and domestic violence are conveniently swept under the carpet as 'private matters', and the errant northeastern tenant is marked out as the source of all the social ills of the locality.

Peter Geshiere and Francis Nyamnjoh write in the context of Cameroon that the questions of autochthony and its assertions are not remnants of the pre-modern past but rather a modern construction, which gained prominence after the 1980s.[43] The claim to autochthony in the context of the urban village in Delhi as well cannot be seen as removed from the culture of accumulation and capitalism that reigns in these villages. It must be noted that within the rhetoric of being the 'farmers who lost their land', their own history of being settlers in these villages needs to be blurred.

The two communities, distrustful of each other and yet bound by compulsions of their own, are forced to live together. While the landlords are dealing with the fear that their small communities will alienate them from their homes, the migrants have the opposite concern. It is an excessively alien, harsh city that many are compelled to begin calling 'home'. Having lived in these villages for long, having started their businesses of grocery, vegetables and meat to be able to cook their own food, and having built social networks to create a community, despite all their precarity, the migrants are here to stay.

[******] 'We oppose the anti-social elements who regularly, after getting drunk, spread bloody violence, sexual misconduct and disturbance on the streets.'

The landlords too, with their own economic compulsions and opportunities, will continue to rent to the same set of people they seemingly despise. The fear of violence, which exists at the level of potentiality, rarely flares into a full-blown confrontation. This violence, underpinned by social conflicts that constitute the city space, when deployed differentially in spaces like Munirka and Shahpur Jat, marks out the geography of accumulation. If politics is the *continuation of war by other means*, then the job of power is to reinscribe force in institutions, social inequalities, language and bodies of individuals.[44] There are sporadic cases of violence, ending up in street brawls or scuffles, but violence in its full-blown form takes place only once in a while—like it did in the case of the rape of the minor girl and the resulting standoff between the local landlords and the northeastern tenants. More often than not, the violence exists not in actuality but in the realm of possibility, always threatening to become real. But what this potentiality of violence allows for is extraction.

The Violence Will Be Televised

Community solidarity, demographic anxiety and even violence seem to be rooted in the way rent operates in the urban villages. This book, however, is not meant to be a study in Marxist determinism, and I am acutely aware of the dangers of falling into such a trap. It is certainly not a one-way traffic where economy precedes everything else. As we have seen, cultural and social norms have a way of determining the nature of rent and how it operates. Be it their proximity to land, or how they negotiated different businesses as the economy changed contours to how rent now works today, I argue that the people are not passive actors condemned to a historic condition. Rent is, therefore, not merely a historic condition. Rent as a social relation owes its genesis to their system of *bhaichara* land tenure, but it evolves its way into contemporary economy to consolidate itself both in Nehruvian command economy and now, in neoliberal economy through human agency.

Geographies of neoliberal capital distinguish the wealthy from the dispossessed, the white from the black. It has increasingly produced segregated cities, cities with privatised security, barbed wires, security cameras and coded locks. Geographies of rent, at least in the case of the urban villages, do not segregate, despite heightened mistrust. We witness here how creating rent becomes an entrepreneurial act, where violence works as a catalyst. However, I would refrain from arguing that questions of caste solidarity and claims of autochthony and racism are used instrumentally for economic purposes. What is important here is to understand how questions of autochthony and belongingness, which might be pre-market in their origin, work alongside the logic of capital. Racism and xenophobia are not products of rational economic decisions, but there are ways in which they do work together. This kind of extraction happens in the nooks and crannies of 'big' capital. This extraction would not have been possible if these village lands had seamlessly entered financial markets. The villages, however, do not see this as a limitation but something desirable. It is only in this 'nook and cranny' that they are able to tap into the opportunities thrown up by capital more or less firmly within the ambit of community pride.

By mid-2018, a new vigilante group had formed in Munirka, which wanted to take matters into their own hands. Tired of the inactivity of the police and the unwillingness of the respective landlords to control their tenants, this group resolved to take care of law-and-order issues late in the night. They patrol the streets in the night, force shops to shut down at 11 p.m. and confront 'troublemakers' who are found openly drinking and creating a ruckus. While much of the group is made up of young men, some older, middle-aged men too are part of this group. 'Hum poochte hain logon se woh kahan ja rahe hain. Koi raat ko dawai lene nikla ho toh usko manahi nahi hai. Koi office se nikla ho toh manahi nahi hai, koi behen kaam se aa rahi hai toh usko bhi manahi nahi hai.'††††† What this group does not acknowledge is the fact that the real problem is in racially profiling people and subjecting them to a series of questions on an everyday basis. Many of these encounters are diligently recorded and posted on YouTube.

One video shows three local men accusing two men from the northeast that they killed a pigeon with a slingshot. The video goes with the tagline 'peigons [sic] ko maar kar khate hain ye log'.‡‡‡‡ Another video is sensationally titled 'Dog Eaters of Munirka'. The video is a long, CCTV grab that shows four men walking by, one of whom is carrying a dog. The videos are often about northeastern tenants being accosted, interrogated and being made to apologise for drinking in public and in parking lots. Other videos show local shops being raided for keeping alcohol. There are even some where people are stopped, interrogated and their bags checked to reveal alcohol bottles inside. Some other videos are taken from afar and posted as 'kinnaron ka aatank',§§§§§

---

††††† 'We ask people where they are going. If someone is stepping out at night to get medicines, there is no problem. If someone has left from office, there is no problem. If a "sister" [woman] is coming back home from work, there is no problem.'
‡‡‡‡ 'They eat peigons [sic] after killing them.'
§§§§§ 'The terror of the transgenders.'

allegedly of transgenders and women soliciting sex work, flashing at men or engaging in loud brawls. While videos bear witness, what is recorded and what is edited out, and the titles and taglines or descriptions that accompany them, are intended to inspire emotions such as hate, disgust, bravado and probably even titillation. It sometimes becomes hard to distinguish these emotions from one other. They are repetitive, trying to reiterate one trope: that of brave, *dabangg* Jat men who are never scared to do the right thing, who are out to clean their society of the 'aatank' of the errant, criminal tenants from the northeast and Africa and sometimes even transgendered people. Nelli Kambouri and Pavlos Hatzopoulos argue that violence is mediated through repetition in the world of YouTube. In the context of generating violence through videos, they write that the latter 'can be cut to pieces, re-assembled, commented on, replicated as many times as possible, and might still be the same'.[45]

Conclusion

The nature of this subliminal violence is such that its visible forms might be sporadic and such vigilante groups ephemeral. Violence, however, continues to fester under the surface of the skin of the locality. This mistrust is, nevertheless, productive for rent—more so in the case of cartelised social control that we see here. Xenophobia and social control go hand in hand to produce extractive relationships as much as they do to produce anxieties about the futures and the bodies of migrant labour. In effect, inequality and violence do not creep into our urban forms; they go on to build these urban forms. Rent goes on to define their social structures, their anxieties, their aspirations and even their built forms. The architecture here is not that of fear,[46] as much as it is of the mistrust which necessitates the surveillance of tenants. The perpetuation of a strong community that exhibits its dominance and re-embeds security in the architecture of these villages does not necessarily slow down the process of accumulation but instead enhances it. The culture of fear and the threat of being evicted has normalised sudden hikes in rent, increased electricity bills and so on to thrive. Thus, the already existing feelings of racism and hierarchy reinforce the process of accumulation; indeed, the fear of violence and caste domination and the process of accumulation are not antagonistic to each other.

The story of rent in its social life, as we have seen, meanders through institutions like caste, racism, domination and exploitation, and is experienced through fear, violence and claims of autochthony. The land being owned by 'villagers' allows them a sense of social cohesion that seems like a continuity from primordial times. And yet we know that this continuity is not natural. Rent, and the way it operates on an urban landscape, has only enlivened this sense of social cohesion. But the same sense of social cohesion, based on caste lines, begins to loosen up as people who are not Jats start to own property. The cartel and the joint-stock company forms are not merely instrumental but rather a deeply ingrained socio-historical form as well. The identity of a landlord that is so closely associated with ownership of land, in the post-liberalisation era, does not remain impervious to how land ownership changes with new market forces. But the use value of land, as much as it is a cause of their collective sense of loss, also pushes up the exchange value of land further. It also shows how global capital has been taken, twisted and appropriated to make global capital their own. But *that* has come with its own set of costs.

Notes

1. Nikhil D. and Tenzin Tsundue Phunkhang, *Boys of Safdarjung*, short film, https://www.vice.com/en_in/article/xwmb5n/boys-of-safdarjung-turns-a-queer-eye-on-delhis-northeast-community (accessed 29 September 2018).
2. Angela McRobbie, 'Reflections on Feminism, Immaterial Labour and the Post-Fordist Regime', *New Formations* 70 (Winter 2010): 71.
3. Maurizio Lazzarato, 'Immaterial Labour', in *Radical Thought in Italy: A Potential Politics*, ed. Paolo Virno and Michael Hardt (Minneapolis: University of Minnesota Press, 1996), 140.
4. Carla Freeman, *High Tech and High Heels in the Global Economy: Women, Work, and Pink-Collar Identities in the Caribbean* (Durham: Duke University Press, 2000).
5. It is not uncommon to see advertisements and posters which demand 'smart and good-looking' women candidates across India. Many of them also specify age bracket.
6. Not just Delhi, but even cities as far as Thiruvananthapuram in Kerala have a sizeable number of workers from the northeast, especially in salons. See Bengt G. Karlsson and Dolly Kikon, 'Wayfinding: Indigenous Migrants in the Service Sector of Metropolitan India', *South Asia: Journal of South Asian Studies* 40, no. 3 (2017).
7. Keya Bardalai, 'Malls versus Streets: North-Eastern Women between Modernity and Marginality', *South Asia: Journal of South Asian Studies* 42, no. 9 (2019).
8. Ibid.
9. Ibid., 5.
10. Jelle J. P. Wouters and Tanka B. Subba, 'The "Indian Face", India's Northeast, and "The Idea of India"', *Asian Anthropology* 12, no. 2 (2013): 134.

11. McDuie-Ra, *North East Migrants in Delhi*, 65.
12. E. G. Dattatreyan, 'Policing the "Sensible" in the Era of YouTube: Urban Villages and Racialised Subjects in Delhi', *Television and New Media* 21, no. 4 (2019).
13. Duncan McDuie-Ra, 'Being a Tribal Man from the North-East: Migration, Morality, and Masculinity', *South Asian History and Culture* 4, no. 2 (2013).
14. McDuie-Ra, *North East Migrants in Delhi*, 98.
15. M. A. Falzon, 'Paragons of Lifestyle: Gated Communities and the Politics of Space in Bombay', *City and Society* 16, no. 2 (2004); Stanely D. Brunn, 'Gated Minds and Gated Lives as Worlds of Exclusion and Fear', *GeoJournal* 66, nos. 1–2 (2006).
16. Caldeira borrows from Michael Taussig to speak of how narratives produce violence. Going back to the period of colonialism, Taussig speaks of how the colonial moment itself was produced by misunderstandings which reproduced the nature of colonialism. These fables, sharply demarcated along the lines of 'good' and the 'evil', produce prejudices which in turn affect social behavior, public policy and political behaviour. See Teresa Caldeira, *City of Walls: Crime, Segregation, and Citizenship in São Paulo* (Los Angeles: University of California Press, 2001), 34–40.
17. Much has been written on the question of women's honour and the making of the national movement. See Partha Chatterjee, 'The Nationalist Resolution of the Woman's Question', in *Recasting Women: Essays in Colonial History*, ed. Kumkum Sangari and Sudesh Vaid (New Delhi: Zubaan Books, 2006). For the creation of the modern state, see Ritu Menon and Kamla Bhasin, 'Recovery, Rupture, Resistance: Indian State and Abduction of Women during Partition', *Economic and Political Weekly* 28, no. 17 (1993); and from the perspective of the creation of the Hindu nationalist project, see Tanika Sarkar, *Hindu Wife, Hindu Nation, Community, Religion and Cultural Nationalism* (New Delhi: Permanent Black, 2001).
18. Rohit Negi and Persis Taraporewala, 'Window to a South–South World: Ordinary Gentrification and African Migrants in Delhi', in *Migration and Agency in a Globalizing World*, ed. Cornelissen S. and Mine Y, 209–230. London: Palgrave Macmillan, 2018.
19. 'Habshi' is Arabic for Abyssinian. But today, it works more as a racist epithet.
20. Duncan McDuie-Ra, 'Leaving the Militarized Frontier: Migration and Tribal Masculinity in Delhi', *Men and Masculinities* 15, no. 2 (2012).
21. Duncan McDuie-Ra. *Debating Race in Contemporary India* (London: Palgrave, 2015), 3.
22. Kathleen Fordham Norr, 'Factions and Kinship: The Case of a South Indian Village', *Asian Survey* 16, no. 12 (1976); George Clement Bond, 'Kinship

and Conflict in a Yombe Village: A Genealogical Dispute', *Africa: Journal of the International African Institute* 42, no. 4 (1972). Both argue that factions within kinship structures depend on specific lineages, and to interactions of rules and pragmatic behaviour of choice. Marshall Sahlins writes how kinship that creates membership on the basis of ancestry, residence, commensality, land use ... engenders a sense of equality. He further writes, 'Because of the equality, a certain measure of conflict—ranging from studied distance to violent rupture—is likely wherever the primary group holds offices, privileges, or objects of differential value." Marshall Sahlins, 'What Kinship Is (Part Two)', *Journal of the Royal Anthropological Institute* 17, no. 2 (2011): 235.
23. Youth Brigade Munirka Pamphlet, dated 13 October 2013.
24. Arjun Appadurai, *Fear of Small Numbers: An Essay on the Geography of Anger* (Durham: Duke University Press, 2006).
25. In the year 2018, the Delhi Commission for Women and Delhi Police were able to bust a trafficking ring that had brought 16 women of Nepali origin to Munirka on the pretext of finding them jobs in the Gulf.
26. Kamala Kempadoo elaborates on the sexual nature of slavery, which not only encouraged sex slavery but also controlled procreation among slaves through 'female breeders' and 'black male studs'. Kamala Kempadoo, *Sexing the Caribbean: Gender, Race and Sexual Labour* (New York: Routledge, 2004), 40. During colonial times, this took shape through oriental discourses around native women and prostitution for the military and so on.
27. Kempadoo, *Sexing the Caribbean*, 3.
28. Kimberley Kay Hoang, *Dealing in Desire: Asian Ascendancy, Western Decline, and the Hidden Currencies of Global Sex Work* (Los Angeles: University of California Press, 2015), 126–29.
29. Staff Correspondent, 'Delhi: 24-yr-old Raped by Landlord in Munirka', *Hindustan Times*, 7 October 2014, https://www.hindustantimes.com/delhi/delhi-24-yr-old-raped-by-landlord-in-munirka/story-as7r9JGjm Gxp3HlN7MPuXM.html (accessed 27 September 2019).
30. Ranabir Samaddar makes the connection between migration, trafficking and extraction of living labour. See Ranabir Samaddar, *Karl Marx and the Postcolonial Age* (Cham: Palgrave Macmillan, 2018), 121.
31. Graeber, 'It Is Value That Brings Universes into Being', 224.
32. Sunil Khanna, 'Shahri Jat and Dehati Jatni: The Indian Peasant Community in Transition', *Contemporary South Asia* 10, no. 1 (2001).
33. Radhika Govinda, '"First Our Fields, Now Our Women": Gender Politics in Delhi's Urban Villages in Transition', *South Asia Multidisciplinary Academic Journal* 8 (2013).

34. Ibid., 13.
35. Zee Media Bureau, 'Somnath Bharti`s Midnight Raid: African Woman Forced to Urinate in Public', *Zee News*, 18 January 2014, https://zeenews.india.com/news/delhi/somnath-bhartis-midnight-raid-african-woman-forced-to-urinate-in-public_905018.html (accessed 19 January 2014). This also emphasises that the urban villages are not the only place where Africans and northeasterners are harassed and discriminated against. Racism is widespread in Delhi and beyond. The argument about racism and accumulation that I am trying to make, however, is limited to these villages to show how these two come together.
36. Tanima Biswas, 'Daylight Attack with Iron Rods Killed College Student Nido Tania', *NDTV*, 10 February 2014, https://www.ndtv.com/india-news/daylight-attack-with-iron-rods-killed-college-student-nido-tania-550373 (accessed 22 November 2016).
37. Shibaji Roychoudhury, 'Racist Mob? No Worse than What Africans Face Every Day in Delhi', *Scroll*, 2 October 2014, https://scroll.in/article/681845/racist-mob-no-worse-than-what-africans-face-every-day-in-delhi (accessed 23 May 2016).
38. Express News Service, 'Congolese Youth Beaten to Death in New Delhi, One Suspect Detained', *Indian Express*, 22 May 2016, https://indianexpress.com/article/india/india-news-india/delhi-african-youth-beaten-to-death-in-vasant-kunj-2811692/ (accessed 23 May 2016).
39. The decision never really came through and could not be implemented because of the media hype that followed. Also, such *panchayat*s on evicting the northeastern tenants have taken place before, but because of the presence of the Dalits who opposed it on grounds of feasibility, it could never be implemented. See Chapter 4 where this is discussed.
40. Jayashree Nandi and Somreet Bhattacharya, 'Anti-northeast Fiat in Munirka, Cops Step In', *Times of India*, 18 February 2014, https://timesofindia.indiatimes.com/city/delhi/anti-northeast-fiat-/articleshow/30580917.cms (accessed 19 February 2014); Binalakshmi Nepram, founder of the Manipur Women Gun Survivors Network, was quoted as saying

> The first panchayat meeting took place on 9th February after the 14-year-old from Manipur was raped. Thanks to media pressure, the rapist was caught. That was a first. At the first meeting, some of the people said that the people from northeast are 'gandey log' (dirty people). Then another meeting was held on Sunday, where they said they wanted to rid of all 'gandey log'. This is similar to the Khirki incident, and they have said that Northeast girls are loose and of bad character.

See Shruti Dhapola, 'Munirka's Campaign against 'Gandey Log' of Northeast', Firstpost, 19 February 2014, https://www.firstpost.com/india/delhi-munirkas-campaign-against-gandey-log-of-northeast-1396833.html (accessed 20 February 2014).

41. Nandi and Bhattacharya, 'Anti-northeast Fiat'.
42. Rhetorically, the influx of Punjabis into Delhi post partition and the resettlement of Tibetans and Bangladeshis is seen as an attack on the Jat existence and the traditional claims that the Jats had on the city. However, what this rhetoric does not acknowledge is that land value could not have increased without the influx of migrants.
43. Peter Geschiere and Francis Nyamnjoh, 'Capitalism and Autochthony: The Seesaw of Mobility and Belonging', in *Millennial Capitalism and the Culture of Neoliberalism*, ed. Jean Comaroff and John Comaroff (New York: Duke University Press, 2001).
44. Michel Foucault, *Society Must Be Defended: Lectures at the Collège de France, 1975–76* (New York: Picador, 2003), 16.
45. Nelli Kambouri and Pavlos Hatzopoulos, 'Making Violent Practices Public', in *Video Vortex Reader: Responses to YouTube*, ed. Geert Lovink and Sabine Nierderer (Amsterdam: Institute of Network Cultures, 2008), 130.
46. Steven Flusty, *Building Paranoia: Proliferation of Interdictory Space and the Erosion of Spatial Justice* (West Hollywood, CA: Los Angeles Forum for Architecture and Urban Design, 1994).

6

The Fringes of the Cartel
How the Marginalised Become Landlords

Writing about cooperation and solidarity means writing at the same time about rejection and mistrust.

—Mary Douglas, *How Institutions Think*

Lakshmi is a woman in her seventies who belongs to the Nai community. She came to Munirka as an 11-year-old bride in the 1960s. Her husband had a barber shop in Tilak Nagar, West Delhi, before he got a job with the Central government. When I spoke to her, Lakshmi seemed oddly fixated on high-lying areas 'jahan paani nahi jamta'.[*] She muses that the capital was moved to Delhi from Calcutta only because the city is situated at a height and therefore water does not stagnate in Delhi. Munirka, according to her, is also a far better place than a suburb like Dwarka for the same reason. Even her memories of her natal place, a village near Palam, are strongly tied to recollections of waterlogging. This impression of a relationship between topography of land and its value stood out for me during our conversation because it was so unique. No other person I had spoken to had made such associations.

I soon got a better sense of the reason for Lakshmi's preoccupation with low-lying areas and waterlogging. She owns a building right in the middle of Munirka village, which one can access only after crossing several meandering narrow lanes. Left to myself, I would never be able to trace my steps back to her house. She lives with her son on the ground floor of the same building. The floors above have been rented out. There is no separate entrance, so there is a constant flow of people going up and down through the living room. In order to ensure that the lanes were not awash with rain and sewage water during the monsoons, resurfacing was done repeatedly to make them higher, so much so that Lakshmi's ground floor has now sunk to a level below that of the lane. This is not a problem unique to Munirka. Unauthorised colonies

---

[*] 'Where stagnant water does not collect.'

across Delhi, built on cheaper, unused, low-lying land increasingly suffer from the same issue.[1] Lakshmi's house faces chronic seepage on the ground floor, and she fears that the entire structure and its foundation have considerably weakened. When we were speaking, she was particularly anxious about a wall that seemed to be slowly tilting towards the inside of the building. She was desperate to secure a loan to carry out necessary repairs. Having already lost close to 5 lakh rupees in committees, she was looking for other avenues to achieve this goal.

Lakshmi kept asking Babloo, who had accompanied me to her house, if he knew of ways to secure housing loans at cheaper rates. She also wanted to buy some property in Faridabad. Babloo responded that he wanted to buy land in Jhajjhar as well, but land prices were currently too high. It was evident to me that Lakshmi was torn between restoring her village property and buying new property elsewhere. There was no way for her to do both. But in order to accomplish either, she needed a housing loan. As we have seen before, Babloo's own story is also about making tough choices of a similar kind. In Chapter 3, we met Babloo's mother who had painstakingly managed to buy property in order to secure a better future. As a trade-off, the family had not been able to fund their son's education. That remorse continues to grate on her till date. Both Babloo and Lakshmi belong to the Nai caste. In fact, the Jatavs, Nais and Kumhars of the village have been able to capitalise on the real estate boom that Munirka witnessed, but this mobility has come at a price. They have had to make a series of difficult choices and continue to live in the shadows of decrepit infrastructure and heavy interest on loans. In the next few pages, we try to trace the journey of some of these communities as they turned into landlords, and what that has meant for them.

Dalits and Their Dispossession

We have earlier alluded to how land acquisition had a very different impact on the Dalits of the village and this needs to be reiterated here. The systematic alienation of depressed classes from their agrarian status during colonial times had a far-reaching consequence. With no land to call their own, Dalits had no stake in much of the wrangling over the compensation to be received. All the same, land acquisition had the impact of accentuating the differences that already existed between the Jats and the Dalits. From the land records, it seems that the system of tenancy was not very popular, at least on paper. Almost all the agricultural land was designated under the category of *khudkasht*, or to be self-cultivated.[2] Many Jatavs, Nais and even Balmikis were either marginal farmers or landless agricultural labourers on lands owned by the Jats. And more often than not, their presence was not even recorded in the land revenue documents.

The presence of Chamars[3] as both occupancy and non-occupancy tenants has been indisputably true across Uttar Pradesh in the 19th century.[4] The Khatik, Lohar and Kumhar communities too have a history of working as agricultural labourers for the Jats.[5] But Chamars were the primary agricultural labourers along with people from the Balmiki caste.[6] Under the Punjab Land Alienation Act, which facilitated the initial acquisition of land around 1957–58, there was no provision made for occupancy tenants. So even when some individuals from the Nai and Jatav communities were able to produce documents which proved that they were indeed occupancy tenants, their claims were turned down.[7] But soon enough, the rights of occupancy tenants came to be recognised. By 1963, the Delhi Land Reforms Act had taken over and had made provisions for compensation for occupancy tenants as well. The award from the year 1963 stated that in the case of occupancy tenants, the compensation would be divided in the ratio of 4:12, whereby 4 annas of a rupee would go to the landlord and 12 annas would go to the occupancy tenant.[8] While it is not very clear from the land acquisition records how many occupancy tenants were awarded the compensation, there are traces that probably such claims were rejected. A Jamadar Manphool (possibly a Balmiki) had claimed 17,000 rupees per *bigha* as compensation in the year 1960, but the claim was rejected because of lack of evidentiary proof.[9] One can only surmise that Jamadar Manphool was not the only one whose claim was turned down. The lack of evidentiary proof only furthered the marginalisation of these already marginalised communities in a variety of ways, land being one of them.

The Jatavs, Nais and Balmikis of the village had little land to seek compensation for. They were either landless peasants or marginal farmers and, at times, occupancy tenants, with little documentary proof. When the Jats were quibbling over compensation and land values (as we saw in Chapter 1), the Jatavs, Nais and Balmikis were dealing with a different situation. Their lives were being profoundly altered as the *shamilat deh*, the parts that the Jatavs were settled on, was also being acquired. In 1961, the Jatavs, who were residents of Khasra no. 825 in Munirka[10] put in a request with the land acquisition collector for their *khasra* to not be acquired.[11] The award notes 'Hukam Singh, Bihari Lal, Ram Kishan, Shankar Lal, Kundan Lal etc. etc. Harijans[12] and other non land owners of the village' as people who had requested the exemption. Clearly their request was not met, and the land was acquired.

But while the Jatavs were making requests that their homestead land be exempted for acquisition, the Jats were claiming that compensation for their share of the *shamilat deh* be anything between 30 rupees to 50 rupees per square yard. It is not clear if compensation was ever paid for the *shamilat deh* land, but what is evident is that the acquisition turned several Dalits into encroachers overnight. The land revenue records even took cognizance of this 'occupation' by using the phrase *hasberasad kabza*, or encroachment by multiple individuals. Referring back to Chapter 1, we can see how a socially recognised *kabza* by the Dalits was turned into an illegal one overnight at this time. In the Jamabandi register of Munirka, till date, the residential part of the village, where the Dalits mostly live, is marked as *hasberasad kabza*.

Clearly the Dalits of the village feel insecure about their ownership not being recognised by the state. The Jats on the other hand, they allege, not only got compensated for their land but also continue to have control over it. Dharamveer, one of the local activists, argued, 'Hum sainkron saalo se reh rahe hain. Par court keh dega ki aap unauthorised ho. Iski muawaza jaato ne le li hai. Par kabza bhi nahi chhora. Khet ka muawaza le liya aur phir market e bhi daal di.'† On the one hand, their occupation of the village land, earlier understood as legitimate, was suddenly illegitimate in the eyes of the law. On the other, as land values transformed rapidly, the marginalised villagers found it extremely difficult to hold on to their establishments on the fringe, or *phirni*, land of the village. In order to understand the impact of these developments better, I trace the journeys of two Dalit caste groups—Jatavs and Balmikis—to show how they fared in this urbanising landscape.

Though the chapter is mainly about the two Dalit groups, there are references to other caste groups as well who are not Dalits. For instance, there are references to Nais who are not Dalits but Kamin caste groups that have traditionally served the Jats and Brahmins. Today, they are classified among the other backward classes (OBCs) in Delhi. Though the Jats consider them lower in social status than themselves, the Kumhars and Nais are ritually higher than both the Dalit groups—Jatavs and Balmikis. Kumhars are traditional potters. Nais have historically worked as barbers.

In the *jajmani* system, however, Nais were also responsible for acting as a conduit for marriage proposals. In the case of Munirka, until very recently, one member of the Nai community would be a designated *hanatiwada*,

---

† 'We have lived here for hundreds of years. But the court will say that you are unauthorised. The Jats have already been compensated for this land. And did not give up their *kabza*. They took compensation money for their farms and then later went about setting up markets.'

a person who would go around the village beating a drum to inform people of *panchayat* meetings and such. Even though Nais are not Dalits, their historic dependence on the landed Jats has kept them marginalised. Not having much land to begin with, their choices for social mobility have been few. Though this chapter mostly speaks of the two Dalit castes, Jatavs and Balmikis, and their internal differences, it is important to keep in mind these other castes, Nais and Kumhars, who may not be Dalits but share the same marginalities in varying degrees.

Collective Memories of the Jatavs

There are numerous stories of forcible dispossession and land grab by the Jats. Dalits in the village allege that the rich landowners also forcibly occupied vacant spaces lying within the village and later constructed buildings there. As the rocky and uneven land on the southern fringe of the village that faces Jawaharlal Nehru University (JNU) rose in value after liberalisation in the 1990s, these areas too became subject to systematic land grabs and speculation. This part of Munirka village, until the early 1990s, had remained an area occupied by the Jatavs and Kumhars precisely because of its rough and uneven terrain. Given its height and rocky topography, water had always been a major concern here. The Jatavs remember having collectively dug a well in the southern craggy end by cutting through a 20-feet-wide rock face. But that community well has now been subsumed into a six-storeyed rental building overlooking JNU.

The Jatavs have a very different memory of Delhi villages. They are suspicious of the popular Jat oral narrative of two brothers arriving from nowhere and then slowly taking the area over from a Muslim nobleman. 'Aap hi bataiye, kaun doodhwala udhaar de-dekar aajtak zameen ka maalik bana hai?' they ask me.‡ Another elderly Jatav man also alludes to foul play. 'Brahmin bahot kam hai. Kshatriya, Vaishya yahan nahi hai, Baniya bhi koi nahi tha. Ab ye zamindar, zamin ke maalik jaat kaise ban gaye, pata nahi. Ye zamin to musalmano ke naam thi.'§

Their understanding of caste geographies is also different. The fact that they are in the southern part of the village is not a coincidence. Himmat Singh, a Jatav man who quotes Ambedkar verbatim, loves to hold court and tell stories.

---

‡ 'You tell me. Which milkman has ever become a landowner just by lending money?'
§ 'Brahmins are very few. Kshatriya, Vaishya are not here. Not even Baniyas. Now how did they become landowners, we don't know. These lands used to belong to the Muslims.'

A staunch believer in Ambedkarite politics and a critic of Hinduism, he converted to Buddhism after his retirement. Himmat Singh quotes *Discovery of India* by Jawaharlal Nehru to argue that all the Dalit communities were settled towards the southern direction of any region. The non-Aryans, the defeated community, had escaped to the south, he says. 'Ravan bhi Dakshin ka raja tha,'** he adds. The south of Delhi, in their collective memory, by extension, was the turf of the Dalits. They remember Mochi Bagh as a village consisting of Chamars, which was acquired, turned into an upper-middle-class government residential locality and renamed a more respectable 'Moti Bagh'.

Growing up in the 1960s, Himmat Singh was part of the glorious age when the villages of Delhi were waking up to the power of Dr Ambedkar. 'Yeh gaon hi shudron ka hai. Jaat bhi shudron mein hi aate hain,'†† he tells me. 'Jat aur Jatav mein dosti hamesha se thi. Par brahmanvaad tha, us wajah se untouchability bhi zoron par thi,' he adds.‡‡ The Dalits were not allowed to use the *johad*, or the pond. Himmat Singh insists that despite the prevalence of untouchability, the Jats considered Jatavs closest to being their equals. While reminiscing about how the Jatavs could not use particular wells and had to face humiliation at the hands of the Jats, he says in the same breath, 'Jatav Samaj pehle se hi kranti karti aayi hai.'§§ He spoke of moments when the Jats were collectively challenged by the Jatavs when the latter took out Holi or wedding processions. In their local legends, Birma Pehelwan, a Jatav bodybuilder in Munirka, epitomises their pride. Old Jatav men, who still use Birma Pehelwan's house as a space for community gathering, to play cards or to just chit-chat, speak of his prowess as being unmatched by any Jat wrestler. He was the only Jatav who could arrange to have an elephant for his son's wedding procession. In his honour, Birma Pehelwan's house has been left untouched.

The Jatavs also maintain that despite the prevalence of untouchability in the past, the Jats never resorted to the kind of caste violence that make headlines in Uttar Pradesh till date. As I was speaking to them, I got a sense of a complex relationship between the Jats and the Jatavs through history. Despite having faced untouchability, they consider Jats at par with themselves,

---

** 'Ravan was also the king of the South.' In *Ramayana*, an important epic in Hindu mythology, Ravan was the king of Lanka, who was defeated by Ram, the Hindu God.

†† 'This village belongs to the Shudras. The Jats also fall within the Shudras.'

‡‡ 'Jats and Jatavs have always been friendly. But there was Brahminism, and that is why untouchability was heavily practised.'

§§ 'The Jatav community has been doing revolutions from the beginning.'

as Shudras. I wondered if perhaps their current economic confidence might have coloured their memories of the past.

The Jatavs are clearly a proud lot. Throughout north India, they have been at the centre of social movements around caste.[13] The impact of Ambedkarite politics has had an impact on their social mobility and caste consciousness. Speak to any Jatav from the villages and they will tell you how many Jatav Central government officers and lawyers come from the village. During my conversations with them, every now and then, I heard someone say, 'Unke [Jaats] paas zameen zyada ho sakti hai, par stamp lagwane unhe hamare hi paas aana hota hai.'**** Himmat Singh recalls how he first heard of Babasaheb (Dr B. R. Ambedkar) around 1956, when the latter passed away. Himmat Singh was 14 years old at that time and he clearly remembers people mourning Babasaheb's death and reflecting on how the 'Doctor' had done so much for their community. The consciousness that education is their way out of discrimination seems to have seeped fast among Jatav boys growing up here in the 1950s and 1960s. Himmat Singh's own struggle to study irrespective of financial and social obstacles speaks volumes. He managed to finish his LLM while holding a job and taking care of a family. He tells a fascinating tale involving an interview with Upendra Baxi, the then vice chancellor of Delhi University, to get admission for a PhD degree. Several individuals I spoke to who belonged to the older generation remember this phase as nothing less than a period of social revolution. Some of them even turned into cultural activists.

Dharamveer, another social activist from the Jatav community, remembers with immense pride the plays he wrote and directed to be performed for the Dalit community. He recalls having written plays against superstition, Hinduism and the caste system. Himmat Singh recalls how younger men would regularly go to Ambedkar Bhavan in Karol Bagh to be groomed by senior Ambedkarites. They were expected to later work for the social upliftment of the Jatav community with the teachings of Ambedkar as their touchstone. In their collective memory, this was a golden period when Jatavs became 'jagruk', or aware. They started to speak the language of rationality and fight superstition. Women too came out of their homes and regularly took part in these meetings.

**** 'They [Jats] may have more land, but they have to come to us for stamping [affidavits].' The reference is to being a class one gazetted officer. Class one gazetted officers are authorised to attest the authenticity of documents and vouch for the truthfulness of individuals for government purposes.

The community has vivid memories of the Buddha Vihar, the Buddhist temple, being built through the concerted effort of the community by the latter half of the 1970s. 'Hum tab chhote the, par apne sar par eent utha kar le jaate the,'††† Kishan Kumar recollects. Till date, many Jatavs, especially the older ones, who were young men in the 1960s and 1970s, identify themselves as social workers, reformers and thinkers. When the Buddha Vihar was built, it was an important source of their community pride—a marker of Dalit assertion. But this period of social revolution did not last very long. They are now bitter about how the community has lost the zeal for social change and have instead turned against each other for petty gains. But ultimately, it was a land dispute that splintered the Jatav solidarity.

The Feud over Buddha Vihar

The Jatavs, inspired by the teachings of Ambedkar and Buddhism, had started doing their own *Buddha Vandana* (Prayers for Lord Buddha) in the village in the 1960s. Together, they started the local chapter of the Buddhist Society of India (BSI) in 1967. In the absence of an assigned space, they would take turns to hold prayer meetings in their own houses. Himmat Singh remembers the time when statues of Buddha would be desecrated each time they tried to set them up, but the Dalit community persevered. By 1976, they had together cleared up the trees and bushes over around 1,600 square yards of land on the craggy southern fringe of the village and set up the Buddha Vihar there under the BSI.

In the meanwhile, a local Jatav man called Puran had returned to Munirka in 1985 after living outside the country for 25 years. Puran was one of the first kids from their community to have finished schooling upto class 10 and get a government job. Himmat Singh still remembers how Puran would contribute his entire salary towards the development of their community. As one of the early generations of young men to have been influenced by Dr Ambedkar, he had converted to Buddhism by 1959. Soon after, he became a Buddhist monk, took the name Bhante Nag Sena and left the country. After returning to India, Bhante Nag Sena took charge of the Budhha Vihar in Munirka. This development, for various reasons, became extremely contentious within the Jatav community of Munirka, to the point that it led to two factions within the community. Both accused the other group of attempting to usurp control

---

††† 'When we were young, we had lifted bricks on our heads [to construct Buddha Vihar].'

over the temple and the land. The other group alleged that Bhante Nag Sena had become grossly corrupt and that he, along with a local landlord, had conspired to wrest control of the Buddhist temple in order to build a hotel there. In the middle of this fracas, the Delhi Development Authority (DDA) got a whiff of unauthorised construction and decided to clamp down heavily. Allegations flew thick and fast about which faction had called the DDA to demolish the temple. As the Buddha Vihar had been built on the *shamilat deh* part of the village, which had been acquired, it was, for all practical purposes, an unauthorised property.

What ensued was a gory set of events. The DDA arrived along with the police in order to take control of not just the Buddha Vihar but the entire area. Close to 2,000 people, mostly from the Dalit community, were left homeless in the demolition drive that followed in 1985.[14] Several Buddhist monks, who were staying in the Buddha Vihar for a community event, were badly beaten by the police. The event sent shockwaves through the city. The fact that Buddhist monks had been injured also ensured that the story made it to international news. Himmat Singh remembers the time vividly:

> Yahan par jab logon ke makaan demolish hue, toh unhone attack kar diya DDA walon par. Lathiya chali goliyan chali. Par uske baad poore baudhh jagat mein krosh ho gaya. Maharashtra se log aaye, UP se aaye. Jabardast pradarshan hue. Rajiv Gandhi ke yahan bhi hue. 10,000 aadmi ikattha hue. Sab community ne saath diya. Jaaton ne 6 busein di. Roz ka 1,000 rupya kharcha hota tha. Wahi dete the.‡‡‡

The 1985 demolition and its aftermath were not just Dalit issues. After all, even Jats had property built on unauthorised land. And if it could happen to the Jatavs, it could happen to them too. Himmat Singh seemed acutely aware of this as he spoke to me. He knew that the only reason Jats rallied with the Jatavs at the time was because it was in their interest to do so.

The event, however, made the differences between the two factions even more acrimonious. Ownership and control over the Buddha Vihar became a bone of contention whose wounds continue to fester till today.

---

‡‡‡ 'When people's houses were demolished here, they attacked the DDA people. They retaliated with lathis and guns. But after that, it was met with a lot of rage from the Buddhist world. People came from Maharashtra and Uttar Pradesh. There were massive protests. Even at Rajiv Gandhi's [the prime minister at the time] residence. Around 10,000 people gathered. All communities supported us. The Jats gave us six buses. The daily expense was close to 1,000 rupees. They [Jats] used to only give [take care of this expense].'

Allegations were levelled tirelessly, and fights and arguments broke out every now and then. Bhante Nag Sena broke away from the BSI and formed his own trust. As far as the Buddha Vihar was concerned, the case of its ownership went to court where the BSI alleged that Bhante Nag Sena had illegitimately attempted to usurp ownership of the structure.[15] In response, Bhante Nag Sena responded by arguing that he had spent 14,000 rupees in constructing four rooms, one toilet, one bath area and had also installed a statue of Lord Buddha in the structure. The court rejected both the claims. The district court judgment noted that the plaintiffs had admitted that the property in suit was government land which had been used and occupied for charitable purposes. However, the plaintiffs had not come clean on how they had come to occupy the property. In response, one plaintiff, Benarasi Lal from the BSI, tried to argue that though the property is situated on *shamilat deh* land, it was approved by the government for the Dalits. However, the BSI could not produce any document that could work as a proof of legal possession. As a result, the court declared the Buddha Vihar premises to be a case of illegal possession. The judgment was challenged in the Delhi High Court, but it refused to turn the previous judgment down.[16]

Being locked in litigation, the Buddha Vihar is technically a defunct institution. Its premises still act as a meeting place and, more importantly, as a parking lot for the Jatavs. Most of my conversations with Himmat Singh happened there on Sunday mornings, which is a fixed time when Jatav men meet here every week. It also serves as a wedding venue for people of the community because of the size of the space and its accessibility from the main road. A BSI noticeboard that hangs outside Buddha Vihar frequently displays the sayings of Dr Ambedkar and the Buddha or details of programmes to be held at Ambedkar Bhavan. The temple and the administration building, however, remain firmly closed.

Jatavs and the State

The relationship between the Dalits and the state is a tenuous one. The state is both a vehicle for social emancipation and an instrument of oppression for them. Influenced by Ambedkar, and his belief in freedom through the means of a liberal, democratic state, the Jatavs have an innate faith in the state. They have also been that one Dalit community, at least in the village, that has been able to make the most of reservations. Avowed Ambedkarites, many Jatavs have managed to bring themselves at par with the rest of society through the state policy of protective discrimination across north India.

The Jatavs have also been the core constituency for the Dalit-based organisation called the Bahujan Samajwadi Party.[17] The idea of social transformation, mediated by the promise of equality made by the postcolonial state, had a tremendous impact on the Jatav community.[18] What Himmat Singh and Dharamveer told me is testimony to this phenomenon. As one is well aware, in many contexts throughout the country, the rise of the Dalits through reservations has caused tremendous heartburn among the upper castes and dominant caste groups. This upward mobility of Dalits has even led to numerous cases of caste atrocities.[19] But in the case of Delhi's villages, where Dalits also have also emerged as landlords, the success of the Jats now also depends on how well they are able to placate these Dalit castes and other erstwhile Kamin castes like the Nais and Kumhars.

The policy of reservations gave an entire generation of Jatavs access to steady and comfortable government jobs. But, ironically, the state that has been central to their social ascendancy has, at the same time, derecognised their possession of land. The fact that the land they have traditionally called their own begins to be read as an unauthorised occupation has led to a different kind of insecurity among the Jatavs. As a result, unlike the Jats, who seem suspicious of the state, the Jatavs have historically had a very different relationship with the state. The Jatavs of Munirka have in fact managed to access the state via different channels.

The craggy southern fringe of the village that remained mostly underdeveloped in the 1960s and 1970s needed state support in order to become hospitable. This fringe, despite being right next to Baba Gangnath Marg, was still inaccessible because of its rocky topography. It is located at least 50 metres above the main road because of the rocks. Around 1975, the BSI had started petitioning the state to build a road that would connect the southern fringe of the village to the main road.[20] As we have seen, the Buddha Vihar was being constructed roughly around the same time at the edge of that southern fringe overlooking the main road. Both the road and the community effort to build the Munirka Buddha Vihar and the litigation that took place over its ownership point to the slowly changing property relations within the village. While this is not to say that the emergence of the Buddha Vihar was motivated by the creation of land value alone, but it invariably ended up doing so. Thus by the 1990s, things were changing fast on the southern side of the village as well.

The other important resource that this area needed was access to water. The multi-storeys that dot the southern edge of the village could come up only after water supply was more or less ensured. Constructions similar to those that had happened at the northern end of the village through the 1960s and 1970s had begun here as well. The only difference was that the northern side of the village had developed as a market, while the southern side, by the 1990s, saw more promise in building for renting purposes. With the heavy influx of students and civil services aspirants who wanted to stay in and around JNU and attend the Indian Administrative Services (IAS) coaching institutions mushrooming in institutions mushrooming in nearby Ber Sarai, the demand for rental housing on the southern side grew exponentially. By 2004, the local councillor from the Jatav community lobbied with the member of legislative assembly (MLA) at the time to get a water tank installed in the upcoming rentier part of the village, where the Jatavs live. The volume of tenants had not grown exponentially in this part until then because it had minimal access to groundwater, being hard and rocky. Once the water tank was built, however, there was no looking back for the Jatav community. It is fairly evident, therefore, that unlike Jats, who have a tenuous relationship with the state marked by suspicion that runs deep, the Jatavs have a more positive relationship with the state. Meghna Chandra's work traces the number of petitions made by the BSI, Munirka, to the government to construct a road that would connect the Dalit part of the village to the adjacent road around the year 1975.[21] Chandra's paper on the Dalits of Munirka argues how convergences and relationships between Ambedkarism and urbanisation in Munirka are thickly linked with claims of land and citizenship at the same time. Furthering Chandra's argument, I see these demands for electricity and water as much as claims of citizenship as they were ways of entering a rent market.

Despite the fact that things have indeed turned around for the Jatavs, however, on scratching the surface, somewhere, the memory of the bloody demolition in 1985 makes its appearance once in a while. This fear and insecurity are not necessarily a prominent, throbbing one, but they continue to fester somewhere deep down in the community's memory. When Sheila Dixit's government, right before its term ended in 2013, initiated a policy of regularising unauthorised colonies, the Jatav community got together and collected money from each Jatav family to prepare the required documents for the application. This process was, however, far from smooth. Dharamveer, one of the many activists among the Jatavs, initiated the process but was accused of embezzlement of funds, and of leaving out people the activists did not quite get along with. The applications were finally submitted with 218 names, but by that time there had been enough bad blood within the community and it was soon forgotten.

Jatavs and Their Rise as Landlords

As real as these cases of land grabs are, it would be misleading to argue that Dalits have only lost out in the process. The time lag of commercial development of the two different sides of Munirka has led to prosperity for different communities at various points. The southern fringe, mostly occupied by the Jatavs, began to emerge as rental property by the mid-1990s and 2000s. Hilly and rocky, with a perennial water problem, this was again a part of the village that was either vacant, or used commonly for dung cakes or occupied by the lower-caste communities. Over a period of time, though Jats started to encroach southwards, the Jatavs and Nais have emerged as communities with significant economic clout.

Some of them also managed to work their way into land speculation. Nathu Lal, a Nai, who had come to Munirka from Wazirabad in Haryana and speaks of his grandfather's barber shop being taken over by the Jats, had continued to retain land in Wazirabad. Delhi Land and Finance (DLF) acquired it in 1991. Nathu Lal also claimed that his family, along with other Nai families, were granted land by the Jats on the condition that the property could not be alienated until the benefactor was alive.[22] Nathu Lal's story may not be exceptional. And it is plausible that many of the families from the Nai community have received compensation for land acquired in Mohammadpur-Munirka and even villages from where they migrated. Their bargaining power increased significantly and more evenly after the real-estate escalation made even the village land valuable.

For Jatavs, the social mobility that they had acquired through education and jobs began to get converted into rent. By the time the first generation of Jatavs inspired by Ambedkarite politics, who had managed to get government jobs in the 1960s, began to retire, the land rush of the 1990s was already underway. It was only common sense for this generation to invest their retirement fund in creating rental property. As a result, the provident fund amounts of the generation which retired between the 1990s and 2000s went straight into the burgeoning land market. Therefore, for the Jatavs of Munirka, the 1990s changed two important things. One, it created demand. More and more tenants wanted to now live on the southern side of the village. Two, the spate of people retiring with hefty provident funds solved their eternal liquid cash problem. Even Himmat Singh, who retired in 2002, constructed a building with 12 rooms for renting purposes in 2003, separate from the one he lived in. Out of the 12 rooms, he uses one as his office, which is now filled with books on law and Ambedkar. Himmat Singh's daughter married a poor schoolteacher and lived in Munirka with her husband in a rented place for years, struggling to make ends meet. But Singh proudly says that over the years, they too have managed to buy land and build a four-storeyed building. He takes pride in the fact that he only gave his daughters 2 lakh rupees each from his retirement money and never tried to help them thereafter, thus keeping their self-respect intact.

A significantly high number, close to 60–80 per cent, of Jatavs own at least two properties in the village. The process of land grab also remained the same—with firewood, cattle and dung cakes. Jamuna Prasad, a retired principal of a government school from the Jatav community, bought a piece of land of around 100 square yards in the 1990s. Today, it is a six-storeyed building. Lakshmi, the Nai woman we met earlier, had also offhandedly mentioned how her sister-in-law had appropriated 525 square yards of land around the southern fringe and sold it off. As I started asking more about these transactions, Lakshmi grew defensive. She almost bellowed at me saying, 'Zameen toh hamari hi thi!'§§§ It was after all the land that had legitimately belonged to their community, not the state, not the Jats.

The southernmost fringe, directly accessible from the JNU North Gate, has sprung up as a commercial and residential hub meant mostly for students by the mid-1990s. A row of shops for photocopying and printing line that craggy hilly edge and is collectively referred to as 'Hilltop'. There is also an attempt on their part to counter the networks of financing and committees by floating their own. Dharamveer claims that in order to support people of their community to build property, he runs the Savitribai Vittlya Sahayata Samiti, or Savitribai Financial Help Committee, which loans out amounts up to 50,000 rupees at 1 per cent interest. Even though others either dismissed it or did not even know of it, it is committees like these that are possibly attempts to counter the committees run by the Jats.

Kiran Kumar's grandfather was a shoemaker who used to make shoes on order. 'Tokri mein joote le kar jaate the,'[23] Kumar reminisces. Kumar attributes Jatav assertion to the fact that they have been entrepreneurial, unlike other castes like Nais and Kumhars who are servile because of their historic dependence on Jats.[24] A Jatav by caste, Kumar's father got a job in the Delhi government and served there between 1952 and 1993. Kiran's first job was in the media industry, but he soon left it to start his own private printing and binding business in 1995. From there, he tried to diversify into a poultry farm business between 2000 and 2008. Just as he had managed to scale up this business, the bird flu epidemic struck. As a result, he had to wind down the

---

§§§ 'The land was ultimately ours!'

business after major losses. He ran a cybercafe from 2008 to 2012, which was later converted into a regular shop selling stationery, gift items, and so on. It is evident though that the shop is not his main source of income. He has now diversified into a property dealership and earns commissions on sale or renting. For properties on rent, he claims the usual commission of a month's rent. For sale of property, he says he gets 2 per cent of the value as commission. In fact, as I spoke to him, I remembered him bursting into another respondent's office with great excitement with news of some property in Najafgarh. My respondent had excused himself from the interview and rushed out with Kumar to check it out immediately. 'In the village, a one-room set is sold for anywhere between 10–15 lakh rupees and a two-room set is sold for 25–30 lakh rupees,' Kumar tells me.

The Jatavs, despite being economically ascendant, have not yet found a steady place in electoral politics. They have stood for the Municipal Corporation of Delhi (MCD) elections only when the seat for councillor was reserved for scheduled castes (SC). There have been cases where Jatavs have stood for elections, but in these cases, they have been explicitly backed by Jat benefactors, both politically and economically. Many a time, it has just been a moneylending exercise. But they collectively feel that there is no way someone from a Dalit community can win an election in an unreserved category. 'Tab yeh naak ki ladai ban jayegi.'**** Given the internal differences and the petty bickering within the Jatav community, aspirants do not feel that they would have the full support of their own community. 'Main doosron se kya vote expect karoon jab khud ke hi log nahi vote karenge?'[25]†††† Kumar asks dejectedly. The property feud over Buddha Vihar has led to all kinds of schisms within the community, which show up across various platforms, including that of elections.

The internal differences notwithstanding, the Jatavs have found a collective voice in the *panchayat* and in the numerous resident welfare associations (RWAs). With respect to the *panchayat*, the Jatav, Nai and Kumhar landlords have been able to collectively find some bargaining power. As discussed in the previous chapter, one reason why the fiat against northeastern tenants allegedly declared by the Munirka RWA did not work was because the Dalit landlords did not agree to it. Even though the Dalit landlords of the village did not have very different views about the northeastern tenants, they clearly could not afford an injunction to not give their rooms to these tenants.

**** 'Then it will become a fight for pride.'
†††† 'What votes can I expect from others when my own people will not vote for me?'

With far fewer rooms to rent out, loans drawn at extremely high rates from committees or local financiers and properties sunk in the depths of the village, they did not have the luxury of turning down anyone who wanted to take their rooms on rent.

Even organisations like the Youth Brigade, as already discussed in the previous chapter, who used the seductive entry point of the plight of the landlords and the erosion of the village culture, had to give up the language of exclusion. The young men from the Jatav and Nai communities who attended these first few meetings began to become increasingly uncomfortable with the Youth Brigade because of its narrow caste-based approach. The Youth Brigade had to eventually tone down the Jat rhetoric and broaden their appeal when faced with questions. The leadership of the young Jat man had not remained unchallenged either. An Ambedkarite Jatav man and another tenant who worked as a social activist had slowly become important decision-makers within the Youth Brigade. It was evidently clear that the ambition to be politically relevant could not be met by only appealing to the Jats. Over two years, partially because of these internal changes, the Youth Brigade had accomplished a complete turnaround. From making emotional pleas of being *mulnivasi*s, as it had during the crisis around the rape case in 2014, it had begun taking up positions in support of the northeastern tenants. As a matter of fact, the Youth Brigade Munirka (YBM) soon got enlisted by the Delhi Police as an organisation that supported the northeastern tenants. Soon, much to the chagrin of the Jats in the village, the YBM, now led by a tenant and a Jatav resident, even launched a campaign for women's inclusion in the RWA elections. They took it up with the authorities, who in turn issued a notice that they would have to include women in the voting process. Grudgingly, the RWA had to register women in the voting process as well.

Clearly, therefore, we would be mistaken to assume that Jats have monopolised power in the urban villages of Delhi and that these marginalised communities have remained voiceless. The very fact that property has also led to the rise of Dalits as landlords has introduced a very different dynamic from the one that existed before. To hark back to Jat pride for issues pertaining to the village does not necessarily work anymore. Jatavs, Nais, Kumhars and even the poorer Jats have been able to build alliances to represent their collective concerns. In the search for a new vocabulary, we see different terms like *gaonwalla* (villager) or 'Munirkavasi' (residents of Munirka) being deployed at different times. The term 'gaonwalla', while translating to 'villager', means much more than that. It implies a sense of belongingness, which translates into being a landlord, but one that is not restricted to the Jats.

The term 'Munirkavasi' applies to all the residents of the village and therefore extends to even the tenants. Both the terms invoke a far broader sense of community than that of caste and are deployed carefully. During political crises, like the case of demolition in 1985, or the rape in 2014, this was even more evident as the villagers had to take recourse to the pride and honour of being *gaonwalla*s and not just Jats.

Though the Jatavs have witnessed a considerable upward mobility in the last two decades, they are still constrained by their economic limitations. In Shahpur Jat, the mobility of the marginalised section of the resident population continues to be even more limited. That is because the fringes of Shahpur Jat, which are the most highly valued, have all been grabbed by the Jats. The Dalits have property mostly in the inner part of the village and are aware that there is little chance of them gentrifying their dingy lanes and attracting higher rents. The Jatavs may have had a similar trajectory of social ascension through government jobs, but their shift into property has not been smooth. The ones who do have houses closer to the outer lanes have little money to tap into the gentrified rental business. As a result, the new RWAs that have mushroomed to mimic the joint-stock company form of the Balliram family have become a cross-caste association of financially weaker families. The RWA in this case is thus compensating for the absent *kunba*. One of the attempts the RWA made towards gentrification, as we saw in Chapter 4, was to paint the entire lane in which these houses are located in one colour. But despite having pumped in money, they have met with limited success in their efforts to gentrify.

The Jatavs, having entered the cartel as members, have now come to enjoy the same protection from the state's wrath that other cartel members receive. Despite not having the protection that *lal dora* property owners have, they effectively know that the expanse of unauthorised construction is such that no state can simply demolish it. They are aware that what was possible in 1985 is no longer possible, and yet the memory and experience of their own precarity, and their subordinate relationship with the state and the Jats, make them archive their documents and demand the state's developmental intervention and even legal recognition. The memory of the application the Jatavs had filed as a community to regularise their unauthorised property in 2013 had all but faded by 2018. Some even alleged that the activists had not duly finished the process and instead embezzled their money. But until I asked about it, the matter seemed a forgotten one. No one, including the ones who had initiated the process, had any clear idea of what the fate of their application had been. The Jatavs, in a way, inhabit a strange middle zone. At one level, they understand the precarity of their ownership, yet they have come to feel comfortable that the protection that the Jats enjoy would be extended to them as well.

Rent, as a result, brings us to a curious juncture. At one level, as previous chapters have argued, rent needs expressions of solidarity and community. Cartels function only because they work as collectives. Before this, we have seen how cartels emerge through readily available community forms. In this chapter, however, we see rent moving in the opposite direction. We see how rent can be far more dynamic, and traditional structures can be loosened up by it at moments. The nature of rent, so closely tied with Jat identity, begins to fray, and we see how the vocabulary of community solidarity has to undergo a whole different set of callisthenics to adapt to the narrative of the Jatavs. Forced open by capital, rent creates a rather slippery, unstable discourse around what community is. Here the idea of community becomes subject to a daily plebiscite depending on economic interests, social networks and most importantly, the issues at hand. And all these have undulating surfaces, which are always susceptible to change. Rent has also become the source of a new-found confidence among the Jatavs. The unequal relationship that the Jats have with Jatavs has been mitigated to a significant extent as Jatavs have become landlords, following which the interests of the two communities seem to have converged. The story is rather different for the Balmikis, another Dalit community that has not witnessed any of this upward mobility.

On the Margins of the Margins: The Balmikis

The story of Jatav upward mobility cannot be understood as a story of all Dalits in the village. The Balmikis of the village, the most underprivileged caste, has had none of the opportunities that the Jatavs or Nais have had. Traditionally associated with waste picking and sanitation work like in most places across north India, the Balmikis have not managed to break out of this debilitating work. The differences between the two Dalit communities are stark: the upwardly mobile Ambedkarite Jatavs, who have managed to channel this mobility into property ownership, as opposed to the Balmikis who are pretty much on the margins of the economy and society. On asking the Jatavs about the Balmikis and why education or social upliftment has eluded them, the answers I received smacked either of resignation or disdain. Almost as if the Balmikis were errant children, a Jatav Ambedkarite person told me disparagingly, 'Unka kuchh samajh nahi aata ji.'#### Some even attributed it to

---

'I don't understand anything about them.'

the 'slave mentality' of the Balmikis. This disparity seems to have long historical roots. Owing to the influence of Ambedkar, the importance of education has percolated into the sensibilities of the Jatavs across north India.[26] The Balmikis, on the other hand, got closer to Hindu identity as they are roped into the Hindu fold by Sant Valmiki, their primary icon.[27] The Balmikis do not seem to have engaged in *kabza*, which is something all castes have indulged in here. On asking the Jatavs why the Balmikis did not do so, the former blame it on the latter's lack of awareness. In effect, the Jatavs ironically attribute the fact that they have managed to grab land and become landlords to their education and political awareness. The Balmikis, however, have consistently depended on municipal jobs, which were more or less assured for this caste.

Vijay Prashad notes that at the beginning of the 20th century, a significant number of Balmikis migrated to Delhi and other cities like Shimla, Jalandhar and Ludhiana.[28] Most of them, having migrated under the pressure of debts and bonded labour, were far more impoverished than the Jatavs. Prashad notes that the expansion of several city municipalities at the turn of the century created a steady demand for *safai karamchari*s in various cities.[29] Increasingly, the Balmikis who were erstwhile agricultural labourers began to be identified with lowly paid municipal work. As a result, to date, most *safai karamchari*s in Delhi continue to be from the Balmiki caste. Though low paying, these jobs assure stability, retirement benefits and even government accommodation at times. As these jobs have been informalised over time, the security that accompanied even low-paid government jobs has dried up. Exploitative *thekedaar*s, or contractors, have entered the fray who, at times, do not even pay the full salaries as stipulated by the government. While the previous generation of Balmikis enjoyed a reasonably assured life, such security has thus waned for the current generation of young men from the community.

I first managed to get in touch with the community through a flex board announcing Valmiki Jayanti, which had the names, photographs and numbers of a few young men displayed on it. I managed to contact one of these young men, Ravi, who agreed to meet me. Throughout our conversation, however, most of his responses were bored monosyllables as he remained mostly distracted by his phone. Ravi is unemployed and has not found a job with the MCD, even though both his parents have held MCD jobs. Ravi lives in a joint family set-up. That is possibly because most Balmiki families have not had the opportunity to make new houses for different units in the family due to the lack of space. Most of them have 25–40-yard plots, and families have grown and expanded within these. When Ravi's father retired around 2014, the retirement money was used to reconstruct their narrow plot into a four-storeyed building. They took a loan with some jewellery on mortgage from Muthoot Finance, which they say is far more transparent than the local financiers. One has to walk through a series of even narrower lanes to reach Ravi's house. His living room is a small one with no windows and a bed and a sofa in the corner. A few steps at the end of the room descend into a kitchen on the left and a dark corridor that opens into the back lane. The house is a compact and poorly built one. But unlike the Jatavs who used their retirement money to create rental property, Ravi's father's retirement fund seems to have gone into making their space more liveable. The walls had been tiled up and an air conditioner installed in the living room-cum-bedroom on the ground floor. The vertical expansion has barely been enough to accommodate the growing joint family, however.

Rameshwar Balmiki also retired in 2014 as an upper division clerk with the Delhi government with an assured pension. He claims that the ones who retired after the 7th Pay Commission ended up with a far better deal than he did. His is a much older house with a limestone wash and wires loosely hanging about. Rameshwar lives with his three sons in the same house. His oldest son has been employed by a contractor to supervise *safai karamchari*s at an educational institution nearby. He did not mention anything about the occupations of the other two sons. Ravi's uncle too declined to answer what jobs the younger generation is engaged in. He gruffly responded, 'Bachhon ke paas naukri toh hai nahi. Sab log bas chhota mota kuchh kaam mein lage hue hain. Ab aap bhi kuchh na kuchh kaam toh karti hongi. Ab insaan khali thodi baith sakta hai.'§§§§

Rental property is not very common among the Balmikis. And even if they happen to have some, they barely have a couple of rooms to rent out. To give me a sense of the difference, Rameshwar Balmiki says, 'Ki agar hamare paas do kamre hain, unke bagalwale Jaat ke paas dus hain.'***** Balmikis, who lived on the northern side of Munirka, were squished into the middle of the village in the 1960s and 1970s. The Jatavs had a geographical advantage of having the southern fringe exclusively to themselves until the 1990s. The Balmikis, who had been pushed inside in the 1960s, were already surrounded by the Jats. The Balmikis complain that the Jats would often pick fights if the former tried to grab land. Ravi's family, in fact, alleges that they had to give up the land on which they had done *kubza* because the neighbouring Jat kicked up a fuss.

---

§§§§ 'Our kids don't have jobs. Everyone is engaged in some minor work. Even you must be working somewhere. Now human beings cannot sit idle.'

***** 'If we have two rooms, the next-door Jat has 10.'

The Balmikis of Munirka used to rear pigs around the Basant Lok area, hardly a kilometre away.[30] In 2000, they were evicted from that space without any compensation. The altercation that followed the eviction also led to seven–eight people from the community ending up in jail. This issue remains a sore point with the Balmikis. They claim that Balmikis from Basant Gaon were allotted 12 yards of land each for rearing pigs and that they should be allocated some land for the same. It is indeed notable that the Balmikis who got left behind in the hustle to grab land not only remember it vividly but also want to be given land in return for it. It is plausible that they are demanding that land in the name of customary pig rearing but intend to use it for real estate purposes—the most obvious way of becoming upwardly mobile in this context. But it is also equally plausible that given pig rearing is an intrinsic part of 'more-than-human ecologies' in informal settlements, where pigs are a means of production as well as infrastructure in their shared margins of a global city,[31] the Balmikis could genuinely be interested in pigsties. Their demand seems fanciful, and their resolve or social capital to pursue it even weaker. But it is not surprising that they are lobbying with the state for land.

Conclusion

The unpredictable, malleable networks of capital have certainly been able to counter caste discrimination to a rather significant extent for the Jatavs in the village. However, it cannot be denied that the same networks of capital have also gone on to create newer coordinates of power, domination and violence in the same milieu. We see how each of these castes hitherto kept away from the source of power—land—begin to break into the networks, and consequently begin to function not very differently from the Jats. But at the same time, the Jatavs retain their opposition to Jats and manage to put forth a collective position at the level of the *panchayat*s or the RWA. The neatly, insularly constructed cartel is clearly a platform with multiple interests, stakes and, most importantly, communities. Different economic interests are mediated through communities within the cartel.

Like the current generation of Jat young men, who have grown up with the certainty of money flowing in from their buildings, the Jatav young men have very different aspirations from their fathers. While their fathers, empowered by Ambedkarite politics, landed government jobs, the younger people have neither seen the fervour around Ambedkarite politics nor have they felt the pressure of getting jobs. Their fathers lament how this generation completely lacks the vision and motivation that they had. Some blame the sudden influx of money in the 1990s for this. Some others blame the television. The young men in the Balmiki community, however, like Ravi, are caught in a far more precarious position. With degrees that hold little importance in the job market, and no sign of the previous generation being able to secure the future of the next, they seem to be stuck in a limbo between gaming apps and community festivals. Clearly the Dalits in the urban villages have not had a homogenous experience with land and rents.

The Jats have also had to come around to these changing dynamics and adapt to a situation where they have to include other communities as 'equals' but at the same time maintain their dominance over the system. With the Jats not being a homogeneous category, a significant section of them find themselves rallying with the Jatavs and Nais when needed. But these collaborations do not iron out the hierarchies between the communities. The Jatavs' own attitude towards the Balmikis also reeks of the older rifts between the two communities historically,[32] which has only been exacerbated in the face of extreme economic inequality.

In this chapter, we have tried to examine how capital's unintended consequences fired by the erratic nature of real-estate speculation have created opportunities for the weaker sections in the urban villages of Delhi. The value attached with becoming a landowner has allowed the Dalits a sense of social mobility despite being splintered. But whether this could be read as a form of collective caste assertion or as democratisation is not an easy question to answer. But it reveals the relationship rent can create with social location. Real estate values pushed upwards by the new financialised economy have forced rent to loosen up its hitherto exclusive relationship with the Jats. Land evidently lends itself to curious, unprecedented speculative methods, which at moments cut across class and caste hierarchies. Landlordism does not map on so neatly to the Jat community alone anymore. Now that the Jatavs, Nais and Kumhars have emerged as landlords, the Jats' notions of being a 'community' have been forced to undergo a change.

The overlap between caste and economic networks is usually understood to be a neat one. Marwaris and Reddys from Andhra Pradesh have been able to manage investments within caste groups. But in our case, as the land held even by Dalits begins to shoot up in value, the tight Jat-based discourse of *panchayats* and associations begins to lose its potency. As others have emerged as landlords as well, the cartel-like *panchayats* have had to begin accommodating them. In fact, sometimes, the poorer Jats have more interests in common with

Jatavs than with their fellow Jats. Quite reminiscent of Partha Chatterjee's articulation of modern, governmental forms of population groups that acquire the 'moral attributes of a community',[33] here we see how these communities get reshaped by stretching the contours of an ethnically bound community into a community that is relevant in the market economy. They continue to be bound by kinship, market and governmentality. Elections, rent, violence and caste-based interests determine their articulation. The expressions of anger or anxiety that seem so rooted in caste and community structures, as seen in the previous chapter, appear to then not merely be defensive and protective. These expressions of anger and anxiety go on to produce new communities and by extension, new adversaries. 'Communities' then begin to have porous borders and amoebic properties. They can stretch themselves and contract as need be. If in the previous chapters we see community forms appropriating capital, in this chapter we see capital reconstituting community forms. In other words, communities almost organically evolve to make new friends and new enemies that the global capital throws up for them.

Notes

1. This is not a very uncommon phenomenon. Several unauthorised colonies built in low-lying places with bad sewage works face this problem. See Ravish Kumar, 'Khora Colony, Ghaziabad: A Town Sinking in Its Own Sewage and Garbage', *Ravish Ki Report*, NDTV India, published on YouTube, 11 June 2013, https://www.youtube.com/watch?v=qamJf39R6_U (accessed 12 November 2018).
2. Eric Stokes, while writing about the Jats in the Rohtak region, says that there was no system of tenancy in that area. The owner-cultivator was the form natural to the Jats and the *bhaichara* system was the most readily adaptable tenure for maximum production. Eric Stokes, *Peasant and the Raj*, 237, 241. Punjab Government, *Gazetteer of the Delhi District, 1883–84* (Gurgaon: Vintage Books, 1988), 84. In the case of Uttar Pradesh, often a lot of land was designated as *khudkasht*, or self-cultivated, although they were worked on by peasants.
3. Jatavs are a sub-caste of Chamars. Compared to other sub-castes among Chamars, the Jatavs have been the most upwardly mobile in the northern region.
4. Ramnarayan S. Rawat, *Reconsidering Untouchability: Chamars and Dalit History in North India* (Bloomington: Indiana University Press, 2011), 56.
5. Prem Chowdhry, *Punjab Politics and the Role of Sir Chhotu Ram* (New Delhi: Vikas Publishing House, 1984), 6; *Gazetteer of Delhi, 1883–84*, 90.

6. Oswald Wood and R. Maconachie, Final Report on the Settlement of Land Revenue in the Delhi District (London: Victoria Press, 1882), 41; *Gazetteer of Delhi*, 1883–84, 92.
7. Department of Revenue, Award No. 889, dated 10 October 1958.
8. Department of Revenue, Award no. 1597, 31 May 1963. Anna is an older currency unit now defunct, whereby 16 annas would be equivalent to one rupee.
9. Department of Revenue, Award no. 1076, dated 15 October 1960.
10. Since the *shamilat deh* was considered outside the *lal dora*, they were given a separate *khasra* number.
11. Department of Revenue, Award no. 1938, date blurred, 1961.
12. *Harijan* was a term coined by Gandhi for members of the depressed classes, now scheduled castes. It was used in administrative documents and political discourses earlier, but the term was met with great resistance later.
13. Owen Lynch, *The Politics of Untouchability: Social Mobility and Social Change in a City of India* (New York: Columbia University Press, 1969); Manuela Ciotti, *Retro-Modern India: Forging the Low-Caste Self* (New Delhi: Routledge, 2010). In the Delhi region, too, agitations against caste oppression have been written about since the 1950s. See Oscar Lewis and Victor Barnouw, 'Caste and the Jajmani System in a North Indian Village', *Scientific Monthly* 83, no. 2 (1956).
14. Staff Correspondent, 'An Inhuman Mess', *Times of India*, 23 August 1985.
15. Tis Hazari Court, *M/S. The Buddhist Society of India vs Bhante Nagasena @ Puran Singh* on 20 February 2010, Suit no. 569/2008.
16. Delhi High Court, *Buddhist Society of India vs Bhante Naga Sena* on 3 June 2011, MANU/DE/2320/2011.
17. Sudha Pai, *Dalit Assertion and the Unfinished Democratic Revolution: The Bahujan Samaj Party in Uttar Pradesh* (New Delhi: Sage Publications, 2002).
18. Ciotti, *Retro-Modern India*.
19. Prem Chowdhry, '"First Our Jobs Then Our Girls": The Dominant Caste Perceptions on the "Rising" Dalits', *Modern Asian Studies* 43, no. 2 (2009). Massacres of Bathani Tola in 1996 and Khairlanji in 2006 are examples of such caste atrocities.
20. Meghna Chandra, 'Munirka Budh Vihara 401/AB: Identity and Democracy, Religion and Real Estate' (Unpublished MA seminar paper, Jawaharlal Nehru University, 2015).
21. Ibid.
22. This seems to be a variation of the *muafidar* system, whereby people would be given land in return for religious or social services by the colonial government. *Muafidar*s were, as a rule, like grantee landowners who retained all the profit of the grant, and if at any time they went out of

favour, the grant of quasi-ownership would be resumed. They had no right to the village *shamilat*, but their ownership was recognized as *malik kabza*. See Punjab Government, *A Gazetteer of Delhi, 1912* (New Delhi: Aryan Publishers, 2011), 179.

23. Kumar did not clarify exactly how his grandfather was a part of the shoe manufacturing chain. However, in the earlier part of the 20th century, the shoe trade in north India was conducted by middlemen buying 'baskets of shoes' from independent shoemakers. Vikram Seth's *A Suitable Boy* makes a reference to such a trade being carried out in the fictitious town of Brahmapur. See Vikram Seth, *A Suitable Boy* (New Delhi: Penguin Books, 2005), 200.
24. This is a sensibility that comes from Jatavs being involved with leather manufacturing in cities like Agra in Uttar Pradesh. It is not clear if the Jatavs in Delhi villages were themselves very involved in shoe/leather manufacturing. In fact, they were also most probably agricultural labourers for the Jats.
25. 'What votes can I expect from others when my own people will not vote for me?'
26. Craig Jeffrey, Patricia Jeffrey and Roger Jeffrey, *Degrees without Freedom? Education, Masculinities and Unemployment in North India* (Stanford: Stanford University Press, 2008); Ciotti, *Retro-Modern India*.
27. Vijay Prashad, *Untouchable Freedom: A Social History of a Dalit Community* (New Delhi: Oxford University Press, 2000), 99–107. Prashad notes that the Balmikis have increasingly become the foot soldiers of the Hindutva agenda in contemporary times.
28. Ibid., 25. Prashad goes on to attribute this move to the commercialisation of agriculture, consolidation of land holdings of landlords, famines and increased taxes.
29. Ibid., 43.
30. Mostly pig rearing is associated with Khatiks in north India. See M. Bellwinkel-Schempp, 'Pigs and Power: Urban Space and Urban Decay', in *Urbanization and Governance in India*, ed. Evelin Hust and Michael Mann (New Delhi: Manohar, 2005).
31. Sneha Gutgutia, 'Pigs, Precarity and Infrastructure', *Society and Space* 38, no. 6 (2020).
32. Vijay Parshad notes these differences between the Chamars and the Chuhras (now called Balmikis) that crop up in the 1920s during the Ad-Dharm movement as the Chamars begin worshipping Ravidas and the Chuhra community develops their leanings towards Valmiki. See Prashad, *Untouchable Freedom*, 90.
33. Chatterjee, *Politics of the Governed*, 57.

7

The Allure of Politics
The Candidates, the Cadre and the Euphoria of Elections

Action alone is the exclusive prerogative of man; neither a beast nor a god is capable of it, and only action is entirely dependent upon the constant presence of others.
—Hannah Arendt, *The Human Condition*

Dheeraj Tokas's entry into Munirka's political landscape has been nothing less than phenomenal. Particularly so because he is not from the wealthiest or the most connected families in the village. Dheeraj started his career under the aegis of a strong Congress leader, a former member of the legislative assembly (MLA) whose patronage, as many allege, helped Dheeraj to act as the broker for a huge land deal with a prominent real estate company.[1] Rumour has it that the windfall from that land deal changed his fortunes overnight. It was this new-found wealth that helped Dheeraj's political ambitions grow, and he soon started challenging his patrons in the Indian National Congress (INC). After he had fallen out with the INC, his wife, Parmila Tokas, stood independently for the seat of councillor from Munirka in 2012 (as that year, that particular ward was reserved for women candidates) and won it by a stupendous margin. Parmila and Dheeraj were, however, more ambitious. It is common for the nouveau riche to enter municipal-level politics. But the real litmus test is the legislative assembly elections. After Parmila's massive victory, Dheeraj fought elections for the state legislative assembly in 2013 from the Bahujan Samajwadi Party, which he lost rather badly.[2] But right before the 2015 state legislative assembly elections, within two months of joining the Aam Aadmi Party (AAP) Parmila won the much-coveted AAP ticket for the R. K. Puram constituency with a massive margin of over 19,000 votes. Dheeraj may not have been very successful himself in winning elections, but together with this wife, they seemed to have figured out the 'trick' to winning them. Dheeraj handles much of the work, and Parmila's connect with people gets her the votes.

Why Politics?

I shift gears to discussing electoral politics in this chapter because it is pivotal to one's understanding of the social life of rent. Money circulates through multiple registers of meanings and social realities. It goes without saying that investing in politics is a gamble and a heady one at that. Risk has for long been the hallmark of neoliberal finance capital. Derivative trading ruled by heavy number crunching is dependent on forecasts that always run the risk of failing.[3] Elections, especially in India, have always been known to be mercurial. These two world views which seem deeply divergent, therefore, actually have far more in common. Risks bring value to both, but differently. In one, it promises financial windfalls and in the other, a form of social presence, a way of asserting one's status. In one, you run the risk of losing all in a fraction of a second, and in the other, you stand the risk of losing money and subjecting oneself to the social humiliation of losing elections. Jat landlords are sceptical of the world of finance capital, but deeply invested in the risks of electoral politics.

As community life and principles of rent become inseparably enmeshed, electoral politics emerges as crucial for three reasons. First, a community that has effectively made use of the state's resources understands that investing in securing one's position within the state machinery wields far more returns than any shares or debentures. Second, permeating government structures at the local level is crucial in minimising the effects of the state's regulatory impulse. Third, electoral politics is vital for creating social distinction within a community structured around rent. This is because rent, both in cartels and vernacular forms of a joint-stock company, depends on effacing personalities and projecting the collectivity; it does not allow shining singular protagonists to emerge. Some try to salvage a sense of distinction and honour by thinking of themselves as entrepreneurs (Chapter 4), but the actual field where that impulse really plays out is that of electoral politics.

This chapter attempts to understand electoral politics as a site, and also an event. It looks at the affects and sociabilities it produces. After all, the Jat community has been able to make the most of the close relationship between money, power and politics. Now that urban real estate has transformed the fortunes of some, and increased the spending power of many, electoral politics does not look like a distant dream. I thus show how the position that politics has come to occupy in these villages is linked to the community's social life of rent. In doing so, we look at cooperation at some level, but also serious forms of jealousy and competitiveness.

By looking at the continuities and discontinuities between two very different ethos of politics—from the older and rural Jat politics of western UP to urban Jat politics of Delhi—the idea is to understand the implications of such a shift. We examine how the principle of *bhaichara* has travelled from the older *khap panchayat* form of political mobilisation to urban electoral politics. While this community has always had influential figures in Delhi politics, their increased wealth has led to an expansion in political aspirations of the nouveau riche within the community as well. In other words, aspirations have travelled beyond the ambit of just the wealthy Jats, and village politics has started involving party workers from weaker Jat families, from among tenants and even Dalits.

***

Dheeraj does not quite exude the authority and stature of the *chaudhary*s from the 1970s. He is more like a deal-broker politician. In fact, Dheeraj Tokas and Parmila are emblematic of the shift from one kind of leader to another. The older idioms of political authority, and the figure of the *chaudhary*, are increasingly being displaced as the villages become more assimilated in the urban fabric. Here I tell a story of the changing nature of Delhi politics in the context of increasing wealth, interwoven with stories of the hopes and aspirations people attach to participation in elections. Different characters in the story—a real estate dealer-turned-politician, a Union Public Service Commission aspirant-turned-*karyakarta*, an erstwhile leader struggling to remain relevant, an unemployed young man flitting from one party to another—together bring into view a rich tapestry of rising and falling fortunes, narratives of hopes and aspirations and most importantly, the rush of victory and the humiliation of defeat, both electoral and otherwise.

Politics is, as many in these villages like to put it, a *nasha*, a form of addiction. The euphoric excitement reaches its crescendo at the time the parties are about to declare their candidates. The street corners and *chai* shops run rife with all kinds of gossip, theories and speculation—people arguing, conjecturing and betting over results. Who will get the party ticket? Whose strategy involved casting their net wide with political parties and who is concentrating all their energy on just courting one party? Who are the new people trying to make their political debut by seeking tickets? Will they stand as independent candidates if denied a party ticket? The presence of so many individuals seeking tickets around them, whom they personally know, lends to the process a nail-biting quality. With winners and losers, smart moves, deft alliances and unexpected twists, politics resembles a sport most closely. The mass excitement dissipates quite a bit after the candidates are declared. The number of contenders reduces significantly, and their moves become relatively more opaque. But this sport is not about spectatorship alone. The rise of a nobody like Dheeraj Tokas gives many the hope and the confidence that they can enter electoral politics too. It has led to a litany of people seeking tickets or becoming lackeys to existing political leaders in order to climb that political ladder.

In my research into the electoral politics of the villages, 'rumours' and 'gossip' have been as crucial as 'verified knowledge'. Information and misinformation merge into each other in ways that make them inseparable. While one person's political rise may be perceived as *vishvaasghaat*, or betrayal, another's is discussed as a purely kickback-based arrangement. One encounters characters struggling to emphasise their honesty and righteousness, only to become an object of scorn and humour in the narrative of another. The field is rife with stories and gossips of kickbacks, alliances and personal enmities translating into political rivalries. The circles of *karyakarta*s are the most active in this regard. They gossip about each other and about various other leaders to whom they are not attached. And as their loyalties shift, the object of their scorn also shifts. Though the individuals I am referring to here are all public figures, their operations and networks remain opaque. Some details make their way into intimate gossip, at times incredulous and exaggerated and at others eerily plausible.

Attributing information derived from gossip to people as truths, however, has its own complications. As a methodology of anonymising, therefore, I have used real names of such public figures only when I have found formally acceptable sources for the rumours circulating about them. But I obfuscate the identities of these public figures when it comes to information derived mostly from the whisper networks and rumours. In cases where I have had both substantiated facts and unsubstantiated rumours about the same individual, I have resorted to obfuscating their identity in the second instance as much as possible. What such a methodology has cost this chapter are some of these connections between facts and rumours. The other challenge with public figures is also that they become hard to anonymise. Because along with their names, the names of political organisations or details of the years in which they contested elections also have to be anonymised. In most cases, I have refrained from giving very precise details. Apart from that, I have obfuscated the names of the village they belong to. I realise that these are far from ideal choices while telling a story like the one I am about to, but a compromise of this sort is probably the most ethical way to make these tales public.

Bhaichara and Its Transition into Modern Regional Politics

As we have seen in the previous chapters, the concept of *bhaichara*, a form of collective land ownership, has travelled a long distance to mean different kinds of solidarities in the modern context. The associational nature of *bhaichara*, as we already know, was centrally rooted in the institution of the *khap panchayat*. In more recent times, it has had its influence on electoral politics as well. *Khap*s are a tiered structure of villages: the village is the basic unit, over which is located the second tier comprising 20, 24, 40 or even 360 villages, which is usually led by one village.[4] The third tier is the conglomerate of these villages. *Khap*s cut across electoral boundaries and together represent the interest of Jats collectively. At the same time, they are important vehicles of modern politics in the region. In the 2014 elections, too, *khap*s were very much a part of electoral politics, especially in Haryana. The head of Ghatwal Khap, Baljeet Malik, was fielded by the Bharatiya Janata Party (BJP) from the constituency of Baroda in 2014.[5] For the same election, Shamsher Kharka, the *sarpanch* of Meham Khap, fought elections from Meham constituency on a BJP ticket, after having lost as an Indian National Lok Dal (INLD) candidate.[6] Kandela Khap *sarpanch* Tekram fought the election from Jind as an independent candidate after he was refused an INC ticket. The deep-rooted hold of *khap*s over electoral politics is evident from the fact that despite being extremely controversial in the matter of honour killings and caste violence, they have hardly drawn any public criticism from local leaders.[7]

*Khap*s bring with them their unique culture of equality stemming from the idea of *bhaichara*. A *chaudhary* as a politician was only the 'first among equals', a direct extension of the Jat social ethic into the modern political structure of the farmer's union.[8] Leaders were expected to be humble and respectful to everyone. This culture of *bhaichara*, despite being hierarchical, especially around wealth, undercuts any tendencies towards a subservient form of patronage politics. At the same time, however, their political landscape has been heavily dominated by the *chaudharys*—big landowners with extensive networks of social capital.[9]

Bhaichara has therefore created a different kind of an ethic for political mobilisation in the agrarian belt of northwest India, which has traditionally valued a demonstration of equality. Since the rise of the rural agrarian regional parties based on Jat participation in the 1970s, *bhaichara* had acquired a semblance of political consolidation. *Khap panchayat*s, organised around clusters of villages, emerged as institutions which sustained this social and economic cohesion. Thus, *khap panchayat*s, the historic institution of Jat landlords, transformed themselves into relevant political institutions as well.

Unsurprisingly, the earliest parties that emerged from this culture spoke essentially of agrarian interest. The Unionist Party, founded in 1923 by Sir Chhotu Ram and others, was seen as a 'Jat Party' with Jats being the single largest supporter of the party in this region, clearly in opposition to the INC, which was perceived as a Bania political party.[10] Prem Chowdhry notes that though it declined in the post-Partition years, and could not iron out differences between the *zamindar*s, the Unionist Party and Chhotu Ram were able to mobilise around the caste 'pride' of the Hindu Jats through entities such as the Jat Mahasabha, *Jat Gazette* and Jat *dharamshala*s.[11] This was key in creating a sense of regional identity, which left a long-lasting impact on the politics of the region itself.

Though the Unionist Party faded away, it marked the politics of the region as being in opposition to the Centre or the INC. The Centre was seen as being urban-centric and antithetical to the interests of the agriculturist class. Much later in the 1970s, the emergence of parties like the Bharatiya Kranti Dal (BKD), Lok Dal and Indian National Lok Dal following the 'roaring success' of the Green Revolution in north India was also built on the fissures between the INC and the agrarian class.[12] This opposition based on agrarian concerns has always been at odds with the Jats of Delhi. As many Jats of urban Delhi had already moved away from agriculture into urban businesses (as we see in Chapter 2), their concerns had become radically different from their counterparts in Haryana and Uttar Pradesh. It needs to be emphasised at this point that Jat politics in Delhi cannot be understood in isolation. It can only be made sense of in its continuities and discontinuities with the politics of the region. The next section explores that tension.

Bhaichara in Delhi Elections

Though most of the literature on the political manoeuvres of the rich, landed Jats pertains to the agrarian belt of Uttar Pradesh, Haryana and Rajasthan, there is little or no scholarship on how the legacy of this politics has left its mark on the political landscape of Delhi. The assertion of Jat identity, therefore, had to happen differently in the case of Delhi. The Delhi villages, even when their lands did not get acquired, knew very well that their relationship with land would have to change eventually. Subject to speculative games or fearing land acquisition as early as the 1960s, the Jat landlords of Delhi knew that they could not continue to remain agrarian. Not just that, they perhaps also realised there was more money in speculating on land. These schisms between the interests of the rural Jats and the urban Jats of Delhi had been long in the making.

One of the watershed moments for *khap*s in Delhi politics was the Kanjhawala Agitation in 1977. One of the biggest *sarv khap mahapanchayat*s (the apex body of *khap*s which invites participation of all the *khap*s) was organised in Kanjhawala in the union territory of Delhi over the issue of the state distributing common grazing land to the landless Dalits. This historic agitation against the state, which was understood to be working against the interest of the landowning Jats, also led to the formation of the Bharat Kisan Union (BKU). Kanjhawala as an issue, therefore, turned out to be much broader than simply that of giving away land to Dalits.[13] This created a major furore culminating in a *sarv khap*, which produced a list of demands, including, among others, the preservation of pasture land in every village, end to caste-based reservation in government jobs, reduction in irrigation rates and a ban on land acquisition of cultivable land by the state.[14] Many of my older respondents, especially from Shahpur Jat, remember being a part of the Kanjhawala *khap panchayat* agitation. Given that Shahpur Jat lost its land in 1978, it is not surprising that the Kanjhawala *sarv khap* is etched in their memory. But ironically, BKU, the organisation that originated in Delhi by mobilising farmers in the 1980s, never managed to become a popular organisation within Delhi.

As time passed, the distinction between the rural Jats of western UP and Haryana and the urban Jats of Delhi started to become more pronounced as land increasingly began to mean different things to them. And yet, it was important that the territorial structure should continue. The Delhi Jats were making their mark in urban politics very differently from the rural Jats in the 1970s. The agrarian parties had forged a politics based on their opposition to parties like the INC for being a 'Brahmin-Bania Party', whereas the Jats of Delhi aspired for positions of importance in the INC. But despite their differences, they maintained good relations with each other. For instance, Jagadish Tokas remained a loyal Congressman all through his political career, but he speaks very highly of Charan Singh and Tau Devi Lal. As the first person to be elected to the erstwhile Metropolitan Council[15] from the R. K. Puram ward (Munirka used to be a part of the larger R. K. Puram) between 1972 and 1977, his association with the INC remained long and steady, including his alleged involvement in the 1984 Sikh riots.[16] But the fondness with which he speaks of Charan Singh and Tau Devi Lal only shows the nature of Jat identity and how it played into politics in the 1970s across party lines. Indeed, Jagadish Tokas speaks of a lot of 'apnapan' in Tau Devi Lal, and even small-time leaders speak of their 'uthna-baithna' with the likes of Mahendra Singh Tikait and Dara Singh.

The presence of 'Outer Delhi'[17] as a Lok Sabha constituency until as late as 2008 had a huge role to play in maintaining these continuities despite these differences. Outer Delhi, comprising rural parts of Delhi, allowed for a rural idiom of a *chaudhary* figure to remain alive. This constituency was traditionally considered a Jat stronghold.[18] Brahm Prakash (Yadav), Chaudhary Dalip Singh Panwar, Sahib Singh Verma and Sajjan Kumar[19] are all leaders who won from this constituency. Though agrarian-based parties never came close to winning elections, it was not uncommon to see candidates from these parties in Outer Delhi. Indeed, till its trifurcation, Outer Delhi would be the constituency that would be bitterly fought over by the *chaudharys* of Delhi. In 1967, Jan Sangh propped up Chaudhary Mir Singh from Munirka village against Chaudhary Brahma Prakash (first chief minister of Delhi, Yadav by caste) from the Outer Delhi constituency.[20]

However, there were pronounced fissures between the two. Even in the 1970s, in the heyday of Jat leaders from Outer Delhi, most of the Delhi Jat *chaudharys* chose mainstream national parties over the agrarian ones. The fact that none of these major agrarian-based political parties could make a significant impact on Delhi politics even in Outer Delhi is an indication that a party mandate based on an agrarian identity could not have any direct impact in urban spaces.[21] The steady suspicion that the owner-cultivator-based politics of northwest UP has had for urban people and their ways of life, and political parties like the INC, may have also extended to the Jats of Delhi.

Liberalisation proved to be the final straw that broke the camel's back. It sounded the death knell for the agrarian Jats, but it spawned an entirely new set of opportunities for the urban ones in a way that was unprecedented. The tensions between the rural agrarian Jats and the urban Jats, which had always existed, thus got exacerbated over time, particularly after the 1990s. The trifurcation of the Outer Delhi Lok Sabha constituency in 2008, which was once the largest Parliamentary constituency in the country, splitting it up into three constituencies—South Delhi, New Delhi and West Delhi—dealt the final blow to the dominance of Jat politics in Delhi.

Even after the trifurcation, however, it is clear that Jat candidates still have a higher chance of winning tickets, especially in the South Delhi constituency.[22] In the 2014 general elections, the candidates for both the

BJP and AAP were Jats while the INC candidate was a Gujjar. In the 2013 elections, 14 Jat MLAs were elected to the Delhi Legislative Assembly, which is about 20 per cent of the total strength of the 70-member house.[23] Clearly, the trifurcation has not cost Jats their political clout. What has suffered, however, is the older language of a regional Jat solidarity and politics. The broader social contiguity of Jat solidarity across the northwest Indian region is strained by modern territorial boundaries. Jats stand not only divided across state borders but also between urban and rural areas, which led to the fragmentation of their political interests.

Slowly, the older feudal *chaudhary* figure had to be replaced by a more urbane, suave South Delhi businessman figure, which many of these newer *neta*s have already become. The weakening of the *panchayat*s has automatically led to the decline of the influence of the *chaudhary*-like figures. Also, given that the average wealth of people has increased significantly in the village, the possibility of commanding that kind of customary authority has become far more difficult. *Khap panchayat*s, being sites of hierarchy and power, are now being undermined by new money, and the rise of the rentier economy appears as a strange kind of democratising force. The erstwhile Chaudhary families have diversified into different businesses and are now owners of businesses like educational institutions, imported cars, tea businesses in London, factories and restaurants. From the older *chaudhary* figure, who was more rural, today's political aspirants are urbane and more like the 'Bania' that the Jats earlier detested the INC for supporting.

*Khap Panchayat*s of Delhi

The most recent *mahapanchayat*s, however, took place over the OBC reservation in 2015 and 2016, where they were able to pressurise the former United Progressive Alliance (UPA) government to give them OBC status just before its term came to an end. The decision was, however, revoked by the Supreme Court in 2015.[24] As a response, the Jats blocked National Highway 1 in Sonepat for days in February 2016. The agitation took a violent turn with mobs destroying property worth 20,000 crore rupees, and 20 people lost their lives.[25]

While the country was rocked with the news of the Jat protests over OBC reservations, it barely touched a chord in the urban villages that I was looking at. If asked, they would vehemently speak in favour of OBC reservations and the discrimination that they had faced at the hands of the state, which justified the reservation; all the same, it barely ever became a topic of conversation or debate at their own behest. It was not an election issue, either. This is because salaried jobs, particularly government jobs, do not have such appeal for the Jats of the Delhi villages.

The rural crisis that has been exacerbated since the 1990s has increasingly threatened rents for rural Jats and made them aspire for government jobs and links with the bureaucracy.[26] The rural Jats have also progressively lost out in the regime of 'Mandir, Mandal and Market'.[27] For the urban Jats of Delhi, however, the movement has been in the opposite direction. As we have seen before, the massive boost to real estate due to liberalisation provided the Delhi Jats with opportunities that made government jobs seem unattractive. In the glittering world of real-estate speculation, OBC reservation is, therefore, not something they are losing sleep over. Indeed, when I travelled to Jind in Haryana to attend a *khap mahapanchayat*, the meeting of *khap panchayat*s across the northwest belt, while leaders of *khap* after *khap* gave riveting speeches, Palam 360, the *khap* that consists of the 360-odd villages in and around Delhi, was conspicuously absent.

Palam 360 was in the news, however, for having organised a *mahapanchayat* on the question of amending the Hindu Marriage Act, banning same-*gotra* marriages in 2010, which was held in Jharoda village in Najafgarh.[28] The *panchayat* was held with the tragic background of around 19 cases of honour killings within a span of 80 days.[29] *Khap* leaders argued that for honour killings to cease, the Indian legal system must declare same-*gotra* marriages unlawful. Ram Kishan Solanki, the Pradhan of Palam 360, argued that allegations of *panchayat*s having ordered honour killings were without any foundation, and that the *panchayat*s only wanted to protect their age-old traditions.[30] Palam 360's enthusiastic participation in banning same-*gotra* marriages makes evident that Delhi villages are more concerned about their women. It is reflective of their anxieties about the bodies of women in their families in the face of increasing urbanisation, as I have discussed in Chapter 5.[31]

Curiously, the same Delhi *panchayat*s which seem so powerful in the economic context, where they are even able to pass diktats on evictions, find themselves increasingly powerless in the political realm. *Khap panchayat*s in Delhi are significantly weaker than some of their counterparts in Uttar Pradesh or Haryana. The power that *khap*s can have in the absence or inaccessibility of the state is immense. In a place like Delhi, it is obviously difficult for *panchayat*s to find that kind of purchase with several other alternative networks being in place. Villagers themselves sounded dismissive about the *panchayat*s

when I enquired. 'Woh? Bas ab shaadiyon mein laddu khaane jaate hain."*
In villages like Shahpur Jat, the village *numberdaar*, a hereditary post, is the local representative to *panchayat*s. In others, they take the shape of resident welfare associations (RWAs) and have to follow a structured electoral process to elect a *panchayat*. Munirka, for instance, has a structured election process for its *panchayat*/RWA election, complete with a voters' list that gets updated every two years. In Chapter 4, we have already discussed how the local village-level *panchayat* had to couch itself as an RWA in order to be legally recognised. What it also did was to make the *panchayat* susceptible to demands to make it a more open organisation. An RWA cannot anymore deny membership to women or tenants, for instance. In 2016, the voting rights for women were secured in Munirka after a sustained effort by a youth organisation in the village, which filed several complaints and petitions. Thus, as the pressure of being relevant urban institutions mounts, *khap panchayat*s keep losing their earlier identity.

All the same, however, *khap panchayat*s are not obsolete or toothless institutions that are relics from the past. Election times always bring out the continuing importance of these institutions. Local *panchayat* meetings are held before elections and there are times when support is expressed for specific candidates. For instance, when Parmila Tokas won the councillor seat, the local *panchayat* placed its entire weight behind her. No election candidate can bypass the *panchayat* or upset them. Another candidate was made to publicly apologise at the insistence of the *panchayat* for having betrayed a fellow Jat from the village in order to get closer to the INC. At the same time, some are of the opinion that these public declarations of support are empty. Some villagers laugh and say that come election day, they (the *panchayat* leaders) will not vote for the ones they have declared support for. It also goes without saying that the hold of *panchayat*s over the villagers in these matters is questionable. Much depends on the *panchayat*'s credibility and the 'hawa'† of politics, as they call it. Though there is no clear correlation between the *panchayat*'s support to the candidate and them winning, *panchayat*s do retain some importance in eliciting votes from the villagers.

'Everybody Wants to Become a *Chaudhary* These Days'

While major shifts were taking place at the scale of the general and assembly elections, the terrain of municipal elections has also been rapidly changing.

---
* 'They? They just go to eat sweets at other people's weddings.'
† Loosely translatable to 'wind' or trend.

The delimitation of the MCD wards in 2007 reduced their sizes considerably, so much so that the MCD elections became truly local for the first time. The emergence of the rent economy has led to a spurt in the general interest in and aspiration of participating in electoral politics. In the 2017 MCD election, for instance, in the Greater Kailash constituency, of which Shahpur Jat is a part, out of 7 candidates, 6 were from urban villages like Shahpur Jat and Zamrudpur. At least 3 of them, while contesting as independents or candidates of insignificant parties, were non-Jat candidates. Political aspirations have also become prominent among people who are technically not locals. In Munirka, out of 11 candidates for the 2017 MCD elections, 9 were from either Munirka or Mohammadpur village, out of which 8 stood as independent candidates. Invariably, many of them list either 'social work', 'business' or 'rental income' as their profession in their declaration forms. More individuals from the villages now aspire to contest in the legislative assembly elections as well.

Philip Oldenberg in his work on local elected representatives in Delhi explains this by observing how local elections are merely administrative exercises and bring little power. This observation holds true till date. The councillor has to be readily available for minor governance issues, sign attestations and look after everyday issues like electricity, water and sanitation. As a result, people with old money, conscious of their social status, have often considered MCD elections below their dignity.[32] Though the post of the councillor may be extremely important, it is not one that exudes authority and status. The wealthier villagers, therefore, mostly channelise their energies into legislative elections. Here, the gamble and the stakes are both bigger.

Landlords jostle with each other, vying for the attention of political parties. But there also has been a clear shift of preference among Jats of Delhi—from the INC to the BJP, both for voting as well as contesting elections. To emerge as the only authoritative figure from among the Jat ranks was probably never a possibility. The structure of the older Jat agrarian politics was mostly about conflict and rivalries among the few richer and more influential Jats. With rent having created more political aspirants, however, the differences that existed between 'leaders' and the Jat community of these villages have been levelled. This has had a far-reaching influence on the political field of these villages. The first time I met one such political aspirant from the village, Ram Pratap, it was for a pre-planned interview. He had asked me to see him in the office of a taxi service. He told me that this office belonged to his friend, and he had come there to see me because it would be more convenient for me. His own office, he said, was the INC office in Safdarjung Enclave. When I mentioned that it would have been no issue for me to come to Safdarjung Enclave to see him, he kept nodding. Much later, he revealed to me that he had been with the District Congress Committee until six months back. Now that he was no longer part of the committee, he did not need to go to the INC office. Ram Pratap Tokas has had a long career in politics. He had first contested in one of the earlier legislative assembly elections[33] from the Janata Dal in the 1990s. In his younger days, he was constantly hanging around people like Chaudhary Mir Singh, Swaroopa Lambardar and Mauji Ram, the stalwarts of the *panchayat* in those days. 'Panchayat mein durrie bichhata tha, ya unki gaadi chalata tha.'‡ It was through Mir Singh that he first met Hira Singh Rana[34] from Mukhmelpur, who was the executive councillor of Delhi from the INC between 1972 and 1977. These stalwarts from the *panchayat* requested Tau Devi Lal to give Ram Pratap Tokas a ticket from the Janata Dal (despite the fact that the village always voted for the INC) and apparently he did so. Locally, however, Tokas is also known to have been close to the BJP. Formally, however, following the Janata Dal debacle, he has always been with the INC.

Ram Pratap Tokas held a massive Deepawali Milan Samaroh and Vichaar Goshthi in his constituency on an October afternoon in 2016 in an auditorium, which I attended. As there was no election around the corner, I wondered what the agenda of the programme really was. I thought it might be a village community meeting where I would get to meet some of my respondents. Once there, I realised that it was neither a festive community gathering nor a platform for discussion. A huge number of slum residents from the R. K. Puram area had been brought there; they sat cramped in the auditorium even as the people on stage went up to the mic one by one, singing paeans to the organiser of the function and how great a leader and how sensitive a person he was.[35] The audience, jostling and shoving each other to find space to sit or stand, had no patience for either the speeches or me. Intermittently, some volunteers shushed and scolded the crowd, whose patience was only wearing thin as lunch kept getting delayed because of the long eulogies. In one glance, I knew that there was no one from the village there.

Ram Pratap is one of many such leaders who once rose to prominence but now find themselves increasingly irrelevant. He climbed to the heights of his success when he managed to get the Janata Dal ticket through his proximity to the *panchayat*. That social network is now hard to replicate. There are many like him who are slightly older and also readily throw money to earn some goodwill but rarely find any. Ram Pratap's *vichar goshthi* was merely a platform of self-promotion, for which he had managed to get an audience

---

‡ 'I used to spread the dhurries before the *panchayat* meetings and also drive their cars.'

from the slums with the promise of food. This was an act of pure patronage, or at least an act of wanting to appear as a patron. However, the rent economy has consolidated a sense of equality where the usual patron-client relationship does not work very well. Having acquired a sense of equality, members of the community hate being patronised, more so by one of their own. Jat villagers find it beneath their dignity to go for events that smack of condescension. In the village, Ram Pratap is often dissed for having no depth. Locals rubbed their hands with glee as they told me that Ram Pratap went to Jawaharlal Nehru University (JNU) twice when the fracas over sedition charges against the Jawaharlal Nehru University Students' Union (JNUSU) President Kanhaiya Kumar and a few other students broke out in 2016; in the morning he accompanied the Bajrang Dal members who congregated at the JNU gate baying for the blood of the anti-nationals, and in the evening he went with Rahul Gandhi to express support for the students. What is evident then is a scenario where leaders are struggling to find legitimacy, on the one hand, from the party, and on the other, the people. In the process, their own political loyalty has little purchase.

Two other political aspirants are the grandsons of ex-politicians from the 1970s who have been struggling for party tickets from the villages. Vijay Tokas's family has been fairly influential from the early days of the Delhi villages. His grandfather was an influential *chaudhary* of the area and was closely associated with at least two political parties. His family has been in the business of importing luxury cars and tea. While Vijay is seen as a promising political candidate in the village, he has not been very successful in winning a party ticket. He entered politics in 2014–15, when AAP was reaching its peak. Quite predictably, he began courting AAP for a ticket for the 2015 election and he even emerged as a strong contender. Many, in fact, presumed he had far better chances than Parmila Tokas because he was young and untainted by corruption charges. His own ancestral home soon became an AAP *mohalla sabha*, although it never quite functioned like one. It remained mostly a space for Vijay Tokas's cronies to hang out in. After losing the party ticket to Parmila Tokas for the 2015 election, he moved closer to the BJP in the hope of winning a party ticket for the 2020 election. Things did not work out for him then either.

Prakash, the grandson of a major INC leader from the 1970s, has also been struggling to find his foot in politics. The local councillor has been from his family over two consecutive terms. The INC offered his mother the ticket for MCD councillor for the 2017 elections, but now the family has more ambitious political aspirations. Of late, Prakash feels that the INC has gradually sidelined his family. The last straw was when the INC legislative assembly ticket was given to his aunt. He accuses the party of not having any intra-party democracy. He says he and his father worked hard on the ground for years but there is little scope to get ahead in the INC anymore. 'You could spend years working on the ground but never get their ticket,' he said to me. Prakash quit the INC a week before the 2013 assembly elections to join the BJP. I asked him if he had considered joining AAP and he responded saying he had thought about it: 'Par AAP ka kuchh samajh nahi aaya.'§ For Prakash, personal ambitions have become enmeshed with a nostalgia for old-world politics, where lineage defined political careers and demanded deference. 'Abhi toh sab chaudhary banna chahte hain,'** he sniggers. And he isn't quite off the mark. As political aspirations have grown with money, competition has only increased. The same institution of the *kunba* that resembles a consolidated force as a vernacular form of the joint-stock company is also a field of extreme rivalries, where cousins, nephews and aunts are pitted against each other, all of whom are trying to claim the true lineage of the old party leader.

Though Dheeraj and Parmila's success has been extraordinary, leaders like Dheeraj are strewn across Delhi villages. He is, in some ways, the epitome of this new crop of leaders who don't need to possess family lineage to contest elections. And in the light of the failure of these political scions to win a ticket, his wife's victory has been definitive. His public image is clearly not that of someone who is clean. References to Dheeraj Tokas elicited chuckles or disdain in public conversations. An ongoing feud over the control of the Baba Gangnath Temple (a local temple in Munirka considered very important by the Jats of the village) between Dheeraj Tokas and a Narinder Tokas took a violent turn when some gunshots were fired.³⁶ Both parties accused each other of having started the fight and firing the shots.

A look at Dheeraj Tokas's asset declaration affidavits also reveals quite a few things. The value of Dheeraj and Parmila's total declared assets stand at 100 crore rupees in 2013. Their wealth has grown within a very short period because the couple's earliest property was purchased as late as 2006 in Parmila's name for 1.05 crore rupees (valued at over 10 crore rupees in 2013).³⁷ A close scrutiny of the declaration shows clearly that a lot of property was bought around 2007–08: nine agricultural, non-agricultural and residential properties. The declaration also shows that they cumulatively own all the equity shares in companies called Veny Properties Private Limited, Veny Developers,

---

§ 'But I did not quite understand what was happening with AAP.'
** 'Nowadays everyone wants to become a chaudhary.'

Veny Real Estates and Veny Farm Land Private Limited. Veny Properties seems to be a firm directly run by them or a family member as the registered address of the company corresponds to one of their properties in Munirka village, which has been declared in their assets.[38] That the firm Veny Properties Private Limited was also registered in the year 2007 only goes to further substantiate the claim that their fortunes started growing around this period. Though Veny Properties Private Limited does not have a website of its own, on another website about 'lifestyle farmhouses', Veny Properties is listed as a partner, stating the following:

> Veny Properties has been in the business of land aggregation since 2004. Since its inception, they have aggregated large tracts of land in South and South West Delhi. Their clients include 'High Networth Individuals and Corporates'. Their credibility stems from a long track record of providing aggregated land with clean legal titles and all government approvals.[39]

Going by the estimates of the income declaration, the couple's property portfolio seems to have doubled between 2012 and 2013, after Parmila Tokas became an MCD councillor. Dheeraj Tokas exemplifies the possibility of the nouveau riche making it big in politics. Given how the grandsons of erstwhile leaders are finding it hard to break into politics, it is clear that the exclusive access to politics that the *chaudharys* had at one time is not essential anymore. Dheeraj and Parmila's success is significant for another reason. Electoral politics in these villages have been, for the longest time, tied to the structure of *khap panchayats* as Delhi was a part of the contiguous political landscape of Jat politics of northwest India. As a result, the Jat community in the city used to largely be a fiefdom of rich agriculturists where different *chaudharys* would go through the rigmarole oscillating between friendships and rivalries. But all that is changing fast in present times, with the entry of petty rentiers in the political class.

Ordinary Party Workers, Part-Time Activists

As political aspirations have soared in the wake of this petty rental economy, not everyone has the means to become a leader. Several work as cadres, or *karyakartas*, and fill the rank and file of different political parties. Though they occupy the lowest level of political work, their presence shapes the ways in which electoral politics get framed. Politicians are no longer distant strangers to the community. A career in politics, getting a party ticket and rising in the hierarchy—all of it now appears achievable and extremely lucrative, especially to the youth. Entering politics has become a matter of aspiration for a number of young men, who do not necessarily have to earn their living but are not particularly wealthy either. They do not belong to politically connected families. Not having taken education seriously but at the same time having reached an economic status where a Delhi Police job or an army job may no longer seem terribly appealing, a lot of these young men choose to be without one. Caught somewhere in the middle, joining electoral politics thus becomes a plausible aspiration and an attractive route to reclaim their masculinity. They latch on to candidates as their cadre, or henchmen, in the hope that if the candidate succeeds, they succeed with them too.

My fieldwork coincided with two extremely dramatic legislative assembly elections, in 2013 and 2015, both of which marked a crest like never before for AAP, a young party, which coalesced around a highly morally charged anti-corruption agenda, that captured the imagination of the nation in a fairly short time.[10] The party first fought the 2013 Delhi elections, held in December, where it emerged as the second largest party and then came to power in a coalition with the INC. After 49 days of government, Arvind Kejriwal resigned as chief minister for not being able to table the Jan Lokpal Bill. Delhi stayed under the president's rule for a year after that, until the assembly was dissolved and fresh elections were held in January 2015. This time, AAP won a whopping 67 out of 70 seats across the capital.

AAP's political trajectory in Munirka was an exceptional one. Riding high on the effervescence of the anti-corruption movement, its volunteers were an enthusiastic bunch. Many AAP volunteers from the village were individuals who had come to Munirka several years ago to prepare for the civil services exams, which they had failed to clear. Disillusioned, some of them subsequently aspired to take the bank/probationary officer exam or get any government job. But several others, having curated fantastically heroic and righteous images of themselves, were attracted to the ethos of AAP. The fact that Arvind Kejriwal, the leader of AAP, was himself an Indian Administrative Service (IAS) officer who had quit to join politics made them even more enthusiastic about the party. Indeed for them, AAP's activism provided renewed hope of reliving their fantasies of changing the world through this new opportunity of a 'merit-based' rise in politics, which needed neither money nor connections and, most importantly, did not require them to clear any exams.

The AAP local office for R. K. Puram constituency (of which Munirka is a part) used to run out of a room in the commercial market, rented to the party for free by Shyam Tokas, who at the time was a party sympathiser. Tired of the INC and its unresponsiveness, Tokas had become one of the benefactors of

AAP. During its heyday, when AAP had just entered the political scene after the anti-corruption movement, the office was always milling with *karyakarta*s. Two people sitting at the computer were always hard at work doing data entry and chalking out campaign schedules. In the run-up to the 2013 assembly elections, AAP's first electoral battle, the enthusiasm and hope in the office was palpable; graduates, tuition teachers and young men who did odd jobs or were preparing for government jobs worked as volunteers here. Banter seemed to be the one thing that mediated these sociabilities. As I began spending time in the office, I realised that apart from the two people busily entering data into the computer and the cashier in the office, who had dedicated work to do, the other *karyakarta*s were mostly sitting around, engaging in banter and waiting for their turn to join the campaign. The office had, in many ways, replaced the local *chai* shops as a space where men could come and spend endless hours chatting, while also feeling like they had a purpose. This moment was, however, short-lived.

After highly charged campaigns, meticulously drawn volunteering responsibilities and high drama, the overheated elections finally ended in a bit of an anticlimax: a hung parliament with AAP winning 28 seats and the BJP winning 31 seats.[41] The R. K. Puram constituency was especially at the centre of much of the drama after a sting operation accused Shazia Ilmi, the AAP candidate from R. K. Puram, of accepting bribes. After many high-pitched accusations and counter accusations and emotionally charged defences, Shazia Ilmi lost by a hairline margin of 340 votes.[42] By the time the heat started to turn up for the 2015 elections, however, AAP had already begun to work like a heavyweight. AAP, in its desperation to win, had already begun to make compromises with its political stance by fielding candidates based on caste-based calculations and money power.[43] Parmila Tokas, winning the AAP ticket, was a clear sign of there being trouble in paradise.[44] It specifically struck party workers who had truly believed in AAP's moral cause of anti-corruption. Some sat in a protest, while the rest slunk back into their disillusionment. The promise that the *aam aadmi* had seen of social change or of becoming a *neta* without necessarily having the financial or social status required to do so evaporated.

In a story I will discuss in detail later, AAP's office in Munirka had to move from its earlier location as the party fell out with Shyam Tokas, its original benefactor. In the brief middle, between the 2013 and 2015 elections, Vijay Tokas, the grandson of a very influential landlord-cum-politician who was courting AAP, offered the party his ancestral home in Munirka. It never became the main office of AAP but ran for a while as the *mohalla sabha* for the locality and was practically inhabited by only the followers of Vijay Tokas. The office was sparsely but well furnished with sofas, chairs, two computers, a huge LCD TV (liquid crystal display television), a desk and several pictures of a turbaned old man who I believe was Vijay Tokas's grandfather. In an adjacent room, there was a large snooker table that covered almost three-quarters of the room. A handful of men who all seemed like novices at the game were huddled over the snooker table at all times. On the many occasions that I went to the AAP office, the room was always full, but I never got to see Vijay Tokas himself. He was clearly a busy leader, with far more important meetings and lobbying to attend to.

By the 2015 elections, Babloo (whom we have met earlier) had become one of the lackeys of Vijay Tokas. Babloo, who often introduces himself as a 'researcher' or a 'social activist', has in fact covered the entire political spectrum through his various memberships.[45] His political career began with Dheeraj Tokas. After a tiff, he distanced himself from Dheeraj Tokas and became close to AAP. On realising that AAP would not be very easy to crack into, he moved closer to Ambedkarite politics. When I met him, he was already a passionate follower of Ambedkar—reading books on him, on caste and Buddhism—and a trenchant critic of the BJP. But probably realising that there was not much future for Dalit politics in Delhi, he decided to swallow his pride and go back to AAP after it won the election in 2013. By this time, Vijay Tokas was already courting AAP for a ticket. Babloo attached himself to Vijay in the hope that the latter would win the ticket.

As already mentioned, local functionaries or *karyakarta*s such as Babloo often introduce themselves as 'social worker'. Being a social worker, either independently or as part of the retinue of a bigger political figure, provides a way of earning legitimacy, which can, in turn, help in consolidating their own political careers.[46] Apart from working as 'fixers' to solve people's problems, the *karyakarta*s float across organisations or attach themselves to particular political figures.

When I met them, Babloo's parents, and especially his mother, seemed upset about his political activities. We have earlier encountered Babloo's mother, Radha, in Chapter 3. His parents moved into Munirka as tenants but with some difficulty were finally able to buy their first piece of property in the village in the year 2000. They made difficult choices, of investing in land and not in their sons' education, to build a semblance of security around their family through property. But Babloo himself does not seem to possess any of his parents' industriousness. When Babloo invited me home for lunch, Radha continuously abused her son while making rotis and serving us food.

She was unhappy about how he wastes time running around political leaders and does not even attempt to stay gainfully employed. It was evident to me that she was partly angry at her son, partly at herself. Through this ordeal of a lunch, Babloo sat upright and ate in stoic silence.

The security of a steady income through rent that these young men saw in their early years had assured them of a very comfortable life owing to their property. But property has over time been divided among brothers, and the money that once looked like a huge amount seems considerably less today. Most property is fiercely guarded by parents who dole out 'pocket money' to their unemployed sons. For those who are unemployed and live off the family income through rent, their insignificance stares them in the face on a daily basis. Even their wives rarely treat them with any regard because they are seen as 'useless'; the wives feel more deference for their in-laws rather than their husbands. One of the few young women I was able to talk to spoke bitterly about the kind of control her in-laws have over her. Her husband, who moves between being a railway ticket agent and an insurance agent, rarely finds much to do: 'Kuchh kaam milta hai toh karte hain, warna sara din bed par pade rehte hain,'[††] she tells me with a sense of disgust.

For men like Babloo, as much as politics is a way of acquiring upward mobility, it is also an immediate escape from the feeling of emasculation that many of them face. Spending time at home also means that the women give them domestic errands to run, which they find further emasculating. Political work gives these unemployed men the reason to appear busy and be absent from their homes. The young leader, the busy hero, is powerful and revered in the eyes of his followers mostly because of his absence. The leader's absence means that he is probably onto bigger things, most likely meeting more important people. They expect their own absence from home for long hours in the name of political work would make them more respectable in the eyes of their families. This rarely happens for them, however. But possibly, the leaders who appear so busy and well networked to their cadres are probably one among the many lackeys to bigger, powerful leaders of different parties. In the next section, we meet some of these 'leaders'.

Rivalry, Cooperation, Rivalry

The coalitions that were built among the *chaudharys* were visible to everyone, and so was the competition.[47] After all, cooperation and conflict often go hand in hand in politics. As already discussed, *bhaichara*'s import into

---

[††] 'He does some work if he gets any, otherwise he stays in bed all day.'

modern politics allowed as much space for cooperation as it did for conflict. As *panchayat*s and *khap*s pushed candidates toward electoral success, they were also mired in rivalries. Even Chaudhary Charan Singh's[48] rise as the district leader of the INC in 1952 could happen only after a 'family feud' between him and a Vijay Pal Singh of the Dahiya Khap.[49] Furthermore, Mahendra Singh Tikait[50] came to lead the Baliyan Khap only after an intense power struggle with his father-in-law.[51]

In the 1970s, owing to the rise of the agrarian parties, the political career of the Jats was quite strong at the national level. If Ram Pratap's (the INC leader whom we have already met earlier in the chapter) claims of having climbed the political ladder through the *panchayat* are to be believed, these networks had continued all the way up to the 1990s. Electoral politics and its networks look very different for Jat political leaders. The events around the 2013 and 2015 elections are only enlightening in this matter.

These elections were phenomenal for Delhi because of the churning that AAP's rise had created. With AAP coming to power in the 2013 election (as we have seen before, Shazia Ilmi, the AAP candidate from the R. K. Puram constituency, lost by some 300-odd votes in 2013), things changed dramatically for the party. By this time, as I have already mentioned before, AAP's original benefactor, Shyam Tokas, had fallen out with the party. But AAP had begun to look like a really attractive option to many landlords who had earlier dismissed the party; many of them now made a beeline for it. AAP's office in Munirka had moved to Vijay Tokas's another property by now, and he was hoping that AAP would give him a party ticket. As I have mentioned earlier, in all those months of visiting the office, I never saw the young leader himself, but heard much about how brilliant he was at the game or how he was the most deserving candidate for the ticket from AAP or the BJP. The 'leader' would only come in once in a while to his 'office', oversee some matters and leave. Meanwhile, Shyam Tokas's premises that had once housed the vibrant AAP office had turned into the BJP youth office by 2015. I went there a couple of times, but never saw anyone. By 2019, the building sported a bright neon-lit banner that screamed 'Cash for Gold'.

When Vijay Tokas failed to get an AAP ticket, it was a major blow to his supporters who had banked on him for at least winning a ticket if not the election. I happened to watch the 2015 election results in Vijay Tokas's office with this bunch of disgruntled men. There was a lot of laughter and friendly banter as counting began. The men seemed sure that Parmila Tokas would lose the election badly. As the day progressed and it started to become clear that AAP was coming to power, the room fell into a deafening silence interrupted by an occasional sigh. One by one, each of them started calling people in the party office, trying to sound exhilarated at their collective win, as if there were no rifts, and that the only reason they were not at the party office celebrating was because they had got held up somewhere and they would definitely drop by in the evening. By the afternoon, the office was empty.

After the 2015 election, Vijay Tokas realised that there was no future for him at AAP and he moved closer to the BJP. When this happened, the set of AAP *karyakarta*s who were loyal to him also found themselves estranged from AAP. The erstwhile AAP office with the snooker table, however, remained open to Vijay Tokas's 'band of men', like Babloo. Like the other *karyakarta*s, Babloo, an Ambedkarite, found himself forced to reconcile with the BJP. His own reconciliation with inadvertently becoming a BJP party worker could only be justified by a sense of instrumentality necessitated by realpolitik. 'Main apne aap ko BJP karyakarta nahi samajhta. Main bas Vijay Tokas ka saath de raha hoon,' he once said to me.‡‡ The circles of these men are full of political gossip, where they volunteer information about each other's political and local leaders. Jibes like 'arre woh? Aajkal Babloo kya BJP samarthak hai?'§§ were fast and frequent.

Parmila Tokas's phenomenal success in the elections, first becoming the MCD councillor in 2012 and then the MLA from R. K. Puram in 2015, had been the stuff of dreams. During the run-up to the 2015 election, most people were full of disdain for both her and her husband. Many complained that she had worked harder for the middle-class colonies and not really for the village. But the most common complaint that many had against the couple was 'ghamand', or arrogance. 'MCD ke election mein poore gaon ne saath diya tha. Ab unka ghamand hi unhe girayega. Unko yeh lagta hai ki paise se sabko khareed lenge.'*** Many also found Parmila to be far more respectful than her husband and were particular about distinguishing between the two. Despite the contempt the villagers may have had for them, Parmila Tokas's electoral success was a clear rebuke. Their dislike had had little or no effect on the couple's political success.

---

‡‡ 'I do not think of myself as a BJP worker. I am only with Vijay Tokas.'
§§ 'Oh him? Is he a BJP supporter these days?'
*** 'For the MCD elections, the entire village supported them. Now their arrogance will cause their downfall. They think they can buy anything with money.'

Conclusion

Money has been a strange leveller in the Jat villages of Delhi. It may not have created a real equality of resources or even rent-seeking opportunities, but it has created aspirations beyond the traditional power wielding. 'Success stories' of the likes of Dheeraj Tokas from being a fixer/*karyakarta* to becoming a political leader while eliciting chuckles also represents hope and a possibility for many. A bevy of fixers/*karyakartas*/social workers roam about the village, hoping to find that one opportunity, that one moment when their lives would be transformed. The leaders, too, are essentially doing the same—networking with different parties and leaders, hoping that one would give them a ticket. Despite the huge economic difference between the two classes of political actors, the leaders and the cadres, they are both suspended in limbo in the corridors of eternal waiting. While having little ideological or political affinities, they have a symbiotic relationship with each other. The leader looks like a leader only if he has five or six men surrounding him all the time. The *karyakarta* thinks of himself as a political figure because of his proximity to the leader. But in many ways, the stakes of the *karyakarta* are always higher because the bets they place on these aspiring leaders are tied to their own aspirations.

The aspect of political participation needs to be understood through the question of territorial influence and its changing forms.[52] The form of territorial influence that could be exhibited and performed through the status of being a landed elite two generations ago cannot work anymore because of the changed nature of Delhi's politics. In effect, the shift from 'land' to 'real estate' being a basis of candidacy has changed the nature of local politics. Delhi's urban politics runs counter to the Jat ethics of *bhaichara*. The sheer number of competing patrons and the urban context in which they operate compel politicians to strike temporary deals with the voters. As the voters in these villages are also not only Jats anymore, with more and more 'outsiders' now getting voting rights from these constituencies, the leaders have little choice but to court them as well, for whom the language of *bhaichara* has little purchase. And yet, that notion of *bhaichara* continues to remain important in the local political scenario.

Rent seekers have always known the force of political power. But politics is more than power. Politics is also aspiration. Politics is a sport. A rent market that is constantly dependent on anonymising individuals in favour of the cartel or the joint-stock company can be emasculating for individuals who have aspired for more than just having money. The transformation has been twofold.

First, the political-economic and territorial contours have had a significant impact on politics. Second, the fact that landlordism has been democratised since the 1990s and the changing nature of rent economy allows more people to stake their claims in the political realm, which they could not earlier. Politics opens up for them both the possibility of adding to their wealth as well as that of creating newer networks of influence and patronage with other urban voters.

As much as patronage politics was looked down upon by the villagers, Ram Pratap's Vichar Goshthi or the several *bhandara*s that various leaders conducted were not at all aimed at the villagers. It is evident that the new crop of leaders has been able to forge different ties that go beyond the approval or disapproval of the villagers who are numerically weaker. *Panchayat*s and *kunba*s that looked completely indomitable in the previous chapters despite all their differences do not appear so once we take the changing nature of politics into account. Furthermore, the basis of the political union of *panchayat*s, of being Jat men, is also slowly getting eroded with women getting entry, at least formally. The struggle to remain relevant as Jat men continues.

In a glance, the story is a familiar one. The rise of a deal-broker politician is not so unique in the landscape of South Asia. Patronage and politics have been hand in glove in this region.[53] This chapter tells us the place of the deal broker in the context of neoliberal urban India and shows how it has transmuted from the older idiom of *bhaichara* politics. Given how subjects are complex products of different subject positions, this new professional politician also tries to imitate the older Jat *chaudhary* figure despite breaking away from it. The *karyakarta*s and party workers, on the other hand, flit between performances of being 'dabangg' to being entirely emasculated figures. As far as rent is concerned, it creates value in politics. It creates incentives for politics. The otherwise risk-averse rent seekers become enthusiastic participants in elections. Rent gets accentuated by urban capital, invigorates competition and creates its own sets of local anxieties, which find their way in politics.

Notes

1. Sanjay Srivastava discusses a similar story of a land agent in Gurgaon, who also gets into politics. See Sanjay Srivastava, *Entangled Urbanism: Slum, Gated Community and Shopping Mall in Delhi and Gurgaon* (New Delhi: Oxford University Press, 2014), 171.
2. Only 7,614 votes were polled in his favour.
3. Edward LiPuma and Benjamin Lee, *Financial Derivatives and the Globalization of Risk* (Durham: Duke University Press, 2004).

4. The conglomerate is usually led by one village, whose headman represents the interest of the entire conglomerate in the larger *panchayat* structure. Meham-24 Khap, Dahiya Khap, Dalal Khap, Rohtak-84 Khap, Jharsa-360 Khap, Sonepat-360 Khap are extremely powerful *khap*s. There are arguably around over 300 such *khap* conglomerates all over north India. For a detailed description of the organisation of *panchayat*s, see M. C. Pradhan, *The Political System of the Jats of Northern India* (Bombay: Oxford University, 1966). It is a detailed but hagiographic study of Baliyan Khap and its continuities since 1580.
5. Staff Correspondent, '92 Khaps Hold the Key in Haryana Assembly Polls', *Indian Express*, 12 October 2014, https://indianexpress.com/article/india/punjab-and-haryana/92-khaps-holds-the-key-in-haryana-assembly-polls/ (accessed 9 September 2016).
6. Founded in 1996, this party is largely based out of Haryana. It was started as the Haryana Lok Dal (Rashtriya) by Chaudhary Devi Lal. It is currently run by his son, Om Prakash Chautala, and his grandson, Ajay Chautala. Though it was a part of the BJP-led government, INLD has been performing badly in Haryana after 2000.
7. The current Chief Minister Manohar Lal Khattar went to the extent of defending *khap panchayat*s in the name of being useful instruments for social reform. PTI, 'Khap Panchayats Useful in Society, Says Haryana CM Khattar', *Indian Express*, 31 January 2016, http://indianexpress.com/article/india/politics/khap-panchayats-useful-in-society-says-haryana-cm-khattar/ (accessed 1 February 2016).
8. Dipankar Gupta, *Rivalry and Brotherhood: Politics in the Life of Farmers in Northern India* (Delhi: Oxford University Press, 1997), 155. Even someone like Mahendra Singh Tikait, despite being the head of Baliyan Khap and the BKU, could not assert his status as a *chaudhary* beyond a point for acquiring deference.
9. Akhil Gupta, *Postcolonial Developments: Agriculture and the Making of Modern India* (Durham: Duke University Press, 1998), 91.
10. Prem Chowdhry, 'Social Support Base and Electoral Politics: The Congress in Colonial Southeast Punjab', *Modern Asian Studies* 25, no. 4 (1991): 817.
11. The Jat Mahasabha is an annual convention that calls all the big community leaders and the representatives of different *panchayat*s to Talkatora Stadium, New Delhi. *Jat Gazette* is a community newspaper run from Agra. Communities especially in north India have had a system of running their own subsidised rest houses, or *dharamshala*s, across the country.
12. Charan Singh's role in various capacities managed to bring forth a voice for the middle peasants through both a rural discourse and by rallying to

bring in acts like the Zamindari Abolition Act. Akhil Gupta argues that Charan Singh, with his tirade against collectivisation and an India vs Bharat discourse, was able to pull together a coalition of 'landlords, patwaris, traders and moneylenders, all of whom managed to extract, through a variety of morally or legally dubious means, the surplus that legitimately belonged to the farmer.' See Gupta, *Postcolonial Developments*, 77.

13. Anjan Ghosh, 'Caste Idiom for Class Conflict: Case of Khanjawala', *Economic and Political Weekly* 14, nos. 5–6 (1979): 185. Kanjhawala happened to be within the region of Green Revolution. The movement around Kanjhawala, mobilised under the name of Kisan Sangharsh Samiti, was aimed at addressing the plight of the middle peasants but ended up articulating the interests of the *kulak*s.

14. Friese, 'Peasant Communities', A-141. Caste-based reservation had directly affected middle peasants as upward mobility among Dalits made agricultural labour more expensive.

15. The Metropolitan Council was formed under the Delhi Administration Act, 1966, which functioned up to 1990. This was introduced under Section 239(A) of the Constitution as introduced by the 14th Amendment of the Constitution. The Metropolitan Council was devised as the highest elected body of Delhi and was the deliberative wing of Delhi.

16. People's Union of Civil Liberties, *'Who Are the Guilty?' Report of a Joint Inquiry into the Causes and Impact of the Riots in Delhi from 31 October to 10 November 1984*, 1984. Sajjan Kumar, another prominent Jat Congress leader, was key in orchestrating the riots.

17. Shakurbasti, Najafgarh, Rampur, Bawana, Madipur, Palam, Mehrauli and Tughlaqabad were all part of the Outer Delhi constituency.

18. According to figures around 1972, the Outer Delhi constituency consisted of 25.8 per cent Jat voters and 19.2 per cent Gujjar and Ahir voters. M. S. A. Rao, 'The Mid-Term Poll in a Village in Outer Delhi Constituency', *Sociological Bulletin* 21, no. 1 (1971): 218.

19. Sajjan Kumar, one of the stalwarts from Congress to have been returned as a member of parliament (MP) three times over from the Outer Delhi constituency.

20. Philip Oldenburg noted that during the 1967 election, Jan Sangh had adopted the policy of not necessarily giving tickets to big names but the ones who were locally influential. Philip Oldenburg, *Big City Government in India: Councilor, Administrator and Citizen in Delhi* (Tucson: University of Arizona Press, 1976).

21. BKD began contesting from Outer Delhi around the year 1962 but could never make a significant impact on Delhi politics. What is interesting is that

BKD could not win significant support even in Outer Delhi constituency, which had a large number of Jat voters and surprisingly a lot of rural villages too. INLD too had only limited success in Delhi elections. Though around the 1970s, regional parties like BKD and Vishal Haryana Party did gain some importance, more so when some of them became a part of the national Janata Party alliance. But the rise was barely one that created any ripples in the political landscape. Not many strong candidates veered towards these political parties because elections in Delhi could not be fought only on the basis of an agrarian identity.

22. Sanjay Kumar writes at length how the Jat and Gujjars of Delhi, being traditionally amply landed, possess high bargaining power in the realm of political representation, making them very competitive ticket seekers. Despite constituting only 5 and 4.5 per cent of the total population of Delhi respectively, 13 candidates from the BJP and 14 from the INC were either Jats or Gujjars, making them almost 20 per cent of the total contestants of the two parties in the 2008 assembly elections. Sanjay Kumar, *Changing Electoral Politics in Delhi: From Caste to Class* (New Delhi: Sage Publications, 2013), 43.

23. Ashok Kumar, 'Jats Continue to Hold Political Ground in Capital', *Hindu*, 25 October 2013, http://www.thehindu.com/todays-paper/tp-national/tp-newdelhi/jats-continue-to-hold-political-ground-in-capital/article5270650.ece (accessed 27 January 2014).

24. Apoorva, Anuja and Gyan Varma, 'Supreme Court Scraps Decision to Include Jats in OBC Category', *Mint*, 18 March 2015, https://www.livemint.com/Politics/9fTdDA17XYfsMLPEWnN4fI/Supreme-Court-scraps-reservation-for-Jat-community.html (accessed 27 February 2016).

25. Shoaib Daniyal, 'Ground Report: The Haryana Protests Are Peaceful (For Now) But Jat Anger Smoulders Underneath', *Scroll*, 10 June 2016, http://scroll.in/article/809587/ground-report-the-haryana-protests-are-peaceful-for-now-but-jat-anger-smoulders-underneath (accessed 11 June 2016). Several cases of rape were reported in Murthal during the protests, which have since been mired in contradictory reports and claims. Jahnavi Sen and Akhil Kumar, 'A Conspicuous Silence in Murthal on Rape Allegations', *Wire*, 12 March 2016, https://thewire.in/politics/a-conspicuous-silence-in-murthal-on-rape-allegations (accessed 16 March 2016).

26. Craig Jeffrey, *Timepass: Youth, Class and the Politics of Waiting in India* (Stanford: Stanford University Press, 2010), 37–51, Satendra Kumar, *Badalta Gaon, Badalta Dehat*.

27. 'Mandir, Mandal and Market' collectively refer to three broad shifts in Indian politics after the 1990s, which continue to bear their impact. 'Mandir' refers

to the Hindutva movement that sinks deeper with the Ram Mandir issue. 'Mandal' refers to the controversial 27 per cent reservation meant for OBCs, and 'Market' refers to the structural adjustment programme that ushered in the market; Kalaiarasan A. and Christophe Jaffrelot, 'The Political Economy of the Jat Agitation for Other Backward Classes', *Economic and Political Weekly* 54, no. 7 (2019).

28. Abhishek Saran, 'Ban Same-Gotra Marriages: Khap', *Hindustan Times*, 26 July 2010, https://www.hindustantimes.com/delhi-news/ban-same-gotra-marriages-khap/story-SOKtlmZIIfxZTVpCE4RlNL.html (accessed 25 October 2016).
29. Avantika Ghosh, 'Honour Killings: North India Wages a Vicious War against Love', *Times of India*, 1 July 2010, https://timesofindia.indiatimes.com/india/Honour-killings-North-India-wages-a-vicious-war-against-love/articleshow/6112387.cms (accessed 25 October 2016).
30. Abhishek Anand, 'Mahakhap Has a Riddle for Rahul Gandhi', *Mid-Day*, 27 July 2010, https://www.mid-day.com/articles/mahakhap-has-a-riddle-for-rahul-gandhi/89537 (accessed 25 October 2016).
31. Some *khap panchayat*s have also spoken against honour killings and the Jharsa Khap stood up to defend the rights of Muslims to be able to offer prayers in public. The *khap*s have been going through their own set of churnings, which is beyond the scope of this work.
32. Oldenburg, *Big City Government in India*, 240–41.
33. The first election took place in 1952. It was abolished soon after and then Delhi was run directly by the Central government through the lieutenant governor. In 1966, it got its own administrative set-up and constituted the Delhi Metropolitan Council in September 1966. With an amendment in the Constitution and the passing of the Government of National Capital Territory of Delhi Act, 1991, the Centre paved the way for a state government in Delhi. The second assembly elections were held in November 1993.
34. Hira Singh too was one of the prominent local leaders of rural Delhi. The Azadpur Fruit and Vegetable wholesale market is named after him. Yoganand Shastri, a Delhi-level Congress leader, is his son-in-law. For more, see 'Chaudhary Hira Singh', JatLand, http://www.jatland.com/home/Ch._Hira_Singh (accessed 12 November 2016).
35. This seems to have become an annual event.
36. Staff Correspondent, 'MLA Involved in Fracas at Temple, Gunshots Fired', *Deccan Herald*, 31 May 2015, https://www.deccanherald.com/content/480759/mla-involved-fracas-temple-gunshots.html (accessed 1 June 2015).

37. 'Dheeraj Kumar Tokas (BSP): Criminal and Asset Declaration', MyNeta, Association for Democratic Reforms, http://www.myneta.info/delhi2013/candidate.php?candidate_id=303 (accessed 12 January 2015). Since the declaration of property in the year 2013 is only an assessment of property owned at that particular time, it is quite possible that the couple could have bought and sold land before. This analysis is based on the income declaration that is being used for plainly indicative purposes.
38. 'Veny Properties Private Limited', AllCompanyData, http://www.allcompanydata.com/in/company/veny-properties-privatelimited/U45200DL2007PTC160508 (accessed 14 January 2015).
39. 'Elements Farmland: About', Elements Farmlands, http://elementsfarmlands.com/about.html (accessed 14 January 2015).
40. Srirupa Roy, 'Being the Change: The Aam Aadmi Party and the Politics of the Extraordinary in Indian Democracy', *Economic and Political Weekly* 49, no. 15 (2014).
41. AAP formed the government with support from the INC, but Arvind Kejriwal resigned after 49 days on account of his government's inability to pass the Lokpal Bill, a major electoral promise made by AAP.
42. Lalit Vachhani's film *An Ordinary Election* is an extremely well-told story of the R. K. Puram constituency election in 2013.
43. Sandipan Sharma, 'Caste Calculations, VIP Candidates: AAP Succumbs to Cong, BJP Ailments', *Firstpost*, 10 March 2014, http://www.firstpost.com/politics/caste-calculations-vip-candidates-aap-succumbs-to-cong-bjp-ailments-1427157.html (accessed 12 March 2014).
44. Zee Media Bureau, 'Prashant Bhushan Submits List of 12 AAP Candidates with Dubious Reputation', *Zee News*, 25 January 2015, http://zeenews.india.com/news/delhi/prashant-bhushan-submits-list-of-12-aap-candidates-with-dubious-reputation_1535473.html (accessed 26 January 2015). This candidature was objected to on the grounds that Dheeraj Tokas had criminal charges against him; Supriya Sharma, 'The Bhushans Aren't the Only Ones Upset with Arvind Kejriwal', *Scroll*, 23 January 2015, http://scroll.in/article/702088/the-bhushans-arent-the-only-ones-upset-with-arvind-kejriwal (accessed 24 January 2015).
45. The term 'social activist' or social worker is a much-abused term in this respect. Both Lisa Bjorkman and Craig Jeffery's work set in Mumbai also speaks at length about these self-appointed social workers. Bjorn Alm, in the context of Tamil Nadu also speaks of similar social activists. Bjorn Alm, 'Creating Followers, Gaining Patrons', in *Power and Influence in India: Bosses, Lords and Captains*, ed. Pamela Price and Arild Ruud (New Delhi: Routledge, 2011), 1–19.

46. Lisa Björkman, '"You Can't Buy a Vote": Meanings of Money in a Mumbai Election', *American Ethnologist* 41, no. 4 (2014): 621. Unlike Björkman's experience where social workers were working more or less independently and only expressing allegiance to particular candidates at the time of the elections, promising a certain number of votes, these social workers have little individual credibility. In fact, their interest of latching on to a party or a candidate is to build one's own credibility through theirs. Björkman writes that the reach and effectiveness of social workers' networks can thus often exceed that of any particular elected corporator. Political parties select candidates from among these social workers or candidates with very good networks with these social workers. Lisa Björkman, *Pipe Politics, Contested Waters: Embedded Infrastructures of Millennial Mumbai* (Durham: Duke University Press, 2015), 225–26.
47. Sucha Singh Gill, 'The Farmers' Movement and Agrarian Change in the Green Revolution Belt of North-West India', *Journal of Peasant Studies* 21, nos. 3–4 (1994): 203.
48. Chaudhary Charan Singh was the fifth prime minister of India who served between 1979 and 1980. He left the INC in 1967 to form his own party, BKD, and become the chief minister of Uttar Pradesh. He was known for active reforms of the middle peasantry.
49. Friese, 'Peasant Communities', A-140.
50. Mahendra Singh Tikait was the leader of the Baliyan Khap but went on to become a major farmer leader under the banner of the BKU. He is known for having led massive rallies and sit-ins, which forced the Central government to bow down several times.
51. Gupta, *Postcolonial Developments*, 98.
52. Jeffrey Witsoe, in the context of the OBC upsurge in Bihar, writes how electoral politics works through a control over territory. Witsoe understands this territorial dominance as a way of perpetuating inequality. Jeffrey Witsoe, *Democracy against Development: Lower-Caste Politics and Political Modernity in Postcolonial India* (London; Chicago: University of Chicago Press, 2013), 109–39.
53. Anastasia Piliavsky, ed., 'Introduction', in *Patronage as Politics in South Asia* (Cambridge; New Delhi: Cambridge University Press, 2014), 1–36; Pamela Price and Arild Ruud, eds., *Power and Influence in India: Bosses, Lords and Captains* (New Delhi: Routledge, 2011).

Epilogue

After the crash of the stock market in 1929 a Great Depression engulfed western society like a grey cloud! … Where they could, people relocated from farm to city or city to farm. Seeking greener pastures like hunter-gatherers of old. But in Bronx, on Dropsie Avenue, most tenement dwellers remained holding fast to their beach-head simply because they had only just arrived from other more hostile places. They carried with them the tabernacle of a life force they hardly understood. It was now, the middle thirties….

—Will Eisner, *The Contract with God Trilogy*

In 1926, a Swiss architect called Hannes Meyer firmly believed he was ushering in the 'new world' by radically reclaiming built structures. The new-world architecture needed to be functionalist, minimalist and fiercely anti-bourgeois. Each age, after all, demands its own form. 'It is our mission to give our new world a new shape with the means of today.'[1] As a Bauhaus architect, Meyer saw democratic power in art. In his famous essay titled 'The New World', Mayer wrote, 'The new work of art is a work for all, not a collector's piece or the privilege of a single individual.' The essay found immense popularity among thinkers and policymakers in the early 20th century as it exhibited the radical potential of modernist architecture. But far more than the piece, the image, *Die Wohnung*, or *The Apartment*, that accompanied the writing became iconic. Instead of predictable pictures of urban plans or even a building plan, Meyer chose to put in a picture of an eerily sparse room: a foldable cot and two foldable chairs, a minimalist shelf and a foldable stool in the corner. The only thing that could qualify as extravagant in the room was a gramophone, which sat atop the foldable stool.

The room in the picture was to become the manifesto for modern 'minimum dwelling': a form of functionalist urban living marked by minimalism and efficiency. Without going into an account of the unravelling of the modernist, utopian dream of heralding in a new world, it can safely be said that this modernist dream has found its way into the Global South as the stuff of nightmares. A vast majority of the urban working class have to live in small, functional living units, but these units are a world apart from Meyer's *Apartment*. Workers' housing constructed as 'one-room sets' in Delhi, the 'coffin homes' of Hong Kong, or the dormitories in Singapore stand testimony to what the 'new world' really looks like in most of the world. While I tell only one such story from Delhi, it is part of the same continuum.

Precarious Infrastructures, Perilous Futures

In the wee hours of the morning of 20 February 2020, residents of a six-storeyed building in Munirka village woke up to debris falling on them (Figure E.1).[2] The building was on the edge of the rocky cliff on the southern side of the village that overlooked the main gate of Jawaharlal Nehru University (JNU). They could see that the wall had a crack running through it. From the outside, it was clear that the building had tilted gravely. An alarm was raised; the Delhi Disaster Management Authority (DDMA) was contacted, and the authorities, for a change, moved swiftly. As the ground floor was 25 feet higher than the road, the structure was as high as an eight-storeyed building. Within a couple of hours, the DDMA had declared that the building would have

Figure E.1 A building that collapsed in February 2020 in Munirka village

Source: Hindustan Times.

to be demolished immediately by the South Delhi Municipal Corporation (SDMC). But demolishing this building was no easy task. Thankfully, the building was on the edge of the village, facing the road next to JNU, which allowed the heavy cranes and JCBs[3] space to enter without any impediment. Yet, because of the congested construction in the locality, bringing down just one tall building without damaging others proved to be a challenge. Along with 45 tenant families, 100 other families were evacuated from neighbouring buildings. It took 40 labourers on 24-hour shifts, 3 JCBs, one crane and 15 engineers to pull the building down over the next two days. The residents of the building, along with several curious bystanders, watched the building that housed all their belongings and worldly possessions come down in front of their eyes.

I happened to be travelling to Delhi on the day the building was brought down. I managed to reach Munirka only by 9:30 at night. The residents had left. The entire lane in Munirka, facing JNU, usually known for its hustle-bustle, was pitch dark. But amidst the rubble, in that darkness, two people were rummaging through what used to be the first floor of the building. I called out to them, but they asked me to keep quiet. They came down a couple of minutes later, with utensils, a wall clock and some other objects stuffed in bags. While one man disappeared with the bags, the other one stayed behind to speak to me. He said he was the landlord of the building. He didn't live there and therefore had not lost anything of his own. But he was helping his tenant retrieve some belongings, he said. He spoke to me in English throughout, even when my questions to him were in Hindi. Cautious, he refused to give me his name but was curious to know if I could help the situation in any way. Later, I found out that the building belonged to someone from the Kumhar community. Other villagers complained that the owners had drilled into the rocks that formed the foundation of the building to make space for two commercial plots, which had made such a tall building vulnerable.

Two months before this, when I was in Delhi for fieldwork, I had visited one of my respondents, Shashi, the Ambedkarite landlord we met earlier in the book, who had written poems lamenting the tall, irregularly built buildings of his locality. That day, too, he was worried about the overburdened, outdated and poorly built sewage system of Munirka that was crumbling. Big sewer rats that had infested the villages have become an added menace as they relentlessly eat into the sewage walls. Often the sewage pipelines were found jammed with pieces of brick and concrete that the rats had eaten into. Shashi claimed that this had led to the weakening of the foundations in some places. Shashi's brother, who was constructing a six-storeyed building, could not complete the structure because the foundation would not support it. They tried propping up the building with extra pillars, but that did not work either. The same thing happened in another building, which could not be built because of a weak foundation. Shashi's own house has beams underneath. But he fears that the floor might collapse if the foundation has been weakened. And what if the building next door was not built on strong beams? Even that could cause damage. It's a ticking time bomb, Shashi said to me. He claimed he had tried to bring the residents together to work to rid the sewage pipelines of the rats, but they were not bothered.

The day the building in Munirka come down, I remembered my conversation with Shashi from two months ago and felt what he had said was prophetic. That evening in Munirka, the landlord too was not sure who to blame. Were the rats to be blamed? Or just the unplanned erection of tall buildings with weak foundations? Or was it the Municipal Corporation of Delhi (MCD)? Obviously, this wasn't the only building in such a state. Munirka was also not the only village facing such a crisis.

When Shashi spoke to me, he had seemed clear about the choices that lay ahead of him. In the coming years, if it got too difficult, he told me, he would not mind selling the house and moving out. He did not want to put in humongous sums of money into the house anymore. That eight-storeyed building, which had pushed him to pen down his thoughts in poetry, had also cut off sunlight to his house. It was getting hard to live. Apart from the crumbling infrastructure, there were several other nagging problems. Air conditioners jutting out of each house in a narrow lane heated up the whole street, and his house as well. There was no separate parking space. If two bikes were not parked properly in the lane, then his bike could not get in. This led to frequent skirmishes among neighbours. I asked him how long he would wait to sell. Because once the rat infestation problems grew, it was clear to me that the real estate prices would fall too. But he seemed confident that not much would change. He said that three–four Jat landlords were ready to buy up any property in the village and refurbish it and put it on rent. One of them had recently bought a house and turned it into a seven-storeyed structure with nine rooms on each floor. They have the money to sink in a building, he said to me, unlike himself.

When I spoke to him, Shashi was already in a significant amount of debt. It is a debt that had dragged him to court. He and his wife had borrowed 20 lakh rupees from a neighbour some years back to reconstruct their house. They got the loan at a whopping 36 per cent annual interest payable at 3 per cent interest each month. He said he paid 60,000 rupees every month.

He claimed that he had already paid back the principal amount along with a heavy interest, and he was not in a condition to pay more. When he requested the lender to enter a settlement and reconsider the interest rate, the latter would not agree. The neighbour filed a case claiming that Shashi's wife runs a committee and owes him around 19 lakh rupees. Today, Shashi has reached a point where he is trying to assess how much time he has. He refuses to sink more money into the house. Already locked in litigation, he seems to be assessing what lies ahead for him.

Meeting and talking to Shashi took me back to another conversation with Savitri who had also built her house to put it on rent. She had seemed worried about her house because her ground floor was technically underground. As the road kept getting levelled higher and higher, the houses, deep in the middle of the village, in the low-lying parts, kept sinking below it. The next house's ground floor was now at the same level as the first floor of Savitri's house. The wall adjoining the neighbour's house was also in a bad shape because of seepage. When she had spoken to me, Savitri was hoping for a bank loan to be able to build pillars to support the damaged wall. She had lamented to me that her house was a literal money-guzzling machine. It frequently needed repairs and the danger of it giving way was ever present. She even asked Babloo, who had accompanied me, if there was a way in which she could procure a home loan for refurbishing the house. But soon the conversation veered towards land prices around Jhajjhar in Haryana.

It is evident that the power of the landlords seems indomitable in the face of the precarity of tenants who are caught at the lower end of blue-collar jobs, which display no signs of letting their livelihoods improve. Much of my work acknowledges the precarity that the migrant working class is doubly exposed to at their workplace and where they live. That tension, that crisis is at the heart of this work. But when I heard of the building crashing down and spoke to the landlord, I was made powerfully aware of the precarity that the landlords face as well. This is because there is another kind of crisis that has been brewing underneath the surface: that of infrastructure. Landlords like Shashi and Savitri still live in the same building that they rent out. Of course, several landlords have made basic improvements to the section of their properties they inhabit. Some have put in marble tiles to their part of the staircase, the paint job looks better on their side and so on. But as we have seen, these are superfluous touches, and the precarity of the condition of the structure is something they face together with their tenants. There is obviously a class of landlords who can insulate themselves from any looming disaster, but landlords like Shashi and Savitri, who are new at this, many from

Dalit and other backward communities, find themselves as vulnerable as their tenants. In this regard, the Dalits especially, who have more recently tasted social assertion after becoming landlords, find themselves at the bottom of the pile once again.

The dramatic demolition of the building in Munirka in 2020 thus forced me to change my perspective on things. My work had been about rent and how thick community forms can create their own networks of extraction. It spoke of extraction that takes place not at the workplace, like capital would, but rather extraction that happens at the place workers call home. It spoke of violence and exploitation that is made possible because of common ownership of the resource called land and, by extension, their homes. The larger work speaks of precarity that is created for migrant workers in a city in places they live. But this incident forced me to acknowledge something that I had not focused on, that rent extraction could also lead to its own precarities, especially for those who are in the lowest rung of the ladder.

Rent in Precarious Economies

For me, understanding how control takes shape through negotiations and fractures is important. Cartels and family-run joint-stock companies come into existence to create a consolidated platform for landlords. Family feuds, interpersonal jealousies, caste and class differences may temper this control, but they never decimate it. Control is central for rent. Rent is an expression of collectivity. So far, the structure of rent allowed the landlords to build their defences. But how does one respond to the risks that no one is individually responsible for? This precarity, in this case exemplified by the collapsed building, quickly unravelled into blame games or a farce of passing the buck within the community.

What happens when control is seen to be floundering? Rent works best in a seller's market, when the resource you hold is at a premium—like oil. But what happens when the demand crashes? At first, it seemed impossible. Oil's demand could never crash. With affordable housing, too, things were not very different. It was a much smaller market than crude oil, but the principles were the same. The demand for affordable housing in an increasingly expensive city could never crash. But then the impossible happened.

The confidence of the early 2000s, in the time of a booming economy, seems to be quickly evaporating in more recent times. The ripple effects of the 2008 housing crisis that hit the US reached India as well. The real estate market since then has taken a hit in the country. Real estate companies have been declaring insolvency,[4] or projects have been getting indefinitely delayed. Middle-class families, which had put in their life savings with the hope of owning a home they could call their own, now find themselves stuck in a situation where they don't know if they should continue to pay their equated monthly instalments (EMIs) in cases of indefinitely stalled projects. The subterranean land market is not unaffected by it either. Prices have plummeted, especially those for commercial property. The cracks are there for everyone to see. But there are several other ways in which the economic slowdown has hit these villages. Shahpur Jat, which had found its way into the global chains of garment manufacture, now finds itself in the throes of a lull. Decembers in Shahpur Jat have always been vibrant and busy. With the wedding season in Delhi at its peak, Shahpur Jat is high on adrenaline in winter. The December of 2019 seemed very different. There were hardly any workers thronging the tea stalls or even the several stores that sell garment supplies like buttons and laces. The posters that used to be everywhere, regarding requirement for *karigar*s and masters, making evident the heavy demand in various workhouses, were fewer and further between.

When I had first met Dharampal, he was trying to convert his old *haveli*, which he had inherited from his father, into a fancy boutique. He was a property dealer by profession too and hoping he would get a Western (read: white) client who would refurbish the place and transform its value. Readers might remember that Dharampal had a plaque hanging outside his building, which read 'Property from Mughal period. Interested in renting to foreigners' (Chapter 3). In five years, no foreigner turned up at his doorstep. The advertisement looking for foreign tenants was now gone. The place was, now, being rented out to *adda*s for sums such as 7,000 rupees and 10,000 rupees. In December 2019, I asked him how his property dealership was going. He appeared dejected as he responded, 'Sab kuchh dheela pada hua hai aarthik mandi ki wajah se."* The *adda*s were locked out because they did not have enough business by this point, so the workers had gone back home. Until a big order came their way, the workhouses would remain closed. The government's expression of intent to carry out a National Register of Citizens (NRC) in 2019 had led to a panic among the Bengali-speaking Muslim *karigar*s all the way from Delhi to Surat.[5] As a result, many of them all along the chain had left. Noida police, he told me, had shut down several *karkhana*s forcibly in the wake of the fervour created around the NRC. As a result, there was also a crunch in the supply chain. But for Dharampal, all was not lost.

---

* 'Everything has slowed down because of economic downturn.'

He saw it as a momentary glitch. 'Aap kuchh saal mein yahan aayengi, toh aapko yahan ek building khadi milegi.'[†] But building is expensive. And he knew it as well as me that it would not happen that easily.

It must also be pointed out that Dharampal's economic situation is nowhere close to that of his Dalit counterparts like Shashi and Savitri, discussed in the previous section. A relatively better-off Jat landlord, he faces precarity of a different kind, one that is far more familiar to the outside world. The economic downturn and the strain in the garment supply chain has subjected him to a precarity where he finds his own fortunes tied with the global, political processes over which he has no control.

Pandemic and Precarity

By February 2020, however, when the building in Munirka was demolished, the COVID-19 crisis was already brewing. By April 2020, what had earlier been considered impossible had happened. Crude oil barrel prices had fallen to negative.[6] Which meant that there were traders ready to pay people to take the oil off their hands. On 25 March 2020, the Government of India declared probably one of the harshest lockdowns in the world with a four-hour notice. This decision sent millions of working-class migrants into a crisis; without wages or food, many of them took to the highways to reach their homes several hundred kilometres away. Massive job losses and the drying up of business opportunities left millions of others in the lurch. Tenants in Munirka were not forced to hit the streets, but several had to depend on charity for food and other requirements.

Cities world over—New York, London, Paris and Washington, DC—have been witnessing rent strikes which have begun to articulate themselves around the universal right to housing. Twitter hashtags like #CancelRent and #CantPayMay rocked the internet. The movement caught on in the face of growing unemployment when cancelling rent was the only way out for millions of Americans and Europeans who were by then queuing up to file for unemployment benefits. But this has also led to other worries. Given how in the West rents are linked to mortgages and mortgages in turn are linked to financialised systems, cancelling rent may just precipitate a larger economic crisis. The smaller landlords are also equally hit because the mortgage holders would not allow more than three months' forbearance and the landlord was still responsible for paying utilities and property taxes.

[†] 'If you come in a few years, you will see a building standing here.'

In India, the situation has not been very different. Across the country, people have expressed their inability to pay rents. But apart from the Student Tenants' Union Delhi (STUD) that has been actively arguing for cancelling rents in Delhi, the rent strike movement has not really caught on here. The government has been appealing to landlords to not charge rent through the lockdown, but these appeals have been honoured at varying levels. While episodes of forced evictions have thronged the news, landlords in Delhi have responded to the situation in numerous ways. In Munirka, while some richer landlords have been magnanimous and cancelled rent for a couple of months, the smaller ones have either deferred rent or given different levels of rent relief. Many have also refused to do anything. In Shahpur Jat, several landlords resorted to accepting rents in smaller amounts spread across a longer period. Some tenants maintain that their landlords are being understanding because 'we are all in this together'. Shahpur Jat, which has been seeing a downturn for a couple of years now since demonetisation,[7] will clearly need concessions and relaxations from its landlords. While the economic downturn clearly hit the wedding business hard, COVID-19 has posed newer uncertainties and a vulnerability that cuts across classes. If the virus continues to stay, as many fear, it will have a significant impact on the scale of weddings in the city, which directly impacts Shahpur Jat. It remains to be seen how these *kunba*s and *panchayat*s respond to the crisis when their usual methods of establishing control do not work.

The post-COVID world may witness a further reduction in real estate prices. It may also shift offices and people into permanent work-from-home models. It may compel designers to move their businesses online. COVID-19 may just precipitate several technological 'disruptions' otherwise not possible. The landlords are quite cognisant of these big shifts that may slowly happen. In Shahpur Jat, the workshops that are tied to particular designers have been dependent on advances from them. But then the people who run the workshops are not formal employees of these design labels. In any case, no designer produces a garment entirely in-house to begin with. So, even the ones who have decided to be charitable during the pandemic feel their limits are being tested. When I asked some of the designers if they were paying their workers, they gave me ambivalent answers about trying to make the situation work for everybody and that they were not, after all, 'funded companies'.[8] The designers have managed to stay afloat on the basis of an everyday inflow and outflow of money, but the lockdown has pushed their own existence to the brink. It has left several *karigar*s of Shahpur Jat in the lurch. Seven hundred such *karigar*s, stuck without any earnings and no relief from either their employers or landlords, wrote an appeal to the chief minister of West Bengal, Mamata Banerjee, to arrange for their travel back home.[9] The real numbers of workers stuck in the village was, it may be presumed, far higher.

While many tell me that the landlords have been understanding and lenient with rent, the real crisis might begin only once the worst of the pandemic is over. Given that rent is not so intrinsically tied here with financialisation but instead built on filial networks as we have seen, it gives more elbow room to the landlords. But then any kind of concession is not sustainable in the long run here as well. Their larger complicity with neoliberal capital will clearly make a dent on their incomes. Once the economy totters back into some shape, when work resumes with the constraints of the post-COVID world, how long will the magnanimity of several landlords last? There is some sense of collectivity and even solidarity here; this time, it has even been extended to the tenants. But for how long? All the same, given the blow that migration has received, landlords might find themselves compelled to make concessions to retain tenants. The value associated with urban property may just be transformed in a radical way in the post-COVID world. At the end, COVID-19 has made apparent how fragile our worlds are. As Clifford Geertz had once written, 'What we need, it seems, are not enormous ideas, nor the abandonment of synthesizing notions altogether. What we need are ways of thinking that are responsive to particularities, to individualities, oddities, discontinuities, contrasts, and singularities.'[10]

This brings me to a question of how much can rent explain the current precariousness and how much it does not. How does precarity, in turn, impact rent? Having now seen the precarity of the landlords themselves, it is important to ask what the limits of the conceptual framings of rent are. Rent and precarity clearly do not work well together. But, historically, it is also true that collectivities like community *panchayat*s emerged the strongest during moments of crises. How rent shapes up after this moment, a crisis thrown up by a neoliberal order, is something that remains to be seen.

The Final(?) Word

Rent has also had a far-reaching impact on the value of the public culture of the city. The exponential rise of the Jats in the post-liberalisation landscape of Delhi, fuelled by increasing real estate values, changed the visible public culture of the city. Delhi's public culture, which had been significantly Punjabi at one point, gave way to one prominently influenced by the Jat community culture by the early 1990s. It may not be too much of a stretch to even point out that the 1984 Sikh riots and the ghettoisation of the Sikh community must have had a significant role to play in this shift as well. The fact that mobs were mobilised from within these Jat villages under the leadership of Indian National Congress–based leaders may also not be a matter of coincidence but instrumental in a community trying to wrest control in an opportunity provided by a political ethnic conflict.[11] But, over the years, once the foot soldiers of the Partition violence and Sikh riots, the Jats have acquired bigger stakes in reshaping the nature of politics in Delhi.

Delhi was never known to be friendly. But prior to the 1990s, its unfriendliness emerged from stereotypes of its people being sweet-talking yet deceitful and money minded. It is still unforgiving as a city, but now it is considered 'rude', 'rough' and 'unsophisticated'. Stories of road rage, of violence with impunity, combined with exhibitionism of brute wealth and power have come to define Delhi's character. I see this shift happening simultaneously with the displacement of the Punjabi business class by Delhi's Jat landed-entrepreneur class by the early 1990s. The rise of Gurgaon, with its own specific sets of stereotypes around new money, fast cars and guns, only supplements this new neoliberal Delhi built on real estate values. Since 2000, the number of cars in Delhi–NCR that display caste names, especially Jats, Gujjars and Yadavs, has gone up significantly. This kind of caste assertion can also be read as a counter to the loss that they experience because of urbanisation. As a result, they have often been at the receiving end of an upper caste–middle class derision, also empowered by the same neoliberal capital. But in isolating these communities as 'violent', we erase the long history of the violence of the state that dragged them unceremoniously into urban modernity.

This is not to mindlessly essentialise people and communities but rather to connect the dots between individual subjectivity, modes of production, knowledge structures and collective value systems.[12] Though being *dabangg* is associated with caste pride and has roots in times much before the contemporary phenomenon of real estate that I discuss in my work, it acquires a new life in these times and circumstances. But if subjectivity is always subject to changing social norms, ethical deliberations and political processes, it is far from being a closed circuit.[13] The open traffic between how experience informs subjectivities takes us back to the question of what experience itself may really constitute. Joan Scott writes, 'Experience is neither self-evident, not straightforward, it is always contested, always therefore political.'[14] Experience does not inhabit some pure, pristine realm of the pre-political. Subjectivities too are then politically constituted.

It needs to be seen how the real estate slump will change these cultures and expressions. If this economic downturn is here to stay, and COVID does go on to change how we live and work permanently, how will the struggling landlords then attract tenants? Will more landlords begin to behave like the ones in Shahpur Jat: warm, friendly and forever eager to please? Or will these buildings morph again, just the way they had morphed from village houses to commercial buildings in the 1990s?[15] Or will renting property also abate as a business, just like construction and transport did before, leaving the villagers ready to use their networks to plough their money into something else? And most importantly, will we see these landlords acting more as individuated entrepreneurs or would we see them depending all the more on their community solidarities in the face of this crisis?

But these are open-ended questions to which an immediate answer may be hard to reach at present. What we do know now is that between money and finance, and between local and global forms of capital, the world of rent reveals a world of social and cultural capital that can be very specific to it. This story is not a story of urban villages alone. Other questions arise meanwhile: how far is vernacular capital determined by rent? Apart from land and property, what are the other spaces in which forms of rent dominate the market? These questions too may have to wait for the time being. But the hope is that the story of the Jats of Delhi and their relationship with rent throws some light on the way rent works, at least with respect to urban property in much of urban India. If the *panchayat*s manage to function as cartels, the way in which elite resident welfare associations (RWAs) pass diktats on not renting out to Muslims also undeniably has the makings of cartels of some kind. One might wonder, what kind of community discourses do those deploy?

I am aware that the present book may be read as a corollary to the kind of World Bank–funded, neoliberal literature on property regimes that pushes for legalisation of informal property because it frees up value, because it can be freely bought and sold, mortgaged and speculated upon.[16] Many scholars have shown us that this is far from the truth. Pulling informal property into formal property markets has helped only bigger players and not the dwellers themselves.[17] The significant rise in property values also pitches such property outside the reach of the informal poor. Though I am clearly not talking of an urban poor population, the formalisation of these property markets would not necessarily make property more egalitarian. The response to the problem of urban villages has to go beyond simplistic notions of formalisation of property. Also, with buildings coming crashing down, the infrastructural aspect of these villages cannot be addressed with mere formalisation.

To come back to a full circle, the draft plan of the new Delhi Master Plan 2041 was released in July 2021. It has deferred a 'composite plan' on urban villages to two years. As a result, there is again precious little in the document that speaks of urban villages. The new Master Plan speaks of a public–private partnership in housing but does not lay down how the local area development is to be done. It also does not make explicit what this public–private partnership would look like when the 'private' could range from being big private developers to petty landlords, which has invigorated the presence of land mafia. The new Master Plan is also silent on the question of providing ownership and has refused to take a principled stand on regularisation.[18]

The Master Plan 2041 also arrives in the moment when a new method of transforming rural land into urban is already underway—land pooling. Unlike land acquisition, land pooling is a method by which parcels of land are collectively handed over to the state for development. The state develops the land and returns it to its owners after deducting around 40 per cent of the land as 'cost'. But the land pooling policy also makes a much greater space for private players as partners. As a result, the 95 villages that are now getting 'developed' through land pooling are now exposed to the vagaries of real estate pricing. The New Master Plan 2041 is not even attempting to solve the systemic problems that make low-cost housing such a challenging urban problem.

At the end, I find I might have ended up with more questions than answers. A lot of our assumptions are coming undone. With the neoliberal dream crumbling in front of our eyes with a global pandemic unfolding before us, what might be the future of global capital? And as an extension, of these subterranean vernacular markets that run on rent? How will this crisis reshape the discourse of who belongs where? Or is there a utopian possibility, at the level of these communities, to allow for broader solidarities to emerge cutting across the identities of landlords and tenants? If this crisis persists, then the language of hurt and anxiety directed at the state will transform too. History has it that Jat solidarity has always been the strongest when faced with an affront. And this clearly is not the first affront that the community has faced. The farmers' movements, which seemed to have lost their steam, has gathered strength once again over the past year and has shown unprecedented opposition to the three farm laws passed by the Indian Parliament in 2020. Even as I write this Epilogue, Mahendra Singh Tikait's (the farmer leader who was figured in Chapter 7) two sons—Rakesh and Naresh Tikait—are currently leading the movement from the front at Delhi's borders. The agrarian leaders, who were getting closer to the BJP and had abdicated their father's anti-communal agenda, suddenly find themselves in radical opposition to the BJP.[19] The Muzaffarnagar *panchayat*, which came to limelight for its anti-Muslim rhetoric and the subsequent riots, is now at the centre of the farmers' agitation. The Jat farmers taking on the government at Delhi's borders may also create pressure on the Jats of Delhi to show moral support to them. But showing open support to the farmers at the Singhu and Ghazipur borders would involve a personal cost that many Delhi Jat leaders would want to avoid. In fact, journalists have been alleging that the groups of men who have been trying to disrupt the movement are BJP supporters, and many among them happen to be Jats.[20] The rift between the rural Jats and the Jats of Delhi could not be more pronounced as they are now.

But perhaps I am jumping the gun here. Politics never ceases to surprise us. The post-pandemic world too appears hazy at the moment. As I finish writing this book, in the middle of the pandemic, when uncertainty over access and efficacy of vaccines reigns supreme, we have little idea how the world may change for us for ever. Vernacular economies will need to change as well, and devise their own ways of survival, especially now that the urban poor and urban precariat labour already find themselves in a corner, with even less room for extraction. It is undeniable, however, that the shape rent takes would have a lot to do with how COVID transforms our world.

Notes

1. Hannes Meyer, 'The New World', in *Hannes Mayer: Buildings, Projects, and Writings*, ed. Claude Schnaidt (Teufen AR/Schweiz: Arthur Niggli Ltd., 1965).
2. Ashish Mishra, 'Leaning Building of Delhi's Munirka Razed in 72-Hour Long Exercise', *Hindustan Times*, 24 February 2020, https://www.hindustantimes.com/cities/munirka-building-razed-in-72-hour-long-exercise/story-PnsNI6KlsAsDdTO7W46O0J.html (accessed 25 February 2020).
3. JCB technically stands for Joseph Cyril Bamford, a UK-based heavy machinery company that makes heavy equipment for construction. JCB has come to stand for these big construction machines also used for demolitions.
4. Bloomberg, 'Number of Distressed Real Estate Developers Doubles after Collapse of IL&FS', *Hindu Business Line*, 3 October 2019, https://www.thehindubusinessline.com/money-and-banking/number-of-bankrupt-real-estate-developers-doubles-after-collapse-of-ilfs/article29582807.ece (accessed 26 November 2020); Dhwani Pandya and Upamanyu Trivedi, 'India's Mini-Lehman Moment: Bankruptcies Double at Real Estate Developers', *Business Standard*, 3 October 2019, https://www.business-standard.com/article/economy-policy/india-s-mini-lehman-moment-bankruptcies-double-at-real-estate-developers-119100300295_1.html (accessed 26 November 2020).

5. The Register was first prepared after the 1951 Census of India for the state of Assam, which borders Bangladesh, and had not been updated until recently. In 2015, the Register was updated again for the state, which led to an extremely messy situation where close to 1.9 million people found themselves excluded from the list. Home Minister Amit Shah also expressed the government's intention to conduct an NRC across the entire country to weed out Bangladeshi infiltrators. This led to a massive scare within the Muslim population, more so among Bengali-speaking Muslims who are frequently accused of being Bangladeshis.
6. Stanley Reed and Clifford Krauss, 'Too Much Oil: How a Barrel Came to Be Worth Less than Nothing', *New York Times*, 20 April 2020, https://www.nytimes.com/2020/04/20/business/oil-prices.html?searchResultPosition=5 (accessed 22 April 2020).
7. There are several other changes that hit the fashion industry in Shahpur Jat specifically. First, more designers have started choosing to go entirely online, which makes them significantly cheaper and affordable. The rise of rental options, where online platforms let you rent a designer ensemble for a couple of days, has also become intensely important.
8. By this they mean that they do not have the luxury of being a corporation, which can raise money through venture capitalists.
9. Shinjini Ghosh, 'Help Us Return Home, Workers in Shahpur Jat Appeal to W. B. Govt.', *Hindu*, 11 May 2020, https://www.thehindu.com/news/cities/Delhi/help-us-return-home-workers-in-shahpur-jat-appeal-to-wb-govt/article31561429.ece (accessed 21 May 2020).
10. Clifford Geertz, *Available Light: Anthropological Explorations on Philosophical Topics* (New Jersey: Princeton University Press, 2001), 224.
11. The PUCL Report *Who Are the Guilty?* has very telling details of the 1984 riots breaking out in these localities of Delhi. The report names not just big leaders like Sajjan Kumar and Jagadish Tytler, already considered close to the Jat constituency, but also implicates the names of even the local representative from Munirka, Jagadish Tokas. See People's Union of Civil Liberties, *Who Are the Guilty? Report of a Joint Inquiry into the Causes and Impact of the Riots in Delhi from 31 October to 10 November 1984*, https://www.legal-tools.org/doc/d9b7c8/pdf (accessed 10 November 2018).
12. Joao Bichl, Byron J. Good and Arthur Kleinman, eds., *Subjectivity: Ethnographic Investigations* (Berkeley, Los Angeles: University of California Press, 2007), 5.
13. Ibid.
14. Joan Scott, 'Experience', in *Feminists Theorise the Political*, eds. Judith Butler and Joan W. Scott (New York; London: Routledge, 1992), 37.

15. Buildings, Stewart Brand argues, are never built to adapt. And yet, buildings persist beyond us. They have a material memory which contributes to their permanence. They are constantly changed through a push and pull of technology, money and fashion. Stewart Brand, *How Buildings Learn: What Happens after They're Built* (New York: Penguin Books, 1995).
16. de Soto, *Mystery of Capital*.
17. Timothy Mitchell, 'The Properties of Markets', in *Do Economists Make Markets? On the Performativity of Economics*, eds. Donald Mackenzie, Fabian Muniesa and Lucia Siu (Princeton; Oxford: Princeton University Press, 2007), 258–60.
18. These criticisms against the Draft Master Plan 2041 have been made most succinctly by the Main Bhi Dilli campaign. See 'The Campaign', Main Bhi Dilli, https://www.mainbhidilli.com/ (accessed 21 August 2021).
19. Aditya Menon, 'Rakesh Tikait's Tears Turn Tables: Why BJP Govt Underestimated Him', *Quint*, 29 January 2021, https://www.thequint.com/news/politics/rakesh-tikait-crying-ghazipur-border-farmers-protest-bku-tractor-rally-red-fort (accessed 29 January 2021).
20. As of 30 January 2021, Mandeep Punia, an independent journalist, was arrested by the police as he was doing a story on the independent groups trying to disrupt the farmers' protests. A video he released before getting arrested named several individuals, many of whom were Jats themselves, but had stakes in the BJP's future in Delhi.

Glossary

atta chakki	flour mill; usually, they are small establishments
abaadi	usually means population; in this case, it means 'residential'
adda	a wooden frame on which embroidery work is usually done; *adda* also stands for smaller workshops that do such work
apnapan	familiarity
badarpur	a coarse, reddish soil, produced by crushing rock; it is used in construction work
bhaichara	brotherhood
bhandara	a feast
Bania	trader caste
banatiwada	a person designated to go around a neighbourhood with a drum to announce important information, community meetings and such
chacha	uncle (younger to father)
chaiwallah	tea seller
chak	a collective piece of land
chaudhary	a prefix to denote Jat patriarch with traditional authority
chaupal	an open meeting square with a roof; now mostly a building
chinky	a derogatory term used for migrants from the northeast; literally means 'small eyes'
chowk	village square
dabangg	an aggressive masculine demeanour
dalal	broker
dangal	a wrestling contest
dhaba	local catery for affordable meals
dharamshala	community-run rest houses
gaon	village
gaonwalla	villager
ghaghra	a traditional skirt

gherna	to capture
gumbad	tomb
haveli	an older kind of a house; usually belonging to the well off
habshi	derogatory term for Africans
hundi	illicit method of money transactions
johad	natural pond or stream
kabza	grab
karigar	artisan
karyakarta	activist/social worker
kameti	colloquial way of saying 'committee'; a form of pooling and investing money
karkhana	factory or workshop; does not denote size
khudkasht	self-cultivated
kirayedaar	tenant
kunba	a family unit
kurta pyjama	a cotton tunic and pants; usually worn by both men and women
lal dora	literally means red thread; in the text, it means land demarcated as village residential land
lassi	a drink made of curd
Limca	a carbonated soft drink
makaanmalik	landlord
malikan deh	the village collective body that technically owned the village commons
mistri	mason
mohalla	neighbourhood
more	a turn; usually named as a marker for location.
mulnivasi	original inhabitant
neta	leader
pahar	hill
pagdi	a lumpsum collateral paid before leasing any commercial property
phirni	the common land circumventing around the village, usually left for village purposes
rangrez	dyer
rishta	marriage prospects
safai karamchari	garbage collectors employed by the municipal corporation

shamilat deh	village commons
satta	a local way of betting
taak	shelf
tau	father's elder brother
thekedaar	contractor
uthna-baithna	literally, 'to get up and sit'; means regular interaction

Bibliography

Government Documents and Reports

Census of India. *Administrative Atlas*. New Delhi, 2011.

Delhi Administration. *Compendium of Delhi Building Bye-Laws 1983 and Building Development Control Regulations as per Master Plan for Delhi 2021*. New Delhi: Nabhi Publications, 2013.

———. *Delhi Gazetteer, 1976*. New Delhi, 1976.

Delhi Development Authority. *Draft Master Plan for Delhi 2041*. New Delhi, 2021.

———. *Master Plan for Delhi*. New Delhi, 1962.

———. *Master Plan for Delhi*. New Delhi, 2021.

———. *Mini Master Plan: Integrated Development of Urban and Rural Villages*. New Delhi, 1985.

———. *Report of the Expert Committee on Lal Dora and Extended Lal Dora*. New Delhi, 2007.

———. *Work Studies Relating to the Preparation of the Master Plan*, vols. 1–3. New Delhi, 1957.

Government of Delhi. *Land Acquisition Papers Ladha Sarai*. Department of Revenue.

———. *Land Acquisition Papers Munirka*. Department of Revenue.

———. *Revenue Records*. 1908–?.

———. *Statistical Abstract of Delhi*. 2012.

Ministry of Urban Development. *Report of the Expert Committee on Lal Dora and Extended Lal Dora in Delhi*. New Delhi, 2007.

———. *Report of the Tejendra Khanna Committee of Experts*. New Delhi, 2006.

Municipal Corporation of Delhi. *Build Your House with a Valid Building Permit: A Guide*. New Delhi, 2011.

Punjab Government. *Gazetteer of the Delhi District, 1883–84*. Gurgaon: Vintage Books, 1988.

———. *Gazetteer of Delhi District, 1912*. New Delhi: Aryan Publishers, 2011.

Wood, Oswald and R. Maconachie. *Final Report on the Settlement of Land Revenue in the Delhi District*. Lahore: Victoria Press, 1882.
Delhi Legislative Assembly Debates. 1993–2015.
Lok Sabha Debates. 1985.
Metropolitan Council Debates. 1966–89.

Acts

Delhi Development Authority Act, 1957.
Delhi Land Reforms Act, 1954.
Delhi Municipal Corporation Act, 1957.

Reports by Independent Collectives

Krantikari Naujawan Sabha. 'Rise in Rage against Massive Factory, Fire in Anaj Mandi, New Delhi: A Report'. Pamphlet, 2019.
People's Union of Civil Liberties. *'Who Are the Guilty?' Report of a Joint Inquiry into the Causes and Impact of the Riots in Delhi from 31 October to 10 November 1984.* https://www.legaltools.org/doc/d9b7c8/pdf. Accessed 10 November 2018.
Rao, Mohan, Ish Mishra, Pragya Singh and Vikas Bajpai. *Communalism and the Role of the State: An Investigation into the Communal Violence in Muzaffarnagar and Its Aftermath: A Report.* December 2013. http://www.countercurrents.org/msfreport.pdf. Accessed 15 November 2015.

Court Cases

Delhi High Court. *Buddhist Society of India vs Bhante Naga Sena* on 3 June 2011. MANU/DE/2320/2011.
———. *Mir Singh and Others vs Union of India Case* on 4 August 1978. 14(1978) DLT 121.
———. *Sarvodaya Coop. Housing Society vs Union of India and Others* on 7 July 2009. MANU/DE/2069/2009.
———. *Shri Ramesh Chand vs Suresh Chand and Another* on 9 April 2012. 188 (2012) DLT 538.
———. *Suresh Prasad Alias Hari Kishan vs Union of India and Another* on 14 March 2012. 2012(129) DRJ 199.
———. *Union of India and Another vs Gopal Seth and Others* on 10 March 2011. MANU/DE/1541/2011.
Supreme Court of India. *Almitra H. Patel and Another vs Union of India and Ors* on 15 February 2000. MANU/SC/2767/2000.

———. *M. C Mehta vs Union of India and Others* on 19 February 2006. AIR2006SC1325.

———. *M. C. Mehta vs Union of India and Ors* on 7 May 2004. MANU/SC/0488/2004.

———. *Olga Tellis and Ors vs Bombay Municipal Corporation and Others* on 10 July 1985. MANU/SC/0039/1985.

———. *R. P. Kapur vs The State of Punjab* on 25 March 1960. 1960 CriLJ 1239.

———. *Shanti Sports Club and Anr vs Union of India and Ors* on 25 August 2009. MANU/SC/1505/2009.

———. *Suraj Lamp and Industries Pvt. Ltd vs State of Haryana and Anr* on 11 October 2011. SLP (C) 13917/2009.

Tis Hazari Court. *M/S. The Buddhist Society of India vs Bhante Nagasena @ Puran Singh* on 20 February 2010. Suit no. 569/2008.

Books and Articles

Abdourahme, Nasser. 'Assembling and Spilling Over: Towards an "Ethnography of Cement" in a Palestinian Refugee Camp'. *International Journal of Urban and Regional Research* 39, no. 2 (2015): 200–17.

Agarwal, Manu. 'Urban Villages: An Oxymoron?' *Down to Earth*, 15 June 2003. http://www.downtoearth.org.in/coverage/urban-villages--an-oxymoron-13014. Accessed 29 June 2013.

Agarwal, Samantha, and Michael Levien. 'Dalits and Disposession: A Comparison'. *Journal of Contemporary Asia* 50, no. 5 (2020): 696–722.

Ahlawat, Neerja. 'Political Economy of Haryana's Khaps'. *Economic and Political Weekly* 47, nos. 47–48 (2012): 15–17.

A., Kalaiarasan, and Christophe Jaffrelot. 'The Political Economy of the Jat Agitation for Other Backward Classes'. *Economic and Political Weekly* 54, no. 7 (2019): 29–37.

Anand, Abhishek. 'Mahakhap Has a Riddle for Rahul Gandhi'. *Mid-Day*, 27 July 2010. https://www.mid-day.com/articles/mahakhap-has-a-riddle-for-rahul-gandhi/89537. Accessed 25 October 2016.

Anand, Abhishek, and Sushant Mehra. 'Regularisation of Unauthorised Delhi Colonies: A Massive Infra and Realty Revamp'. *India Today*, 19 November 2019. https://www.indiatoday.in/mail-today/story/regularisation-of-unauthorised-delhi-colonies-a-massive-infra-and-realty-revamp-1621440-2019-11-22. Accessed 12 December 2020.

Anderson, Matthew B. 'Class Monopoly Rent and the Contemporary Neoliberal City'. *Geography Compass* 8, no. 1 (2014): 13–24.

Andreucci, Melissa Garcia-Lamarca, Jonah Wedekind and Erik Swyngedouw. 'Value Grabbing: A Political Ecology of Rent'. *Capitalism, Nature, Socialism* 28, no. 3 (2017): 28–47.

ANI. 'Delhi Polls: AAP Releases Final List of Candidates'. *DNA*, 2 January 2015. http://www.dnaindia.com/india/report-delhi-polls-aap-releases-final-list-of-candidates-2049082. Accessed 3 January 2015.

Anwar, Tarique. 'From Local Goondas to Full-Fledged Mafia: Land Grabbing, Extortion Fuel Gang Wars in Delhi'. *Firstpost*, 27 August 2015. http://www.firstpost.com/india/from-local-goondas-to-full-fledged-mafia-land-grabbing-extortion-fuel-gang-wars-in-delhi-2410176.html. Accessed 1 September 2015.

Anwer, Nausheen H. 'Receding Rurality, Booming Periphery: Value Struggles in Karachi's Agrarian–Urban Frontier'. *Economic and Political Weekly* 53, no. 12 (2018): 46–54.

Apoorva, Anuja, and Gyan Varma. 'Supreme Court Scraps Decision to Include Jats in OBC Category'. *Mint*, 18 March 2015. https://www.livemint.com/Politics/9fTdDA17XYfsMLPEWnN4fI/Supreme-Court-scraps-reservation-for-Jat-community.html. Accessed 27 February 2016.

Appadurai, Arjun. 'Disjuncture and Difference in the Global Political Economy'. *Public Culture* 7, no. 2 (1990): 295–310.

———. *Fear of Small Numbers: An Essay on the Geography of Anger*. Durham: Duke University Press, 2006.

———. 'How Moral Is South Asia's Economy? A Review Article'. *Journal of Asian Studies* 43, no. 3 (1984): 481–97.

———. 'Introduction: Commodities and the Politics of Value'. In *The Social Life of Things: Commodities in Cultural Perspective*, edited by Arjun Appadurai, 3–63. Cambridge: Cambridge University Press, 1988.

———. 'Spectral Housing and Urban Cleansing: Notes on Millennial Mumbai'. *Public Culture* 12, no. 3 (2000): 627–51.

———. 'The Ghost in the Finance Machine'. *Public Culture* 23, no. 3 (2011): 517–39.

———. 'Theory in Anthropology: Centre and Periphery'. *Comparative Studies in Society and History* 28, no. 1 (1990): 356–61.

Arendt, Hannah. *The Human Condition*. Chicago; London: University of Chicago Press, 1998.

Baden-Powell, B. H. *The Land Systems of British India*. Vol. 1. Oxford: Oxford University Press, 1974.

Bagchi, Soumen. 'Governance in Delhi: Too Many Cooks'. *Economic and Political Weekly* 38, no. 46 (2003): 4831–32.
Balakrishnan, Sai. *Shareholder Cities: Land Transformations along Urban Corridors in India*. Philadelphia: University of Pennsylvania Press, 2019.
Ball, Michael. 'Differential Rent and the Role of Landed Property'. *International Journal of Urban and Regional Research* 1, nos. 1–3 (1977): 380–403.
———. 'The Built Environment and the Urban Question'. *Environment and Planning D: Society and Space* 4, no. 4 (1986): 447–64.
Banerjee, Banashree. 'Security of Tenure in Indian Cities'. In *Holding Their Ground: Secure Land Tenure for the Urban Poor in Developing Countries*, edited by Alain Durand-Lasserve and Lauren Royston, 37–58. London: Earthscan Publications, 2002.
Bannerjee-Guha, Swapna. *Accumulation by Dispossession: Transformative Cities in the New Global Order*. New Delhi: Sage, 2010.
———. 'Space Relations of Capital and Significance of New Economic Enclaves: SEZs in India'. *Economic and Political Weekly* 43, no. 47 (2008): 51–59.
Baran, Paul A., and Paul M. Sweezy. *Monopoly Capital: An Essay on the American Economic and Social Order*. New York; London: Monthly Review Press, 1966.
Bardalai, Keya. 'Malls versus Streets: North-Eastern Women between Modernity and Marginality'. *South Asia: Journal of South Asian Studies* 42, no. 9 (2019): 1078–94.
Basile, Elisabetta. *Capitalist Development in India's Informal Economy*. Oxon; New York: Routledge, 2013.
Baviskar, Amita. 'Between Violence and Desire: Space, Power, and Identity in the Making of Metropolitan Delhi'. *International Social Science Journal* 55, no. 175 (2003): 89–98.
———. 'Cows, Cars and Cycle-Rickshaws: Bourgeois Environmentalists and the Battle for Delhi's Streets'. In *Elite and Everyman: The Cultural Politics of the Indian Middle Classes*, edited by Amita Baviskar and Raka Ray, 391–418. New York: Routledge, 2011.
———. 'Dreaming Big: Spectacular Events and the "World-Class" City: The Commonwealth Games in Delhi'. In *Leveraging Legacies from Sports Mega-Events: Concepts and Cases*, edited by Jonathan Grix, 138–61. London: Palgrave Macmillan, 2014.
———. 'What the Eye Does Not See: The Yamuna in the Imagination of Delhi'. *Economic and Political Weekly* 45, no. 50 (2011): 45–53.
Bayly, Christopher. *Rulers, Townsmen and Bazaars: North Indian Society in the Age of British Expansion 1770–1870*. New Delhi: Oxford University Press, 2012.

Bear, Laura. 'Capitalist Divination: Popularist Speculators and Technologies of Imagination on the Hooghly River'. *Comparative Studies of South Asia, Africa and the Middle East* 35, no. 3 (2015): 408–23.

Bear, Laura, Ritu Birla and Stine Simonsen Puri. 'Speculation: Futures and Capitalism in India'. *Comparative Studies of South Asia, Africa and the Middle East* 35, no. 3 (2015): 387–91.

Bellwinkel-Schempp, M. 'Pigs and Power: Urban Space and Urban Decay'. In *Urbanization and Governance in India*, edited by Evelyn Hust and Michael Mann, 201–26. New Delhi: Manohar, 2005.

Benda-Beckmann, Franz von. 'Mysteries of Capital or Mystification of Legal Property?' *Focaal-European Journal of Anthropology* 41 (2003): 187–91.

Benjamin, Solomon. 'Occupancy Urbanism: Radicalizing Politics and Economy beyond Policy and Programs'. *International Journal of Urban and Regional Research* 32, no. 3 (2008): 719–29.

———. 'Touts, Pirates and Ghosts'. In *Sarai Reader 5: Bare Acts*, edited by Monica Narula, Shuddhabrata Sengupta, Jeebesh Bagchi, Geert Lovink and Lawrence Liang, 242–54. New Delhi: CSDS, 2005.

———. 'Urban Land Transformation for Pro-Poor Economies'. *Geoforum* 35, no. 2 (2004): 177–87.

Benjamin, Solomon, and Bhuvaneshwari Raman. 'Illegible Claims, Legal Titles, and the Worlding of Bangalore'. *Revue Tiers Monde* 206 (2011/12): 37–54.

Bentall, Jim, and Stuart Corbridge. 'Urban–Rural Relations, Demand Politics and the "New Agrarianism" in Northwest India: The Bharatiya Kisan Union'. *Transactions of the Institute of British Geographers* 21, no. 1 (1996): 27–48.

Berenschot, Ward. 'Everyday Mediation: The Politics of Public Service Delivery in Gujarat, India'. *Development and Change* 41, no. 5 (2010): 883–905.

———. 'On the Usefulness of Goondas in Indian Politics: "Moneypower" and "Musclepower" in a Gujarati Locality'. *South Asia: Journal of South Asian Studies* 34, no. 2 (2011): 255–75.

Bhan, Gautam. 'Planned Illegalities: Housing and the Failure of Planning 1947–2010.' *Economic and Political Weekly* 48, no. 24 (2013): 58–70.

Bhan, Gautam, and Kalyani Menon-Sen. *Swept off the Map: Surviving Eviction and Resettlement in Delhi*. New Delhi: Yoda Press, 2008.

Bharadwaj, Suraj Bhan. 'Myth and Reality of the Khap Panchayats: A Historical Analysis of the Panchayat and Khap Panchayat'. *Studies in History* 28, no. 43 (2012): 43–67.

Bhatt, Virendra Nath. 'What Led to the Muzaffarnagar Communal Riots'. *Tehelka*, 8 September 2013. http://www.tehelka.com/2013/09/what-led-to-the-muzaffarnagar-communal-riots/. Accessed 16 November 2015.

Bhattacharya, Neeladri. *The Agrarian Conquest: The Colonial Reshaping of a Rural World*. Ranikhet: Permanent Black, 2018.

Bhattacharyya, Debjani. *Empire and Ecology in the Bengal Delta: The Making of Calcutta*. New Delhi: Cambridge University Press, 2019.

Bhuwania, Anuj. Courting the People: *Public Interest Litigation in Post-emergency India*. New Delhi: Cambridge University Press, 2016.

Biehl, Joao. *Vita: Life in a Zone of Social Abandonment*. Berkeley; London: University of California Press, 2013.

Biehl, Joao, Byron J. Good and Arthur Kleinman, eds. *Subjectivity: Ethnographic Investigations*. Berkeley, Los Angeles: University of California Press, 2007.

Birla, Ritu. *Stages of Capital: Law, Culture, and Market Governance in Late Colonial India*. New Delhi: Orient Blackswan, 2011.

Biswas, Tanima. 'Daylight Attack with Iron Rods Killed College Student Nido Tania'. NDTV, 10 February 2014. http://www.ndtv.com/india-news/daylight-attack-with-iron-rods-killed-college-student-nido-tania-550373. Accessed 11 February 2014.

Björkman, Lisa. *Pipe Politics, Contested Waters: Embedded Infrastructures of Millennial Mumbai*. Durham: Duke University Press, 2015.

———. '"You Can't Buy a Vote": Meanings of Money in a Mumbai Election'. *American Ethnologist* 41, no. 4 (2014): 617–34.

Blomley, Nicholas. 'Landscapes of Property'. *Law and Society Review* 32, no. 3 (1998): 567–612.

———. 'Law, Property, and the Geography of Violence: The Frontier, the Survey, and the Grid'. *Annals of the Association of American Geographers* 20, no. 1 (2003): 121–41.

———. 'Making Private Property: Enclosure, Common Right and the Work of Hedges'. *Rural History* 18, no. 1 (2007): 1–21.

———. *Unsettling the City: Urban Land and the Politics of Property*. New York; London: Routledge, 2004.

Bloomberg. 'Number of Distressed Real Estate Developers Doubles after Collapse of IL&FS', *Hindu Business Line*, 3 October 2019. https://www.thehindubusinessline.com/money-and-banking/number-of-bankrupt-real-estate-developers-doubles-after-collapse-of-ilfs/article29582807.ece. Accessed 26 November 2020.

Bond, George Clement. 'Kinship and Conflict in a Yombe Village: A Genealogical Dispute'. *Africa: Journal of the International African Institute* 42, no. 4 (1972): 275–88.

Bose, Ashish, and Chaman Singh. 'New Rich in a Delhi Fringe Village'. *Economic and Political Weekly* 4, no. 10 (1969): 464–70.

Brand, Stewart. *How Buildings Learn: What Happens after They're Built*. New York: Penguin Books, 1995.

Brass, Paul R. 'Congress, the Lok Dal, and the Middle-Peasant Castes: An Analysis of the 1977 and 1980 Parliamentary Elections in Uttar Pradesh'. *Pacific Affairs* 54, no. 1 (1981): 5–41.

———. 'The Politicization of Peasantry in a North Indian State: I'. *Journal of Peasant Studies* 7, no. 4 (1980): 395–426.

———. 'The Politicization of Peasantry in a North Indian State: II'. *Journal of Peasant Studies* 8, no. 1 (1980): 3–36.

Brenner, Neil. 'Beyond State-Centrism? Space, Territoriality and Geographic Scale in Gobalisation Studies'. *Theory and Society* 28, no. 1 (1999): 39–78.

———. 'Theses on Urbanisation'. *Public Culture* 25, no. 1 (2013): 85–114.

Brown, Wendy. *States of Injury: Power and Freedom in Late Modernity*. New Jersey: Princeton University Press, 1995.

Brunn, Stanely D. 'Gated Minds and Gated Lives as Worlds of Exclusion and Fear'. *GeoJournal* 66, nos. 1–2 (2006): 5–13.

Byres, Terence J. 'Charan Singh (1902–1987): An Assessment'. *Journal of Peasant Studies* 15, no. 2 (1988): 139–89.

Caldeira, Teresa. *City of Walls: Crime, Segregation, and Citizenship in São Paulo*. Los Angeles: University of California Press, 2001.

Caro, Robert. *The Power Broker: Robert Moses and the Fall of New York*. New York: Knopf, 1974.

Castree, Noel. 'Invisible Leviathan: Speculations on Marx, Spivak and the Question of Value'. *Rethinking Marxism* 9, no. 2 (1997): 45–78.

Chakrabarty, Dipesh. *Provincializing Europe: Postcolonial Thought and Historical Difference*. New Jersey: Princeton University Press, 2000.

Chakravarty, Surajit. 'Between Informalities: Mahipalpur Village as an Entrepreneurial Space'. In *Space, Planning and Everyday Contestations in Delhi*, edited by Surajit Chakravarty and Rohit Negi, 113–36. Springer India, 2016.

Chakravarty-Kaul, Minoti. *Common Lands and Customary Law: Institutional Change in North India over the Past Two Centuries*. New Delhi: Oxford University Press, 1996.

———. 'Land Reforms or a Tragedy of the Commons? Kanjhawala Cluster in Delhi and the Punjab'. Conference paper, Indiana University, 2004. https://dlc.dlib.indiana.edu/dlc/handle/10535/1720. Accessed 16 September 2014.

———. 'Market Success or Community Failure? Common Property Resources in North India and a Case Illustration from a Cluster'. *Indian Economic and Social History Review* 36, no. 3 (1999): 355–87.

———. 'Two Centuries of Change on the Commons: Twenty Villages in the Delhi Region'. Paper submitted for Workshop in Political Theory and Policy Analysis, Indiana University, Bloomington, 1990.

Chakravorty, Sanjay. *Price of Land: Acquisition, Conflict, Consequence.* New Delhi: Oxford University Press, 2013.

Chandravarkar, Raj Narayan. *The Origins of Industrial Capitalism in India: Business Strategies and the Working Classes in Bombay, 1900–1940.* Cambridge: Cambridge University Press, 1994.

Chari, Sharad. *Fraternal Capital: Peasant Workers, Self-Made Men and Globalisation in Provincial India.* Stanford; New Delhi: Permanent Black, 2004.

———. 'Marxism, Sarcasm, Ethnography: Geographical Fieldnotes from South India'. *Singapore Journal of Tropical Geography* 24, no. 2 (2003): 169–83.

Chatterjee, Partha. 'Democracy and Economic Transformation in India'. *Economic and Political Weekly* 43, no. 16 (2008): 53–62.

———. *Lineages of Political Society: Studies in Postcolonial Democracy.* New Delhi: Permanent Black, 2011.

———. 'The Nationalist Resolution of the Woman's Question'. In *Recasting Women: Essays in Colonial History*, edited by Kumkum Sangari and Sudesh Vaid, 233–53. New Delhi: Zubaan Books, 2006.

———. *The Politics of the Governed: Reflections on Popular Politics in Most of the World.* New York: Columbia University Press, 2004.

Chaturvedi, Abha, and Anil Chaturvedi. *ACC: A Corporate Saga.* The Associated Cements Companies Limited, 1997.

Chibber, Vivek. *Locked in Place: State-Building and Late Industrialization in India.* New Jersey: Princeton University Press, 2003.

Chitlangia, Risha. 'BSP's Tokas Second Richest Candidate'. *Times of India*, 19 November 2013. http://timesofindia.indiatimes.com/assembly-elections-2013/delhi-assembly-elections/BSPs-Tokas-second-richest-candidate/articleshow/26013347.cms. Accessed 28 February 2014.

Choi, Eun Kyong, and Kate Xiao Zhou. 'Entrepreneurs and Politics in the Chinese Transitional Economy: Political Connections and Rent-Seeking'. *China Review* 1, no. 1 (2001): 111–35.

Chowdhry, Prem. 'Caste Panchayats and the Policing of Marriage in Haryana: Enforcing Kinship and Territorial Exogamy'. *Contributions to Indian Sociology* 38, nos. 1–2 (2004): 1–42.

———. '"First Our Jobs Then Our Girls": The Dominant Caste Perceptions on the "Rising" Dalits'. *Modern Asian Studies* 43, no. 2 (2009): 437–79.

———. *Political Economy of Production and Reproduction: Caste, Custom and Community in North India*. New Delhi: Oxford University Press, 1991.

———. *Punjab Politics and the Role of Sir Chhotu Ram*. New Delhi: Vikas Publishing House, 1984.

———. 'Social Support Base and Electoral Politics: The Congress in Colonial Southeast Punjab'. *Modern Asian Studies* 25, no. 4 (1991): 811–31.

Ciotti, Manuela. *Retro-Modern India: Forging the Low-Caste Self*. New Delhi: Routledge, 2010.

Comaroff, Jean, and John L. Comaroff. *Law and Disorder in the Postcolony*. Chicago: University of Chicago Press, 2006.

———. 'Millennial Capitalism: First Thoughts on a Second Coming'. In *Millennial Capitalism and the Age of Neoliberalism*, edited by Jean Comaroff and John L. Comaroff, 1–56. Durham; London: Duke University Press, 2001.

Corbridge, Stuart. 'The Political Economy of Development in India Since Independence'. In *Routledge Handbook of South Asian Politics: India, Pakistan, Bangladesh, Sri Lanka, and Nepal*, edited by Paul Brass, 305–20. London; New York: Routledge, 2010.

Coronil, Fernando. *The Magical State: Nature, Money and Modernity in Venezuela*. Chicago; London: University of Chicago Press, 1997.

Cowan, Tom. 'Subaltern Counter-Urbanism: Work, Dispossession and Emplacement in Gurgaon, India'. *Geoforum* 92 (2018): 152–60.

———. 'The Urban Village, Agrarian Transformation, and Rentier Capitalism in Gurgaon, India'. *Antipode* 50, no. 5 (2018): 1244–66.

———. 'The Village as Urban Infrastructure: Social Reproduction, Agrarian Repair and Uneven Urbanisation'. *Environment and Planning E: Nature and Space* 4, no. 3 (2021): 736–55.

Cronon, William. *Nature's Metropolis: Chicago and the Great West*. New York; London: W. W. Norton and Company, 1991.

Damodaran, Harish. *India's New Capitalists: Caste, Business, and Industry in a Modern Nation*. New York: Palgrave MacMillan, 2008.

Daniyal, Shoaib. 'Ground Report: The Haryana Protests Are Peaceful (For Now) But Jat Anger Smoulders Underneath'. *Scroll*, 10 June 2016. http://scroll.in/article/809587/ground-report-the-haryana-protests-are-peaceful-for-now-but-jat-anger-smoulders-underneath. Accessed 11 June 2016.

Das Gupta, Chirashree. *State and Capital in Independent India: Institutions and Accumulation*. New Delhi: Cambridge University Press, 2016.

Das, Ritanjan. 'Narratives of the Dispossessed and Casteless: Politics of Land and Caste in Rajarhat, West Bengal'. *Journal of Contemporary Asia* 50, no. 5 (2019): 806–30.

Das, Veena, and Deborah Poole, eds. *Anthropology at the Margins of the State*. Santa Fe: School of American Research Press, 2004.

Datta, Nonica. *Forming an Identity: A Social History of Jats*. New Delhi: Oxford University Press, 1999.

Dattatreyan, E. G. 'Policing the "Sensible" in the Era of YouTube: Urban Villages and Racialised Subjects in Delhi'. *Television and New Media* 21, no. 4 (2019): 1–13.

DeFillipis, James. 'The Myth of Social Capital in Community Development'. *Housing Policy Debate* 12, no. 4 (2001): 781–806.

de Soto, Hernando. *Mystery of Capital: Why Capitalism Triumphs in the West and Fails Everywhere Else*. New York: Basic Books, 2003.

Desmond, Matthew. *Evicted: Poverty and Profit in the American City*. London: Penguin, 2016.

Dey, Ishita, Ranabir Samaddar and Suhit K. Sen. *Beyond Kolkata: Rajarhat and the Dystopia of Urban Imagination*. New Delhi: Routledge, 2013.

Dhapola, Shruti. 'Munirka's Campaign against "Gandey Log" of Northeast', *Firstpost*, 19 February 2014. http://www.firstpost.com/india/delhi-munirkas-campaign-against-gandey-log-of-northeast-1396833.html?utm_source=ref_article. Accessed 20 February 2014.

DHNS. 'MLA Involved in Fracas at Temple, Gunshots Fired'. *Deccan Herald*, 31 May 2015. https://www.deccanherald.com/content/480759/mla-involved-fracas-temple-gunshots.html. Accessed 1 June 2015.

Dirlik, Arif. 'The Postcolonial Aura: Third World Criticism in the Age of Global Capitalism'. *Critical Inquiry* 20, no. 2 (1994): 328–56.

Doron, Assa. 'Caste Away? Subaltern Engagement with the Modern Indian State'. *Modern Asian Studies* 44, no. 4 (2010): 753–83.

Doshi, Sapana. 'The Politics of the Evicted: Redevelopment, Subjectivity, and Difference in Mumbai's Slum Frontier'. *Antipode* 45, no. 4 (2013): 844–65.

Dupont, Véronique. 'Slum Demolitions in Delhi since the 1990s: An Appraisal'. *Economic and Political Weekly* 43, no. 28 (2008): 79–87.

Dupont, Véronique, and Usha Ramanathan. 'The Courts and the Squatter Settlements in Delhi: Or the Intervention of the Judiciary in Urban Governance'. In *New Forms of Urban Governance in India: Shifts, Models, Networks, and Contestations*, edited by I. S. A. Baud and Joop de Wit, 312–43. New Delhi: Sage, 2008.

Eiss, Paul K., and David Pederson. 'Introduction: Values of Value'. *Cultural Anthropology* 17, no. 3 (2002): 283–90.
Express News Service. 'Congolese Youth Beaten to Death in New Delhi, One Suspect Detained'. *Indian Express*, 22 May 2016. http://indianexpress.com/article/india/india-news-india/delhi-african-youth-beaten-to-death-in-vasant-kunj-2811692/. Accessed 23 May 2016.

———. 'In Chhatarpur Village, 4 Attacks in 30 Mins: Mob "Targets" Africans, 7 Injured'. *Indian Express*, 29 May 2016. http://indianexpress.com/article/india/india-news-india/african-nationals-attacked-congo-latest-updates-2823603/. Accessed 30 May 2016.

———. 'Know Your Neta: Newcomers to Neo-Rich'. *Sunday Standard*, 24 November 2013. http://www.newindianexpress.com/thesundaystandard/Know-your-neta-Newcomers-to-neo-rich/2013/11/24/article1907521.ece. Accessed 27 October 2015.

———. 'Levy Higher Property Tax on Those with More than Two Kids: Delhi Councillor'. *Indian Express*, 3 December 2019. https://indianexpress.com/article/delhi/levy-higher-property-tax-on-those-with-more-than-two-kids-councillor-6147529/. Accessed 7 January 2020.

Falzon, M. A. 'Paragons of Lifestyle: Gated Communities and the Politics of Space in Bombay'. *City and Society* 16, no. 2 (2004): 145–67.
FAO. 'Public Distribution System in India: Evolution, Efficacy and Need for Reforms'. http://www.fao.org/3/x0172e/x0172e06.htm. Accessed 24 November 2019.
Feinstein, Susan. 'Financialisation and Justice in the City: A Commentary'. *Urban Studies* 53, no. 7 (2016): 1503–08.
Ferguson, James. *The Anti-Politics Machine: 'Development', Depoliticization, and Bureaucratic Power in Lesotho*. Cambridge: Cambridge University Press, 1990.
Flusty, Steven. *Building Paranoia: Proliferation of Interdictory Space and the Erosion of Spatial Justice*. West Hollywood, CA: Los Angeles Forum for Architecture and Urban Design, 1994.
Foucault, Michel. *Society Must Be Defended: Lectures at the Collège de France 1975–76*. New York: Picador, 2003.

———. *The Birth of Biopolitics: Lectures at the Collège de France 1978–79*. New York: Picador, 2004.

Frankel, Francine. *India's Green Revolution. Economic Gains and Political Costs*. Pennsylvania: Princeton Legacy Library 2016.

———. *India's Political Economy: 1947–2004*. New Delhi: Oxford University Press, 2006.

Freed, Stanley A., and Ruth Freed. 'Urbanization and Family Types in a North Indian Village'. *Southwestern Journal of Anthropology* 25, no. 4 (1969): 342–59.

Freeman, Carla. *High Tech and High Heels in the Global Economy: Women, Work, and Pink-Collar Identities in the Caribbean*. Durham: Duke University Press, 2000.

Friese, Kal. 'Peasant Communities and Agrarian Capitalism'. *Economic and Political Weekly* 25, no. 39 (1990): A135–A143.

Geertz, Clifford. *Available Light: Anthropological Explorations on Philosophical Topics*. New Jersey: Princeton University Press, 2001.

———. 'Deep Play: Notes on Balinese Cockfight'. In *The Interpretation of Cultures: Selected Essays by Clifford Geertz*, 412–54. New York: Basic Books, 1973.

Geschiere, Peter, and Francis Nyamnjoh. 'Capitalism and Autochthony: The Seesaw of Mobility and Belonging'. In *Millennial Capitalism and the Age of Neoliberalism*, edited by Jean Comaroff and John L. Comaroff, 159–90. New York: Duke University Press, 2001.

Ghertner, David A. 'Gentrifying the State, Gentrifying Participation: Elite Governance Programs in Delhi'. *International Journal of Urban and Regional Research* 35, no. 3 (2011): 504–32.

———. *Rule by Aesthetics: World-Class City Making in Delhi*. New York: Oxford University Press, 2015.

Ghosh, Anjan. 'Caste Idiom for Class Conflict: Case of Khanjawala'. *Economic and Political Weekly* 14, nos. 5–6 (1979): 184–86.

———. 'The Role of Rumour in History Writing'. *History Compass* 6, no. 5 (2008): 1235–43.

Ghosh, Avantika. 'Honour Killings: North India Wages a Vicious War against Love'. *Times of India*, 1 July 2010. https://timesofindia.indiatimes.com/india/Honour-killings-North-India-wages-a-vicious-war-against-love/articleshow/6112387.cms. Accessed 25 October 2016.

Ghosh, Shinjini. 'Help Us Return Home, Workers in Shahpur Jat Appeal to W. B. Govt.'. *Hindu*, 11 May 2010. https://www.thehindu.com/news/cities/Delhi/help-us-return-home-workers-in-shahpur-jat-appeal-to-wb-govt/article31561429.ece. Accessed 21 May 2020.

Ghosh, Shrimoyee Nandini. '"Not Worth the Paper It's Written On": Stamp Paper Documents and the Life of Law in India'. *Contributions to Indian Sociology* 53, no. 1 (2019): 19–45.

Gibson-Graham, J. K. 'Diverse Economies: Performative Practices for "Other Worlds"'. *Progress in Human Geography* 32, no. 5 (2008): 613–32.

Gidwani, Vinay. *Capital, Interrupted: Agrarian Development and the Work of Politics in India*. Minneapolis; London: University of Minnesota Press, 2008.

———. '"Waste" and the Permanent Settlement in Bengal'. *Economic and Political Weekly* 27, no. 4 (1992): PE 39–PE 46.

Gill, Sucha Singh. 'The Farmers' Movement and Agrarian Change in the Green Revolution Belt of North-West India'. *Journal of Peasant Studies* 21, nos. 3–4 (1994): 195–211.

Gohain, Manash Pratim. 'Campaign for DUSU Elections Kickstarts'. *Times of India*, 6 September 2014. http://timesofindia.indiatimes.com/city/delhi/Campaign-for-DUSU-elections-kick-starts/articleshow/41822889.cms. Accessed 12 December 2014.

———. 'JNU Row: Landlords Tell Students to Go'. *Times of India*, 18 February 2016. http://timesofindia.indiatimes.com/city/delhi/Landlords-tell-students-to-go/articleshow/51031496.cms. Accessed 18 February 2016.

Goldman, Michael. 'Speculative Urbanism and the Making of the Next World City'. *International Journal of Urban and Regional Research* 35, no. 3 (2011): 555–81.

Govinda, Radhika. '"First Our Fields, Now Our Women": Gender Politics in Delhi's Urban Villages in Transition'. *South Asia Multidisciplinary Academic Journal* 8 (2013).

Govindarajan, Radhika. 'Electoral Ripples: The Social Life of Lies and Mistrust in an Indian Village Election'. *HAU: Journal of Ethnographic Theory* 8, nos. 1–2 (2018): 129–43.

Graeber, David. *Debt: The First 5000 Years*. New York: Melville House, 2011.

———. 'It Is Value That Brings Universes into Being'. *HAU: Journal of Ethnographic Theory* 3, no. 2 (2013): 219–43.

———. *Toward an Anthropological Theory of Value: The False Coins of Our Own Dreams*. Hampshire: Palgrave, 2001.

Granovetter, Mark. 'Economic Action and Social Structure: The Problem of Embeddedness'. *American Journal of Sociology* 91, no. 3 (1985):481–510.

Gudeman, Stephen. *The Anthropology of Economy: Community, Market and Culture*. Massachusetts; Oxford: Blackwell Publishers, 2001.

Guha, Ranajit. *A Rule of Property: An Essay on the Idea of Permanent Settlement*. Ranikhet: Permanent Black, 2016.

Guha, Sumit. *Beyond Caste: Identity and Power in South Asia Past and Present*. Ranikhet: Permanent Black, 2016.

Gupta, Akhil. 'Blurred Boundaries: The Discourse of Corruption, the Culture of Politics, and the Imagined State'. *American Ethnologist* 22, no. 2 (1995): 375–402.

———. *Postcolonial Developments: Agriculture and the Making of Modern India*. Durham: Duke University Press, 1998.

———. *Red Tape: Bureaucracy, Structural Violence and Poverty in India*. Durham: Duke University Press, 2012.

Gupta, Dipankar. *Rivalry and Brotherhood: Politics in the Life of Farmers in Northern India*. Delhi: Oxford University Press, 1997.

Gururani, Shubhra. 'Cities in a World of Villages: Agrarian Urbanism and the Making of India's Urbanizing Frontiers'. *Urban Geography* 41, no. 7 (2020): 971–89.

———. 'Flexible Planning: The Making of India's "Millennium City", Gurgaon'. In *Ecologies of Urbanism: Metropolitan Civility and Sustainability*, edited by Anne Rademacher and K. Sivaramakrishnan, 119–44. Hong Kong: Hong Kong University Press, 2013.

Gururani, Shubhra, and Rajarshi Dasgupta. 'Frontier Urbanism: Urbanisation beyond Cities in South Asia'. *Economic and Political Weekly* 53, no. 12 (2018): 41–45.

Gutgutia, Sneha. 'Pigs, Precarity and Infrastructure'. *Society and Space*, 30 November 2020. https://www.societyandspace.org/articles/pigs-precarity-and-infrastructure. Accessed 30 November 2020.

Haila, Anne. 'Land as a Financial Asset: The Theory of Urban Rent as a Mirror of Economic Transformation'. *Antipode* 20, no. 2 (1988): 79–101.

———. 'Real Estate in Global Cities: Singapore and Hong Kong as Property States'. *Urban Studies* 37, no. 12 (2000): 2241–56.

———. 'The Theory of Land Rent at the Crossroads'. *Environment and Planning: International Journal of Urban and Regional Research* 8, no. 3 (1990): 275–96.

———. *Urban Land Rent: Singapore as a Property State*. Chicester: Wiley-Blackwell, 2015.

Hann, C. M. 'Introduction: The Embeddedness of Property'. In *Property Relations: Renewing the Anthropological Traditions*, edited by C. M. Hann. Cambridge: Cambridge University Press, 1998.

Hansen, Thomas Blom. 'Performers of Sovereignty: On the Privatization of Security in Urban South Africa'. *Critiques of Anthropology* 26, no. 3 (2006): 279–95.

Hansen, Thomas Blom, and Finn Steppurat. *States of Imagination: Ethnographic Explorations of the Postcolonial State*. Durham; London: Duke University Press, 2001.

Hardgrove, Anne. *Community as Public Culture: The Marwaris of Calcutta c. 1897–1997*. New York: Columbia University Press, 2001.

Hardt, Michael, and Antonio Negri. *Empire*. Cambridge; London: Harvard University Press, 2001.

Harris-White, Barbara. *India Working: Essays on Society and Economy*. Cambridge: Cambridge University Press, 2003.

Hartle, D. G. 'The Theory of "Rent Seeking": Some Reflections'. *Canadian Journal of Economics* 16, no. 4 (1983): 539–54.

Harvey, David. 'Class-Monopoly Rent, Finance Capital and the Urban Revolution'. *Regional Studies* 8, nos. 3–4 (1974): 239–55.

———. *Conditions of Postmodernity: An Enquiry into the Origins of Cultural Change*. Cambridge; Oxford: Blackwell, 1989.

———. *Enigma of Capital and the Crises of Capitalism*. New York: Oxford University Press, 2010.

———. 'Land Rent and the Transition to the Capitalist Mode of Production'. *Antipode* 14, no. 3 (1982): 17–25.

———. *Paris: Capital of Modernity*. New York; London: Routledge, 2003.

———. *The Limits to Capital*. London; New York: Verso, 2006.

———. *The New Imperialism*. New York: Oxford University Press, 2003.

———. *Urbanization of Capital*. Baltimore: Johns Hopkins University Press, 1985.

Hoang, Kimberley Kay. *Dealing in Desire: Asian Ascendancy, Western Decline, and the Hidden Currencies of Global Sex Work*. Los Angeles: University of California Press, 2015.

Hu, Winnie. '"Hostile Architecture": How Public Spaces Keep the Public Out'. *New York Times*, 8 November 2019. https://www.nytimes.com/2019/11/08/nyregion/hostile-architecture-nyc.html. Accessed 20 March 2020.

Hull, Matthew S. 'Communities of Place, Not Kind: American Technologies of Neighbourhood in Postcolonial Delhi'. *Comparative Studies in Society and History* 53, no. 4 (2011): 757–90.

———. *Government of Paper: The Materiality of Bureaucracy in Urban Pakistan*. Berkeley: University of California Press, 2012.

Irani, Lilly. *Chasing Innovation: Making Entrepreneurial Citizens in Modern India*. New Jersey: Princeton University Press, 2019.

Islam, M. Mufakharul. 'The Punjab Land Alienation Act and the Professional Moneylenders'. *Modern Asian Studies* 29, no. 2 (1995): 271–91.

Jackson, Peter. 'Commercial Cultures: Transcending the Cultural and the Economic'. *Progress in Human Geography* 26, no. 1 (2002): 3–18.

Jaffe, Rivke. 'The Hybrid State: Crime and Citizenship in Urban Jamaica'. *American Ethnologist* 40, no. 4 (2013): 734–48.

Jäger, Johannes. 'Urban Land Rent Theory: A Regulationist Perspective'. *International Journal of Urban and Regional Research* 27, no. 2 (2003): 233–49.

Jaoul, Nicholas. 'Casting the "Sweepers": Local Politics of Sanskritisation, Caste and Labour'. In *Cultural Entrenchment of Hindutva: Local Mediations and Forms of Convergence*, edited by Daniela Berti, Nicholas Jaoul and Pralay Kanungo, 273–306. New Delhi: Routledge, 2011.

Jeffrey, Craig. '"A Fist Is Stronger than Five Fingers": Caste and Dominance in Rural North India'. *Transactions of the Institute of British Geographers* 26, no. 2 (2001): 217–36.

———. 'Are Rich Rural Jats Middle Class?' In *Elite and Everyman: The Cultural Politics of the Indian Middle Classes*, edited by Amita Baviskar and Raka Ray, 140–63. New Delhi: Routledge, 2011.

———. 'Caste, Class, and Clientelism: A Political Economy of Everyday Corruption in Rural North India'. *Economic Geography* 78, no. 1 (2002): 21–41.

———. *Timepass: Youth, Class and the Politics of Waiting in India*. Stanford: Stanford University Press, 2010.

Jeffrey, Craig, Patricia Jeffrey and Roger Jeffrey. *Degrees without Freedom? Education, Masculinities and Unemployment in North India*. Stanford: Stanford University Press, 2008.

Jeffrey, Craig, and Jens Lerche. 'Dimensions of Dominance: Class and State in Uttar Pradesh'. In *The Everyday State and Society in Modern India*, edited by C. J. Fuller and Veronique Benei, 91–113. New Delhi: Social Science Press, 2009.

Joseph, Miranda. *Against the Romance of the Community*. Minneapolis; London: University of Minnesota Press, 2002.

Kambouri, Nelli, and Pavlos Hatzopoulos. 'Making Violent Practices Public'. In *Video Vortex Reader: Responses to YouTube*, edited by Geert Lovink and Sabine Nierderer, 125–32. Amsterdam: Institute of Network Cultures, 2008.

Karlsson, Bengt G., and Dolly Kikon. 'Wayfinding: Indigenous Migrants in the Service Sector of Metropolitan India'. *South Asia: Journal of South Asian Studies* 40, no. 3 (2017): 447–62.

Katz, Steven. 'Towards a Sociological Definition of Rent: Notes on David Harvey's The Limits to Capital'. *Antipode* 18, no. 1 (1986): 64–78.

Kaviraj, Sudipta. 'Indira Gandhi and Indian Politics'. *Economic and Political Weekly* 21, nos. 38–39 (1986): 1697–1708.

———. 'On State, Society and Discourse in India'. *IDS Bulletin* 21, no. 4 (1990): 10–15.

———. 'The Imaginary Institutions of India'. In Sudipta Kaviraj, *The Imaginary Institution of India: Politics and Ideas*, 167–209. Ranikhet: Permanent Black, 2010.

Kempadoo, Kamala. *Sexing the Caribbean: Gender, Race and Sexual Labour*. New York: Routledge, 2004.

Khan, Mushtaq H., and Jomo K. S., eds. *Rents, Rent-Seeking and Economic Development: Theory and Evidence in Asia*. Cambridge: Cambridge University Press, 2000.

Khan, Naveeda. *Muslim Becoming: Aspiration and Skepticism in Pakistan*. Durham: Duke University Press, 2012.

Khanna, Sunil. 'Shahri Jat and Dehati Jatni: The Indian Peasant Community in Transition'. *Contemporary South Asia* 10, no. 1 (2001): 37–53.

King, Anthony D. *Urbanism, Colonialism and the World-Economy: Cultural and Spatial Foundations of the World Urban System*. London; New York: Routledge, 1990.

Kipnis, A. B. *Producing Guanxi: Sentiment, Self, and Subculture in a North China Village*. Durham: Duke University Press, 1997.

Kohli, Atul. 'Politics of Economic Liberalisation in India'. *World Development* 17, no. 3 (1989): 305–28.

Krueger, Anne O. 'The Political Economy of the Rent-Seeking Society'. *American Economic Review* 64, no. 3 (1974): 291–303.

Kumar, Ashok. 'Jats Continue to Hold Political Ground in Capital'. *Hindu*, 25 October 2013. http://www.thehindu.com/todays-paper/tp-national/tp-new delhi/jats-continue-to-hold-political-ground-in-capital/article5270650.ece. Accessed 27 January 2014.

Kumar, Mukul. 'Erstwhile Villages in Urban India'. *Development in Practice* 25, no. 1 (2015): 124–32.

Kumar, Rajesh. '39 Villages under SDMC to Be Made "Urban Villages"'. *Pioneer*, 9 February 2015. http://www.dailypioneer.com/city/39-villages-under-sdmc-to-be-made-urban-villages.html. Accessed 10 February 2015.

Kumar, Sanjay. *Changing Electoral Politics in Delhi: From Caste to Class*. New Delhi: Sage Publications, 2013.

Kumar, Satendra. *Badalta Gaon, Badalta Dehat: Nai Samajikta Ka Uday*. New Delhi: Oxford University Press, 2018.

Kumar, Sunalini. 'Chronicles of a Death Untold: The Lethal Geographies of Delhi's Peripheries'. In *Critical Studies in Politics: Exploring Sites, Selves and Power*, edited by Aditya Nigam, Nivedita Menon and Sanjay Palshikar, 113–65. New Delhi: Orient Blackswan, 2013.

Lackman, Conway L. 'The Modern Development of Classical Rent Theory'. *American Journal of Economics and Sociology* 35, no. 3 (1976): 287–300.

Lama-Rewal, Stephanie Tawa. 'Neighbourhood Associations and Local Democracy: Delhi Municipal Elections 2007'. *Economic and Political Weekly* 42, no. 47 (2007): 51–60.

Lapavistas, Costas. 'The Financialization of Capitalism: 'Profiting without Producing'. *City* 17, no. 6 (2013): 792–805.

Lazzarato, Maurizio. 'Immaterial Labour'. In *Radical Thought in Italy: A Potential Politics*, edited by Paolo Virno and Michael Hardt, 133–148. Minneapolis: University of Minnesota Press, 1996.

Lefebvre, Henri. *The Production of Space*. Translated by Donald Nicholson-Smith. Oxford: Blackwell, 1998.

Leitner, Helga, and Byron Miller. 'Scale and the Limitations of Ontological Debate: A Commentary on Marston, Jones and Woodward'. *Transactions of the Institute of British Geographers* 32, no. 1 (2007):116–25.

Levien, Michael. *Dispossession without Development: Land Grabs in Neoliberal India*. New York: Oxford University Press, 2018.

———. 'Special Economic Zones and Accumulation by Dispossession in India'. *Journal of Agrarian Change* 11, no. 4 (2011): 454–83.

———. The Politics of Dispossession: Theorizing India's "Land Wars"'. *Politics and Society* 41, no. 3 (2013): 351–94.

Lewis, Oscar. *Village Life in Northern India: Studies in a Delhi Village*. Urbana: University of Illinois Press, 1958.

Lewis, Oscar, and Victor Barnouw. 'Caste and the Jajmani System in a North Indian Village'. *Scientific Monthly* 83, no. 2 (1956): 66–81.

Lin, Sharat G., and Nageshwar Patnaik. 'Migrant Labor at ASIAD '82 Construction Sites in New Delhi'. *Bulletin of Concerned Asian Scholars* 14, no. 3 (1982): 22–31.

LiPuma, Edward, and Benjamin Lee. *Financial Derivatives and the Globalization of Risk*. Durham: Duke University Press, 2004.

Locke, John. *Two Treatises of Government*. London: Everyman's Library, 1993.

Lund, Christian. 'Property and Citizenship: Conceptually Connecting Land Rights and Belonging in Africa'. *Africa Spectrum* 46, no. 3 (2011):71–75.

———. 'Rule and Rupture: State Formation through the Production of Property and Citizenship'. *Development and Change* 47, no. 6 (2016): 1199–1228.

Lynch, Owen. 'Review of M. C. Pradhan, The Political System of Jats of Northern India'. *American Anthropologist* 70, no. 3 (1968): 593–94.

———. *The Politics of Untouchability: Social Mobility and Social Change in a City of India*. New York: Columbia University Press, 1969.

Marazzi, Christian. *The Violence of Finance Capitalism*. Translated by Kristina Lebedeva. Los Angeles: Semiotext(e), 2010.

Marcus, George. *Ethnography through Thick and Thin*. New Jersey: Princeton University Press, 1998.

Marston, Sallie. 'The Social Construction of Scale'. *Progress in Human Geography* 24, no. 2 (2000): 219–42.

Marston, Sallie, John Paul Jones III and Keith Woodward. 'Human Geography without Scale'. *Transactions of the Institute of British Geographers* 30, no. 4 (2005): 416–32.

Marx, Karl. *Capital: A Critique of Political Economy*. Vol. 1. Translated by Ben Fowkes. London: Penguin Classics, 1994.

———. *Capital: A Critique of Political Economy*. Vol. 3. Translated by David Fernbach. London: Penguin Classics, 1991.

———. *The Eighteenth Brumaire of Louis Bonaparte*. Moscow: Progress Publishers, 1972.

Mathur, Nayanika. *Paper Tiger: Law, Bureaucracy and the Developmental State in Himalayan India*. New Delhi: Cambridge University Press, 2016.

Maunder, D. A. C., and T. C. Mbara. 'Liberalisation of Urban Public Transport Services: What Are the Implications?' *Indian Journal of Transport Management* 20, no. 2 (1996): 16–23.

Mazzucato, Mariana. *The Value of Everything: Making and Taking in the Global Economy*. London: Allen Lane, 2018.

McDuie-Ra, Duncan. 'Being a Tribal Man from the North-East: Migration, Morality, and Masculinity'. *South Asian History and Culture* 4, no. 2 (2013): 250–65.

———. *Debating Race in Contemporary India*. London: Palgrave Macmillan, 2015.

———. 'Leaving the Militarized Frontier: Migration and Tribal Masculinity in Delhi'. *Men and Masculinities* 15, no. 2 (2012): 112–31.

———. *Northeast Migrants in Delhi: Race, Refuge and Retail*. Amsterdam: Amsterdam University Press, 2012.

McFarlane, Colin. 'Rethinking Informality: Politics, Crisis, and the City'. *Planning Theory and Practice* 13, no. 1 (2012): 89–108.

McGee, Terrance. 'The Spatiality of Urbanization: The Policy Challenges of Mega-Urban and Desakota Regions of Southeast Asia'. Working paper no. 161, Institute of Advanced Studies, United Nations University, 2009.

McRobbie, Angela. 'Reflections on Feminism, Immaterial Labour and the Post-Fordist Regime'. *New Formations* 70, no. 1 (Winter 2010): 60–76.

Mehra, Ajay K. 'Urban Villages of Delhi'. In *Urbanization and Governance in India*, edited by Evelyn Hust and Michael Mann, 279–310. New Delhi: Manohar, 2005.

Mehra, Diya. 'Planning Delhi ca. 1936–1959'. *South Asia: Journal of South Asian Studies* 36, no. 3 (2013): 354–74.

———. 'Protesting Publics in Indian Cities: The 2006 Sealing Drive and Delhi's Traders'. *Economic and Political Weekly* 47, no. 30 (2012): 79–88.

Menon, Aditya. 'Rakesh Tikait's Tears Turn Tables: Why BJP Govt Underestimated Him'. *Quint*, 29 January 2021. https://www.thequint.com/news/politics/rakesh-tikait-crying-ghazipur-border-farmers-protest-bku-tractor-rally-red-fort. Accessed 29 January 2021.

Menon, Ritu, and Kamla Bhasin. 'Recovery, Rupture, Resistance: Indian State and Abduction of Women during Partition'. *Economic and Political Weekly* 28, no. 17 (1993): WS2–WS11.

Merrifield, Andy. 'The Urban Question under Planetary Urbanization'. *International Journal of Urban and Regional Research* 37, no. 3 (2003): 909–22.

Meyer, Hannes. 'The New World'. In *Hannes Mayer: Buildings, Projects, and Writings*, edited by Claude Schnaidt, 91–94. Teufen AR/Schweiz: Arthur Niggli Ltd, 1965. https://modernistarchitecture.wordpress.com/2010/10/20/hannes-meyer%E2%80%99s-%E2%80%9Cthe-new-world%E2%80%9D-1926/. Accessed 29 March 2021.

Mezzadra, Sandro, and Brett Neilson. *Border as Method, Or, The Multiplication of Labour*. Durham: Duke University Press, 2013.

———. 'On the Multiple Frontiers of Extraction: Excavating Contemporary Capitalism'. *Cultural Studies* 31, nos. 1–3 (2017): 185–204.

———. 'Operations of Capital'. *South Atlantic Quarterly* 114, no. 1 (2015): 1–9.

Mishra, Ashish. 'Leaning Building of Delhi's Munirka Razed in 72-Hour Long Exercise'. *Hindustan Times*, 24 February 2020. https://www.hindustantimes.com/cities/munirka-building-razed-in-72-hour-long-exercise/story-PnsNI6KlsAsDdTO7W46O0J.html. Accessed 25 February 2020.

Mishra, H. M. 'Red Line Bus Fleet Wreaks Havoc in Delhi'. *India Today*, 15 June 1993. https://www.indiatoday.in/magazine/indiascope/story/19930615-red-line-bus-fleet-wreaks-havoc-in-delhi-811185-1993-06-15. Accessed 17 November 2019.

Mitchell, Timothy. *Rule of Experts: Egypt, Techno-Politics, Modernity*. Berkeley; Los Angeles: University of California Press, 2012.

———. 'The Limits of the State: Beyond the Statist Approaches and Their Critics'. *American Political Science Review* 85, no. 1 (1991): 77–96.

———. 'The Properties of Markets'. In *Do Economists Make Markets? On the Performativity of Economics*, edited by Donald Mackenzie, Fabian Muniesa and Lucia Siu, 244–75. Princeton; Oxford: Princeton University Press, 2007.

Mitra, Iman, Ranabir Samaddar and Samita Sen, eds. *Accumulation in Postcolonial Capitalism*. Singapore: Springer, 2016.

Muelbach, Andrea. *The Moral Neoliberal: Welfare and Citizenship in Italy*. Chicago: University of Chicago Press, 2012.

Mukul, Akshaya. *Gita Press and the Making of Hindu India*. New Delhi: Harper Collins, 2016.

Murari, Krishna. 'Farmers' Movements in Independent India'. *Indian Journal of Public Administration* 61, no. 3 (2015): 457–79.

Naik, Mukta, and Eesha Kunduri. 'The Role of Housing Finance Actors in Regenerating Delhi's Unauthorised Colonies: An Examination of State–Citizen–Market Boundaries'. *Urbanisation* 5, no. 2 (2020): 1–19.

Naik, Mukta, and Manish. 'BJP and AAP Know Regularising Delhi Colonies Is Smart Policy, But It's an Incomplete Plan'. *Print*, 26 January 2020. https://theprint.in/opinion/bjp-aap-know-regularising-delhi-colonies-is-smart-policy-but-incomplete-plan/354709/. Accessed 15 April 2020.

Nandi, Jayashree, and Somreet Bhattacharya. 'Anti-northeast Fiat in Munirka, Cops Step In'. *Times of India*, 18 February 2014. http://timesofindia.indiatimes.com/city/delhi/Anti-northeast-fiat-/articleshow/30580917.cms. Accessed on 18 February 2014.

Natrajan, Balmurali. 'Caste, Class, and Community in India: An Ethnographic Approach'. *Ethnology* 44, no. 3 (2005): 227–41.

———. 'From Jati to Samaj'. *Seminar* 633 (2012): 54–57.

Negi, Rohit, and Persis Taraporewala. 'Window to a South-South World: Ordinary Gentrification and African Migrants in Delhi'. In *Migration and Agency in a Globalizing World*, edited by S. Cornelissen and Y. Mine, 209–30. London: Palgrave Macmillan, 2018.

Nielsen, Kenneth Bo, Siddharth Sareen and Patrik Oskarsson. 'The Politics of Caste in India's New Land Wars'. *Journal of Contemporary Asia* 50, no. 5 (2020): 684–95.

Nigam, Aditya. 'Dislocating Delhi: A City in the 1990s'. In *Public Domain, Sarai Reader 01*, edited by Raqs Media Collective and Geert Lovink. New Delhi: CSDS, 2001.

Norr, Kathleen Fordham. 'Factions and Kinship: The Case of a South Indian Village'. *Asian Survey* 16, no. 12 (1976): 1139–50.

Oldenburg, Philip. *Big City Government in India: Councilor, Administrator and Citizen in Delhi*. Tucson: University of Arizona Press, 1976.

Oldenburg, Veena Talwar. *Gurgaon: From Mythic Village to Millennium City.* New Delhi: Harper Collins, 2018.

Ong, Aihwa. *Neoliberalism as Exception: Mutations in Citizenship and Sovereignty.* Durham; London: Duke University Press, 2006.

Ong, Aihwa and Stephen J. Collier. *Global Assemblages: Technology, Politics, and Ethics as Anthropological Problems.* Oxford: Blackwell Publishing, 2005.

Ortega, Andre C. 'Manila's Metropolitan Landscape of Gentrification: Global Urban Development, Accumulation by Dispossession and Neoliberal Warfare against Informality'. *Geoforum* 70 (2016): 35–50.

Osburg, John. *Anxious Wealth: Money and Morality among China's New Rich.* Stanford: Stanford University Press, 2013.

Pai, Sudha. Dalit Assertion and the Unfinished Democratic Revolution: The Bahujan Samaj Party in Uttar Pradesh. New Delhi: Sage Publications, 2002.

Palat, Nipesh Narayan, and René Véron. 'Informal Production of the City: Momos, Migrants, and an Urban Village in Delhi'. *Environment and Planning D: Society and Space* 36, no. 6 (2018): 1026–44.

Palshikar, Suhas. 'Caste Politics through the Prism of Region'. In *Region, Culture and Politics in India,* edited by Vora Rajendra and Anne Feldhaus, 271–98. New Delhi: Manohar, 2006.

Pandit, Ambika, and Paras Singh. '12 Years after Bulldozers Ended Dream Run of MG Road, New Malls Rising Again'. *Times of India,* 10 May 2018. https://timesofindia.indiatimes.com/city/delhi/12-years-after-bulldozers-ended-dream-run-of-mg-road-new-malls-rising-again/articleshow/64101807.cms. Accessed 27 November 2020.

Pandya, Dhwani, and Upamanyu Trivedi. 'India's Mini-Lehman Moment: Bankruptcies Double at Real Estate Developers'. *Business Standard,* 3 October 2019. https://www.business-standard.com/article/economy-policy/india-s-mini-lehman-moment-bankruptcies-double-at-real-estate-developers-119100300295_1.html. Accessed 26 November 2020.

Parnell, Susan, and Jennifer Robinson. '(Re)Theorizing Cities from the Global South'. *Urban Geography* 33, no. 4 (2012): 593–617.

Parry, Jonathan, and Maurice Bloch. 'Introduction: Money and the Morality of Exchange'. In *Money and the Morality of Exchange,* edited by Jonathan Parry and Maurice Bloch, 1–32. Cambridge; New York: Cambridge University Press, 1989.

Patel, Geeta. 'Risky Subjects: Insurance, Sexuality, and Capital'. *Social Text* 24, no. 4 (89) (2006): 25–65.

Pati, Sushmita. 'Accumulation by Possession: Political Economy of Urban Villages of South Delhi'. In *Accumulation in Postcolonial Capitalism*, edited by Iman Mitra, Ranabir Samaddar and Samita Sen, 93–108. Singapore: Springer, 2016.

———. 'Anxieties of "Dabanggai": Tales from Delhi's Urban Villages'. Special issue edited by Madhura Lohokare on Masculinities of Urban India: Of Contradictions, Dilemmas and Uncertainties for *Café Dissensus* (35).

———. 'Jagmohan: The Master Planner and the "Rebuilding" of Delhi'. *Economic and Political Weekly* 49, no. 36 (2014): 48–54.

———. 'The Making of the "Rentier" Jat: Land, Rent and the Social Processes of Accumulation of Capital in South Delhi'. *Policies and Practices: Mobile Labour and the New Urban* 67 (2014): 30–45.

———. 'The Productive Fuzziness of Land Documents: The State and Processes of Accumulation in Urban Villages of Delhi'. *Contributions to Indian Sociology* 53, no. 2 (2019): 249–71.

———. 'The Regime of Registers: Land Ownership and State Planning in Urban Villages in South Delhi'. SOAS South Asia Institute Working Papers 1, 2015, 17–31.

Perelman, Michael. 'Primitive Accumulation from Feudalism to Neoliberalism'. *Capital, Nature, Socialism* 18, no. 2 (2007): 44–61.

Piketty, Thomas. *Capital in the Twenty-First Century*. Translated by Arthur Goldhammer. Cambridge, MA; London: The Bellknap Press of Harvard University Press, 2017.

Piliavsky, Anastasia, ed. *Patronage as Politics in South Asia*. New Delhi; Cambridge: Cambridge University Press, 2014.

Polanki, Pallavi. 'Sheila Dikshit's Trump Card: The Voting Power of Unauthorised Colonies'. *Firstpost*, 1 July 2013. http://www.firstpost.com/politics/sheila-dikshits-trump-card-the-voting-power-of-unauthorised-colonies-917777.html. Accessed 24 November 2013.

Polanyi, Karl. *The Great Transformation: The Political and Economic Origins of Our Time*. Boston: Beacon Press, 2001.

Poovey, Mary. *A History of the Modern Fact: Problems of Knowledge in the Sciences of Wealth and Society*. Chicago: Chicago University Press, 1998.

Pradhan, M. C. 'The Jats of Northern India: Their Traditional Political System'. *Economic and Political Weekly* 17, no. 50 (1965): 1821–24.

———. 'The Jats of Northern India: Their Traditional Political System—II'. *Economic and Political Weekly* 17, no. 51 (1965): 1855–64.

———. *The Political System of the Jats of Northern India*. Bombay: Oxford University Press, 1966.

Prakash, Aseem. *Dalit Capital: State, Markets and Civil Society in Urban India.* New Delhi: Routledge, 2017.

Prashad, Vijay. *Untouchable Freedom: A Social History of a Dalit Community.* New Delhi: Oxford University Press, 2000.

Price, Pamela. 'Changing Meaning of Authority in Contemporary Rural India'. *Qualitative Sociology* 29, no. 3 (2006): 301–16.

Price, Pamela, and Arild Ruud, eds. *Power and Influence in India: Bosses, Lords and Captains.* New Delhi: Routledge, 2011.

PTI. '90% Buildings in Delhi Illegal, Panel Tells HC'. *Pioneer,* 5 October 2017. https://www.dailypioneer.com/2017/page1/90-buildings-in-delhi-illegal-panel-tells-hc.html. Accessed 7 November 2018.

———. '92 Khaps Hold the Key in Haryana Assembly Polls'. *Indian Express,* 12 October 2014. http://indianexpress.com/article/india/punjab-and-haryana/92-khaps-holds-the-key-in-haryana-assembly-polls/. Accessed 9 September 2016.

———. 'Delhi Government Notifies 80% Reduction in Water, Sewer Charges'. *DNA,* 28 June 2015. http://www.dnaindia.com/delhi/report-delhi-government-notifies-80-reduction-in-water-sewer-charges-2099707. Accessed 19 April 2016.

———. 'Good News for Delhi's Unauthorised Colonies! Govt Exempts Property Owners from Income Tax'. *Financial Express,* 30 June 2020. https://www.financialexpress.com/money/good-news-for-delhis-unauthorised-colonies-govt-exempts-property-owners-from-income-tax/2009230/. Accessed 19 August 2020.

———. 'Hauz Khas Village Is a Ticking Time Bomb: High Court'. *Economic Times,* 15 September 2017. https://economictimes.indiatimes.com/news/politics-and-nation/hauz-khas-village-is-ticking-time-bomb-high-court/articleshow/60517338.cms. Accessed 20 March 2018.

———. 'HC Refuses to Stay Delhi's MG Road Demolitions'. *Outlook,* 3 February 2006. https://www.hindustantimes.com/india/hc-refuses-to-stay-delhi-s-mg-road-demolitions/story-EPCB8ngjp1EW66b01MP1uK.html. Accessed 29 December 2015.

———. 'Khap Panchayats Useful in Society, Says Haryana CM Khattar'. *Indian Express,* 31 January 2016. http://indianexpress.com/article/india/politics/khap-panchayats-useful-in-society-says-haryana-cm-khattar/. Accessed 1 February 2016.

Pugh, Cedric. 'Housing and Land Policies in Delhi'. *Journal of Urban Affairs* 13, no. 3 (1991): 367–82.

Purcell, Thomas, Alex Loftus and Hug March. 'Value–Rent–Finance'. *Progress in Human Geography* 44, no. 3 (2020): 437–56.

Rabinow, Paul. *Reflections on Fieldwork in Morocco*. Berkeley; London: University of California Press, 1977.

Rai, Usha. 'Illegal Colonies Mushrooming in Delhi'. *Times of India*, 2 August 1982, 7.

Rajagopal, Krishnadas, and Smita Gupta. 'SC Removes Jats from OBC List'. *Hindu*, 17 March 2015. http://www.thehindu.com/news/national/supreme-court-sets-aside-jat-quota/article7002786.ece. Accessed 18 March 2015.

Raman, Bhavani. *Document Raj: Writing and Scribes in Early Colonial South India*. Durham: Duke University Press, 2012.

Ramanathan, Usha. 'Demolition Drive'. *Economic and Political Weekly* 40, no. 27 (2005): 2908–12.

Ramani, Bina. *Bird in the Banyan Tree: My Story*. New Delhi: Rupa Publications, 2013.

Rao, M. S. A. 'The Mid-Term Poll in a Village in Outer Delhi Constituency'. *Sociological Bulletin* 21, no. 1 (1972): 17–34.

———. 'Urbanisation in a Delhi Village: Some Social Aspects'. *Economic and Political Weekly* 1, no. 9 (1966): 365–70.

Rawat, Ramnarayan S. *Reconsidering Untouchability: Chamars and Dalit History in North India*. Bloomington: Indiana University Press, 2011.

Reed, Stanley and Clifford Krauss. 'Too Much Oil: How a Barrel Came to Be Worth Less than Nothing'. *New York Times*, 20 April 2020. https://www.nytimes.com/2020/04/20/business/oil-prices.html?searchResultPosition=5. Accessed 22 April 2020.

Roohi, Sanam. 'Anticipating Future Capital: Regional Caste Contestations, Speculation and Silent Dispossession in Andhra Pradesh'. *Journal of Contemporary Asia* 50, no. 5 (2020): 723–42.

Roy, Ananya. 'Postcolonial Urbanism: Speed, Hysteria and Mass Dreams'. In *Worlding Cities: Asian Experiments and the Art of Being Global*, edited by Ananya Roy and Aihwa Ong, 307–35. Sussex: Wiley Blackwell, 2011.

———. 'Slumdog Cities: Rethinking Subaltern Urbanism'. *International Journal of Urban and Regional Research* 35, no. 2 (2011): 223–38.

———. 'The 21st-Century Metropolis: New Geographies of Theory'. *Regional Studies* 43, no. 6 (2009): 819–30.

———. 'Why India Cannot Plan Its Cities. Informality, Insurgence and the Idiom of Urbanization'. *Planning Theory* 8, no. 1 (2009): 76–87.

Roy, Srirupa. 'Being the Change: The Aam Aadmi Party and the Politics of the Extraordinary in Indian Democracy'. *Economic and Political Weekly* 49, no. 15 (2014): 45–54.

Roychoudhury, Shibaji. 'Racist Mob? No Worse than What Africans Face Every Day in Delhi'. *Scroll*, 2 October 2014. http://scroll.in/article/681845/racist-mob-no-worse-than-what-africans-face-every-day-in-delhi. Accessed 23 May 2016.

Rudner, David. 'Banker's Trust and the Culture of Banking among the Nattukottai Chettiars of Colonial South India'. *Modern Asian Studies* 23, no. 3 (1989): 417–58.

Rutten, Mario. *Farms and Factories: Social Profile of Large Farmers and Rural Industrialists in West India*. Delhi: Oxford University Press, 1995.

Sahlins, Marshall. 'What Kinship Is (Part Two)'. *Journal of the Royal Anthropological Institute* 17, no. 2 (2011): 227–42.

Salahuddin, Mohammad. 'Committee: An Informal Financial Institution'. *Abhinav National Monthly Refereed Journal of Research in Commerce and Management* 4, no. 3 (2015): 6–11.

Samaddar, Ranabir. *Karl Marx and the Postcolonial Age*. Cham: Palgrave Macmillan, 2018.

Sami, Neha. 'From Farming to Development: Urban Coalitions in Pune, India'. *International Journal of Urban and Regional Research* 37, no. 1 (2013): 151–64.

Sampat, Preeti. 'Special Economic Zones in India: Reconfiguring Displacement in a Neoliberal Order?' *City and Society* 22, no. 2 (2010): 166–82.

Sanyal, Kalyan. *Rethinking Capitalist Development: Primitive Accumulation, Governmentality and Post-Colonial Capitalism*. New Delhi: Routledge, 2007.

Sarkar, Swagato. 'Beyond Dispossession: The Politics of Commodification of Land under Speculative Conditions'. *Comparative Studies of South Asia, Africa and the Middle East* 35, no. 3 (2015): 438–50.

Sarkar, Tanika. *Hindu Wife, Hindu Nation, Community, Religion and Cultural Nationalism*. New Delhi: Permanent Black, 2001.

Sassen, Saskia. *Territory, Authority, Rights: From Medieval to Global Assemblages*. Princeton; Oxford: Princeton University Press, 2006.

———. 'Visible Formalizations and Formally Invisible Facticities'. *International Journal of Global Studies* 20, no. 1 (2013): 3–37.

Satish, D. P. 'Delhi Elections: BJP, AAP and Congress Bank on Caste in Chhattarpur and Mehrauli; AAP Fields BJP Defectors'. *News18*, 28 January 2015. https://www.news18.com/news/india/delhi-elections-bjp-aap-congress-bank-on-caste-in-chhattarpur-mehrauli-aap-fields-bjp-defectors-964298.html. Accessed 29 January 2015.

Saxena, Astha. 'JNU Row: Innocent Students Face the Hate Wave'. *Mail Today*, 18 February 2016. http://indiatoday.intoday.in/story/jnu-row-innocent-students-face-the-hate-wave/1/599080.html. Accessed 18 February 2016.

Schraff, Christina. 'The Psychic Life of Neoliberalism: Mapping the Contours of Entrepreneurial Subjectivity'. *Theory, Culture and Society* 33, no. 6 (2016): 107–22.

Scott, James C. *The Art of Not Being Governed: An Anarchist History of Upland Southeast Asia*. New Delhi: Orient Blackswan, 2010.

Scott, Joan. 'Experience'. In *Feminists Theorise the Political*, edited by Judith Butler and Joan W. Scott, 22–40. New York; London: Routledge, 1992.

Scott, Julie. 'Property Values: Ownership, Legitimacy and Land Markets'. In *Property Relations: Renewing the Anthropological Tradition*, edited by C. M. Hann, 142–59. Cambridge: Cambridge University Press, 1998.

Searle, Llerena Guiu. *Landscapes of Accumulation: Real Estate and the Neoliberal Imagination in Contemporary India*. Chicago: University of Chicago Press, 2016.

Sehran, Sohail. 'Capital's Vegetable Basket Is Now a Fashion Farm'. *Hindustan Times*, 24 May 2016. http://www.hindustantimes.com/delhi/capital-s-vegetable-basket-is-now-a-fashion-farm/story-X9FtmHoLkUnOGEbfMFfpcL.html. Accessed 25 May 2016.

Sen, Jahnavi, and Akhil Kumar. 'A Conspicuous Silence in Murthal on Rape Allegations'. *Wire*, 12 March 2016. http://thewire.in/24635/a-conspicuous-silence-in-murthal-on-rape-allegations/. Accessed 13 March 2016.

Seth, Vikram. *A Suitable Boy*. New Delhi: Penguin Books, 2005.

Shankar, Aranya. 'Munirka Reserved Constituency: In All-Women Constituency, Candidates "Nowhere in Sight", Male Kin Woo Voters'. *Indian Express*, 18 May 2016. http://indianexpress.com/article/cities/delhi/delhi-mcd-bypolls-munirka-reserved-constituency-in-all-women-constituency-candidates-nowhere-in-sight-male-kin-woo-voters-2802666/. Accessed 19 May 2016.

Sharan, Abhishek. 'Ban Same-Gotra Marriages: Khap'. *Hindustan Times*, 26 July 2010. http://www.hindustantimes.com/delhi/ban-same-gotra-marriages-khap/story-SOKtlmZIIfxZTVpCE4RlNL.html. Accessed 29 August 2015.

Sharan, Awadhendra. *In the City, Out of Place: Nuisance, Pollution and Dwelling in Delhi, c. 1850–2000*. New Delhi: Oxford University Press, 2014.

———. 'One Air, Two Interventions: Delhi in the Age of Environment'. In *Ecologies of Urbanism: Metropolitan Civility and Sustainability*, edited by Anne Rademacher and K. Sivaramakrishnan, 71–91. Hong Kong: Hong Kong University Press, 2013.

Sharma, Sandipan. 'Caste Calculations, VIP Candidates: AAP Succumbs to Cong, BJP Ailments'. *Firstpost*, 10 March 2014. http://www.firstpost.com/politics/caste-calculations-vip-candidates-aap-succumbs-to-cong-bjp-ailments-1427157.html. Accessed 12 March 2014.

Sharma, Supriya. 'The Bhushans Aren't the Only Ones Upset with Arvind Kejriwal'. *Scroll*, 23 January 2015. http://scroll.in/article/702088/the-bhushans-arent-the-only-ones-upset-with-arvind-kejriwal. Accessed 24 January 2015.

Shatkin, Gavin. *Cities for Profit: The Real Estate Turn in Asia's Urban Politics*. Ithaca; London: Cornell University Press, 2017.

———. 'Planning to Forget: Informal Settlements as "Forgotten Places" in Globalising Metro Manila'. *Urban Studies* 41, no. 2 (2004): 2469–84.

Sheth, Sudev. 'Historical Transformations in Boundary and Land Use in New Delhi's Urban Villages'. *Economic and Political Weekly* 52, no. 5 (2017): 41–49.

Simone, AbdouMaliq. 'At the Frontier of the Urban Periphery'. In *Sarai Reader: Frontiers*, edited by M. Narula, S. Sengupta, J. Bagchi and R. Sundaram, 462–70. New Delhi: CSDS, 2007.

———. *For the City Yet to Come: Changing African Life in Four Cities*. Durham: Duke University Press, 2004.

———. 'People as Infrastructure: Intersecting Fragments in Johannesburg'. *Public Culture* 16, no. 3 (2004): 407–29.

Sinclair, Robert. 'Von Thünen and the Urban Sprawl'. *Annals of the Association of American Geographers* 57, no. 1 (1967): 72–87.

Singh, Karunakar. 'Inclusive Policy of Reservation and Occupational Mobility of Dalits: A Study of Jatavs of Munirka Village in New Delhi'. *Eastern Anthropologist* 66, nos. 3–4 (2013): 315–27.

Singh, Sandeep. 'Delhi: Demolitions and Sealings'. *Outlook*, 20 September 2006. http://www.outlookindia.com/website/story/delhi-demolitions-and-sealings/232582. Accessed 20 June 2016.

Singh, Yashveer. 'DUSU Elections 2015: Caste Fillip Works in Student Elections Too?' *DNA*, 31 August 2015. http://www.dnaindia.com/delhi/report-dusu-elections-2015-caste-fillip-works-in-student-elections-too-2120515. Accessed 2 September 2016.

Sinha, Bhadra. 'Sealing Scare Back in Delhi: SC Revives Panel that Sealed Thousands of Illegal Properties'. *Hindustan Times*, 16 December 2017. https://www.hindustantimes.com/delhi-news/sealing-scare-back-in-delhi-sc-revives-panel-that-sealed-thousands-of-illegal-properties/story-0WvHS30WeGr50Spdih6P2J.html. Accessed 20 December 2017.

Sisson, Richard. 'Peasant Movements and Political Mobilization: The Jats of Rajasthan'. *Asian Survey* 9, no. 12 (1969): 946–63.

Smart, Alan. 'Gifts, Bribes, and Guanxi: A Reconsideration of Bourdieu's Social Capital'. *Cultural Anthropology* 8, no. 3 (1993): 388–408.

Smith, Neil. 'Gentrification and the Rent Gap'. *Annals of the Association of American Geographers* 77, no. 3 (1987): 462–65.

———. *New Urban Frontier: Gentrification and the Revanchist City*. London; New York: Routledge, 1996.

Soni, Anita. 'Urban Conquest of Outer Delhi: The Case of the Mehrauli Countryside'. In *Delhi: Urban Space and Human Destinies*, edited by Véronique Dupont, Emma Tarlo and Denis Vidal, 75–96. New Delhi: Manohar, 2000.

Srinivas, M. N. 'The Dominant Caste in Rampura'. *American Anthropologist* 61, no. 1 (1959): 1–16.

Srivastava, Sanjay. *Entangled Urbanism: Slum, Gated Community and Shopping Mall in Delhi and Gurgaon*. New Delhi: Oxford University Press, 2014.

Staff Correspondent. 'An Inhuman Mess'. *Times of India*, 23 August 1985.

Staff Correspondent. 'Delhi: 24-yr-old Raped by Landlord in Munirka'. *Hindustan Times*, 7 October 2014. https://www.hindustantimes.com/delhi/delhi-24-yr-old-raped-by-landlord-in-munirka/story-as7r9JGjmGxp3HlN7MPuXM.html. Accessed 27 September 2019.

Staff Correspondent. 'Delhiites Can Now Register General Power of Attorney-Based Properties'. *Firstpost*, 23 July 2013. http://www.firstpost.com/business/economy/good-news-delhiites-can-now-register-general-power-of-attorney-based-properties-978359.html. Accessed 24 July 2013.

———. 'Lal Dora Is Meant for Villagers, Not for Building Shopping Malls'. *Hindu*, 4 February 2006. https://www.thehindu.com/todays-paper/tp-national/tp-newdelhi/lal-dora-is-meant-for-villagers-not-for-building-shopping-malls/article3173924.ece. 12 April 2017.

Staff Correspondent. 'Lethal Misgovernance: On Anaj Mandi Fire Tragedy'. *Hindu*, 10 December 2019. https://www.thehindu.com/opinion/editorial/lethal-misgovernance/article30259827.ece. Accessed 10 December 2019.

———. 'Sealing Drive Continues in Delhi'. *Hindu*, 5 September 2006. http://www.thehindu.com/todays-paper/tp-national/tp-newdelhi/sealing-drive-continues-in-delhi/article3071121.ece. Accessed 20 June 2016.

Staff Correspondent. 'What, When, How of Delhi Sealing Drive and the Politics Over It'. *India Today*, 2 February 2018. https://www.indiatoday.in/india/story/what-when-how-of-delhi-sealing-drive-and-the-politics-over-it-1160485-2018-02-02. Accessed 9 March 2018.

Stokes, Eric. *The Peasant and the Raj: Studies in Agrarian Society and Peasant Rebellion in Colonial India*. Cambridge: Cambridge University Press, 1978.

Sundaram, Ravi. *Pirate Modernity: Delhi's Media Urbanism*. Oxford; New York: Routledge, 2010.

Suykens, Bert. 'The Land that Disappeared: Forceful Occupation, Disputes and the Negotiation of Landlord Power in a Bangladeshi Bastee'. *Development and Change* 46, no. 3 (2015): 486–507.

Sweezy, Paul M. *The Theory of Capitalist Development: Principles of Marxian Political Economy*. New York; London: Modern Reader Publication, 1968.

Szeman, Imre. 'Entrepreneurship as the New Common Sense'. *South Atlantic Quarterly* 114, no. 3 (2015): 471–90.

Tarlo, Emma. '"Ethnic Chic": The Transformation of Hauz Khas Village'. *India International Centre Quarterly* 23, no. 2 (1996): 30–59.

———. 'Fashion Fables of an Urban Village'. In *Clothing Matters: Dress and Identity in India*, 284–317. London: Hurst and Company, 1996.

———. *Unsettling Memories: Narratives of the Emergency in Delhi*. Ranikhet: Permanent Black, 2003.

Taussig, Michael. *The Devil and Commodity Fetishism in South America*. Chapel Hill: University of North Carolina Press, 1980.

Taylor, Keeanga-Yamahatta. *Race for Profit: How Banks and the Real Estate Industry Undermined Black Homeownership*. Chapel Hill: University of North Carolina Press, 2019.

Thompson, E. P. 'The Moral Economy of the English Crowd in the Eighteenth Century'. *Past and Present* 50, no. 1 (1971): 76–136.

Thrift, Nigel. 'Intensities of Feeling: Towards a Spatial Politics of Affect'. *Geografiska Annaler* 86, no. 1 (2004): 57–78.

Tian, Li. 'The Chengzhongcun Land Market in China: Boon or Bane? A Perspective on Property Rights'. *International Journal of Urban and Regional Research* 32, no. 2 (2008): 282–304.

Tiemann, Gunter. 'Cattle Herds and Ancestral Land among the Jat of Haryana in Northern India'. *Anthropos* 65, nos. 3–4 (1970): 480–504.

———. 'The Four-Got-Rule among the Jat of Haryana in Northern India'. *Anthropos* 65, nos. 1–2 (1970):166–77.

Tilly, Charles. 'Space for Capital, Space for States'. *Theory and Society* 15, nos. 1–2 (1986): 301–09.

Tsing, Anna Lowenhaupt. *Friction: An Ethnography of Global Connection*. New Jersey: Princeton University Press, 2005.

———. 'Supply Chains and the Human Condition'. *Rethinking Marxism: A Journal of Economics, Culture and Society* 21, no. 2 (2009): 148–76.

———. *The Mushroom at the End of the World: On the Possibility of Life in Capitalist Ruins*. New Jersey: Princeton University Press, 2017.

Unnikrishnan, Dinesh. 'Regulations Yet to Catch Up with India's Illegal Chit Fund Industry'. *Mint*, 24 May 2016. http://www.livemint.com/Money/PYvp2nBSpJJZ2IK9vsJwNP/Regulations-yet-to-catch-up-with-Indias-illegal-chit-fund-i.html. Accessed 19 August 2016.

Upadhya, Carol. 'Social and Cultural Strategies of Class Formation in Coastal Andhra Pradesh'. *Contributions to Indian Sociology* 31, no. 2 (1997): 169–93.

———. 'The Concept of Community in Indian Social Sciences: An Anthropological Perspective'. In *Community and Identities: Contemporary Discourses on Culture and Politics in India*, edited by Surinder S. Jodhka, 32–58. New Delhi; Thousand Oaks; London: Sage Publications, 2001.

———. 'The Farmer-Capitalists of Coastal Andhra Pradesh'. *Economic and Political Weekly* 23, no. 27 (1988): 1376–82.

Vanaik, Anish. *Possessing the City: Urban Space and Property Relations in Delhi 1911–1947*. Oxford: Oxford University Press, 2020.

Varley, Anne. 'Private or Public: Debating the Meaning of Tenure Legalization'. *International Journal of Urban and Regional Research* 26, no. 3 (2002): 449–61.

Venugopal, Rajesh. 'Neoliberalism as Concept'. *Economy and Society* 44, no. 2 (2015): 165–87.

Vercellone, Carlo. 'The Becoming Rent of Profit? The New Articulation of Wage Rent and Profit'. *Knowledge Cultures* 1, no. 2 (2013): 25–32.

———. 'The Crisis of the Law of Value and the Becoming-Rent of Profit'. In *Crisis in Global Economy: Financial Markets, Social Struggles and New Political Scenarios*, edited by Andrea Fumagalli and Sandro Mezzadra, 85–118. Los Angeles: Semiotext(e), 2010.

Verdery, Katherine. 'Property and Power in Transylvania's Decollectivisation'. In *Property Relations: Renewing the Anthropological Tradition*, edited by C. M. Hann, 160–80. Cambridge: Cambridge University Press, 1998.

———. *What Was Socialism, and What Comes Next?* New Jersey: Princeton University Press, 1996.

Verdery, Katherine and Caroline Humphrey. 'Introduction: Raising Questions about Property'. In *Property in Question: Value Transformation in the Global Economy*, edited by Katherine Verdery and Caroline Humphrey, 1–28. Oxford; New York: Berg, 2004.

Vidyasagar, N. 'Demolition Man'. *Times of India*, 22 June 1997.

Virno, Paulo and Michael Hardt, eds. *Radical Thought in Italy: A Potential Politics*. Minneapolis: University of Minnesota Press, 2006.

Waghmore, Suryakant. 'Beyond Depoliticization? Caste, NGOs and Dalit Land Rights in Maharashtra, India'. *Development and Change* 43, no. 6 (2012): 1313–36.

Ward, C., and M. B. Aalbers. '"The Shitty Rent Business": What's the Point of Land Rent Theory?' *Urban Studies* 53, no. 9 (2016): 1760–83.

Watts, Michael J. 'Antinomies of Community: Some Thoughts on Geography, Resources and Empire'. *Transactions of the Institute of British Geographers* 29, no. 2 (2004): 195–216.

———. 'Economies of Violence: More Oil, More Blood'. *Economic and Political Weekly* 38, no. 48 (2003): 5089–99.

———. 'Petro-Insurgency or Criminal Syndicate? Conflict and Violence in the Niger Delta'. *Review of African Political Economy* 34, no. 114 (2007): 637–60.

Weber, Max. 'Politics as Vocation'. In *From Max Weber: Essays in Sociology*, edited by H. H. Gerth and C. Wright Mills, 77–128. New York: Oxford University Press, 1946.

Weber, Rachel. 'Extracting Value from the City: Neoliberalism and Urban Redevelopment'. *Antipode* 34, no. 3 (2002): 519–40.

Whitehead, Judith. 'John Locke, Accumulation by Dispossession and the Governance of Colonial India'. *Journal of Contemporary Asia* 42, no. 1 (2012): 1–21.

Wirth, Louis. 'Urbanism as a Way of Life'. *American Journal of Sociology* 44, no. 1 (1938): 1–24.

Witsoe, Jeffrey. *Democracy against Development: Lower-Caste Politics and Political Modernity in Postcolonial India*. London; Chicago: University of Chicago Press, 2013.

Wouters, Jelle J. P., and Tanka B. Subba. 'The "Indian Face", India's Northeast, and "The Idea of India"'. *Asian Anthropology* 12, no. 2 (2013): 126–40.

Yadava, J. S. 'Kinship Groups in a Haryana Village'. *Ethnology* 8, no. 4 (1969): 494–502.

Yanagisako, Sylvia Junko. *Producing Culture and Capital: Family Firms in Italy*. Princeton; Oxford: Princeton University Press, 2002.

Zee Media Bureau. 'Prashant Bhushan Submits List of 12 AAP Candidates with Dubious Reputation'. *Zee News*, 25 January 2015. http://zeenews.india.com/news/delhi/prashant-bhushan-submits-list-of-12-aap-candidates-with-dubious-reputation_1535473.html. Accessed 26 January 2015.

———. 'Somnath Bharti's Midnight Raid: African Woman Forced to Urinate in Public'. *Zee News*, 18 January 2014. http://zeenews.india.com/news/delhi/somnath-bhartis-midnight-raid-african-woman-forced-to-urinate-in-public_905018.html. Accessed 19 January 2014.

Unpublished Works

Benjamin, Solomon. 'Neighbourhood as Factory: The Influence of Land Development and Civic Politics on an Industrial Cluster in Delhi'. PhD diss., Massachusetts Institute of Technology, 1996.

Bhagat, Kumar Krityanand. 'The Country-Town Nexus in an Urban Village: A Study of Social and Cultural Transition in Village Munirka'. PhD diss., Jawaharlal Nehru University, 1994.

Chandra, Meghna. 'Munirka Budh Vihara 401/AB: Identity and Democracy, Religion and Real Estate'. Unpublished MA seminar paper, Jawaharlal Nehru University, 2015.

Chatterjee, Radhika. 'Urbanisation in "Unplanned" Mehrauli'. MPhil diss., Jawaharlal Nehru University, 2015.

Kataria, Dinesh. 'Moving Frontiers: Delhi's Hinterlands in 1890s–1910s'. MPhil diss., Jawaharlal Nehru University, 2013.

Kumar, Sunalini. 'Planning, Politics and Protest: A Study of Urban Development in the National Capital Region'. PhD diss., Delhi University, 2013.

Lohokare, Madhura. 'Making Men in the City: Articulating Masculinity and Space in Urban India'. PhD diss., Syracuse University, 2016.

Nambiar, Ranjan. 'Conflict, Law and Governance: The Case of Tenure Conversion in New Delhi'. PhD diss., Massachusetts Institute of Technology, 1994.

Soni, Anuj Kumar. 'Housing Market and Transformation in Urban Villages of Delhi'. Master's diss., School of Planning and Architecture, 2014.

Stefan Tetzlaff. 'The Motorisation of the "Mofussil": Automobile Traffic and Social Change in Rural and Small-Town India, c. 1915–1940'. PhD diss., University of Göttingen, 2015.

Tiku, Vikram. 'Urban Villages of Hauz Rani and Khirki: A Study of the Process of Transformation'. Masters diss., School of Planning and Architecture, 1994.

Other Sources

D., Nikhil, and Tenzin Tsundue Phunkhang. *Boys of Safarjung*. Short film.

Prime Time, NDTV India. *Dilli Mein Afriki Log Nishane Par Kyun?* Published on YouTube, 30 May 2016. https://www.youtube.com/watch?v=YZ1EgsRT1zk. Accessed 17 July 2018.

Ravish Kumar. 'Dilli: Gaon, Gotra Aur Gurjar Ki Kahani'. *Ravish Ki Report*, NDTV India. Published on YouTube, 10 May 2014. https://www.youtube.com/watch?v=LrXuWoKunwA. Accessed 8 November 2018.

———. 'Khora Colony, Ghaziabad: A Town Sinking in Its Own Sewage and Garbage'. *Ravish Ki Report*, NDTV India. Published on YouTube, 11 June 2013. https://www.youtube.com/watch?v=qamJf39R6_U. Accessed 12 November 2018.

Vachani, Lalit. *An Ordinary Election*. A Wide Eye Film, 2015.

Index

1963 DDA circular on *lal dora* villages, 5, 88, 104, 116, 138
2008 housing crisis
  effect on real estate sector, 234–235
Aam Aadmi Party (AAP), 113*n*29, 162, 199, 207, 212–217, 219–220, 227*n*41, *n*44
abadi, 3, 44
  deh, 44
accumulation, 7, 50, 63, 79, 93, 98, 117, 119, 125, 127, 134, 137, 153, 165–166, 168, 172*n*35
  by dispossession, 2, 15, 18, 20, 24*n*2
  method of, 98
  practices, 50
  primitive, 2, 19, 24*n*2, 52
  process, 137, 168
  strategies, 79
  through rent and capital, 11, 21, 119, 134
  vernacular, 139*n*1
adda, 4, 89, 94–98, 112*n*17, 133, 235
African migrants, 145, 149, 152, 163, 172*n*35
agricultural/agriculture/agrarian, 8, 10, 13–14, 19, 36, 38–39, 61, 72, 81*n*12, 83, 90, 107–108, 115*n*43, 120, 175, 198*n*28, 203–205, 213, 219, 225*n*21, 241
  -based political parties, 206
  capital, 110, 119
  class, 204
  colonial land documentation for, 46
  and Dalits upward mobility, 224*n*14
  and industrialisation, 5
labourers, 176, 192, 198*n*24
lands, 2–3, 5, 10, 40, 44–45, 64–66, 68, 82*n*20, 91, 94, 145, 175
political economy, 36
tax, 37
urbanism, 16
agriculturist
  rich/wealthy, 17, 61, 64, 214
alienation, 22, 30*n*61, 149
  Punjab Land Alienation Act, 1900, 14, 45, 176
All India Jat Mahasabha, 118, 223*n*11
Ambedkar Bhawan, 180, 183
Ambedkar, B. R., 38, 163, 178–179, 181, 183, 192
Ambedkarism, 185
Ambedkarite politics, 179–180, 183, 217, 220, 231
  Jatavs, 186, 189, 194
angel funder, 136
anger, 15, 17, 44, 83*n*42, 89, 105–110, 164, 196
anthropology/anthropological, 18, 110
Anthropologists, 154, 160
anxiety, 11, 21, 119, 121, 154, 159, 168, 196, 208, 222, 241
  social/cultural, 134, 148
  deep, 147
  demographic, 166
  over northeastern tenants, 158–159
  and violence, relationships between, 149–150
army, 2, 67, 72, 80, 127, 129, 215
  Rajputana Rifles, 70
Arya Samaj Movement, 13

Asiad/Asian Games, 82, 4, 24n8, 34, 91, 94, 112n13, n14
Village, 4, 91
Associated Cement Company Limited (ACC), 69

Baba Gangnath Marg, 184
Baba Gangnath Temple, 213
badarpur, 67–68, 82n29
Bahujan Samajwadi Party (BSP), 184, 199
Balakrishnan, Sai, 8, 16, 27n28, 31n77, 83n43
Balmiki, 12, 32n94, 175–178, 191–195, 198n27, n32
Bania, 62, 72, 204, 207
bank, 61, 76, 78–79, 81n12, 116, 128, 130, 142n30, 215, 233
Bayly, Christopher, 13, 29n59
belongingness, 10, 18, 55n33, 136, 138, 167, 189
bhaats, 28n43
Bhagidari scheme, 140n15
bhaichara (brotherhood) system, 11–15, 18, 21, 35–36, 44–45, 116, 118, 154, 166, 196n2, 201, 203–207, 218–219, 221–22
Bharatiya Kisan Union (BKU), 61, 118, 223n8, 228n50
Bharatiya Kranti Dal (BKD), 204, 224–225n21, 228n48
Bharatiya Janata Party (BJP), 84n46, 113n29, 161, 203, 207, 210–213, 216–217, 219–220, 223n6, 225n22, 241–242, 244n20
  decision to regularise unauthorised colonies in Delhi, 114n31
Bhattacharya, Neeladri, 12, 25n15, 36, 53n8, 56n40, 82n25
Bidhuri, Shispal, 107
Birla, Ritu, 16, 31n74, 54n20, 128, 139n1, 141n22
boutique, 4, 20, 90–91, 94–95, 97, 99–100, 124, 126, 235

bodybuilder, 179
bourgeois environmentalists, 2
Brahmins, 12, 28n45, 72
brick kiln, 63–64, 67–71, 73–74, 77–79, 82n22, 144,
broker, 70, 199
  deal-broker politician, 201, 222
  land, 41, 48
building bye-laws, 7, 88, 104–105, 138
builder, 38, 71, 79, 92, 94, 98, 100, 107, 112n16, 132, 150
Burma Shell Company, 37
Buddha Vihar, 181–184, 188
Buddhist Society of India (BSI), 181, 183–185
Buddhism/Buddhist, 179, 181–182, 217
bureaucracy, 43, 87, 102, 208
  porous, 57n41
bus, 63, 67, 80, 182
  Blue Line (killer) buses, 75–76
  private operators, 72
  Red Line buses, 73–75

cadre, 214–215, 218, 221
capital, 2–3, 9–10, 15, 20, 51, 68, 101, 104, 109, 139n1, 148, 167, 174, 191, 195, 215, 23
  agrarian, 110, 119
  big theory of, 18
  cultural, 145, 149, 165, 240
  definition of, 136
  economic, 15
  finance/financial, 10, 14, 28n42, 89, 100, 128, 136–138, 142n30, 200
  global, 7, 10–11, 14–19, 21, 80, 110, 117, 132, 134, 136, 169, 196, 240–241
  informal, 43
  mercantile, 16
  monopoly, 122
  neoliberal, 16, 24n2, 118, 136, 166, 200, 238–239
  non-capital, 9, 20

in real estate, 52
regional, 60
relationship with, 80, 134, 240
social, 12, 15, 31n75, 45, 62, 66, 78, 105, 118–119, 124, 158–159, 194, 203, 240
speculative, 128–129, 137–138
urban, 222
vernacular, 240
capitalism, 100, 157, 165
Chinese, 16
financial, 128
global, 16
Indian, 16
Italian, 16
postcolonial, 9, 139n1
rentier, 17
state led, 13
vernacular, 16, 21, 117–119, 121, 125, 127–128, 135–138, 139n1
cartel, 21, 109, 116–117, 121, 134–135, 168–169, 190, 194, 200, 221, 234, 240
functioning of, 191
-*like panchayats*, 20, 121–124, 127, 195
village, 138
caste, 7–9, 11–17, 29n53, n57, 37, 50, 60, 72, 80, 117–119, 121, 139n10, 140n12, 145, 149, 153, 163, 166, 168–169, 175–180, 184, 186–187, 189–192, 194–196, 196n3, 197n19, 203–206, 216–217, 234, 239
cattle, 6, 45, 108, 129, 187
cement, 65, 69–71, 76, 80, 83n39, 109, 132, 136
Central Public Works Department (CPWD), 55n37, 68, 71, 80
Chamars, 176, 179, 196n3, 198n32
Chaudhary, 201, 203, 207, 209–214, 214
Chaudhary Balliram, 124–125
Chaudhary Brahma Prakash, 206

Chaudhary Charan Singh, 205–206, 219, 223–224n12, 228n48
Chaudhary Chhotu Ram, 204
Chaudhary Hira Singh Rana, 211
Chaudhary Mir Singh, 206, 211
Chaudhary Prem, 140n13, 196n5, 197n19, 204, 223n10
citizenship, 51, 101, 105–106, 185
chak, 64–66, 82n25, 129
chakbandi, 82n25
Chatterjee, Partha, 27n29, 139n9, 170n17, 196, 198n33
closed-circuit television (CCTV), 152, 163, 167
coal, 67, 70, 74–76, 80
coloniser, 38, 42
definition of, 54n27
colonial, 5, 9, 12, 36–37, 44–47, 118, 128, 157, 170n16, 171n26, 175, 197n22
administrators on Jats, 13, 29n55, n57
obsession over congestion, 24n9
Settlement Report from 1885, 13
Comaroff, John and Jean, 51, 58n51, 109, 115n45, 128, 141n20, 173n43
command economy, 60, 110, 166
committees, 4, 77, 116–117, 119, 121, 129–130, 132, 135, 137, 141n25, 175, 187, 189, 211, 233
commons
village, 20, 36, 44–45
Commonwealth Games, 101, 112n13
compensation, 16, 33–35, 37–41, 43–44, 54n25, 59, 61, 63–64, 67–68, 105, 108, 175–177, 186, 194
competition, 75, 118–119, 123, 126–127, 154, 213, 218, 222
compulsion, 109, 149, 165–166
Congress/INC, 1, 73, 84n46, 159, 199, 203–207, 209–213, 215, 219, 223n10, 224n16, n19, 225n22, 226n34, 227n41, 228n48, 239

construction, 2, 4, 20, 34–35, 38–39, 41, 43, 47, 61, 67–71, 73, 77–79, 86, 88, 91, 94, 97, 102–103, 107, 109, 112n14, n16, 114n43, 120, 127–128, 132, 141n18, 165, 182, 184–185, 190, 231, 240, 242n3
contract, 70–71, 78, 94, 196
contractors, 68–69, 71, 75, 79–80, 192–193
control, 10, 17–19, 21, 29n57, 47, 52, 60–61, 68–69, 71–72, 75, 88–89, 100, 104–105, 110, 118, 123–127, 129, 131, 133–138, 148–149, 155, 157, 161, 167–168, 171n26, 177, 181–182, 213, 218, 228n52, 234, 236–237, 239
Coronil, Fernando, 9, 27n31, 135, 142n32
corruption, 160, 212
Cowan, Tom, 17, 31n80, 111n7
councillor, 56n41, 103, 185, 188, 199, 209–212, 214, 220
COVID-19, 236–238, 240, 242
credit, 77, 92, 117, 127, 130–131
crisis/crises, 60, 84n55, 131, 155, 162–166, 189–190, 208, 232–234, 236–238, 240–241

dabangg, 158–159, 168, 222, 239
Dalits, 21, 44–45, 51, 117, 163–164, 172n39, 175–186, 188–191, 195, 201, 205, 217, 224n14, 234, 236
Damodaran, Harish, 60–61, 81n9, n13
dangal, 121
Das Gupta, Chirashree, 60–61, 71–72, 81n11, 83n41, 84n47, n52
Delhi Commission for Women, 171n25
Delhi Development Authority (DDA), 3, 5, 26n18, 25n11, 38, 42–44, 52, 53n4, n12, 57n47, 78, 92, 99, 101–102, 104, 106, 114n32, 182
Delhi High Court, 47, 53n15, n19, 54n24, 55n37, 57n42, 85n63, 111n8, 112n12, 114n43, 183, 197n16

Delhi Jal Board, 7
Delhi Land and Finance (DLF), 186
Delhi Land Reforms Act, 1954, 44, 54n32, 107, 115n43, 176
Delhi Legislative Assembly, 161, 207
Delhi Metro, 75
Delhi Metropolitan Council, 226n33
Delhi Police, 62, 67, 79, 94, 171n25, 189, 215
Delhi Transport Corporation (DTC), 63, 72–73, 80
delimitation, 210
demolition, 94, 101–106, 108, 112n13, 113n24, 114–115n43, 116–117, 182, 185, 190, 234, 242n3
demonetisation, 133, 237
Desakota, 6, 25n17
Diplomatic Enclave, 39–40
district court, 183
dominant caste, 7, 11–12, 80, 117–118, 184

economic reforms of 1990s, 110
elections, 196, 200–202, 204–207, 222, 224n20, 225n21, n22, 226n33, 227n42, 228n46
  legislative assembly, 114n31, 161, 199, 207, 210–213, 215–217, 219–220
  Lok Sabha, 203, 206
  Municipal, 140n15, 188, 209–210, 212, 220
  RWA, 122, 189, 209
emotion, 6, 17, 76, 145, 147, 168, 189, 216
entrepreneur/entrepreneurial, 6, 13, 22, 60, 63, 72, 79–80, 91, 98, 100, 119, 133, 135, 137–138, 166, 187, 200, 239–240
environment/environmentalism, 5, 75, 86–87, 108, 118, 134, 158
Essential Commodities Act, 1955, 70
eviction, 194, 208, 237
exemption, 7, 88, 104, 106, 108, 110, 116, 119, 138, 176

extraction, 9, 18, 93, 110, 137, 166–167, 171n30, 234, 242
Expert Committee on Lal Dora Report, 35

factory, 4–6, 13, 15, 20, 26n24, 63, 69, 78, 91, 94–97, 99, 112n18, 113n20, 124, 136, 142n33, 207
family, 12, 16, 21–22, 26n24, 41, 45, 51–52, 53n18, 63–66, 68–71, 73–79, 92, 98–100, 118–120, 123–126, 133, 135, 138, 149, 151, 155, 160–161, 175, 180, 185–186, 190, 192–193, 199, 201, 207–208, 212–215, 217–219, 231, 234–236
farmers' movements, 241–242
fear, 6, 11, 120–121, 134, 149, 154–156, 158, 163, 165–166, 168, 175, 185, 204, 232, 237
femininity, 145
feudalism, 117
Financing, 62, 66, 71, 73, 76–77, 80, 85, 116–117, 129–133, 137, 144, 187
financialisation, 9–10, 24n2, 31n87, 40, 87, 238
financier, 76–77, 79–80, 131, 136, 149, 189
Food and Civil Supplies Department (FCSD), 70
Fordism, 26n24
Foucault, Michel, 47, 86, 144, 173n44
fraud, 34, 39, 43, 130
frontier, 3, 89, 105
　agrarian–urban, 83
　urbanism, 16

Gandhi, Indira, 81n5
Gandhi, Rahul, 212, 226n30
Gandhi, Rajiv, 182
gang, 151
gaonwalla, 189–190

garment manufacture, 4, 78, 97, 235
gender, 17, 22–23, 126, 149, 159, 161
General Power of Attorney (GPA), 36, 49–50, 57n42, n44, 109
gentrification, 2, 18, 32n89, 52, 87–88, 123–124, 134, 154, 190
Gentrification theory, 18
Global South, 11, 60, 87, 110, 115n47, 132, 229–230
gotra/got, 14, 28n44, 208
Government of National Capital Territory of Delhi Act, 1991, 226n33
Graeber, David, 7, 26n25, 58n53, 142n27, 160, 171n31
Greater Kailash, 210
greed, 23, 150
Green Revolution, 16, 60–61, 69, 204, 224n13
　definition of, 81n6
guilt, 149
Gujjars, 3, 22, 29n57, 68, 70, 83n34, 84n46, 107, 207, 224n18, 225n22, 239
Guha, Ranajit, 36, 53n6
Gurgaon, 16–17, 31n80, 65–66, 68, 78, 87–88, 222n1, 239
Gururani, Shubhra, 8, 16, 27n28, 31n79

haveli, 32n95, 74–75, 124–125, 235
Harris-White, Barbara, 60–61, 72, 81n2, n12, n15, 84n51
Harvey, David, 2, 18, 24n2, 31n82, n86, n87, 32n88, 113n24, 137, 143n36
Hauz Khas, 65, 90–91, 111n10, 112n12
hire and purchase company, 84n53
homestead land, 10, 19, 66, 119, 177
honour killing, 122, 140n13, 203, 208, 226n31
hurt, 15, 17, 44, 89, 106–110, 241

Ilmi, Shazia, 216, 219
Indian Administrative Services (IAS), 185, 215
Indian National Lok Dal (INLD), 203–204, 223n6, 225n21
indigenous, 128
  argument, 165
  capitalists, 72
  land systems, 36
  people, 164
Industrial Policy 1956, 69
informality, 59, 108–109, 121–122
infrastructure, 24n9, 43, 87, 105, 112n13, 127, 136, 140n15, 175, 194, 230–234
innovation, 49, 92–93, 99–100, 120, 128–129, 137
institution, 6, 13–15, 26n18, 33, 37, 48, 51, 83n39, 87, 106, 109, 116–122, 124–125, 132, 135, 142n30, 164, 166, 168, 183, 185, 193, 203–204, 207, 209, 213
intermediate class, 66, 69, 80, 82n19
  Jats as, 60–63
investment, 19, 23, 53n10, 61–65, 68–69, 71, 77, 98, 125, 127, 129–130, 132, 138, 141n25, 142n30, 195

jajmani system, 177
jamabandi, 46, 49, 177
Jan Lokpal Bill, 215
Janata Dal, 211
Jan Sangh, 206, 224n20
Jatavs, 12, 28n45, 32n94, 153, 155, 175–196, 196n3, 198n24
Jat(s), 7, 10, 13–14, 29n55, 34, 44, 51, 60, 66, 78, 80, 82n28, 118–119, 122, 124, 129, 142n27, 145, 149–150, 154–155, 158–159, 161, 163, 169, 173n42, 175–180, 182, 185–190, 193, 195–196, 201, 206, 208, 210, 213–214, 219, 221–222, 238–242, 244n20

*dharamshala*s, 204, 223n11
Gazette, 204, 223n11
intermediate class, 60–63, 69
landlords, 11, 120, 135–137, 200, 204–205, 232, 236–237
Mahasabha, 223n11
pride, 29n57
rural, 21, 63–64, 205, 208
urban, 21, 134, 164, 206
voters, 224n18, 225n21
Jawaharlal Nehru University (JNU), 22, 69, 83n42, 160, 162, 178, 185, 187, 212, 230–231
Jawaharlal Nehru University Students' Union (JNUSU), 212
Jawaharlal Nehru National Urban Regeneration Programme, 104
Jhajjhar, 175, 233
job(s), 12, 28n46, 63, 77, 79–80, 88, 94–95, 99, 130, 145–148, 159, 166, 171n25, 174, 180–181, 184, 186–187, 190, 192–195, 205, 208, 215–216, 233, 236
joint stock (or cartel) form company, 20, 40, 109, 116–117, 121, 124–127, 134–135, 138, 169, 190, 200, 213, 221, 234
Jomo, K. S., 60, 81n7

kabza, 16, 20, 129, 192–193
  hasberasad, 177
  illegal, 35
  malik, 198n22
  polar opposite register of valuation, 36
  as property making, 44–46
  recorded spaces and values, 50–52
  sarkari, 35
  speculation in land records, 46–50
Kalecki, Michael, 60, 81n2
Kanjhawala
  Agitation in 1977, 205, 224n13
*karigar*s, 133–134, 235, 237

*karkhana*s, 95–96, 100, 112*n*17, 235
Karol Bagh, 73, 180
*karyakarta*s, 201–202, 214, 216–217, 220–221
Kejriwal, Arvind, 141*n*17, 162, 215, 227*n*41, *n*44
Khan, Mushtaq H., 60, 81*n*7
khap
  Baliyan, 219, 223*n*4, *n*8, 228*n*50
  Dahiya, 219, 223*n*4
  Dalal, 223*n*4
  definition of, 139*n*11
  Jharsa-360, 223*n*4, 226*n*31
  khap panchayat, 13, 29*n*57, 118, 122, 140*n*12, *n*13, *n*14, 163–164, 201, 203–205, 207–209, 214, 219, 223*n*7, 226*n*31
  Meham-24, 223*n*4
  Rohtak-84, 223*n*4
  *sarv khap mahapanchayat*s, 205
  Sonepat-360, 223*n*4
Khatik, 176, 198*n*30
Kinship, 11–15, 21, 27*n*29, 30*n*62, 52, 63, 79, 124, 130, 135, 137–138, 154, 171*n*22, 196
  associations, 7, 9
  -based networks, 6
  -bound community, 11, 118
Kumar, Sajjan, 206, 224*n*16, *n*19, 243*n*11
Kumar, Satendra, 8, 26*n*26, 225*n*26
Kumhar, 12, 175–178, 184, 187–189, 195, 231
kunba, 11, 14, 20, 63–65, 116–117, 119, 121, 124–127, 135, 149, 161, 190, 213, 222, 237

labour, 2, 6, 9, 17, 28*n*41, 46, 55*n*35, 77, 87, 94–98, 116, 134, 145, 147, 158, 176, 198*n*24, 224*n*14, 242
  bonded, 192
  congealed, 19
  housing for new, 92–94
  human, 36
  immaterial, 145
  informal, 5
  migrant, 168
  precariat, 116, 242
lal dora, 3, 5, 7, 10, 34–35, 44, 49, 88, 94, 104–105, 107, 109, 114*n*43, 190, 197*n*10
Lal, Tau Devi, 205–206, 211
land acquisition, 1, 17, 20, 33–38, 40–41, 44, 46, 50–52, 60–65, 67, 69, 73, 89–90, 107–108, 118, 127, 131, 175–176, 206, 241
Land Acquisition Act 1894, 3, 33–34, 41–42
land grab/grabbing/grabbers, 7, 35, 37, 44–46, 50, 52, 101, 153, 178, 186–187
land market, 36–37, 40, 42–43, 49, 109, 124, 186, 235
land record, 22, 37, 44, 46–50, 52, 56*n*38, 104, 109, 113*n*26, 175
law, 3, 16, 35–36, 43, 45, 52, 57*n*42, 89, 101, 103–106, 108–109, 116, 138, 158, 177, 186, 241
leader, 1, 73, 107, 120, 189, 199, 201–203, 206, 210–215, 217–222, 223*n*11, 224*n*16, 226*n*34, 228*n*50, 239, 241–242, 243*n*11
legislative assembly, 107–108, 114*n*31, 161, 199, 207, 210–211, 213, 215
lesbian, gay, bisexual, transgender, queer (LGBTQ), 145
liberalisation, 6, 10, 20, 60, 80, 169, 178, 206, 208, 238
license, 69–70
  permit raj, 67
Lohar, 28*n*45, 176
Lok Sabha, 101, 113*n*25, 206
Lok Dal, 118, 204
loss, 15, 20–21, 44, 49, 55*n*33, 57*n*44, 65, 67, 70, 90, 108, 119, 149–150, 153–158, 163, 169, 188, 236, 239

Mahipalpur, 6, 26n23, 35, 68, 71
Manipuri, 145, 151–152, 163
Manipur Women Gun Survivors Network, 172n40
manufacture/manufacturing units, 24n9, 26n24, 61, 77, 83n38, 87–88, 98, 136–137, 198n24
   garment manufacture, 4, 76, 78, 91, 95, 97, 235
market, 2, 4, 10, 14–15, 19, 21, 30n65, 33–34, 36–40, 42–43, 45, 49–50, 60, 67, 69–70, 73, 78, 80, 87, 89, 91, 94, 97, 99, 101, 103, 105, 109, 111n10, 116–119, 122–126, 128, 133, 135–138, 147, 151, 157, 160, 167, 169, 177, 185–186, 195–196, 215, 221, 226n34, 229, 234–235, 240–241
   governance, 16
   informal, 41, 52, 72, 88
Marwaris, 15–16, 117–118, 139n1, 195
Marx, Karl, 1, 9–10, 19, 24n1, n2, 27n30, n37, 28n41, 32n90, 53n10, 62, 82n16, 113n19
masculinity/emasculated, 13, 29n57, 32n93, 62, 148–149, 158–160, 163, 215, 218, 221–222
Master Plan 1962, 3–8, 24n9, 25n18, 43, 62, 86, 88, 104
Master Plan of Delhi 2021, 104
Master Plan of Delhi Draft 2041, 241, 244n18
Mazzucato, Mariana, 9, 27n34, n35, 142n30
McDuie-Ra, Duncan, 25n10, 147–148, 170n11, n13, n14, 170n20, n21
M. C. Mehta case/judgment in 2004, 57n47, 85n62, 86, 88, 101, 103, 111n1, n9
Mehrauli–Gurgaon Road, 114n43
member of legislative assembly (MLA), 185, 199, 207, 220

memory, 12, 34, 95, 108, 178–180, 185, 190, 205, 244n15
Metropolitan Council, 106, 205, 224n15, 226n33
Middle class, 20–21, 50, 77, 87, 91–93, 108, 120, 140n15, 145, 150, 164, 179, 220, 235, 239
migration/migrant, 4, 8, 17, 20, 22, 25n10, 28n45, 77, 88, 91–94, 98, 107, 112n14, 130, 138, 145, 147–149, 151–152, 157–158, 162–163, 165, 168, 171n30, 173n42, 233–234, 236, 238
Mini Master Plan 1985, 104
mistrust, 14, 166, 168, 174
mobility, 22, 175
   social, 63, 79, 99, 178, 180, 186, 195
   upward, 66, 73, 161, 184, 190–191, 218, 224n14
Mohammadpur, 12, 22, 30n62, 33, 35, 40, 43, 52n1, 53n18, 186, 210
monetisation, 110
money, 19, 118–119, 125–133, 136–137, 145, 157, 159–160, 200, 215–216, 218, 220–221, 237, 240
moneylending, 20–21, 72, 85n58, 127–128, 130–133, 142n27, 188
Monopolies and Restrictive Trade Practices Act, 61
monopoly, 9–10, 18, 43, 122–123
moral/morality, 15, 40, 151, 158–159, 196, 215–216, 242
   corruption, 160
   economy, 14, 30n65
mulnivasi, 164, 189
Municipal Corporation of Delhi (MCD), 86, 88, 102–104, 113n26, 121, 134, 188, 192, 210, 212, 214, 220, 232
Muslim, 13, 29n57, 72, 95, 133, 140n13, 148, 150, 162, 178, 226n31, 235, 240, 242, 243n5

Index   291

Naga, 145
Nais, 98, 28*n*45, 155, 174–178, 184, 186–189, 191, 195
National Highway (NH 1), 207
National Insurance Company, 37
National Register of Citizens (NRC), 235, 243*n*5
Nehru, Jawaharlal, 1, 179
   Nehruvian Command Economy, 60, 110, 166
   Nehruvian modernity, 5
   Nehruvian socialism, 1
neoliberal/neoliberalism, 10, 14–17, 21, 24*n*2, 51, 73, 87, 89, 110, 118–121, 136, 147, 166, 200, 222, 238–241
new money, 59, 207, 239
northeast India, 4, 25*n*10, 98, 145–149, 151–155, 157–160, 163, 165–168, 169*n*6, 172*n*35, *n*39, *n*40, 188–189
northwest India, 12, 36, 61, 69, 82*n*28, 122, 203, 207, 214
numberdaar, 209

Oldenburg, Philip, 224*n*20
Ong, Aihwa, 15, 30*n*73, 110, 115*n*48
other backward classes (OBC), 177
   reservation, 207–208, 226*n*27
one-room set, 4, 76–77, 89, 92–94, 98, 100, 122–123, 126, 150–151, 188, 230
Outer Delhi, 206, 224*n*17, *n*18, *n*19, *n*21

Palam, 35, 107, 174, 224*n*17
   panchayat, 22
Palam 360, 122, 208
panchayat, 9, 14, 116–117, 119, 127, 135, 138, 163–164, 172, 178, 188, 208, 209, 211, 219, 223*n*4
   as a cartel, 121–124
   Muzaffarnagar, 242
   Palam, 22
party ticket, 201, 212, 214, 219

party worker, 201, 214–218, 220, 222
Parshad, Vijay, 198*n*32
patriarchal control, 149, 161
patron, 199, 221
   -client relationship, 212
patronage, 119, 199, 212
   politics, 203, 222
patwari, 47–49, 56*n*38, 224*n*12
Pay Commission
   Fourth, 73
   set up by Government of India, 84*n*55
   7th, 193
permits, 72–74, 83*n*38, 119
   licence-permit *raj*/state, 20, 67, 80, 88
Permanent Settlement, 36
phirni, 45, 177
pigs, 194
Piketty, Thomas, 10, 27*n*33, *n*38
plot(s), 42, 54*n*24, *n*27, 76, 94, 98, 192
   agricultural, 64
   alternative, 41, 43, 54*n*25, 55*n*37, 64, 70, 77–78, 107
   commercial, 67, 99, 231
   kubza over smaller, 46
   residential, 38, 53
   urban, 43
police, 75, 80, 155–157, 162–163, 167, 182, 235, 244*n*20
political economy, 2, 9–10, 14, 17–20, 22, 36, 59, 79, 89, 110, 116, 222
Pradhan, 111*n*10, 121, 208
precarity/precarious, 26*n*24, 88, 107, 116, 123, 136, 142*n*33, 165, 190–191, 195, 242
   infrastructures, 230–234
   COVID-19 pandemic and, 236–238
   rent in economies, 234–236
prejudice, 148, 170*n*16
pride, 10–11, 13, 15, 29*n*57, 75, 77–78, 100, 145, 149–150, 158, 167, 179–181, 187–190, 204, 217, 239
proof, 34, 57*n*44, 65, 102, 124, 176, 183

property, 2, 14, 17, 23, 35–37, 44–46, 48, 51–52, 55n35, 57n42, n44, n47, 61–67, 77, 80, 85n60, 88, 91–92, 99, 101, 104–109, 112n16, 113n26, 120–121, 123–127, 134–135, 137–138, 141n18, 149–151, 161–162, 169, 175, 183–184, 187, 189–190, 191, 196, 207, 213–214, 217–219, 227n37, 232–233, 236
  authorised, 50
  boom in 1990s, 128
  commercial property, 71, 76, 78–79, 102, 132, 235
  contemporary ownership of Jats, 13
  formal, 240
  heritage, 100
  informal, 240
  landed, 9–10
  private, 20, 40, 46, 49, 55n36, 118, 153
  property feuds, 122, 153, 188
  regimes, 2
  renting, 10, 82n19, 92, 117, 119, 128–129, 132, 155, 186, 188, 193, 240
  residential property, 113n26, 213
  rural, 20, 38
  unauthorised property, 49, 98, 182, 190
  urban, 20, 38–43, 46, 60, 238
property dealer, 23, 103, 150, 188, 235
prostitution, 157–158, 162, 171n26
Public Distribution System
public interest litigation (PIL), 85n62, 86–87, 112n12

quarry/quarrying, 68–69, 71
quota, 12, 73

race/racial, 9, 21, 25n10, 45, 54n31, 99, 145, 148–150, 153, 158–160, 162–164, 167
  critical race theory, 158

hierarchies, 152
hostility, 147
intersectionalities of, 17
martial, 13, 29n57, 62
neoliberal, 87
and prostitution, relationship between, 157
strife, 152
surcharge, 151, 158
regularisation, 103–105, 107, 113n29, 114n31, n33, 133, 136, 241
regulation, 17, 70–72, 89, 104–105, 112n12, 136
rent/rental, 4, 8–12, 14–23, 27n34, 31n87, 52, 53n10, 56n38, 61–63, 67, 72–73, 77–79, 82n19, 87–88, 90–92, 94, 97–101, 105, 113n20, 117–119, 122–128, 130–138, 139n1, 147–153, 155–158, 160, 166, 168–169, 174, 178, 185–186, 188–191, 193, 195–196, 207–208, 210, 212, 214–215, 218, 221–222, 232–238, 240–242, 243n7
  class-monopoly, 18
  extraction, 93
  ground, 54n24, 66, 74, 76, 80, 85n60, 89, 100
  income, 74
  redistributive, 60
  seeking, 20, 60–62, 72, 80, 88, 118–119, 125, 221
  social life of, 23, 149, 168, 200
  strike, 236–237
  vernacular, 28n42
rentier, 101, 119, 185, 214
  capitalism, 17
  economy, 207
  elite, 17
  finance, 72
  village, 17
reservation, 183–184, 205, 207–208, 224n14, 226n27

resident welfare association (RWA), 106, 120–123, 126, 129, 135, 140n15, 157, 163–164, 188–190, 194–195, 209, 240
revenue, 5, 10, 22, 28n47, 36–37, 44–45, 47–50, 52n1, 53n18, 54n31, 56n38, 72–73, 103–104, 135, 176–177
revenue office, 22, 47–48, 50, 56n8
Ricardo, David, 9
Ring Road, 3, 34, 38–39, 41–42, 45, 51, 68, 90
risk, 11, 66, 94, 98–101, 120, 128–129, 137–138, 149, 200, 222, 234
rivalry(ies), 118, 127, 154, 202, 210, 213–214, 218–220
R. K. Puram, 34, 67, 74, 90, 199, 205, 211, 215–216, 219–220, 227n42
rural Jats, 21, 201, 205, 208, 242

*safai karamchari*s, 192–193
Sanyal, Kalyan, 9, 27n32, 32n92, 139n1
Scott, James C., 109, 115n46, 239, 243n14
security, 105, 124, 133–135, 147–148, 166, 168, 192, 217–218
shamilat deh, 36, 44, 176–177, 182–183, 197n10
Sharan, Awadhendra, 5, 25n9, n13
shikast, 47–48
Singh, Dara, 206
Siri Fort auditorium, 91
Smith, Adam, 9
Smith, Neil, 58n52
  rent gap theory, 32n89, 111n4
speculation, 6, 10–11, 14–16, 34, 37–43, 46–50, 63, 66, 82n27, 87, 98, 128, 131, 178, 186, 195, 201, 208
sports, 12, 21, 24n8, 28n46, 42–43, 63, 92, 112n13, 121, 128, 159, 161, 202
social media, 8, 163

solidarity, 13–14, 116–118, 123, 154, 166, 174, 181, 191, 203, 207, 238, 240–241
Sonepat, 65, 207, 223n4
South Delhi, 3, 11–12, 34, 39, 43, 62, 70, 98, 120, 144–145, 164, 206–207
South Delhi Municipal Corporation (SDMC), 103, 231
Srinivas, M. N., 117, 139n2, 163
State Trading Corporation (STC), 69
Stokes, Eric, 13, 29n51, n52, n53, n55, 139n7, 196n2
Student Tenants' Union Delhi (STUD), 237
subjectivity, 15, 137–138, 239
suburbanisation, 9, 16
Supreme Court of India, 43, 49, 54n29, n30, 57n45, n47, 84n46, 85n62, 88, 111n1, 207
surveillance, 22, 148, 152, 168
suspicion/suspicious, 19, 23, 103–104, 120–121, 134, 136–138, 152–153, 178, 184–185, 206

Tauru, 65–66, 94
tax(es), 26n19, 37, 105, 118, 198n28
  house, 102, 107, 113n26
  property, 103, 236
taxation, 36, 44, 104–105, 107, 130, 141n25
taxi, 70, 74, 76, 79, 210
tehsildar, 47–48
tenant(s), 4, 21–22, 54n24, 56n38, 76, 98–99, 101, 123–124, 126, 130–131, 133, 149–150, 176, 185–186, 190, 201, 209, 217, 231, 233–236, 238, 240–241
  African, 152
  commercial, 127, 134–135
  criminal, 168
  foreigner, 100

northeast, 147, 151–155, 158, 160, 163, 165–167, 172n39, 188–189
young, 161
territory/territorial, 12–15, 21–22, 25n10, 82n28, 110, 122, 205, 207, 221–222, 228n52
Tetzlaff, Stefan, 71–72, 84n48, n50, n53
Thünen, Von
location theory, 53n10
Tikait, Mahendra Singh, 206, 219, 223n8, 228n50, 241
Tsing, Anna, 15, 17, 27n36
Tokas
Dheeraj, 199, 201–202, 213, 217, 221, 227n37, n44
Jagadish, 205–206, 243n11
Narinder, 213
Parmila, 199, 209, 212, 214, 216, 219–220
Ram Pratap, 211
Shyam, 215–216, 219
Vijay, 212, 216–217, 219–220
tombs (or *gumbad*), 12, 90, 99
transgender, 167–168
transport, 20, 23, 53n10, 61, 65, 67–69, 78–80, 81n12, 84n53, n55, 132, 144, 240
fall of, 74–77
rise of, 71–73
trust, 49, 119, 128–130, 137, 183
Tytler, Jagdish, 73, 84n56, 243n11

unauthorised colony/construction/localities, 7, 35, 41–42, 49–51, 54n27, 57n47, 86, 88, 94, 98, 103–104–105, 107, 113n26, 114n31, 174–175, 177, 182, 185, 190, 196n1
The Unionist Party, 204
United Progressive Alliance (UPA), 207
Upadhya, Carol, 16, 31n77, 139n3
urban poor, 7, 87, 240, 242

urbanisation, 2–3, 10, 15, 18, 34–35, 51, 90–91, 134, 154, 165, 185, 208, 239

value, 5–7, 9–11, 14, 16, 18–20, 22, 27n34, 31n87, 34–41, 49–52, 54n31, 65–66, 86–87, 91–92, 97, 99, 104, 110, 118–119, 123, 126, 128, 132, 134, 136–137, 154, 157, 169, 171n22, 173n42, 174, 176–178, 184, 188, 190, 195, 200, 203, 213, 222, 235, 238–240
of daughters, 160–162
Vanaik, Anish, 40, 54n22, 63, 82n18, n19
venture capitalists, 136, 243n8
Verdery, Katherine, 50, 57n48
Verma, Sahib Singh, 206
vernacular, 110, 241
capitalism, 16, 21, 117–119, 121, 125, 127–128, 135–138, 139n1, 240
economic system/economies, 10, 104, 242
institutions and practices, interaction between, 15
joint-stock companies, 20, 109, 117, 200, 213
rent, 10, 28n42
state, 57n41
system to invest money, 85n65
victim/victimhood, 30n65, 84n56, 165
vigilantism, 157, 167–168
violence, 22, 112n13, 123, 149, 151, 153, 158, 166–168, 170n16, 194, 196, 234, 239
caste, 179, 203
communal, 140n13
domestic, 165
of *kabza*, 52
racial, 9, 21, 148, 162
sexual, 21, 147
towards working classes, 15
voter, 209, 221–222, 224n18, 225n21

wealth, 10–11, 62–63, 158–159, 165, 201, 203, 213, 222, 239
  new-found, 156, 199
  risk-free generation, 149
women, 21–23, 33, 46, 90, 122, 129, 134, 146–153, 157, 159–162, 168, 169n5, 170n17, n25, n26, 180, 189, 199, 208–209, 218, 222
worker(s), 89, 92, 96–97, 136, 142n33, 169n6, 201, 220, 222, 230, 234–235, 237–238
  adda, 95
  blue-collar, 6, 88
  construction, 67, 91
  field, 130
  garment, 4, 91
  migrant, 17, 112n14, 130
  northeastern, 147
  party, 214–218
  pink-collar, 146
  social activist, 98, 180–181, 189, 217, 221, 227n45, 228n46
workshop, 4, 6, 90, 95–97, 124, 237

xenophobia, 156, 167–168

YouTube, 21, 148, 152–153, 157, 167–168, 170n12, 196n1
youth, 215
  activism and politics of loss, 153–158
  Jat, 159
  organisation, 209
Youth Brigade Munirka (YBM), 144, 154–155, 164, 189